CEMETERIES OF SOUTHERN DAKOTA COUNTY, MINNESOTA

Includes cemeteries located within the Cities of Farmington and Lakeville, and the Townships of Castle Rock, Douglas, Empire, Eureka, Greenvale, Hampton, Marshan, Randolph, Ravenna, Sciota, Vermillion, and Waterford.

Transcribed and Compiled by Debbie Boe

Cover Photograph: Highview Christiania Lutheran Cemetery, Eureka Township, Dakota County, Minnesota

ISBN 978-0-9844089-1-7

Table of Contents

Table of Maps

Introduction

I have been compiling cemetery burial information in the counties lying south and southwest of the Minneapolis / St. Paul, Minnesota area since 1990. The work started out as an off-shoot of my own love of genealogy and my desire to collect and contribute information to the genealogical community.

I started out by copying down information at a couple of cemeteries near my home and researching the history of the cemetery. Over time this developed into an interest and a hobby. I continue this hobby today. It just seems important. To date, I have created lists for over 100 cemeteries.

Portions of my cemetery lists have been available online within Debbie's Genealogy Library for many years. I have received a great deal of e-mail in response to my website from all across the United States and several foreign countries. Many of these e-mails start out with *'thank you for the great website'* or *'I never thought I would find so and so.'* Debbie's Genealogy Library has proven to be very popular in genealogical circles throughout the world. The website address is www.debbiesgenealogy.com.

The online versions of the cemetery compilations are scaled down versions of the cemetery transcription books I created. The main difference between the online version and the paper version is the paper version includes the row numbers I assign and a general map of the cemetery. The online versions do not include the row numbers or the corresponding map.

This particular book contains cemetery transcriptions for the cemeteries in Southern Dakota County. These cemeteries were visited during 1996, 2000, or 2001.

General Information

The cemetery burial monument compilations are grouped in alphabetical order. Each individual listing is from a burial monument. Unmarked burials are not included.

General maps of each cemetery were created during my visits. These general maps were solely based upon my walk through the cemetery, and are not intended to be official maps or records, nor a substitute for any sort of official cemetery map or record. My maps are best used as a research tool to help locate a particular burial monument.

I attempted to spell information written is native languages (e.g. names, towns, and places) the same. "Born" and "Died" have been translated into English. Dates are listed in a day-month-year style. World War II is listed as World War 2. Titles, like Dr., Rev., etc. are typically not included.

Some cemeteries have sections or plots with a central surname monument. These surname monuments are frequently surrounded by individual burial monuments with only given names. These people are usually related, but may or may not share the same surname. I arbitrarily assign the surname from the central surname monument followed by (?) when no surname is included.

I list the most likely transcription followed by a (?) when a burial monument was difficult to read. If an entry has "?" listed without parenthesis it generally means a letter or number was present, but I was not able to get a good reading.

Works in this series:

Cemeteries of Eastern Carver County, Minnesota
     By Debbie Boe, © 2010
     ISBN: 978-0-9844089-2-4

Cemeteries of Western Carver County, Minnesota
     By Debbie Boe, © 2010
     ISBN: 978-0-9844089-3-1

Cemeteries of Central and Northern Dakota County, Minnesota
     By Debbie Boe, © 2010
     ISBN: 978-0-9844089-0-0

Cemeteries of Southern Dakota County, Minnesota
     By Debbie Boe, © 2010
     ISBN: 978-0-9844089-1-7

LAKESIDE CEMETERY

Randolph township, Dakota county, Minnesota: T112N-R18W, sections 8 & 9?

     This cemetery is upkept and in good shape. It is within one mile, to the east, of the town on Randolph, Minnesota. It boarders the northwest area of Lake Byllesby. When I numbered the rows I divided the cemetery in half along an east - west line. The rows numbered 1 - 12 are in the southern part of the cemetery. The southern area is the older area. The numbers 13 - 31 are the northern rows.

     The Dakota county cemetery records compilation lists this cemetery as: Lakeside Cemetery. Owned by lot owners. First burial in 1857. 3 acres. Located NE & NW 1/4 of Section 8 and 9. Run by a cemetery board.

     In the book "History of Dakota County and the city of Hastings" by Rev. Edward D. Neill, written in 1881, he wrote the following about Randolph: The cemetery is the property of the town, and is under the control of the town board. It is situated in the north-east quarter of section 8, and the north-west quarter of section 9, and contains about three acres. The land was donated by D.H. Morrill and J.W. Pennimann. The first internment made in this ground, was that of a Miss Reinhardt, of Hampton; the second was Mrs. James Hassan, who died in December 1857, which was the first death within the limits of this town. This cemetery was for a time enclosed within the farm of Mr. Pennimann. In 1877, it was enclosed by a wire fence, and in 1879, was surrounded by shade trees. It contains about thirty graves (page 449).

     Everyone is listed in alphabetical order. The number before each entry is the row number. There is a map at the back of this section.

     This cemeteries burial monuments were transcribed during 1996.

13	Leona F. Aamodt 17 September 1910 - 7 September 1977
06	Anton Anderson 1853-1947
06	Pauline Anderson 1865-1941
05	Kenneth Alexander 29 May 1899 - 10 December 1900
16	Anne Fleming Banks 1911-1992
18	Ruth, wife of W.E. Bowen 1895-1932
31	Linda Boysen 25 March 1955 - 26 June 1995
	married Haven W. 14 August 1974
09	Clarence Brown 1899-1927
09	Cora Brown 1895-1922
09	Dora Brown 1902-1924
21	Edmund C. Brown 1906-1967
21	Evelyn D. Brown 1910-1974
09	George Brown (?) (could be Gray (?)) 1880-1963

09	Henry Brown 1897-1931
09	Lily Brown 1904-1921
09	Lydia Brown (?) (could be Gray(?)) 1875-1943
03	Margaret Brown 1865-1963
27	Donald W. Bueling 1912-1983
27	Lois M. Bueling 1918- __
06	Michael Bull 21 June 1801 - 17 December 1876

04	W.O.C.
15	N. Edward F. Carpenter 1945-1966
15	N. Edward F. Carpenter (?) 1945-1966
04	Charlotte E. Church 1843-1920
04	William O. Church 1842-1915
23	Clara M. Cords 1890-1985
23	William C. Cords 1884-1967

30	Charlotte B. Dalaska 1912-1970
30	Harry E. Dalaska 1909-1981
16	Frieda C. Davisson (?) 1898-1973
16	Julia B. Davisson 1925-1926
16	Oscar E. Davisson (?) 1890-1981
17	Ann S. Day (?) 1874-1966
18	Beth I. Day (?) 1907-1928
19	Donald G. Day (?) 1904-1974
19	Dorothy M. Day (?) 1914-1965
17	George Day (?) 1867-1936
18	Leslie H. Day (?) 1897-1916
07	Mary E. Dibble 1864-1945
07	W.S. Dibble 1864-1917
28	Lorraine K. Distad 1944-1984
12	Brianna Marie Dockter 23 January 1984 - 4 June 1984
28	Laura C. Dreager 1910-1980
28	Vernon H. Draeger Sr. 1906- __

02	Charles W. Ekstrom, Minnesota SGT. Co. A 411 Infantry Regt.
	10 December 1930 - 11 April 1959
04	Sylvester C. Ennis (?) 1902-1917
14	Helen Weinel - Erickson 1925-1991
18	Evelyn C. Errington 1906-1978
18	George E. Errington 1897-1980
26	Holly Ann Errington 20 November 1973 - 13 April 1975
04	Aurilla, wife of Franklin Erwin, died 21 October 1885
	age 68 years, 2 months, 15 days
04	Franklin Erwin, died 3 February 1890
	age 71 years, 10 months, 2 days

06	Albert Fay, died 9 March 1888 age 55 years, 17 days
06	Sarah Fay, died 9 July 1883 age 65 years
27	Ella Felton 1901-1978
04	Elmer Felton 28 August - 4 September 1923
04	Olive H. Felton, died 23 March 1902 age 2 months, 16 days
27	William Felton 1895-1981
27	William Felton, PVT United States Army World War 1
	4 November 1895 - 13 May 1981
16	Blanche H. Fleming (?) 1882-1959
16	Daniel A. Fleming 28 August 1958 - 20 February 1982
16	Helen M. Fleming 1911- __
16	Jane Fleming 1948-1949
16	John A. 'Jack' Fleming 1904-1989
16	John B. Fleming (?) 1878-1965
28	Lillian M. Fleming 1903-1986
	married William C. 3 July 1939
28	William C. Fleming 1907-1980
	married Lillian C. 3 July 1939
11	Mary E. Ferguson 19 April 1914 - __
11	Robert E. Ferguson 2 October 1907 - 13 October 1986
07	Abram Foster, died 9 June 1887 age 76 years
08	Alice A. Foster (?) 1853-1926
06	baby daughter of J. & M. Foster
	30 April 1889 - 10 August 1889
05	Carl W. (?), son of (?) Foster (?) , died (?) September 1882, age 11 years
08	Charles R. Foster (?) 1852-1922
08	daughter of (?) & L. Foster (?)
05	E.N. Foster, died 17 September 1876, age 1 year, 5 months
06	George Foster 1844-1914 veteran *
06	Hannah Foster 1842-1913
07	Henry Foster, died 8 June 1877, age 17 years
07	Jane Foster, died 21 April 1877, age 56 years
05	Roga (?) B., daughter of G. & A. Foster (?), died 29 August 1876 (?)
07	Septemoz (?) Foster, died 23 March 1885, age 10 years, 10 months
07	Septemas, son of A. & J. Foster, died 23 March 1865
	age 10 years, 10 months
13	Peter J. Gerber 22 June 1895 - 11 June 1974
25	Theophil Emil Gieschen, United States Navy World War 2
	18 May 1910 - 28 April 1987
10	Dorcas, wife of J. Gottenberg, died 31 July 1877
	age 39 years, 25 days
04	(?), wife of W. L. Gouper, died 10 July (?) 1890 (?), age 27 years (?)
09	George Gray (?) (could be Brown (?)) 1880-1963
09	Lydia Gray (?) (could be Brown (?)) 1875-1943
18	Fred C. Guildner 1877-1951

18	Lizzie M. Guildner 1885-1955
17	Paul L. Guildner 1927-1982
17	Wayne P. Guildner 25 June 1959 - 2 November 1991
03	Haedecke (nothing else)
17	Dale F. Hand 1931-1955
25	Nancy K. Hannah 1929-1986
09	Amy, wife of James Hassan, died 3 February 1859, age 44 years
04	Elizabeth Erwin Hassan 1851-1925
13	Nellie M. Helmbrecht 1885-1974
25	Oneva (Eiesland) Helgerson 8 May 1907 - __
25	Otto F. Helgerson 27 July 1906 - 14 July 1995
17	Gertrude A. Heren 1887-1985
17	Herman E. Heren 1882-1955
05	Cecelia Grace Hickman 1886-1950
30	Jeff Holm 19 November 1964 - 14 October 1992
25	Justin D. Hudak, PVT United States Army World War 2
	8 March 1927 - 20 April 1989
07	W.H. James, died 1 June 1896, age 29 years
07	F.M. Jenkins, died 15 April 1866, age 76 (?) or 16 (?) years, 9 months
03	Albert Johnson 1881-1963
05	Frank J. Klahr 1891-1982
05	Lena M. Klahr 1901-1986
03	Maude Kline (?) 1889-1952
03	Merritt Kline (?) 1888-1954
11	Jack Randall Knox, F1 United States Navy World War 2 veteran *
	31 January 1923 - 16 January 1995
11	Jack R. Knox 31 January 1923 - 16 January 1995
11	Ruth A. Knox 26 October 1927 - __
27	Marilyn A. Kolstad 1927 - __
27	Vernon R. Kolstad 1919-1979
27	Vernon R. Kolstad, Pfc United States Army World War 2
	3 April 1919 - 7 October 1979
26	Chester Konzidka 1926-1984
22	Alice F., wife of Dr. O.A. Kuello (?) 1893-1928
18	Edward A. Lauer 1895-1970
18	Louise M. Lauer 1897-1967
29	Lydia (Redman) Law 12 February 1902 - 25 September 1993
	preceded by husbands Archie Farnum & Willard Law
28	Lydia M. Law 1903-1993
15	Walter T. Law, Minnesota S. Sgt. Co. C 89 Infantry World War 2
	7 February 1913 - 10 November 1972
28	Willard N. Law 1904-1979

29	Willard N. Law, Pvt United States Army World War 2
	29 November 1904 - 14 January 1979
20	Max Curwin Leir, AOM3 United States Navy World War 2
	26 January 1926 - 27 June 1945
05	Emma Lueben (?) 1858-1935
17	Nancy Lueben 1890-1967
17	Walter W. Lueben, Minnesota Pvt. 1 Cl. 13 Engrs.
	17 September 1887 - 13 June 1945
05	William Lueben (?) 1857-1934
06	Martin Lieske 1835-1899
06	Wilhelminne Lieske 1835-1900
09	Dorothy Martin, beloved daughter of W.H. & E.J. Martin
	17 May 1901 - 3 February 1907
09	Eller Martin 1859-1908
27	Hazel A. Martin 1892-1978
27	M. Leroy Martin 1892-1968
03	Felix Mauer 1840-1911
08	Betty Ann McEathron 17 September 1928 - 14 February 1986
13	Carol I. McEathron 1920- __
14	Clifford R. McEathron 1907-1953
07	Genevieve S. McEathron 1904-1981
07	Genevive S. McEathron 10 January 1904 - 2 December 1981
14	George S. McEathron 1881-1965
07	Gerald McEathron 1923-1933
07	Gerald George McEathron 25 December 1923 - 30 June 1933
13	Leonard O. McEathron 1912-1965
08	Leslie W. McEathron 14 November 1926 - __
14	Mary E. McEathron 1879-1951
07	Walter McEathron 1903-1962
07	Walter L. McEathron 1903-1962
19	Ambrose A. McElrath 1853-1930
09	Daisy H., wife of W.L. McElrath, died 1 march 1893, age 23 years
05	Foster B. McElrath 1911- 1914
14	Helen I. McElrath 1891-1973
23	Lillie McElrath 1875-1962
19	Maria E. McElrath 1855-1930
14	Percy L. McElrath 1887-1947
19	baby Vernon Richard McElrath - 2 February 1940 -
23	William McElrath 1866-1953
02	J.H. McKane 1889-1933
20	Florence Millard (?) 1901-1943
20	Lillas L. Millard 1922-1937
19	Mabel Millard 1878-1951
19	Peter Millard 1876-1949
19	William B. Millard, South Dakota Pfc United States Army World War 1

19 April 1896 - 28 October 1971

08	Alice Miller 1870-1957
19	Amanda Miller (?) 1892-1979
05	baby Miller (?) -1916-
17	Clarence F. Miller 1894-1965
19	Elmer J. Miller (?) 1894-1985
20	John J. Miller (?) 1867-1954
17	Lavina B. Miller 1904 -__
05	Louis R. Miller (?) 1859-1936
20	Martha Miller (?) 1872-1927
05	Raymond Miller (?) 1891-1917
05	Sarah E. Miller (?) 1864-1937
03	Arianna M. Morrill 1882-1974
03	Charles L. Morrill 1871-1962
10	D.H. Morrill, died 24 April 1874, age 36 years
27	Glen F. Morrill 1887-1975
04	Hattie J., daughter of (?) R.C. & S.J. Morrill, died 11 June 1887 (?) age (?) 13 years (?) 11 days (?)
27	Helen E. Morrill 1895-1993
03	Ida M. Morrill 1889-1957
11	John O., son of R. & M. J. Morrill, died 9 December 1863, age (?)
22	Leona Morrill 1917 - __
10	little boy (?), son of D.H. & R.M. Morrill, died 20 August 1876 (?) age 3 years, 5 days (?)
22	Lynn Morrill 1912-1988
11	Mary J. Morrill 26 September 1810 - 28 October 1874
03	Minnie, wife of Charles L. Morrill 4 March 1874 - 17 November 1904
03	R.B. Morrill, POST 92 G.A.R., 1842-1925
11	Richard Morrill 19 June 1806, died (nothing listed)
10	Rosetta M. Morrill 1840-1914
03	Sarah J. Morrill 1845-1919 'She done what she could'
10	(?) son of D.H. & R.M. Morrill, died 16 August 1864 (?) age 2 years (?)
03	William D. Morrill 1914-1964
03	William H. Morrill 1869-1919
18	Anna Murray 1856-1936
18	Luke Murray 1856-1925
18	Reuben Carmen Murray 1900-1960
08	Ingrid Nelson 1861-1946
08	Nels A. Nelson 1 February 1856 - 11 February 1909
08	Richard Nelson 1883-1948
26	Victor A. Norstad 1918-1987
05	Abert George Oberdorf 1903-1919
05	Catherine Oberdorf 1862-1935

05	John Thomas Oberdorf 1857-1928
16	Bradley George Ohs 30 April - 10 May 1950
20	Caroline M. Ohs (?) 1879-1945
20	Charles W. Ohs (?) 1878-1946
16	Dorothy M. Ohs 1909-1982
19	Emma E. Ohs (?) 1877-1966
19	Frank A. Ohs (?) 1875-1974
16	George R. Ohs 1908-1994
07	Christina E. Olson (?) 1833-1926
07	Gustave Olson (?) 1863-1941
07	John G. Olson (?) 1841-1940
23	Clinton B. Otte (?) 1908-1981
30	Dorothy M. Otte 1918 - __
24	Edwin Henry Otte (?) 1873-1938
24	Emma Ohde Otte (?) 1875-1951
24	Kenneth A. Otte 29 April 1938 - 27 March 1995
	married Janet I. 23 July 196?
30	Milton C. Otte 1913-1989
04	Bunny (?), son of (?) P.F. & C.I. Pennimann, died 15 June 1871
	age 1 year (?) 1 month (?)
04	Elizabeth Gouper (?), wife (?) of Jesse Penniman 1820-1898
04	Harry (?) Penniman 7 October 1865 - 14 November 1890
04	baby Hettie (?) Penniman, died 20 May 1891, age 14 months
04	Jesse W. Penniman 3 March 1814 - 25 June 1886
04	Marion S., daughter of P.F. & C.I. Penniman, died 5 September 1861
	age (?) 15 days (?)
05	Merton E., son of Charlie & Ida Penniman, (?)
	age 11 years, 11 months (?)
24	Edward Peter 1868-1944
23	Elaine G. Peter 29 April - 8 May 1926
24	Hulda E. Peter 1871-1936
23	Loyd P. Peter 1900-1989
01	Margaret L. Peter (?) 1896-1960
23	Olga F. Peter 1896-1977
01	Walter J. Peter (?) 1884-1923
30	Dennis Podritz (?) 1949-1968
24	Clifford A. Popp 1922-1967
24	Eleanor P. Popp 1928 - __
29	Randy C. Popp 31 May - 28 August 1968
02	Keith E. Porter 15 October 1904 - 11 September 1926
27	Archie R. Pressnall 1886-1974
28	Archie R. Pressnall 1919-1977
28	Charlotte L. Pressnall 11 August 1921 - __
28	Marion R. Pressnall 1916- __
27	Minnie M. Pressnall 1886-1975

28	Ray M. Pressnall 19 October 1921 - 26 October 1987
16	Mary L. Rambo (?) 1899-1955
16	Roy C. Rambo (?) 1886-1933
10	E.J. Tonlinson, wife of J. Richmond, died 26 March 1880, age 67 years (?)
10	Rob. B. Richmond, died 16 November 1867, age 19 years (?) POST 92 G.A.R.
24	Sophia M. Ritzenthaler (?) 1858-1922
22	Emma Schulz 1872-1940
11	B.F. Scofield 1871-1881
11	E.M. Scofield 1833-1918
08	Edward Roy Scofield (?) 1862-1935
11	I.H. Scofield 1829-1881
11	J.L. Scofield 1873-1881
08	Orlin S. Scofield 1858-1924
11	R.I. Scofield 1876-1881
11	S.E. Scofield 1869-1881
28	Eva M. Scott (?) 1937-1975
02	Leroy H. Scott 1919-1983 veteran *
02	LeRoy H. Scott, Pfc United States Army World War 2 1919-1983
02	Myrl E. Scott 1921 - __
22	Hattie C., wife of Henry O. Senn 1872-1927
22	Henry O. Senn 1866-1923
01	Edward I. Shue 1913-1984
02	John James Siless (?) 1867-1927
02	Mary Helen Siless (?) 1870-1919
26	Gladys M. Skaar 10 February 1911- __ married Iroll 3 December 1929
26	Iroll S. Skaar 7 September 1902 - 2 October 1987 married Gladys M. 3 December 1929
29	Janice A. Skaar 27 August 1934 - 16 February 1987
14	Harry W. Slininger 1889-1964
14	Hazel A. Slininger 1894-1965
13	Myrl C. Slininger 1917-1987
13	Myrl C. Slininger, TEC 5 United States Army World War 2 1 July 1917 - 27 March 1987
13	Ola Jane 'Casey' (?) Slininger 1925 - __
27	C. Audrey Smith 1921 - __
27	Elwood C. Smith 1919-1976
02	Georgina Spillmann (?) 1851-1919
02	Henry Spillmann (?) 1843-1921
21	Julius A. Spillmann (?) 1874-1953
21	Martha Spillmann (?) 1879-1945
22	Caroline E. Spillmann (?) 1902-1927

01	Alma J. Spooner 1885-1964
01	Bernard M. Spooner 1908-1920
01	Martin L. Spooner 1884-1953
14	Gerald L. Stafford 14 June 1932 - 15 January 1983
13	Jessie L. Stafford 1891-1980
14	Julie May Stafford 25 February 1950 - 17 September 1951
13	Walter H. Stafford 1889-1957
08	F.A. Steele 1870-1953
08	F.V. Steele 1859-1924
08	L.P. Steele 1827-1900
08	Sophia T., wife of L.P. Steele, died 22 July 1898, age 68 years
01	Elaine Taylor 1924-1958
01	Norma L. Taylor 1928 - __
01	Robert W. Taylor 1919 - __
01	Warren A. Taylor 1924-1958
27	Estella M. Truair 1909-1956
27	Harold F. Truair 1905 - __
27	Marvin G. Truair, MM2 United States Navy
	28 May 1940 - 14 June 1991
09	Alice Eva Trichie 1875-1912
05	LeNora M. Tyner 1890-1914
20	Lorena Tyner 1865-1931
20	John Tyner 1858-1924
31	Fred L. Watkins 10 March 1941 - 25 November 1978
31	John R. Watkins 1910-1972
31	Margaret M. Watkins 1921- __
14	Daniel Weinel 1893-1987
14	Gladys W. Weinel 1904-1974
14	John Wesley Weinel 1927-1945
31	Kathy 'Shorty' Wichser 27 June 1951 - 13 July 1990
09	Allie R., wife of C.E. Wilson (?) 10 June 1871 - 3 July 1904
09	Elmer, son of C.E. (?) & A.R. (?) Wilson (?), died 27 June 1891
	age 2 months (?)
22	Emma Witthans 1884-1959
22	Joseph Witthans 1878-1950
29	Arnold M. 'Red' Ziemer 2 April 1933 - 10 June 1995
29	Danny Ziemer 14 November 1960 - 3 October 1979
30	Josiah Daniel Ziemer 9 July 1990 - 13 October 1990
29	Mert M. Ziemer 15 November 1933 - 5 March 1981
29	baby Shandy Ziemer (?) - 15 November 1983 -
28	Shawn (?) Ziemer (?) - 25 August 1982 -
03	Fred L. Ziervogel 1865-1935

The following names did not list a surname nor were they near another surname.

04   Inez May, died 27 April 1890, age 7 years, 6 months, 25 days
08   Hattie M., 1906-1907
12   Mary R., 1865-1954
12   Mercy A., 1853-1934

To Randolph

Dakota County Road 88

Rail Road

entrance gate

fence

Open Area

N
W —|— E
S

Lakeside Cemetery
Section 8 + 9?
Randolph township,
Dakota County, Minnesota

T112N - R18W

Rows 13-31

Begin Row 13

Drive Area

Rows 1-12
Older Part

Small building

Begin Row 1

Trees

Lake Byllesby

KIBBE CEMETERY

Scotia township, Dakota county, Minnesota: T112N - R19W, section 14

     This cemetery is in poor shape. The area is fenced off with a mix of wooden and cement posts. The area is not mowed. It appears the lilacs were cut back in the last year or two as they have grown to about two feet tall. The only reference to possible burial information was a pair of burial marker stones with the initials JKK and ABK. These were located near the base of a large tombstone. The only other bit of information was a loose piece of another slab style burial stone with: Elm?? and son of ?, the rest was missing. This did not appear to be over a grave. I do not know what became of the tombstones or how many there were. I did notice in the center of the area there was a small mound that had been covered with the regrowth of grass and weeds. The grass patterns gave the appearance that the earth had been scraped and piled in that area. It did not appear the be a burial mound.

     The Dakota county cemetery compilation lists this cemetery as: Kibbe Cemetery. Private. First burial 1856. About 1 acre. Located NW 1/4 of Section 14. Alta Street (County Road 59) and north of 302nd Street. E. (Abandoned).

     This was visited during 1996.

RED ROSE CEMETERY

Waterford township, Dakota County, Minnesota: T112N - R19W, Section 17

This cemetery is upkept and in good shape. Many of the burials do not line up into rows very well. Be especially careful with my row numbers as they are at best an approximation of burial location. Rows 1 - 9 begin with row 1 at the east edge and continue up to the eastern edge of the drive loop. Rows 10 - 18 are rows that are inside the drive loop. All entries listed as 19 are the newer burials at the west edge of the cemetery up to the western edge of the drive loop.

The Dakota county cemetery records compilation lists this cemetery as: Red Rose Cemetery. (Formerly called Rose Leaf). Land donated in 1856, 1 1/2 acres. In 1959 an additional 3/10th acre was purchased. Located NE 1/4 of Section 17. 1 mile east on Highway 3 on 300th St. West.

In Rev. Edward D. Neill's book, "History of Dakota County and the city of Hastings", he writes the following: Rose Leaf Cemetery is situated in the north-east quarter of section 17. It contains one and one-half acres of land, and was given to the town by Dr. Z.B. Nichols, in 1856. The first person buried there was George Swaile, who was browned in the Canon River (page 494). To the best of my knowledge Red Rose and Rose Leaf Cemetery are one and the same.

Everyone is listed in alphabetical order. The number before each entry is the row number. There is a map at the back of this section.

This cemeteries burial monuments were transcribed during 1996.

07	Elizabeth Ackerson 1916-__
07	David F. Ackerson 1910-1990
08	Andrew Ackerson (?) 1873-1959
07	John M. Ackerson 1918-__
08	Judith E. Ackerson (?) 1906-1990
07	Rose L. Ackerson 1921-__
08	Sophia E. Ackerson (?) 1883-1975
18	Florence C. Anderson 1898-1920
19	Jeffrey Paul Anhald 22 July 1983 - 20 December 1985
19	Harry F. Baker 1915-__
19	Martha K. Baker 1917-1985
19	Donna L. Bakken 1933-1972
08	Adelin, wife of (?) H. Barber, died 3 March 1873 (?), age 43 years
15	Jason H. Bates 1848-1881
15	Mrs. Lydia Bates 1881-1921
07	Nettie Bates (?) 1865-1939
07	Roy Bates (?) 1881-1951

07	William W. Bates (?) 1844-1918
14	Phebe, wife of Dr. (?) ? Reuben Beaen (?), died 22 July 1867, age ?
19	Clara M. Beyer 1919-__
19	Paul F. Beyer 1918-__
19	Rosanna P. Beyer 1953-1972
06	Carlton E. Bill 1880-1962
14	Edwd. S. Bill 1833-1919 Co. F 8 Minnesota Inf. G.A.R.
15	Elizabeth, widow of Rufus Bill and W.S. Richards
	died 20 September 1879, age 79 years
06	Margaret M. Bill 1878-1942
02	Russell L. Bill 16 August 1889 - 8 September 1905
14	Theressa A. Bill 1839-1928
14	Josie Laura Blood 9 July 1877 - 4 July 1924
04	?, son of J.W. & E. Boath, died 12 October 1867
	age 3 years 7 months 2 days
14	Clarence F. Bodger 1898-1902, age 3 years 8 months 8 days
14	Clarence J. Bodger 1860-1938
09	Earl Bodger 1900-1902
13	Elizabeth Bodger 1836-1907
09	Hattie Bodger 1876-1948
09	Herbert Bodger 1867-1946
09	Horace Bodger 1898-__
13	Joseph H. Bodger 1831-1906
14	Mary E. Bodger 1873-1968
19	Mildred Hussey Boe 1900-1978
04	Eugene R. Bolin (?) 1905-1957
03	Helen M. Bolin 1880-1945
04	Marjorie A. Bolin (?) 1910-1991
03	Robert E. Bolin 1935-1936
03	Robert F. Bolin 1877-1973
03	Ada A. Bogue 1864-1865
03	Arthur L. Bogue 1860-1863
19	Rev. Arnold J. Borchardt 1904-1979
19	Hazel G. Borchardt 1908-1989
18	?, son of E.D. & M.S. Bowe, died 12 November 1890
	age 3 years 9 months 7 days
18	Bert D. Bowe 1850-1926
18	Leroy R. Bowe 1882-1960
18	Lorena R. Bowe 1879-1973
17	Lucius R. Bowe 1877-1961
18	Mary S. Bowe 1855-1930
10	Ethel C. Boyle 1901-1981
18	Francis J. Boyle 1872-1955
10	Harold E. Boyle 1903-1976
18	Sarah A. Boyle 1866-1953
08	Frank W. Briggs 1872-1911

08	James P. Briggs 1827-1899
08	Mary Briggs 1834-1919
19	Bethel Bussey 1888-1958

15	Wm. W. Campbell, died 25 November 1871, age 51 years
08	Christiana, wife of Geo. C. Chamberlain, died 5 March 1891
	age 66 years
08	Geo. C. Chamberlain 17 July 1823 - 19 April 1898
03	Mark Chamberlain (?), died 11 December 1899
	age 17 years 2 months 8 days
08	Willes N., son of G.C. & C.P. Chamberlin, died 26 December 1870
	age 20 years 8 months 7 days
01	Ruth Cheesman 1 April 1802 - 1 January (?) 1897
	age 89 years 23 days
01	William Cheesman, died 15 July 1880, age 88 years
08	Eliza R. Child 8 March 1888 - 26 November 1911
08	Florence Child (?), died ?? 1862, age 1 year (?) 6 months 12 days (?)
08	Henry E. Child 17 October 1830 - 19 February 1904
08	Herbert E., son of H.D. & E.R. Child, died 9 April 1881
	age 21 years 3 months 8 days
08	Temple A. Child 9 November 1872 - 30 December 1913
15	Franklin Church 1815-1896
15	Sarah A. Church 1818-1915
06	Alexander Clark 1819-1867
06	Chauncey Parker Clark 1874-1948
06	Hannah Clark 1863-1907
06	Jennie Clark 1834-1922
06	Jeremiah Clark 1831-1907
06	John Clark 1860-1913
06	William Clark 1858-1921
09	Gladys L. Conklin 1908-1995
09	Raymond E. Conklin 1902-1990
06	Albert A., child of T.T. & E. Cowell, died 2 September 1874
	age 13 years
12	Ann Cowell 7 August 1825 - 2 August 1909
09	Caroline E. Cowell 1892-1918
06	Charles T., child of T.T. & E. Cowell, died 14 June 1862
	age 7 years
12	Charles W. Cowell (?) 3 January 1865 - 20 April 1932
09	Cyril W. Cowell 1895-1986
12	Edward F. Cowell 19 October 1826 - 9 July 1886
09	'Father' Cowell (?) 1857-1916
06	'Father' Cowell (?) 1833-1925 veteran * 61-65
12	Flroence Cowell (?) 10 March 1876 - 6 September 1933
09	G. Arthur Cowell (?) 1884-1909
06	Ida L., daughter of T.T. & E. Cowell, died 27 November 1880

```
                    age 15 years
16    James E. Cowell  1889-1965
12    Lucy Cowell (?)  1898-1980
12    Minnie Cowell  8 October 1869 - 1 March 1908
09    'Mother' Cowell (?)  1861-1955
06    'Mother' Cowell (?)  1836-1931
09    Myrtle L. Cowell  1896-1991
09    Rexford D. Cowell (?)  1900-1913
16    Rose A. Cowell  1889-1962
06    Thos. Cowell    -no dates


08    Celestia Daniels, died 21 July 1895
                    age 71 years 5 months 19 days
08    George Daniels, died 27 March 1883, age 62 years 5 months 24 days
                    member of Co. F Minnesota Mounted Rangers and
                    Co. D Bracketts Battalion of Calvary    Veteran * 61-65
02    Frances, daughter of G.W. & E. Dilley, died 18 June 1862, age 23 days
03    W.H. Dinson (?), died 1 December 1855, age ??
                    -hard to read
03    William H., son of G.A. & D.A. Dinson, died 14 December 1863, age ??
                    -hard to read
04    A.E. Dixson, died 6 August 1874,   age 38 years
04    A.L. Dixson  1814-1902
13    Adam L. Dixson  1843-1930
03    D.A. Dixson  1839-1913
03    G.A. Dixson  1838-1924
04    Lawrence, infant son of Parentha (?) & I.L. Dixson Jr.
                    died 18 September 1872 (?), age 2 days   -hard to read
04    Margaret A., wife of A.L. Dixson, died 17 March 1879
                    age 64 years 2 months 22 days
13    Parentha Eckles Dixson  1850-1932
04    Samantha Dixson  1833-1908
03    W.H. Dixson  1863-1864
16    Clarence L. Dodds (?)  7 August 1894 - 15 March 1946  Veteran *
17    Dr. Robert M. Dodds  21 October 1852 - 27 May 1930
12    Roscoe Dodds  7 September 1883 - 11 June 1889
17    Sophia S. Dodds  15 July 1853 - 4 November 1940
04    baby Drentlaw  -1949-
08    Dan Dunlap  1848-1912
08    John R. Dunlap  1802-1885
08    Sybil M. Dunlap  1885-1901


19    Edwin P. Ebeling, Pvt United States Army World War 1
                    12 June 1894 - 11 October 1974
19    Eleanor W. Ebeling  18 June 1895 - 24 July 1990
14    Lawrence, son of William & Mary Eckles
```

	10 August 1859 - 27 February 1882
14	Mary A. Eckles, wife of Capt. W.H. Eckles 1820-1911
13	Hazel B. Elliott 1889-1908
10	Elizabeth Ewing 1830-1918
09	Mary E. Ford 1854-196?
09	Edward W. Fort 1847-1922
12	Evalena, child of W.H. & M.C. Freeman, died 16 February 1881
	age 10 years 3 months 21 days
12	Geo. E., child of W.H. & M.C. Freeman, died 9 February 1881
	age 2 years 7 months
12	Mary Ann Freeman, died 12 August 1902
	age 83 years 9 months 16 days
12	Mary C. Freeman, died 21 November 1915
	age 64 years 3 months 21 days
19	? Gibson (?), age 23 days
19	baby Beverly Ann Gibson (?) 11 August - 3 September 1931
17	Bessia Gibson (?) 1889-1987
19	Glennys F. Gibson (?) 1902-1985
19	Harold F. Gibson (?) 1901-1946
17	J. Murray Gibson (?) 1889-1969
16	Ina Gray (?) 1851-1931
16	W.A. Gray 1831-1919 O.D. 194 Reg. N.Y.V.I. G.A.R.
16	A.B. Hale 4 August 1815 - 9 December 1897
16	E.L.B. Hale 10 August 1818 - 6 July 1898
15	Amanda W. Hammond 1817-1875
19	Eleda L. Hand 10 March 1905 - 27 August 1986
19	Frank M. Hand 30 September 1904 - __
04	Mary M. Hansen 1893-1970
04	Matt H. Hansen 1896-1957
12	Frank Harknes 1888-1972
12	James R. Harknes -1924-
12	Sarah E. Harknes 1893-1943
19	Barbara E. Harkness 1922-1992
09	Edwin J. Harkness 1914-1985
19	John M. Harkness 1921-1984
09	May E. Harkness (?) 1889-1980
19	Mayvis A. Harkness 1930-1995, married Lloyd W. 17 June 1950
09	Mildred A. Harkness 1928-__
09	R. Francis Harkness (?) 1920-1940
09	William L. Harkness (?) 1875-1965
12	Evelyn Simpson Harmer 1901-1986
09	George E. Harmer 1875-1949
09	Myrtle A. Harmer 1883-1925

08	William H. Harmer, CPL United States Army World War 2
	24 February 1916 - 3 December 1980
01	John W. Hatten, child of R. & S.A. Hatten, died 5 September 1858
	age 3 years 3 months 3 days
01	Ralph Hatten 25 July 1815 - 20 August 1895
	age 80 years 26 days
01	Ruth O., child of R. & S.A. Hatten, died 17 February 1864
	age 2 years 2 months 2 days
01	Sarah A., wife of R. Hatten, died 9 September 1882
	age 51 years 6 months 6 days
19	Arnold V. Henderson 1921-__
19	Clarice E. Henderson 1919-__
03	Beatrice Hill (?) 1919-1920
03	Hilma S. Hill (?) 1889-1928
04	Jessie O., wife of G.D. Holmes 1887-1920
16	Fannie E. Holt 1869-1902
10	Bertha A. Hovland 1883-1962
10	Daniel J. Hovland 1880-1960
11	Florence L. Hovland, married Ruben G. 21 November 1940
10	Helen G. Hovland 1908-1955
10	James Hovland 1905-1984
11	Ruben G. Hovland 1915-19991, married Florence L. 21 November 1940
19	Shirley M. Hovland 1931-1984
13	Abbie M. Howland 1865-1932
07	Adella M., wife of Jessie J. Howland 1886-1913
	mother of infant sons James F. and Fredrick J.
09	Alice D. Howland (?) 1869-1953
06	Almon F. Howland 1869-1947
13	Clinton J. Howland (?) 1888-1959
14	Elmer E. Howland (?) 1894-1971
13	Frank B. Howland 1859-1909
09	Fred W. Howland (?) 1865-1929
09	infant Howland (?) -1891-
09	infant Howland (?) -1893-
08	James W. Howland 1826-1902
07	Jesse J. Howland (?) 1877-1947
16	John F. Howland (?) 1903-1986
13	Lucia Howland 1901-1902
06	Mary E. Howland 1875-1947
19	Mary E. Howland 1910-1976
14	Phebe S. Howland (?) 1891-1981
16	R. Blanche Howland (?) 1898-1978
08	Rosetta P. Howland 1837-1907
19	Russell H. Howland 1910-1986
14	Sarah S. Howland (?) 1896-1984
06	Warren A. Howland 5 February 1909 - 13 June 1909

01	Pernella Howell 15 April 1820 - 16 November 1892
01	Simeon C. Howell 6 June 1813 - 28 January 1873
17	Dorsey 'Doc' Hussey 1928-1980
11	?, daughter of W. & E. Ingham (?), died 21 February 1881
	age 11 years 8 months ? days
10	Albert Ingham (?) 1869-1948
17	Edwin Ingham (?) 1873-1950
11	Elmira Ingham 1840-1919
16	Florence Ingham 1876-1957
10	Hugh Ingham (?) 1877-1941
16	Jestus Ingham 1875-1943
17	Mary Ingham (?) 1873-1950
11	William F. Ingham 1831-1909 G.A.R.
16	A. Isabel 1905-1984
19	Louis C. Issel 1906-1982
19	Lucille M. Issell 1911-__
14	Elizabeth Laura Johnson 25 August 1856 - 18 February 1916
14	Jerome Leonard Johnson 21 March 1850 - 24 February 1920 G.A.R.
15	Merton Jerome Johnson 29 November 1879 - 14 November 1942
04	Betty Jorgensen (?) 1873-1927
04	Rasmus Jorgensen (?) 1864-__
06	Pauline A. (Triche) Jorgenson 29 February 1912 - 11 August 1991
12	Daniel B. Kelsey 11 March 1830 - 10 July 1875
12	Elizabeth Withers Kelsey 16 August 1836 - 29 April 1932
12	Jessie I. Kelsey (?) 21 February 1868 - 8 December 1889
09	Joseph J. Kielen 1910-1993
09	Marion J. Kielen 1911-1995
12	Amy, wife of Wm. L. Kinyon, died 9 May 1892, age 51 years
12	Wm. L. Kinyon, died 31 July 1894
	age 61 years 6 months 13 days G.A.R.
01	Charlotte, wife of L.S. Lake, died ? -buried to deep to read
04	Nellie B. Lamphea 1867-1928
09	Abel Lanphear, died 27 March 1872, age 98 years
09	Althear L., wife of John Lanphear 1831-1917
17	Edgar C. Lanphear 21 January 1891 - 26 November 1956
	Minnesota PFC 228 Mil. Police Co. World War 1
09	Eva Lanphear, wife of L.A. Lanphear 1864-1916
09	Georgia Lanphear, daughter of L.A. Lanphear -no dates
09	Hannah, wife of Abel Lanphear, died 9 March 1863, age 70 years
09	John Lanphear 1830-1900
09	L.A. Lanphear 1858-1930
10	Esther E. Legare 1897-1964

19	Eloise M. Legare 1919-__
10	Joseph J. Legare 1887-1966
19	Leo O. Legare 1920-1996
16	Elizabeth M. Lemmon 1893-1971
01	Anna T., infant daughter of E. & S. Lincoln, died 14 February 1863 age 24 days
01	Sara, wife of E. Lincoln, died 2 February 1863 age 17 years 10 months 23 days
06	Henry Loop 1871-1939
06	Margaret Loop 1878-1960
15	Edward J. Lundquist 15 February 1897 - 28 September 1980
15	Laura L. Lundquist 25 December 1906 - __
08	Ida McLouth 1857-1893
19	Esther Mackay 1912-1987
19	Sandy Mackay 1909-1976
11	Nancy A., wife of R.C. Masters, died 25 February 1870, age ?
14	Arthur L., son O. & E.C. Mattison, died 30 April 1869 age 2 years 3 months 12 days
03	George Dizson, son of H.A. & S.D. Monser, died 16 August 1866 age 3 years 2 months
16	C.A. Muckey 1858-1902
17	Charles A. Muckey 1856-1901
16	David Muckey, died 31 October 1891 age 66 years 10 months 3 days
16	Elizabeth F., wife of David Muckey, died 14 August 1889 age 58 years 8 months 5 days
16	Euretta D. Muckey 1855-1936
19	Harold A. Muckey 1898-1977
17	Jean L. Muckey 1863-1948
19	Verna G. Muckey 1906-1986
12	Alice K. Nease 1869-1957
12	William R. Nease 1868-1939
02	Andrew Nelson 12 November 1861 - 23 December 1926
02	Amelia Nelson 9 June 1859 - 30 October 1929
02	Arvid Nelson 1894-1972
02	Harriet Nelson 1896-1991
15	Effie A. Nichols 1859-1927
15	Lucy A., wife of A.M. Nichols, died 17 August 1877, age 66 years
15	Newell S. Nichols 1852-1928
13	Catherine J. Oakins 1835-1914
13	J.W. Oakins 1836-1903
02	Charles H. Ozmun 1875-1935
02	Dora A. Ozmun 1885-1975

19	Rosella P. Ozmun 1944-1995
15	Adaline, wife of E.A. Page, died 3 March 1884, age 72 years
15	Eli A. Page, died 28 January 1896, age 81 years
18	Cyrus F. Parker (?) 1864-1927
18	Dora E. Parker (?) 1869-1928
18	Grace (Drentlaw) Weicht Parker 2 May 1908 - 6 April 1976
18	Roy D. Parker 1892-1957
18	Bessie M. Partch 1892-1924
18	Francis W. Partch 1892-1904
18	Herbert O. Partch 1861-1896
02	Helen Pickett 24 June 1913 - 1 December 1913
12	Martha (?) A. Sneil, wife of Moses Porter, died 1 January 1886
	age 79 years 10 months
12	Moses Porter (?), died 10 April 1876, age 76 years 6 months
01	David E. Radgliffe, died 16 September 1875
	age 77 years G.A.R. *
14	R.F. Randolph, died 13 November 1861, age 44 years
04	Jorgen Rasmusen 1835-1916
01	Fred Rathke 1885-1960
01	Mary Rathke 1885-1965
16	Lucius H. Raymond (?) 1846-1936
16	Mary J. Raymond (?) 1846-1923
04	Elizabeth Record 1826-1898
04	John B. Record 1856-1918
04	Walter Record 1823-1874
19	Linda M. Reineke 13 March 1948 - 24 July 1995
04	Ira Rice 1835-1922 G.A.R.
15	Elizabeth, widow of Rufus Bill and W.S. Richards
	died 20 September 1879, age 79 years
10	Betsy C. Riddle 10 March 1811 - 13 January 1890
10	Hiram Riddle 11 January 1809 - 22 February 1883
13	Mattie G. Dakins, wife of J.E. Rige, died 18 July 1879
	age 20 years 6 months
02	Janice Robinson 1939-1973
09	Kathleen Ann Rollins -30 September 1946-
09	Mary E. Rollins 1886-1948
09	Melville W. Rollins 1880-1942
08	Archie W. Rosengren 1899-1965
08	Verle I. Rosengren 1900-1982
02	Chancey B., son of J. & J.E. Sackett, died 11 June 1863
	age 18 years
02	G.W. Sackett, died 8 December 1863, age 30 years G.A.R.
02	baby Sawatzky -20 July 1921-

05	Albert Schade 1885-1967
05	Anna Schade 1893-1991
05	Helen Schade 1914-1927
05	Irene Schade 1921-1924
19	Cora J. Schultz 1909-__, married T. Elmer 1 September 1932
19	T. Elmer Schultz 1907-1980, married Cora J. 1 September 1932
19	Gretchen Widder Schwartz 1946-1988
19	Howard Schwartz 1907-1984
19	Lillian Schwartz 1909-1992
15	David Scofield, died 27 July 1880, age 91 years
17	Ruth Parker Lanphear Sellers 16 August 1904 - 30 January 1989
12	Vashtia, daughter of G. & C.E. Siers, died 12 June 1881
	age 10 years 8 months 20 days
06	Fannie Sleeth 1849-1894
05	Grant M. Sleeth 1906-1978
06	Grant M. Sleeth 1906-1978
05	Ida M. Sleeth 1881-1970
06	Ida M. Sleeth 1881-1970
05	Lucious R. Sleeth 1867-1945
06	Lucious R. Sleeth 1867-1945
06	Samuel Sleeth 1841-1901 G.A.R.
19	Allen D. Simpson 1916-__
12	Charles A. Simpson 19 September 1855 - 24 September 1889
04	E. Kathryn Simpson 1883-1971
15	Frank A. Simpson 1874-1951
11	George C. Simpson 13 September 1860 - 16 February 1941
11	Ida M. Simpson 4 October 1865 - 22 August 1932
12	James P. Simpson -buried and hard to read G.A.R.
12	James P. Simpson (?) 1 April 1871 - 2 April 1871
15	Jennie J. Simpson 1873-1905
12	John Simpson, died 19 May 1885, age 59 years
12	John E. Simpson 1850-1902
12	Lawrance E., son of Mr. & Mrs. E.W. Simpson, died 3 March 1903
	age 6 weeks 1 day
12	Martha Alice, daughter of J. & S.P. Simpson, died 10 February 1874
	age 15 years 6 months
12	Mary E. Simpson 1860-1937
19	Randi B. Simpson 1909-__
12	Robert J. Simpson 1884-1969
04	Russell J. Simpson 1882-1964
12	Sarah S. Porter, wife of John Simpson
	died 26 March 1899, age 67 years
12	Warren W. Simpson 1897-1932
11	Dale R. Skluzacek 1960-1982
18	E.B. Slocum 1832-1908
09	Eddie E., child of B.C. & M.C. Slocum, died 24 January 1879

	age 9 years 5 months 9 days
18	Eleazer Slocum Sr. 1793-1877 soldier of 1812
04	Emma E. Slocum - no dates
09	Ida M., child of B.C. & M.C. Slocum, died 8 January 1879
	age 16 years 5 months 12 days
04	J.M. Slocum 1858-1916
09	Jessie B., child of B.C. & M.C. Slocum, died 18 January 1879
	age 6 years 3 months 19 days
04	John C. Slocum -no dates
18	Lucretia S. Slocum 1836-1923
09	William Edward, only son of Mr. & Mrs. J.M. Slocum
	died 12 February 1892, age 8 months
09	Willie J., child of B.C. & M.C. Slocum, died 17 January 1879
	age 12 years 1 month 2 days
04	Zella Slocum 1874-1948
02	Edna C. Sommers 1886-1929
02	Fred S. Sommers 1887-1968
08	Libbie Spaulding 1838-1916
08	Phebe Spaulding 1804-1899
13	Drew Stephens (?), died 11 December 1899, age 17 years 2 days
13	Florence R. Stephens (?) 1850-1926
13	William L. Stephens (?) 1837-1914
14	William R. Stephens 1881-1927
16	J.T. Stocking 1817-1887
16	Jane Chambers Stocking 1825-1906
11	Arthur A. Thibodeau 25 May 1889 - 24 May 1967
06	C. Fred Trichie 1864-1948
06	Eldo A. Trichie (?) 1897-1917 veteran World War *
01	Ann Tripp, died 25 August 1859, age 16 years
10	Carl D. Tripp (?), died 3 November 1889, age 1 year
10	Caroline Tripp (?), age 83 years
10	George Tripp, died 19 November 1879, age 62 years
10	Mary G. Tripp (?), died 17 May 1902, age 22 years
10	Ray, son of E.W. & J.A. Tripp, died 17 August 1884
	age 4 months 24 days
19	Agnes P. Turner (?) 1864-194?
18	Florence I. Turner 1886-1979
19	Florence H. Turner 15 November 1923 - __
19	George E. Turner (?) 1862-1926
18	George W. Turner 1891-1959
19	Harry D. Turner, T. Sgt. United States Army World War 2
	3 March 1922 - 24 February 1986
18	infant daughter of C.W. & F.I. Turner -22 October 1924-
11	George Ueberlee 9 August 1801 - 1 August 1884

06	Dimple (?) M. VanGuilder 1895-1901 (?)
06	Henry W. VanGuilder 1890-1915
06	Maria VanGuilder 1866-1942
06	Walter VanGuilder 1867-1957
07	Charles E. Wales 1878-1967
06	George S. Wales, died 9 July 1859, age 21 years
07	Mabel F. Wales 1882-1959
07	Pearl V. Wales 1912-__
07	Stanley L. Wales 1908-1975
08	Julia A. Wallace 1836-1890
15	Joseph Pierce Warner 29 March 1907 - 29 March 1957
10	Anna L. Waters, child of C.L. & Hellin Waters 1868-1882
10	Robert John Waters, child of C.L. & Hellin Waters 1877-1882
06	Emma L., wife of L.N. Wilson, died 18 June 1880
	age 26 years 7 months 15 days
16	?, son of A.T. & L.D. Withers 12 June 1888 - 13 June 1888
16	Albert T. Withers (?) 1857-1941
16	Lola C. Withers (?) 1866-1953

Trees

Dakota County Road 92

Rows 1-9

Gravel
Driveway

Rows 10-18

Red Rose Cemetery, section 17
Waterford township, Dakota Co., MN.
T112N-R19W

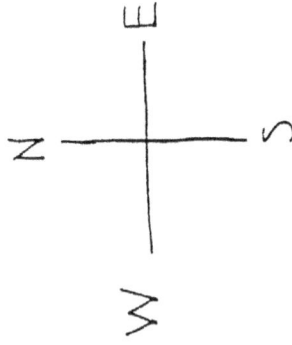

W

N

E

S

Gravel
Driveway

Gravel
Driveway

Gravel
Driveway

3rows
designated
as
19

27

Waterford Cemetery

Waterford township, Dakota county, Minnesota: T112N - R19W, section 20

  I was not able to locate the original location of this cemetery. My assumption is that it no longer exists. The only reference I was able to find in reference to its existence was the following: In the book "History of Dakota County and the city of Hastings", by Rev. Edward D. Neill lists the following about Waterford township: ... R.C. Masters also gave a piece of land in section 20, at the north-west corner of the village plat. Arrangements were made to transfer the bodies from this spot to Rose Leaf Cemetery. A number have been removed, and the remainder will probably be conveyed there during the present year (1881), [when] according to the original contract, the land will revert to R.C. Masters, or his heirs (page 494).

GREENVALE CEMETERY

Greenvale township, Dakota County, Minnesota: T112N – R20W, section 1

This cemetery is well kept and in good shape. It appears that many of the older headstones have been replaced. As with many older cemeteries there are some areas where the headstones do not line up well with the rows. My row numbers are a rough approximation for the burial location. I have numbered the rows beginning on the eastern edge with row 1. Between rows 7 and 8 there is a central drive area.

The Dakota county cemetery records compilation lists this cemetery as: Greenvale (Union) Cemetery, established 1873. 3 acres Section 1, NE 1/4 280th St. W. & Dunbar Avenue.

Rev. Edward D. Neill's book "The History of Dakota County and the city of Hastings" lists the Greenvale Cemetery as Union Cemetery (page 387). To my knowledge these are the same cemetery.

Everyone is listed in alphabetical order. The number before each entry is the row number. There is a map at the back of this section.

This cemeteries burial monuments were transcribed during 1996.

08	C.B.
08	Geofrey N. Barsness, Sgt. United States Army 15 January 1948 - 28 August 1983
08	Robin M. Barsness, SP4 United States Army 7 April 1957 - 28 August 1983
01	Bertha B. Batson 1884-1978
11	Edwin Batson (?) -no dates
01	H. Arthur Batson 1879-1963
12	Jane J. Batson 1847-1919
12	Joseph Batson 1832-1914
12	Josiah Batson (?) -no dates
01	Florence A. Berg 1905-1960
01	Minton L. Berg 1901-1972
19	Anna Berge 1859-1944
19	Erick L. Berge 1860-1947
19	Ernest A. Berge (?) 1903-1982
19	Laura G. Berge 11 September 1899 - 25 September 1984
19	Marion G. Berge (?) 1912-__
04	Maria L. Berlin, died 11 March 1889, age 23 years
15	J. Arthur Billey 1933-1959
15	John E. Billey -1929-
15	Lulu Rose (could be Nelson ? or Billey ?) 1888-1944

15	Stanley P. Billey 1899-1959
15	Verna F. Billey 1902-1991
17	Luella Roach Bingham 1923-1993
01	Jean Ann Blackwell 1926-1961
01	Roy E. Blackwell 1901-1973
09	Alice Bogue 1872-1947
09	Drusilla Bogue 1889-1964
09	Edgar L. Bogue 1866-1936
09	Ira S. Bogue 1874-1947
01	Gladys L. Bogue 1899-1989
04	Lyle G. Bogue 1898-1965
04	Mary Bogue (?) 1869-1950
04	Minerva J. Bogue (?) 1842-1923
01	Ralph E. Bogue 1899-1972
11	Richard Bogue -1925- 'twin'
11	Robert Bogue -1925- 'twin'
09	Roger L. Bogue 1909-1962
09	Ruth I. Bogue 1922-1990
04	Winifred A. Bogue 1900-1986
04	Zachariah Bogue (?) 1833-1911
11	Candace E. Bolin (?) 1847-1923
11	Effie M. Bolin (?) 1890-1965
11	George W. Bolin (?) 1844-1913 G.A.R.
11	Percy A. Bolin (?) 1887-1950
13	Ardath Borchert 1923-1988
13	Charles R. Borchert 1923-__
02	Inez L. Boyd 1893-1978
02	Oakley W. Boyd 1890-1960
12	Anna N. Brady 1870-1958
12	U. J. Brady 1866-1912
01	Travis Peter, son of Mr. & Mrs. Warren W. Brandon -28 February 1968-
19	Warren A. Brandon 5 September 1911 - 28 May 1993
01	William Joseph Brandon 21 September 1963 - 18 October 1980
08	M. Grace Brockway 1873-1900
02	Mattie H. McNeill, wife of Adam Brown, died 14 December 1893
	age 49 years 6 months 3 days
08	Denenda P. Burke 1853-1929
02	Charlie E., son of J.J. & M.J. Campbell, died 18 August 1865
	age ? 3 months 4 days -hard to read
17	Laura Roach Chadwick 1892-1967
07	Henry, son of E. & M.L. Chapman (?), died ?? 1874 (?)
	age 2 years 1 month 5 days
07	John Arthur Chapman (?), died 3 August 1871
	age 1 year 2 months 27 days -hard to read
07	Sarah Ann Chapman (?), died 17 October 1868

       age 1 year 2 months 5 days   -hard to read

18   Morris Chester 22 March - 20 April 1935

18   Phyllis Marie Chester 1936-1945

06   Alfred C. Clague 1857-1923

07   E.T. Clague 1859-1908

06   Isabella Clague, wife of William Clague
          3 November 1817 - 13 June 1907

07   James Clague 1825-1861

07   Sophia VanSlyke, wife of James Clague 1831-1901

06   W. George Clague 1851-1922

06   William Clague 5 April 1805 - 20 December 1884

07   William P. Clague 1856-1867

13   Elizabeth Closson 1915-1982

13   Warren F. Closson 1916-1982

18   Ada Mae Cowell 1875-1965

15   Arthur H. Cowell 1883-1958

15   Augusta B. Cowell 1887-1948

14   Charles Cowell (?) -1918-

14   Charles L. Cowell 1886-1956

01   Ethelyn G. Cowell 1897-1981

14   Herbert Cowell (?) -1920-

01   John P. Cowell 1899-1962

18   Lawrence W. Cowell 1872-1962

14   Pearl E. Cowell 1888-1970

03   Richard J. Cowell, F1 United States Navy World War 2
          21 February 1926 - 23 November 1993

03   S.J. Cowell 1855-1931

03   T.W. Cowell 1856-1910

19   Donelda A. Damann (?) 1916-__

19   Florence G. Damann 1893-1992

19   Gustav B. 'Bright' Damann 1891-1976

19   Kenneth E. Damann (?) 1915-1978

18   Mabel R. Degler (?) 1891-1977

18   Oscar A. Degler, Minnesota CPL 358 Field Arty. BN World War 2
          6 September 1901 - 17 October 1951

18   Otto E. Degler (?) 1889-1946

14   Aletha E. Dilley 1881-1954

16   Amy Lace Dilley 1887-1961

09   Blanche E. Dilley, nee Eigenbrodt
          29 August 1916 - 14 March 1989

08   Charlotte J. Dilley 1855-1935

08   Clara E. Dilley 1877-1881

10   Ephriam C. Dilley (?) 1846-1933

10   Gerald E. Dilley (?) 1857-1941

02   Gerald H. Dilley (?) 3 February 1920 - 16 April 1984

14	Gloa Dilley (?) 1879-1959
09	Harriet, wife of P.A. Dilley, died 15 December 1892
	age 71 years 6 months 11 days
02	Harvey A. Dilley (?) 1890-1965
09	James N. Dilley, died 18 December 1867
	age 5 years 9 months 26 days
08	Jehu B. Dilley 1849-1910
10	Jennie C. Dilley 1858-1931
16	John Perry Dilley 1907-1941
17	Lynn Waldo Dilley 1909-1945
02	Nora E. Dilley (?) 1893-1974
09	P.A. Dilley, died 26 January 1905
	age 83 years 7 months 25 days
08	Paul C. Dilley 1886-1963
14	Scott C. Dilley 5 June 1917 - 8 March 1994
02	Steven G. Dilley (?) 16 October 1945 - 10 August 1963
14	Theron Dilley (?) 1882-1918
10	W.P. Dilley 1854-1937
05	Elzora Doub (?) 1870-1930
05	Henry Doub (?) 1857-1925
13	Joseph Doub 1879-1935
14	Lynn Ann Doub 1852-1919
14	Samuel Doub 1850-1926
12	Edmund F. Dunlap 1874-1923
12	Lucy Gill Dunlap 1882-1934
01	Richard T. Eldred 1934-1957
01	Shirley Ann Eldred 1936-1957
16	Anna E. Farrar 1885-1946
16	Herman F. Farrar 1878-1957
15	Alice O. Frame 1915-1935
08	baby Frame (?) -no dates
11	Betty Frame 1925-1991
11	Donald Frame 1912-__
08	Elizabeth Frame 1863-1925
13	Gertrude Frame (?) 1879-1957
07	Howard Frame 1908-1987
15	James Frame 1908-1967
08	John Frame 1858-1930
15	Lulu Frame (?) 1881-1955
07	Margaret Frame 1912-__
13	Margaret Helen Frame 1943-1954
13	Matt. Frame (?) 1871-1955
12	Matthew T. Frame 1948-1980
15	Robert F. Frame, SSGT United States Army

15 June 1913 - 24 February 1975
07   Ross C. Frame, GM2 United States Navy World War 2   1914-1979
06   Thomas A.H. Frame 1907-__
15   William Frame (?) 1873-1940
06   Wretha M. Frame 1907-1988

11   Emma Roach Gill 1858-1925
09   George W. Gill (?) 1864-1930
10   J. Nelson Gill (?) 1860-1922
10   Jane Gill (?) 1823-1892
10   John Gill (?) 1847-1872
09   Mary E. Gill (?) 1867-1946
10   Thomas Gill (?) 1824-1899
11   Thomas H. Gill (?) 1850-1913
11   Thomas L. Gill (?) 1884-1941
10   William J. Gill (?) 1853-1922
03   Clifford S. Gilomen (?) 29 August 1918 -__
03   Kay A. Gilomen (?) 7 September 1945 - 6 May 1992
05   Michael B. Gilomen 31 March 1959 - 31 December 1979
03   Vivian A. Gilomen (?) 19 May 1917 - __

14   Clifford Harmer 1892-1975
14   John C. Harmer (?) -1915-
14   Neva B. Harmer 1894-1989
14   Ralph H. Harmer (?) -1918-
06   Arthur Hodgson (?) or could be Hutchinson (?), age 9 months 10 days
06   baby Hodgson 1886-1886
05   Charlotte Louise Hodgson 1888-1960
06   Charollet Hodgson 1815-1901
06   Drusilla S., wife of Wm. Hodgson, died 10 May 1878
              age 30 years 5 months 8 days
04   E.J. H. (could be Hodgson ?) 1841-1903
06   Edith Clare Hodgson 20 March 1878 - 4 February 1883
06   Effie Hodgson (?) or could be Hutchinson (?), age 8 months
06   Hannah Hodgson 1883-1884
06   James Hodgson Sr. 1850-1891
06   James Hodgson Jr. 1885-1885
06   Lulu Hodgson 1878-1881
06   Olena Hodgson 1855-1949
06   Thomas Hodgson 1800-1874
06   Walter T., son of Thomas G. & Eliza Hodgson
              14 September 1873 - 15 March 1891
08   Margaret (Dilley) L. Hoeft 1903-1993
19   Ralph W. Holbrook, Minnesota PFC United States Army World War 1
              17 September 1895 - 10 September 1971
03   Hattie Howell 1851-1933

08	Jasper M. Howell 1857-1899
08	Mary L. Howell 1862-1919
03	Russell Howell 1845-1926 G.A.R. 1861-1865
11	Kay I. Hughitt 1957-1995
07	M. Hunter, died 13 December 1875 (?), age 77 years
06	Arthur Hutchinson(?) or could be Hodgson (?), age 9 months 10 days
06	Effie Hutchinson (?) or could be Hodgson (?), age 8 months
06	Mary A. Hutchinson, died 17 November 1875, age 44 years
01	John Johnson 1888-1969
01	Lillian Johnson 1889-1972
02	baby Julie Ann Kimber (?) -18 March 1958-
03	Doris M. Kimber 3 September 1896 - 26 October 1973
03	George N. Kimber 27 November 1896 - 23 September 1936
17	James P. Kirkham 1843-1941
	'Nationality American'
17	James P. Kirkham 1843-1941 Civil War 61-65
	Co. F Captain Co. Minnesota 1st Inf.
	Co. H 5th Reg Minnesota Vol. Inf.
	Co. H 11th Reg Minnesota Vol. Inf.
13	J. Harold Klemenhagen 1921-1991
01	Glenn A. Kuyper 1913-__
01	Marcelle Kuyper 1917-1969
08	Annie J. Lace 1877-1879
08	Catherine L. Lace (?) 1873-1946
08	Edward N. Lace 1876-1880
12	Eliza J. Lace 1855-1884
12	Ellen S. Lace 1858-1942
08	Harry C. Lace 1881-1972
14	infant Lace (?) 1915-1915
14	Irving Charles lace (?) 1885-1975
08	Jane E. Lace 1848-1921
12	John Lace 1840-1922
14	Laura Lace 1889-1980
14	Owen Douglas Lace (?) 1916-1937
12	Philip Lace 1878-1914
08	William Lace 1838-1911
08	William T. Lace (?) 1872-1945
09	Alvin C., son of H. & M. Lundgren, died 21 June 1878
	age 2 years 3 months
09	Ida M., daughter of H. & M. Lundgren, died 2 June 1878
	age 3 years 11 months 17 days
09	infant son of H. & M. Lundgren, died 4 February 1881
	age 1 month 26 days

12	Anna C. McCallum 1847-1935
12	Florence McCallum (?) 1890-1955
12	John McCallum 1846-1913
08	Ann E. McGannon 1899-1985
16	Effie McKague 1870-1949
16	J. Win McKague 1874-1956
15	Jos. H. McKague 1847-1926
15	Mary V. McKague 1838-1931
15	Roy H. McKague 1876-1949
08	E.M.
08	P.M.
08	W.M.
04	Missouri Masters 1836-1907
04	Richard H. Masters 1835-1906 veteran *
12	Abby Mattison (?) 1839-1912
12	S.W. Mattison (?) 1825-1910 Co. F 8 Minnesota
10	Maude D. Megarry 1893-1953
02	baby Miller (?) -1902-
02	Floa A. Miller (?) 1870-1918
03	Arthur G. Moore 1881-1946
10	Christina Moore 1861-1954
03	Ella B. Moore 1886-1968
08	Emma Moore 1859-1938
19	Everett R. Moore 1914-1971
08	Freddie E., son of R. & J.A. Moore, died 25 July 1879
	age 5 years 6 months 19 days
09	Freemont Moore 1886-1950
19	Hazel Moore (?) 1916-__
08	J. Penfield Moore 1892-1934
08	Joseph P., son of R. & J. A. Moore, died 26 July 1879
	age 2 years 9 months
08	Julia Ann, wife of Robert Moore 11 October 1836 - 3 June 1902
08	Laurine, son of R. & J.A. Moore, died 29 July 1875 (?)
	age 10 months (?) -hard to read
08	Robert Moore 1827-1912 veteran *
02	Robert K. Moore, Pvt United States Army World War 2
	14 October 1923 - 3 May 1994
01	Synola B. Moore 6 July 1926 - 6 May 1990
	married Warren A. 20 March 1948
10	Thomas E. Moore 1857-1936
03	Thomas L. Moore 1899-1982
10	Thomas L. Moore 1927-1928
03	Violet E. Moore 1901-1993
08	Wm. Moore 1855-1944

19	Bert E. Morgan 1888-1967
19	Eva L. Morgan 1891-1985
19	Clyde E. Morris 1891-1960
19	Julia Morris 1880-1931
19	Walter J. Morris 30 January 1878 - 14 December 1952
17	Jeffrey Nelsen -1956-
15	Agnes A. Nelson 1875-1929
15	baby Nelson (?) -1929-
12	Casper Nelson 1883-1920
05	Eva Nelson (?) 5 July 1888 - 14 August 1973
06	Glen A. Nelson 8 May 1892 - 10 June 1893
05	Harlan H. Nelson (?) 26 October 1865 - 6 November 1949
06	Hazel I. Nelson 1903-1989
05	Ida M. Nelson (?) 6 May 1869 - 11 September 1942
15	Lulu Rose Nelson (?) or could be Billey (?) 1888-1944
15	Oscar L. Nelson 1874-1966
05	Ray W. Nelson 1894-1984
07	Catherine Olinger 1860-1957
01	Catherine C. Olinger 1886-1962
14	Dora Olinger 1900-1982
14	Earl M. Olinger 1885-1980
07	Ezra L. Olinger 1863-1932
07	Guy O. Olinger 1887-1924 veteran *
19	John A. Olinger 1913-1956
14	Lillian Olinger 1891-1918
19	Lois Jean Olinger (?) 1936-1967
01	Loyd H. Olinger 1890-1961
07	Stacy A. Page -3 May 1973
08	baby Phare (?) -1899-
08	James M. Phare 1834-1908
08	Louise A. Phare 1846-1913
08	Myrtle S. Phare (?) 1872-1900
09	D.W. Phillips 2 December 1839 - __
14	Elizabeth S. Phillips 1844-1919
09	Hattie L. Phillips (?) 29 June 1874 - 26 August 1874
09	Mary Phillips 6 February 1810 - 15 March 1901
09	R.E. Phillips 29 November 1844 - 21 October 1900
14	Robert W. Phillips 1845-1922
04	Alexander Pryor, died 6 December 1880, age 71 years
04	Ann Pryor, died 28 November 1890, age 73 years
02	Elizabeth Pryor 1845-1943
07	Genevieve E. Pryor 1889-1984
02	'Father' Pryor (?) 1837-1937

03	Frederick C. Pryor 1874-1960
02	Henry Pryor 1837-1937
02	Henry Levern Pryor 1877-1899
03	Henry Levern Pryor 1877-1899
04	Mary Pryor, died 30 December 1913, age 72 years
02	'Mother' Pryor (?) 1845-1943
02	Nellie B. Pryor 1883-1979
07	Robert K. Pryor 1885-1976
06	George C. Quilliam (?), died 4 June 1881
	age 6 years 3 months 1 day
06	Josiah W. Quilliam (?), died 24 March 1881
	age 13 years (?) 2 days
06	Mary I. Quilliam (?), died 21 May 1881
	age 15 years 1 month 17 days
17	Verne Riddle 1892-1946
15	Abram Woodward Roach 1849-1932
15	Altie Pratt Roach 1865-1935
17	Byron Roach 1887-1943
16	Byron Roach 1887-1943
04	Joanna Roach 1820-1892
16	Laura Roach 1892-1967
04	Lydia Ardell Roach 1859-1881
04	Phineas Roach 1819-1897
02	Janie B. Smith, wife of Joseph Roberts, died 10 July 1894
	age 52 years
17	Clark A. Robinson 1923-1943
17	Elmer C. Robinson Sr. 1887-1951
17	Evelyn Hatt Robinson 1896-1985
17	Harold B. Robinson 1914-1939
01	Harry W. Ruff 1891-1960
01	Isabel S. Ruff 1895-1967
17	Dorothy Roach Sanford 1917-1959
04	Clark Shellenbarger (?) 1842-1921 G.A.R.
07	Elizabeth Shellenbarger (?) 1851-1933
04	Esther Shellenbarger (?) 1849-1930
04	Florence Shellenbarger (?) 1887-1954
19	Frank R. Shellenbarger 1887-1946
07	Freer Shellenbarger (?) 1845-1922 veteran *
04	John Shellenbarger (?) 1886-1970
19	Lena G. Shellenbarger 1897-1957
06	Minnie, daughter of P. & M. Shepherd, died 30 October 1881
	age 6 years
06	Pet (?), son of ?? -next to Shepherd -to worn to read

02	Aaron Shideler 1841-1903
19	Ella M. Shumway 1866-1957
19	Oscar D. Shumway 1867-1957
05	Dorothy F. Simpson 1907-1930
05	Florence H. Simpson (?) 1879-1936
05	Willis A. Simpson (?) 1881-1966
15	Ed Sommers 1908-1989
15	Ora Sommers 1910-__
04	Arthur J. Steadman 1903-1958
04	Bonnie G. Steadman 1904-1991
15	Loretta H. Steele 1860-1930
07	Alvin D. Strachan 1917-1993, married Joyce L. 8 January 1938
07	Joyce L. Strachan 1915-__, married Alvin D. 8 January 1938
10	Esther E. Switzer 20 November 1912 - __
10	Troy D. Switzer 1962-1985
10	William R. Switzer 15 January 1906 - 14 April 1990
09	William R. Switzer, PFC United States Marine Corps 15 January 1906 - 14 April 1990
14	Kathryn T. Torbenson (?) 1909-1937 and baby -1937-
14	Robert L. Torbenson, A1C United States Air Force Korea 1933-1976
07	Nicholas VanSlyke 1867-1874
04	Ackley C. Wager 1856-1942
04	Annette Wager (?) 1840-1929
04	Cornelius H. Wager (?) 1831-1911
06	Ervin L. Wager 1858-1954
06	Jennie L. Wager (?) -no dates
04	Lillian L. Wager (?) 1862-1938
04	William Wager (?) 1874-1896
18	baby White -1961-
17	Arthur C. Wood 1877-1964
13	Curtiss L. Wood 1908-1976
14	Dean O. Wood, Minnesota PFC 20 Inf. 6 Div. World War 2 7 June 1920 - 22 June 1944
02	Edwin H. Wood 1836-1907
14	Elliot D. Wood 1916-1917
07	George H. Wood 1854-1924
17	Mabel E. Wood 1880-1969
07	Mary Ellen Wood 1856-1937
14	Nellie E. Wood 1883-1957
07	Stanley G. Wood 1883-1954
02	Susan A. Wood 1843-1932

17   Wallace M. Wood (?) 1903-1969
14   Walter R. Wood 1879-1949

I was no able to determine a surname for the following.
12   Carrie Alice 1873-1945   -close to Mattison (?)
12   Henry Burt 1867-1945   -close to Mattison (?)

Dakota County Road 86

Dunbar Avenue
turns into Drexel Ave.

Rows 8-19

Rows 1-7

Drive Area

Drive Area

Trees

Greenvale Cemetery 1873
Section 1, Greenvale Township,
Dakota County, Minnesota
T112N-R20W

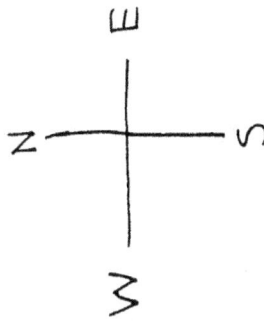

N
W —|— E
S

Solar Lutheran Cemetery

Greenvale township, Dakota county, Minnesota: T112N - R20W, section 9

I was not able to determine if any burials remain at this location. The WPA records list: ... Solor's Lutheran Cemetery in SWNW area of section 9 and that it was moved to Webster township, Rice county, Minnesota.

The Dakota county cemetery records compilation lists this cemetery as: Solar Lutheran Cemetery, established 1881. 1 acre, located Section 9, NW 1/4. Holyoke Avenue. (Abandoned).

John Clague Cemetery

Greenvale township, Dakota county, Minnesota: T112N - R20W, section 11

I was not able to determine if any burials remain at this site. There is a John Clague buried in the Union/Greenvale Cemetery in section 1, as well as other Clague's. I have also came across a reference to the Clague cemetery in the book "History of Dakota County and the city of Hastings" by Rev. Edward D. Neill. He wrote: .... An acre of ground was set apart by John Clague, in the north-east quarter of section 2, in the spring of 1861. The first person buried in it was James Clague, who died 22 February 1861 (page 387). [the Andreas 1874 Atlas Map shows John Clague in the NW corner of NE section 11].   I was not able to find any more information about a cemetery in section 2.

The Dakota County cemetery compilation lists the section 11 John Clague cemetery as: John Clague private cemetery, 1861. 1 acre, located Section 11, NW 1/4. 290th Street. (Abandoned).

ST. JOSEPH'S CATHOLIC CHURCH CEMETERY

Douglas township, Dakota county, Minnesota: T113N - R17W, section 11

This cemetery is a block or so west of the intersection of highways 91 and 61. The grounds are upkept and in good shape. There is evidence of previous vandalism. Some of the old slab headstones were broke at one time. This appears to have been some time ago, as the broken edges are already very worn. There is also some evidence that someone has traced in the names with a black permanent marker. This also appears to have been done some time ago. The vandalism and name tracing only affected a few headstones. Other than these instances the remaining headstones are in good shape.

The Dakota county cemetery records compilation lists this cemetery as: St. Joseph's Catholic Cemetery. First used in 1874. 3 acres. Located SE 1/4 of Section 11.

In Rev. Edward D. Neill's book, "History of Dakota County and the city of Hastings" he wrote the following about St. Joseph's Catholic Church: The cornerstone of this church was laid in May, 1872, and a church completed in the fall of 1873 ... is located on the south-east corner of section 11. The site, with ten acres of land for church and cemetery. ... The cemetery was first used in 1874. In 1876, C.B. Lowell surveyed and staked out three acres on the west end of the lot. This yard contains 357 lots and at the present (1881) only about twenty-five graves (page 344).

This is a large cemetery.   When I wrote down the burials I divided the cemetery into three sections. The first section contains rows 1 - 19. The second section contains rows 20 - 39. The third and newer section contains rows 40 - 48.

Everyone is listed in alphabetical order. The number before each entry is the row number. There is a map at the back of this section.

This cemeteries burial monuments were transcribed during 1996.

45	Bernard J. Ahlers 1904-1983
45	Olive C. Ahlers 1899-1968
22	Johann Anton, born at Reuland (?), Luxemburg 24 March 1810 died 3 October 1884
28	Bernard Bartelmey 1879-1962
28	Christine Bartelmey 1890-1972
28	Elizabeth Bartelmey 1874-1958
27	John L. Bartelmey 1886-1896
27	Johnnie Bartelmey 29 November 1886 - 1 July 1896
27	Mary Bartelmey (?) 1852-1936
27	Peter Bartelmey(?) 1872-1939

27	Theodore Bartelmey 4 November 1844 - 6 March 1891
28	Theresa Bartelmey 1884-1972
45	Alois J. Bauer 1916-1965
42	Catherine Bauer 1905-1992
42	Harold Bauer 1918-1985
45	Irene Bauer 1922-__
43	Mary Bauer 1883-1971
43	Mathias Bauer 1879-1952
42	Paul Bauer 1911-1982
46	Randal Bauer 1951-1971
26	Genevieve, wife of John Bihner 28 September 1843 - 13 July 1922
42	Hannah J. Bihner(?) 1885-1961
26	John Bihner 8 December 1841 - 29 September 1906
42	John L. Bihner(?) 1876-1939
26	Louise C. Bihner 3 May 1879 - 6 November 1893
26	Maria Anna Bihner 21 February 1874 - 17 October 1891
39	Regina Schaffer Bihner 1904-1994
37	Jeanne Susan Birk 3 September 1945 - 16 March 1951
37	Marie Birk 1915-__
37	Randy Birk -18 December 1961-
37	Ted Birk 1910-1990
03	Agnes N. Black 1845-1929
14	Daniel Boland (?) 1863-1927
14	'Father' Boland (?) 1830-1914
14	James F. Boland (?) 1874-1944
14	Jane Boland (?) 1865-1912
14	'Mother' Boland (?) 1835-1911
20	Carl, son of Dionis & Cecilia Boser 7 August 1869 - 19 April 1875
21	Dennis J. Boser 1897-1958
21	Frank A. Boser 14 February 1855 - 20 January 1922
21	George A. Boser 1885-1959
20	Johann Boser 21 April 1863 - 3 July 1898
21	Mary Boser 3 May 1857 - 18 June 1920
04	Catherine Brennen (?) 1837-1924
01	Florence E. Brennen 1898-1994
02	James Brennen (?) 1853-1930
03	Lillian Brennen 1902 - 1996 (recent burial - August 1996 ?)
02	Mary Brennen (?) 1855-1939
02	Mayme S. Brennen (?) 1878-1957
03	Patrick Francis Brennen 1883-1935
03	Thomas Brennen 2 December 1814 - 13 May 1876 county Roseoninoa (?), Ireland
03	Thomas Brennen, husband of Agnes Black 1840-1922
03	Thomas Brennen 1894-1970

03	Winefred, wife of Thomas Brennen 13 May 1813 - 25 May 1893
46	Annella Bretschneider 1927-1988
46	George Bretschneider 1925-__
46	Leland M. Bretschneider 1951-1969
21	Lorenz Burr 14 December 1863 - 30 May 1918
21	Theresa Burr, died 1894, age 32 years
43	Blanche Caneff 1903-1949
16	Catherine Ryan Caneff 7 March 1847 - 2 February 1922
16	John J. Caneff, his wife Catherine Ryan
	18 June 1842 - 19 March 1911
43	John V. Caneff 1884-1960
10	Edward E. Cleary, LCDR United States Navy World War 2 1910-1991
10	Emma O'K (O'Keefe ?) Cleary (?) 1866-1956
10	Edward J. Cleary (?) 1868-1934
10	Gerald Edward Cleary 2 October 1900 - 25 September 1906
11	Harold F. Cleary 1897-1970
10	Mary Theresa Cleary (?) 1950-1981
11	Naomi S. Cleary 1899-1994
40	Cecelia M. Costello 1870-1953
40	Dorothy C. Costello 1898-1984
40	Frederick F. Costello 1872-1934
23	Rev. M.J. Duehr D.D. 1876-1946, born at Ahn, Luxembourg, G.D.
	Pastor at Miesville 1928-1946
24	Dorothea Eckart 10 February 1834 - 15 February 1906
15	Helen Eckart (?) 1867-1951
15	baby Henry Eckart (?) Jr. 1891-1891
15	Henry Eckart (?) 1858-1931
24	Johann U. Eckart 17 June 1827 - 1 March 1906
24	Joseph Eckert 1866-1946
38	baby Eilen (?) born & died 1889
38	George Eilen 18 February 1846 - 14 March 1923
38	George Eilen (?) 1899-1900
39	George Eilen born & died 26 August 1919
38	Margaret Eilen 16 December 1857 - 9 March 1921
09	James A. Elder (?) 1888-1972
09	John D. Elder (?) 1886-1945
09	Mary A. Elder (?) 1853-1929
09	Mary C. Elder (?) 1884-1956
09	Monica M. Elder (?) 1881-1906
09	William H. Elder (?) 1838-1928
09	William T. Elder (?) 1889-1976
18	Zita E., daughter of J.S. & E. Elder, died 11 July 1881
	age 4 months, 15 days

15	Cecelia Caneff Eldred 19 December 1874 - 26 March 1926
15	Ozro Warren Eldred 9 May 1870 - 18 September 1929
09	Patrick C. Fahey, born in county Galway, Ireland
	17 February 1865 - 16 October 1896
09	Ridget Fahey 1863-1947
46	Ruth Ann Nauer Ferraro 1944-1979
32	Dorothy T. Fischer, nee O'Shaughnessy 1925-1993
32	Julius A. Fischer 1909-1994
32	Madeline A. Fischer 1912-1995
14	Frank Ford 1807-1897
27	Agnes C. Fox (?) 1903-1981
36	Albert Fox 1879-1946
47	Alois Fox 1905-1994
36	Anne M. Fox 1883-1969
47	Annett Fox 1917-__
47	August J. Fox (?) 1875-1948
43	Bessie Fox 1915-__
46	Brian Fox 1962-1976
34	Carl Fox 19 October 1901 - 6 July 1970
27	Caroline M. Fox (?) 1878-1932
34	Charles Fox (?) 28 November 1871 - 17 April 1924
36	Ernestine M. Fox 1916-1916
17	baby Eugene Fox 3 January - 12 February 1942
17	Eugene Fox -1942-
43	Fay Ann Fox 9 October - 28 December 1957
48	George J. Fox 1909-1990
	married Rosella M. 25 September 1935
17	Gladys Fox 1914-1991
17	Gladys Fox 1914-1991
47	infant son Fox -1944-
21	John Fox, son of Alvis & Marian Fox
	22 September 1883 - 1 June 1893
44	Kathryn E. Fox 1908-1986
43	Leo G. Fox 1905-1986
17	Leo M. Fox 1911-__
46	Mary E. Fox 1951-1975
36	Myron J. Fox 1920-1953
46	Natalie Ann Fox -24 May 1988-
36	Raymond G. Fox 1922-1929
17	Robert Fox 1949-1969
17	Robert Fox 1949-1969
48	Rosella M. Fox 1914-__ married George J. 25 September 1935
44	Stephen A. Fox 1908-1964
45	Alice M. Freier 1914-1965
45	Bernard W. Freier 1920-1970

44	Katherine A. Freier 1892-1963
45	Rynold C. Freier 1932-1971, married Lois M. 7 May 1949
44	Walwin H. Freier 1891-1961
46	Frances Freiermuth 1909-1937 'mother & child'
44	Helen Freiermuth 1940-1962
48	Robert Friesen 1940-1989, married Elaine 22 July 1961
20	Alois Fuchs 31 August 1830 - 28 April 1909
34	David Fuchs 6 December 1899 - 24 February 1901
21	Johann, son of A. & M.A. Fuchs
	2 February 1869 - 11 October 1876
20	Maria Anna Burr, wife of Alois Fuchs
	9 February 1845 - 4 November 1897
44	Stephen J. Furlong 1956-1992
15	Anna Caneff Garman 9 July 1877 - 28 April 1953
41	Christine C. Gergen 1885-1976
41	Ernestine L. Gergen 1911-1976
41	Martin N. Gergen 1884-1936
41	Robert A. Gergen 1909-1959
35	Anna Gerlach 4 September 1877 - 25 September 1962
33	Anna Gerlach 1880-1966
27	Betty Lou Gerlach 1929-1935
27	Carl S. Gerlach 1902-1977
33	Charles Gerlach 1868-1951
26	Charles Gerlach 22 August 1893-2 September 1893
26	Frank Gerlach 10 January 1901 - 7 April 1901
20	G. Heinrich (?), son of ? & ? Gerlach (?)
	October 1873 (?) - to worn to read
35	George Gerlach 8 November 1870 - 21 August 1920
20	Gottfried Gerlach 19 March 1828 - 19 June 1904
27	Grace V. Gerlach 1904-1983
35	John J. Gerlach 2 December 1902 - 21 January 1903
26	Joseph Gerlach (?) 1864-1928
45	Kathryn Gerlach 1915-1965
26	Louise Gerlach (?) 1867-1942
33	Maria Gerlach 16 July 1898 - 9 March 1901
45	Matt Gerlach 1903-__
27	Nicholas Gerlach 17 June 1886 - 9 August 1892
20	Theresia M. Gerlach 4 June 1831 - 11 May 1903
37	George Ginther (?) 1906-1924
37	Irene Ginther (?) 1920-1921
37	Joseph Ginther (?) 1875-1940
37	Margaret Ginther (?) 1880-1962
03	Bridget, wife of Michael Graney, died 23 June 1883
	age 36 years, 1 month, 2 days, Native of Parish of Crossboyle, county Mayo, Ireland

02	Michael Graney 12 May 1880 - 29 March 1909
40	Lawrence John Hammes 24 October 1913 - 1 March 1995
04	James Hart (?) 1824-1911
04	James Hart (?) -1878-
04	John Hart (?) 1836-1920
04	Michael Hart (?) 1820-1916
04	Thomas Hart (?) 1880-1917
06	Annie E. Henry 17 February 1860 - 31 October 1888
06	George A. Henry 7 April 1869 - 3 August 1891
06	Mary, wife of M. Henry 2 June 1837 - 23 January 1890
06	Mary Honora Henry (?) 13 December 1873 - 25 January 1890
06	Ellen Hicke 1897-1900
43	Jeannette M. Hickey 1904-1967
16	Stephen J. Hickey 1899-1942
16	Winifred Hickey 1863-1942
16	Winifred Hickey 1868-1942
40	Agatha M. Hoffman 1915-__
40	Frank M. Hoffmann 1912-1994
40	Frank M. Hoffmann, TEC 5 United States Army World War 2 26 August 1912 - 19 January 1994
02	Jane Almira Hogan 1895-1987
02	Michael C. Hogan 1891-1980
32	Barbara W., daughter of Peter & Barbara Husting 3 August 1886 - 13 February 1891
31	Catherine Illa 1895-1983
31	Mary Illa 1862-1904
31	Michael Illa 29 September 1859 - 11 November 1898
31	Michael Illa 1859-1898
31	Michael Illa 1891-1966
25	Adam Ille 26 June 1833 - 10 August 1896
11	Steven H. Isaacson 3 January 1952 - 9 March 1991
38	Susanna, wife of Michael Iulen 24 May 1814 - 11 April 1878
36	Ase J. Johnson 1892-1942
36	Veronica K. Johnson 1907-1936
40	Gertrude Mainz Jones 1906-1991
27	Anna M. Karicher 5 January 1835 - 11 January 1916
27	Lambert Karicher, born 20 March 1820 in Bowingen Grossherzog thum Luxemburg, died 3 January 1899
23	Joseph, child of Julia & Joseph Kehlnhofer 21 November 1879 - 21 November 1879
23	May, child of Julia & Joseph Kehlnhofer 28 June 1875 - 24 August 1877

47	Edward Kelly 1926-1992
47	Hedwig Kelly 1927-__
31	Anna Kieffer 1871-1940
32	Anna Kieffer (?) 1880-1945
41	Eliza Kieffer 1899-1946
41	Eliza Kieffer (?) 1899-1946
34	Elizabeth Kieffer 14 February 1848 - 11 January 1915
41	Frances Kieffer 1903-1984
34	Frank Kieffer 1872-1954
34	George Kieffer 17 February 1837 - 21 August 1910
32	George Kieffer (?) 1874-1958
33	Henry G. Kieffer born & died 1905
33	John W. Kieffer born & died 1907
44	Louis J. Kieffer 1904-1962
44	Louis K. Kieffer 1902-1991
45	Madeline L. Kieffer 1916-1969
45	Martin H. Kieffer 1913-1980
34	Mary Kieffer 1881-1955
31	Wilhelm F. Kieffer 26 June 1902 - 25 November 1903
31	Wm. Kieffer 1869-1923
19	Bernardine Kimmes 1924-__
40	Catherine Kimmes 29 January 1900 - 4 May 1900
44	Catherine Kimmes 1911-1995
48	Edward Kimmes 1938-1989
19	George Kimmes 1911-1984
40	John Kimmes 7 September 1898 - 28 September 1898
37	Joseph Kimmes 1902-1934
40	Katherine Kimmes 1874-1953
40	Lena R. Kimmes 1910-__
37	Maria L. Kimmes ? 1904 - 5 February 1909 (?)
40	Maria Kimmes -1908-
37	Mark E. Kimmes 1956-1959
40	Michael M. Kimmes 1909-1993
44	Nick J. Kimmes 1906-__
46	Rosella Kimmes 1914-1971
46	Sylvester Kimmes 1913-1991
40	Theodore Kimmes 1874-1956
39	Catherine King 1835-1918
39	Clara C. King (?) 1877-1950
39	John L. King 1828-1919
29	John M. King 1868-1942
30	Marie C., daughter of Mrs. & Mr. J.M. King 16 December 1896 - 22 December 1896
46	Martin A. King 1919-1978
11	Mary King -no dates listed
29	Mary Ann King 1866-1937

39	Mathew M., son of Mr. & Mrs. J.L. King
	27 August 1875 - 8 June 1907
44	Raymond F. King 1916-1964
44	Sarah L. King 1926-1988
39	Thomas E. King (?) 1873-1951
41	Henry Klein 1872-1935
22	son Klemens 1898-1959
41	Joseph C. Klien 1878-1968
33	Mary Knoblauch 1870-1886
33	Susan Knoblauch 1880-1880
47	Florence M. Kocur 1928-__
47	Joseph A. Kocur 1919-1981
47	Joseph A. Kocur, PFC United States Army World War 2 1919-1981
43	Emily J. Kramer 1924-__, married Eugene J. 28 April 1947
43	Eugene J. Kramer 1921-1995, married Emily J. 28 April 1947
32	baby Allen Kruse 1950-1951
22	Alvina Kruse 1879-1958
32	Anton Kruse 15 January 1859 - 19 September 1918
32	Augusta Kruse 16 September 1884 - 25 July 1954
32	Frank J. Kruse 14 August 1889 - 12 February 1928
22	Joseph Kruse 1872-1920
43	Joseph C. Kruse 1893-1953
12	Karl (?), son of Anton & Katharina Kruse
	16 August 1887 (?) - 11 March 1890 (?)
43	Marie M. Kruse 1900-1976
32	'Mother' A. Kruse (?) 10 June 1870 - 10 April 1942
12	Valentin (?), son of Anton & Katharine Kruse
	15 August 1890 - 18 August 1891
32	Alfred Kuhn 1860-1937
32	Catherine Kuhn 1866-1946
32	George Kuhn 1905-1965
23	George E. Kuhn 5 April 1869 - 15 September 1908
23	Helen Kuhn 28 February 1836 - 18 March 1911
23	John Kuhn 23 October 1828 - 19 June 1881
32	Leo Kuhn 1901-1935
23	Louis Kuhn, died 7 February 1897, age 35 years
41	James F. Kuhns 1927-1930
40	Arthur Kummer 1894-1994
40	Arthur L. Kummer, PVT 5 United States Army World War 1
	2 November 1894 - 30 April 1994
40	Lena M. Kummer 1899-__
35	Phyllis, daughter of Mr. & Mrs. Arthur Kummer 1925-1926
12	Franz, son of M. & V. Kump 6 September 1886 - 16 November 1886
23	John Ladwig (?) 1844-1941
23	Mary Ladwig (?) 1850-1930

25	Henry Lang 8 December 1847 - 21 September 1928
43	Francis Lang 1920-1992
43	John C. Lang 1893-1957
43	Katherine Lang 1893-1980
25	Mary Lang 7 December 1861 - 5 November 1922
12	Franz Lange 2 January 1880 - 15 April 1884
46	Lillian G. Langenfeld 11 July 1925 - 12 November 1976
46	Raymond J. Langenfeld, Minnesota SGT United States Marines Corp.
	World War 2 30 July 1922 - 10 May 1972
29	Christine Riegert, wife of Jacob Lano
	21 March 1862 - 27 December 1891
48	Elizabeth M. Larson, nee Foley
	3 July 1916 - 5 June 1991
01	Anthony Francis Leifeld, son of Robert & Caroline -3 December 1966-
01	August B. Leifeld 1911-__, married Marie C. 8 September 1936
43	baby Leifeld -7 February 1957-
01	Marie C. Leifeld 1915-1994, married August B. 8 September 1936
01	Robert A. Leifeld, son of Robert & Caroline -15 January 1965-
16	Mathew B. Ley 1887-1940
30	Emma Engel, wife of Peter Lorentz
	12 October 1861 - 1 March 1892
30	Peter Lorentz 15 April 1861 - 9 November 1891
42	Charles Lucius 1868-1944
42	Mary T. Lucius 1874-1957
47	Eileen M. Ludwig 1923-__
47	Gilbert N. Ludwig 1916-1980
39	Nicholas Ludwig 15 October 1813 - 8 march 1885
15	Ann McDermoth, died 20 February 1909
15	Michael McDermoth, died 4 June 1898
15	Patrick McDermoth, died 8 August 1912
15	James McDermott -1 February 1957-
15	John McDermott, died 12 August 1940
15	Teresa McDermott -18 February 1954-
15	Winifred McDermott -26 November 1936
47	Kevin M. McDonald 28 March 1989 - 14 February 1990
40	Ethel Mainz 1907-1948
40	John S. Mainz 1909-1992
40	Mathilda Mainz 1873-1964
40	Simon Mainz 1857-1930
13	Jacob T., son of Chn. & Barbara Mamer
	2 April 1880 - 26 May 1885
43	Peter J. Marschall 1887-1958
43	Theresa F. Marschall 1896-1978
28	Ann Meisch 1875-1940

28	Catherine Bertrance, wife of Philip Meisch 1839-1922
41	Clara Meisch 1877-1961
41	Evelyn Meisch 1918-1989
23	Jerome P. Meisch 25 October 1919 - 26 October 1919
41	John P. Meisch 1868-1952
41	Joseph Meisch 1901-1973
41	Madeline A. Meisch 1910-__
41	Peter Meisch (?) 1902-1935
28	Philip Meisch 1841-1928
41	Philip Meisch 1899-1979
41	Philip Meisch 1899-1979
41	Raymond J. Meisch (?) 1912-1940
41	William I. Meisch 1907-1988
20	Franky Miller, son of Peter & Caroline -1884-
35	Theresa M. Molitor 1897-1921
39	Lucy M. Moravec 1 October 1905 (?) - 26 march 1907
39	Rosa Moravec 25 March 1876 - 29 June 1908
48	Mason Murch Jr., PVT United States Army World War 2 1929-1980
46	Arnold J. Nauer 1908-1971
43	Francine M. Nauer 10 May 1950 - 14 October 1950
23	Catherine Kuhn, beloved wife of John Nicola, born in Miesville, Dakota County, Minnesota 3 April 1864, died Minor, North Dakota 13 April 1894
47	Agatha A. Niebur 1926-1986
47	Carrol Niebur, United States Army World War 2 1918-1991
47	Ethel Niebur 1927-__
46	Vernon O. Niebur 1956-1975
47	Verona Niebur 1923-1990
01	Catherine A. Nilan (?) 1897-1940
03	Edward Nilan, Native of Parish of Kilkarton (?) county Galway, Ireland 5 August 1822 - 25 April 1885, age 62 years, 9 months, 20 days
03	Edward P. Nilan, born in Pittsburg, Pa. 18 July 1857 - 15 October 1901 age 44 years, 2 months, 27 days
01	Hanorah R. Nilan 2 December 1868 - 9 October 1942
02	Jane Almira Nilan (?) 1887-1894
01	John M. Nilan (?) 1861-1926
02	Katie F., daughter of Michael T & Jane A. Nilan 15 April 1887 - 13 January 1894, age 6 years, 8 months, 29 days
42	Lena M. Nilan 1897-1988
42	Madeline M. Nilan 1912-1990
01	Mary Jane Nilan (?) 1860-1934
42	Owen S. Nilan 1909-1950
03	Patrick Nilan, Native of Kiltarton (?) Parish county Galway, Ireland November Eve. 1819 - 28 March 1903 age 83 years, 4 months 28 days

02	Patrick, son of John & Mary Jane Nilan
	5 November 1888 - 5 August 1889, age 9 months, 21 days
01	Patrick H. Nilan (?) 1892-1913
42	Patrick J. Nilan 1865-1939
42	Patrick R. Nilan 1895-1963
03	Sarah Nilan, wife of Patrick, native of Crossboyle Parish
	county Mayo, Ireland 23 August 1823 - 21 March 1901
	age 77 years, 6 months, 29 days
42	Sarah A. Nilan 1867-1949
01	Sarah J. Nilan 1873-1955
02	Thomas F. Nilan 23 August 1870 - 14 June 1942
01	Thomas J. Nilan (?) 1900-1937
02	William J. Nilan 26 October 1866 - 16 April 1933
44	Leonora B. Oberg 1926-1995
44	Wilbur Oberg 1924-__
07	Ann, wife of Wm. O'Connell, born 14 January 1831 at Williamsport, Pa.
	died 13 March 1887
07	Ann O'Connell (?) 1831-1887
07	Eliza L., daughter of Wm. & A. O'Connell
	11 January 1856 - 17 February 1872
07	Elizabeth L. O'Connell (?) 1855-1872
07	Jane M. O'Connell, born 9 September 1859 at Willmore, Pa.
	died 1 September 1930
07	John C. O'Connell, born 12 May 1857 at Willmore, Pa.
	died 3 May 1926
07	John G. O'Connell (?) 1857-1926
07	Thomas B. O'Connell, born 16 August 1862 at Willmore, Pa.
	died 19 December 1897
07	Thomas Bernard O'Connell, born 14 December 1822 at Ebensburg, Pa.
	died 2 December 1909
07	William O'Connell (?) 1822-1909
02	Jerome O'Connor, infant of Tom & Katie
	4 January - 5 January 1976
07	Alice O'Keefe 1854-1933
07	Amelia O'Keefe 1856-1927
40	Daniel A. O'Keefe 1857-1942
07	Rev. Dennis F. O'Keefe, son of Jeremiah & Mary O'Keefe, 17 May 1859
	ordained priest 5 November 1885, died 4 December 1886
40	Grace M. O'Keefe 1907-__
40	Helen Maher O'Keefe 1872-1931
07	Jeremiah O'Keefe 1817-1898
07	Jeremiah Vincent, son of Jeremiah & Mary O'Keefe
	17 September 1864 - 31 May 1891
40	Joseph M. O'Keefe 1905-__
07	Mary Ryan O'Keefe 1833-1904

07	Nellie O'Keefe 1862-1936
08	P.H. O'Keefe 1870-1924
08	Mrs. P.H. O'Keefe 1876-1928
33	Leth A. Olin 1882-1941
33	Alvin Olson 1882-1954
33	Caroline Olson 1884-1964
33	Conrad August, son of Alvin & ? Olson
	7 February 1911 - 15 December 1911
43	Mary 'Mamie' Ellen Olson 1880-1962
43	S. August 'Gus' Olson 1878-1948
13	Alice Fallon O'Rourke 1872-1960
13	Bernice Riley O'Rourke 1910-__
13	Edward O'Rourke 1864-1919
12	Edward F. O'Rourke 1914-__
35	Emma O'Rourke 1887-1926
13	Helen Hanley O'Rourke 1907-1972
12	Hannah O'Rourke 1826-1910
35	James O'Rourke 1852-1931
12	John O'Rourke 1858-1889
12	John, son of M. & H. O'Rourke 25 June 1858 - 12 March 1889
13	Katherine H. O'Rourke 1900-1977
35	Lucy A. O'Shaughnessy, wife of James O'Rourke 1851-1923
12	Margaret O'Rourke 1863-1955
05	Margret O'Rourke, born in Kings county Ireland 15 October 1824
	died 30 November 1906, age 82 years, 1 month, 15 days
12	Michael O'Rourke 1823-1893
12	Michael O'Rourke, born in county Galway, Ireland
	died 21 August 1893, age 70 years
13	Michael P. O'Rourke 1898-1987
05	Patrick O'Rourke, born in county West Meath, Ireland 8 April 1816
	died 30 January 1879, age 63 years, 9 months, 22 days
12	Thomas, son of M. & H. O'Rourke
	25 August 1854 - 4 May 1890
12	Thomas O'Rourke 1854-1890
13	Thomas L. O'Rourke 1901-1982
23	Reverend Frederick A. Ortner, born Oberaudorf, Germany 24 May 1904
	ordained Banz, Germany Seminary 26 April 1936
	Pastor of the church of St. Joseph Meisville, Minnesota
	1864-1975, died 1 September 1980
04	Eliza O'S. -no dates
04	Martin O'S. - no dates
04	Eliza J., daughter of Thomas & Eliza O' Shaughness
	died 21 January 1870, age 2 years (?)
04	Michael, son of Thomas & Eliza O'Shaughness
	died 28 February 18??, -broken and hard to read
05	William T, O'Shaughness 3 September 1891 - 21 January 1892

32	Agnes M. O'Shaughnessy 1915-1921
04	Eliza O'Shaughnessy 15 December 1829 - 26 December 1908
05	Helen O'Shaughnessy 1906-1995
05	John O'Shaughnessy 1897-1973
04	John, son of E. & E. O'Shaughnessy
	28 September 1859 - 20 December 1884
44	Louise T. O'Shaughnessy 1899-1987
44	Martin L. O'Shaughnessy, Minnesota PEC HQ Co. 318 Field Arty
	World War 1 31 August 1895 - 25 November 1960
04	Martin, son of E. & E. O'Shaughnessy
	4 September 1863 - 13 July 1890
32	Michael R. O'Shaughnessy 1889-1964
42	Olivia O'Shaughnessy 1895-1982
45	Regina O'Shaughnessy 1904-1967
	married William 25 May 1925
05	Theresa O'Shaughnessy 17 January 1866 - 2 June 1956
32	Theresa O'Shaughnessy 1888-1987
04	Thomas O'Shaughnessy, died 29 September 1879
	age 62 years, 9 months. A Native of Parish of
	Kiltarton, county Galway, Ireland
42	Thomas O'Shaughnessy 1892-1977
44	Venita M. O'Shaughnessy 1923-__
45	William O'Shaughnessy 1902-1967, married Regina 25 may 1925
05	William O'Shaughnessy Sr. 13 July 1861 - 16 June 1905
22	Martin, son of P. & M. Otting (?)
	1 September 186? - 1 November 1878 - very hard to read
46	Richard G. Otto 1966-1972
46	Richard N. Otto 1921-1985, married Viola E. 29 June 1946
46	Viola E. Otto 1926-__ , married Richard N. 29 June 1946
37	Anna Peine 1884-1958
45	Christine Peine 1905-__
37	Margaret Peine 1905-1923
37	Monica Peine -1920-
37	Peter Peine 1876-1959
45	Theodore C. Peine 1908-1981
10	Mary Cleary Peland 17 December 1898 - 16 May 1996
10	George A. Pelant, Minnesota PVT. Co. C. 311 Field SIG BN
	World War 1 24 April 1889 - 30 October 1957
15	Aloysius Raway, son of Louis & Barbara -6 June 1922-
17	Barbara Raway 1898-1989
24	Ben J. Raway 1895-1961
41	Florence Raway 1924-__
41	Francis Raway 1923-1990
24	Kenneth M. Raway (?) 1929-1929

17	Louis Raway 1891-1969
41	Lyle Raway 1955-1977
24	Martha T. Raway 1900-1984
07	Mary Ann O'Connell, wife of John Riley 1853-1875
07	Mary Ann, daughter of Wm. & A. O'Connell, wife of John Riley
	31 January 1853 - 10 February 1875
35	Margaret Robert -no dates
17	Martin M. Robert 1859-1941
35	Mathias Robert -no dates
35	Mathias, son of Nicholas & Magaretha Robert
	4 January 1884 - 29 August 1884
35	Matthew Robert -no dates
35	Michael Robert -no dates
35	Elizabeth Roberts 4 July 1879 - 10 October 1922
35	Margaretha Roberts 13 October 1854 - 28 January 1906
35	Mathias Roberts 28 September 1847 - 7 July 1929
34	Adam Rohr 1878-1965
34	Conrad Rohr (?) 1827-1887
19	Conrad Rohr 16 January 1865 - 5 February 1917
19	Elizabeth Rohr 20 September 1870 - 1 October 1949
34	Henry Rohr (?) 1875-1943
19	Joseph A. Rohr 29 October 1897 - 25 October 1916
19	Leonard P. Rohr 1915-1990
34	Louise Rohr 1882-1954
34	Margaret Rohr (?) 1847-1897
19	Mathias P. Rohr 1878-1944
45	Peter Rohr 1882-1968
19	Teresa Grace Rohr 1882-1972
24	Agnes M. Ruhr (?) 1893-1977
25	Bernard Ruhr 17 March 1824 - 23 July 1903
25	Eduard, son of F.N. & Th. Ruhr, died 20 September 1897
	age 1 month, 19 days
27	Ferdinand F. Ruhr 5 June 1848 - 14 September 1909
20	Frank Ruhr 1873-1874
20	Frank J. Ruhr 1882-1954
25	Frank N. Ruhr 1858-1940
24	Gordon Ruhr 14 June 1934 - 28 December 1937
45	John T. Ruhr 1892-1966
24	Joseph Ruhr 7 March 1921 - 10 May 1942
24	Kenneth Ruhr 28 June 1929 - 20 March 1934
27	Lisetta M. Ruhr 16 January 1885 - 24 April 1909
25	Maria Ruhr 2 April 1820 - 28 September 1910
27	Mary A. Ruhr 22 April 1851 - 13 October 1911
20	Susanna K. Ruhr 1889-1956
20	Theresa Kranz Boser Ruhr 1868-1930
45	Theresa C. Ruhr 1894-1976

25	Theresia Lubbesmeier, wife of F.N. Ruhr
	11 April 1858 - 24 February 1899
24	William A. Ruhr (?) 1888-1960
30	Charles Saam 1870-1948
30	Elizabeth Saam 1872-1950
30	George A. Saam 1908-1980
30	Gertrude Saam 24 July 1824 - 24 March 1900
30	Kasper Saam 6 January 1823 - 11 February 1911
29	Louis J. Saam 1912-1986
30	Maria Saam 26 April 1899 - 15 July 1899
29	Theresa C. Saam 1905-__
46	James P. Salkowicz 1947-1971
26	A. Beatina, daughter of George & Catherine Schaefer
	8 October 1909 - 9 January 1910
18	A. Irene Schaffer 1905-1988
18	Adam J. Schaffer 1870-1946
37	Agnes Schaffer 1900-1958
35	Ambrose Joseph, son of George & Lucy Schaffer
	21 October 1911 - 4 May 1912
26	Anna Schaffer (?) 1853-1939
26	Anna Maria, daughter of Conrad & Anna Schaffer
	4 February 1879 - 4 April 1890
31	August Schaffer 1888-1944
36	Augusta M. Schaffer 1889-1969
39	baby Schaffer 1905-1905
36	baby Schaffer 1929-1929
42	baby Schaffer -1957-
25	Catherine Schaffer 1883-1974
31	Clara Schaffer 1891-1933
26	Conrad Schaffer (?) 1855-1937
39	Elizabeth Schaffer 1880-1947
27	Ernestina A. Schaffer 5 February 1850 - 19 May 1936
18	Frances Schaffer 1902-1932
43	Frank X. Schaffer 1896-1960
43	Gertrude Schaffer 1893-1986
42	Gerve Schaffer 1923-1969
25	Georg P. Schaffer 1881-1970
35	George G. Schaffer (?) 1880-1964
35	Harold Schaffer 1907-1995
18	Henry Schaffer 1896-1916
27	Henry Schaffer 21 February 1845 - 6 October 1913
31	Herbert Schaffer 1911-1947
26	Hilarion N. Schaffer 1922-1935
42	Jean Schaffer 1924-__
36	Joseph M. Schaffer 1889-1986

18	Kathryn Schaffer 1869-1928
46	Kathryn Schaffer 1896-1986
39	Louis G. Schaffer 1882-1956
35	Lucy Ann Schaffer (?) 1881-1948
26	Margaret Schaffer (?) 1857-1927
18	Paul Schaffer 1908-1924
31	Raphael Frances, son of August & Clara Schaffer
	19 November 1910 - 21 November 1910 (?)
45	Regina T. Schaffer 1897-1980
46	William Schaffer 1895-1976
45	William C. Schaffer 1894-1972
46	Lawrence Schauer 1901-1988
46	Leona Schauer 1907-1978
43	baby Schiller -May 1958-
47	Joseph Schiller 1913-__
47	Odelia Schiller 1916-1995
23	Catherine Schmitz 1864 - 28 October 1918
36	Peter Schweich 18 September 1803 - 7 March 1877
13	Liborius S. Schweitzer, son of Wilhelm & Mathilde Schweitzer
	2 September 1860 - 1 October 1891
06	Catherine Sherry (?) 1874-1880
44	Elizabeth A. Sherry 1880-1963
44	Elizabeth A. Sherry 1880-1963
06	Ellen Sherry (?) 1840-1922
06	James Sherry (?) 1828-1898
06	James Sherry (?) 1872-1935
44	Jane Sherry 1868-1967
06	John Sherry (?) 1870-1936
16	Mary Sherry 1866-1947
15	Mary Caneff Sherry 23 February 1872 - 7 August 1915
06	Steve Sherry (?) 1884-1930
44	Thomas A. Sherry 1877-1950
43	Thomas A. Sherry 1877-1950
31	Del A. Shoemaker 1911-__
31	Loretta M. Shoemaker 1913-__
40	Gerald Smiley 1932-1996
40	Patrick Smiley 1965-1983
08	Agnes O'K. (O'Keefe ?) Spencer 1873-1931
08	Albert E. Spencer 1862-1946
46	Joseph Stoffel 1906-1992
46	Martha Stoffel 1904-1986
09	Catherine Toner (?) 1854-1936
09	Frank Toner (?) 1880-1949
09	John Toner (?) 1841-1934
09	Rose I. Toner (?) 1890-1977

04	John Tully, died 11 May 1892, age 80 years (?)
	Native of county Galway, Ireland
04	Mary, wife of John Tully, died 14 March 1896, age 77 years
	Native of county Galway, Ireland
42	Irene J. Voelker 1921-1984
42	Joseph J. Voelker 1912-1989
43	baby Wagner -1952-
28	Joseph J. Wagner 22 November 1889 - 25 November 1892
43	George H. Wallace 1898-1976
17	Charles Waters (?) 1868-1920
17	John Waters (?) 1870-1922
17	Ida M. Waters (?) 1863-1950
17	Thomas Waters 10 April 1827 - 19 March 1915
37	Anna Weber (?) 1863-1935
37	Barbara Weber (?) 1890-1906
37	Bernard Weber (?) 11 April 1923 - 12 September 1928
45	David Charles, son of Mr. & Mrs. John N. Weber Jr. 1965-1968
37	Edward M. Weber 1903-1988
45	Jeanette Weber 1898-__
45	John Weber 1895-__
45	John N. Weber, PVT. United States Army 1895-1981
37	Mary Weber 1898-1992
37	Nick Weber (?) 1860-1934
43	Phyllis Weiss 1937-1994, married Leonard 12 September 1959
28	E. (?) Weibehold 5 January 1903 - 23 January 1904
28	T. Weiberhold 30 December 1891 - 30 June 1892
30	Clara (?) Wiederhold 4 February 1835 - 15 March 1902
14	John T. Wiederhold 8 August 1890 - 30 July 1916
30	Karl Wiederhold 8 September 1832 - 20 December 1907
30	Michael Wiederhold - no dates
30	Michael Wiederhold 18 March 1882 - 26 September 1907
31	Catherine Wiederholt (?) 1877-1925
43	Catherine Wiederholt 1896-1983
14	Charles B. Wiederholt 24 August 1886 - 5 August 1918
31	Charles E. Wiederholt (?) 1875-1943
14	Clara Wiederholt 1888-1890
13	'Father' F. Wiederholt (?) 1858-1929
43	Gary S. Wiederholt, son of Sylvester & Harriet 1966-1985
43	George Wiederholt 1889-1954
43	George E. Wiederholt, son of Mr. & Mrs. Sylvester Wiederholt
	1947-1964
43	Harriet Wiederholt 1924-__
45	Margaret Wiederholt 1899-1970
13	'Mother' F. Wiederholt(?) 1866-1945

31   Raymond C. Wiederholt (?) 1903-1929
43   Sylvester Wiederholt 1920-1972
43   Sylvester F. Wiederholt, Minnesota SGT. United States Army
            World War 2   23 July 1920 - 6 July 1972
45   William J. Wiederholt 1901-1965
46   Frank A. Wellman 1888-1973
46   Gertrude Wellman 1890-1991
44   Dolores M. Witzke 1918-__
44   Merrill E. Witzke 1915-1987

43   Catherine Zimmerman (?) 1896-1974
43   Gerald H. Zimmerman (?) 1939-1947
43   John Zimmerman (?) 1889-1959

The following stones were very worn and hard to read. I was not able to determine a surname.

22   Dorfine (?) ? April 1873 - June 1875 (?)
22   Goreine (?) March 1854 - 8 February (?) 1874 (?)
22   John & Helen (?) - unable to read the rest.

St. Joseph Catholic Church Grounds

St. Joseph's Catholic Church Cemetery
Douglas township, Dakota Co, Minnesota
Section 11 - T113N-R17W

Section 1
Rows 1-19

Section 2
Rows 20-39

Drive Area

Drive Area
(part of section 2)

Drive Area

Section 3
Rows
40-48

Highway 61

67

HAMPTON CEMETERY ??

Hampton township, Dakota county, Minnesota: T113N-R18W, section 4

   This cemetery is upkept and in poor shape. There is no name at the gate of this cemetery. Many of the stones have been broken over the years. It is hard to tell if what remains is actually over the grave. Many of the stones are lying flat at ground level. Some stones are surrounded by bushes or lilacs. The fenced area which comprises the cemetery is much more expansive than the headstones are. There are two obvious family sections, these are for the Bell and Hopkins families. Each had a piped off area to mark their relatives graves. Both are now weedy and have overgrown shrubs or small trees growing in the area. None of the damage appears to have been done recently. The area is mowed. I have not numbered the burials with row numbers. The burials are at the northern half of the area and are spread throughout this northern half.

   The Dakota county cemetery records compilation lists this cemetery as:
Hampton Township Cemetery, established January 1875. 2 acres. Located Section 4, NW 1/4, Township 113, Range 18. 225th St. East. (Abandoned).

   This cemetery may have at one time been located in section 9 of Hampton township. In "History of Dakota County and the city of Hastings" by Rev. Edward D. Neill, he wrote: ... Hampton cemetery was first situated on section 9, the first grave being that of Stephen D. and Amelia Bell. In 1876 the yard was removed to section 4, and contains about seventy-five graves,[in 1881] (page 398). The Andreas 1874 Atlas of Minnesota has a map of Dakota county which shows this area, in section 4, containing a school house.

Everyone is listed in alphabetical order.

This cemeteries burial monuments were transcribed during 1996.

Bettie, Wife of Eli Ballard, died 21 October 1863, age 19 years
Elias Ballard 1835-1904
Julia A. Ballard 15 February 1839 - 16 September 1895
Rebecca, wife of Elias Ballard, died 13 October 1862
         age 28 years 3 months
Susan A., daughter of Eli & Nettie Ballard, died 1 June 1863
         age 1 year 6 days (?)
William M., son of Elias & Rebecca Ballard, died 8 January 1862
         age 1 year (?) 10 months
Daniel Bartelt 14 January 1843 - 18 May 1902
Alice L., daughter of ? & ? Bell, died 21 June 1871 (?)
infant, son of S.D. & M.P. Bell, died 21 August 1853
Princis A., wife of S.D. Bell, died 28 May 1887, age 61 years
S.D. Bell, died 30 June 1895, age 73 years

?, son of B. & M. Burroughs (?) -broken and buried stone
W.H. Burroughs C 6 Minnesota Inf. (?), died 15 August 1865
     21 years his age

Fanny Cain 1809-1876
George Cain 7 July 1832 - 3 May 1909
     married M. A. Curtiss 25 February 1863 (?)
George W. Cain 21 March 1909 - 3 June 1909
Hazel M. Cain 15 July 1895 - 22 January 1897
Jennie B. Cain 1873-1932
Katie, wife of Tom Cain, died 11 April 1896
     age 61 years 3 months (?)
Marion Beth Cain 3 May 1910 - 1 April 1911
Melissa A. Cain, wife of George Cain 5 June 1841 - 9 November 1924
Seth Cain 1806-1881
Seth B. Cain 1872-1945
Caroline N., wife of Jonas Carlson, died 15 December 1898, age 76 years
Jonas P. Carlson, died 24 June 1883, age 67 years
baby Clark, died 18 April 1906 (?), age 18 days (?)
Ralph H. Clark 17 May 1906 - 5 December 1906
Annah, wife of J.J. Cropper (?), died 4 December 1879,
     age 52 years 11 months 21 days -broken stone
?, wife of Madison Cropper (?), died 8 July 1865
     age 29 years 6 months

Donald W. Duff 1872-1956
Emma J. Duff 1851-1929
James Duff 28 December 1809 - 6 February 1872 -broken stone
Joseph (?) P. (?), son of John & Mary Duff
     18 August 1861 - 28 July 1863
Robert Duff 1 January 1848 - 13 February 1854
William Duff 1850-1931
James, son of Wm. & E. Dunkerley, died 18 February 1860
Mary, daughter of W. & ? Dunkerley, died 5 January 1870, age 10 months
Wm. Dunkerley 30 March 1826 - 7 January 1875

J.H. Ferris, died 1 April 1891, age 12 years
P.B. Ferris, died 29 July 1879, age 54 years
Sarah M. Ferris, died ? 1867, age 30 years

William S. Greene 1839-1908

?, son of I.N. & N. Holden (?) -rest of stone is missing
Edith Charity, child of G.J. & E.S. Hopkins
     1 August 1897 - 24 September 1902
Florence J. Hopkins 23 September 1859 - 11 September 1914

George G. Hopkins 4 March 1885 - 3 June 1906
Gilbert J. Hopkins 17 October 1857 - 13 November 1929
Joseph L. Hopkins 28 January 1881 - 9 February 1887
Joseph W. Hopkins 24 December 1831 - 2 August 1919
Lilly E., child of G.J. & E.S. Hopkins
        15 October 1899 - 22 October 1899
Linna M. Hopkins 31 October 1861 - 12 March 1937
Lizzie M. Hopkins 7 November 1891 - 5 September 1914
Sarahett Perrin, wife of J.W. Hopkins 26 May 1832 - 16 July 1905
William W. Hopkins 22 June 1867 - 3 May 1918

Mary J. Johnson 15 April 1815 - 29 February 1904
Wm. H. Johnson, died 9 February 1892, age 80 years
Isaac W. Jones 1806-1893

Christina S., wife of Jos. A.A. Kirk (?), died 18 March 1900
        age 56 years
Elmer A. Kirk, died 22 May 1882, age 6 months
Achsah E. Klaus 1876-1906
Raymond, son of R.C. & A.E. Klaus 9 April 1902 - 14 June 1902
Robert C. Klaus 1876-1954

Mary Ann, wife of James Lee 2 March 1833 - 25 March 1875
        age 42 years 23 days

Alexander McKay 20 October 1809 - 1 April 1862
Catherine, wife of Alexander McKay
        2 August 1816 - 5 July 1898
Albert P., son of Nathaniel & Rhoda Martin
        21 March 1818 - 4 April 1907 , age 89 years 14 days
baby Martin -1908-
Bernice Martin (?) 1896 - 1921
Lillie, daughter of (?) Martin (?), died 18 May 1877
        age 17 years 9 months 29 days -in a bush & hard to read
Nathaniel Martin, died 15 June 1877, age 87 years 4 months 2 days
Perry Martin (?) 1901-1924
Phoda (?) Perry, wife of Nathaniel Martin, died 29 November 1876
        age 84 years 8 months

?, son of J.S. & E.R. Paselton (?) - rest is missing
Nancy Perrin, died 5 May 1860
?, son of ? Perrin - rest is buried in cement
Wm. Perrin, died 13 February 1865, age 70 years
Addie Belle Porter (?), died 29 July 1863
        age 4 months 11 days (?)   -broken stone
Ann Porter (?), died 20 May 1865, age 11 months -broken stone

?, son of Wm. Porter, died 11 July 1862
 age 1 year 1 month -broken stone
Wilhelmina, born Porter (?)

Alexander Records 14 August 1805 - 3 May 1877
Nancy A., daughter of A. & S.A. Records, died 4 July 1866
        age 3 years 4 months 13 days
Francis L. Renslow 28 March 1880 - 14 March 1915

James Smart 23 July 1819 - 28 October 1890
'Father' Smithberger (?) 1831-1920

Levi Taft (?) 1813-18??
Susan F., wife of L. Taft, died 1 June 1872, age ? -broken & worn stone

Rosie Wilson, died 9 November 1869, age 5 months

St. MATHIAS CATHOLIC CHURCH CEMETERY

Hampton township, Dakota county, Minnesota: T113N-R18W, section 8

     This cemetery is located within the town of Hampton, Minnesota. The cemetery is upkept and in good shape. There is a great map and directory with listings of persons that were buried in the cemetery located behind plastic as a permanent part of the cemetery. The burial lists are alphabetized. The list contains year of death, block, lot, and grave numbers for everyone. If you visit the cemetery I would definitely recommend that you use their information as it was copied from the churches original records. I did not use their records to compile my list. I began numbering my rows at the southern edge. The rows seemed to line up well. The only stone that was placed in an odd spot was the burial stone of B. Peters. This stone appeared to be all by itself in the NE corner.

    The Dakota county cemetery records compilation list this cemetery as: St. Mathias Catholic Cemetery, established October 1900. 2 acres. Located Section 8, NE 1/4. Highway 47 and 50.

    Everyone is listed in alphabetical order. The number before each entry is the row number. There is a map at the back of this section.

    This cemeteries burial monuments were transcribed during 1996.

16	Bernadett Bailey, daughter of Jacob & Helena
	23 February 1929 - 10 February 1985
04	Anna Becker 1878-1943
25	Anna Becker 1871-1948
03	Barbara Becker 7 September 1837 - 3 March 1913
04	Emma Becker 12 June 1872 - 18 February 1909
04	Emma Rieger Becker 1870-1909
04	Johann Becker 17 March 1833 - 7 January 1906
04	Johan N. Becker 25 August 1899 - January 1900
04	Johann P. Becker 8 September 1832 - 29 June 1911
09	John A. Becker 1894-1971
03	John P. Becker 1832-1911
25	Joseph L. Becker 1900-1917
04	Joseph S. Becker 25 August 1899 - January 1900
03	Margaret S. Becker 1879-1960
04	Maria Becker, born Schmitt
	26 November 1832 - 25 July 1905
08	Mary Anne Becker 1923-1934
03	Mary Schmid Becker 1832-1905
03	Nicholas P. Becker 1871-1969
03	Nicolaus Becker 1 January 1826 - 25 January 1911

04	Peter Becker 1869-1905
04	Peter Becker 13 January 1867 - 5 June 1905
09	Rose M. Becker 1899-1989
04	Susanna Elsen, wife of Johann Becker
	8 February 1840 - 1 October 1892
04	William E. Becker 24 November 1904 - 1 November 1876
27	William Edward Becker, United States Navy 1958-1982
05	Bernice Beissel 1927-1941
17	Frank Beissel 1904-1984
17	John Beissel 1900-1986
17	Lena Beissel 1888-1957
17	Sophie O. Beissel 1914 - __
11	Anna Bennett 1867-1929
11	Bernard Bennett 1869-1925
10	James L. Bennett 1903-1992
10	John E. Bennett 1907-1955
19	Theresia M. Ber 20 August 1905 - 11 January 1906
19	Johan Berg 24 March 1867 - 24 March 1906
17	Joseph F. Bielen (?) 1873-1925
17	Noretta Bohart 1895-1984
17	William Bohart 1883-1960
16	Dean E. Bowe 1909-1954
16	Marie Bowe 1906 - __
10	Annie K. Burns - no dates
11	'Father' Burr (?) 19 January 1866 - 19 October 1919
11	'Mother' Burr (?) 16 January 1861 - 2 May 1937
20	Caroline M. Cain 1909 - __
20	Lyndle S. Cain 1904 - __
18	Susan Schaffer Campbell 1906-1959
09	Rose K. Carlson 2 October 1898 - 25 September 1966
08	Rose K. Carlson 1898-1966
23	Helen Casawski 18 March 1847 - 3 May 1908
19	Catherine Berg Classen 16 June 1880 - 12 May 1950
23	Anna Cysiewski 1872-1956
18	John V. Cysiewski 1904-1982
18	Marie M. Cysiewski 1905-1991
23	Nicholas Cysiewski 1898-1963
23	Thomas Cysiewski 20 December 1861 - 28 April 1922
33	Gertrud 'Peg' Dailey 1902-1972
06	Cornelius Daleiden 1873-1966
21	Emma Daleiden 1906-1989
06	Gertrude A. Daleiden 1902-1992
06	Katherine Daleiden 1882-1969
05	Alohfius (?) F/ (?) Daletsen (?) 2 April 1900 - 20 February 1905

06	John Delfeld 15 August 1855 - 22 October 1922
06	Maria Delfeld 21 September 1858 - 14 May 1910
10	Beverly R. Deutsch 1953-1981
17	John Dimmers 1840-1922
20	Anna Doffing 1870-1947
09	Cecelia Doffin (?) 1873-1960
12	Donald Doffing 1921-1933
22	Elizabeth A. Doffing 1930 - 1996 (recent burial)
30	Fred R. Doffing 1899-1972
06	George A. Doffing 1896-1967
13	Gertrude Doffing 1870-1941
22	Harold J. Doffing 1927-1977
06	Helen M. Doffing 1902-1992
13	John P. Doffing 1867-1941
33	Lawrence Peter Doffing, PFC United States Army World War 2 4 October 1922 - 12 April 1994
06	Lillian C. Doffing (?) 1907-1986
02	Margaretha Doffing (?) 14 November 1839 - 19 April 1918
07	Maria Doffing 8 August 1846 - 16 February 1911
30	Mary M. Doffing 1902 - __
02	Mathias Doffing (?) 28 February 1839 - 9 December 1924
31	Mathilda Doffing 1898-1972
09	Nicholas Doffing (?) 1871-1931
20	Nicholas P. Doffing 1869-1945
06	Philip J. Doffing (?) 1880-1950
31	William A. Doffing 1901-1970
17	Michael, twin son of Mr. & Mrs. Gery Dohmen 21 september - 27 September 1969
17	Timothy, twin son of Mr. & Mrs. Gery Dohmen - 21 September 1969 -
21	Hallard Drake 1899-1964
02	Darold Gene Dunn 10 January - 8 February 1936
04	Marcella C. Dunn 1912-1973
03	Ralph (Gene) Dunn 1934-1960
04	Roger V. Dunn 1912-1988
02	John Eck 1881-1948
21	Loretta M. Eckes (Daleiden) 30 June 1910 - 25 February 1992
21	Raymond N. Eckes 23 December 1914 - __
19	Gerhard Eich, born in Germany 6 April 1862 - 17 April 1940
25	Elizabeth Eilen (?) 23 January 1891 - 2 April 1929
25	John Eilen (?) 13 January 1891 - 31 March 1967
24	Nicholas Eilen (?) 10 February 1895 - 22 March 1972
06	Alvin Endres 1928-1930
15	Ambrose Endres (?) 1921-1929
23	Anna Endres 1906-1990

23	Conrad, twin son of Mr. & Mrs. Melvin Endres - 10 July 1964 -
22	Duane Endres 1959-1981
15	Emma Endres (?) 1889-1961
22	Gertrude Endres 1927 - __
06	Helena Kranz, wife of Joseph Endres
	11 June 1845 - 13 February 1911
07	Henry Endres 1863-1946
06	Joseph Endres 1 May 1843 - 22 October 1921
05	Joseph Endres 1917-1984, ordained 29 January 1944
23	Joseph Endres 1902-1993
22	Julius Endres 1918-1977
07	Marie Theresa Endres 1898-1949
06	Mathias A. Endres 1872-1945
05	Nicholas Endres 1884-1945
07	Odelia Endres 1867-1949
15	Paul Endres (?) 1867-1942
07	Paul F. Endres 1887-1959
07	Philomena Endres 1894-1930
06	Regina Endres 1892-1969
23	Steven, twin son of Mr. & Mrs. Melvin Endres
	10 July - 15 July 1964
16	Marcella Erickson 1915-1974
03	Francis Feipel 1904-1904
04	Franziskus Feipel 9 August 1904 - 11 December 1904
03	Henry Feipel 1910-1911
03	Joseph M. Feipel 1875-1932
03	Louis Feipel 1899-1907
03	Mary B. Feipel 1876-1972
02	George Foss 17 December 1876 - 29 June 1961
02	George Foss 2 August 1834 - 7 July 1904
02	Katherine Foss 1880-1954
02	Mary Foss 4 April 1880 - 27 April 1943
02	Mathias Foss 1881-1966
02	Stephan Foss 31 January 1875 - 10 October 1903
02	Theresa Foss 16 August 1840 - 15 July 1920
22	Arnold Fox 1912-1971
22	Rita Fox 1920 - __
04	Frank H. Furst 5 April 1868 - 16 August 1902
04	Lucy M. M. Furst 30 July 1897 - 27 April 1898
04	Mary M. Furst 21 September 1865 - 7 July 1939
18	Ralph H. Gergen 1930-1930
18	Teresa M. Gergen 1897-1995
34	Thomas A. Gergen 1958-1978
18	William M. Gergen 1896-1977

22	Dorothy E. Gerster 1895-1974
22	Edward A. Gerster 1889-1983
16	Adolph Giefer 1904-1983
09	Bernard Giefer 10 September 1887 - 20 October 1918
09	Bernard J. Giefer 1887-1918
08	Catherine Giefer (?) 10 March 1897 - 20 October 1934
09	Elizabeth Giefer (?) 25 December 1864 - 14 September 1941
16	Florence Giefer 1908 - __
09	Gertrud, wife of Ludwig Giefer, born in Rohr Kreis Schleiden
	Reg. Bez. Aaghen 14 May 1836 - 29 May 1911
09	John G. Giefer (?) 15 September 1898 - 20 December 1968
09	John J. Giefer (?) 16 February 1861 - 15 October 1939
09	Leo P. Giefer 1906-1981
09	Ludwig Giefer, born in Freilingen Kreis Schleiden Reg. Bez. Aachen
	19 September 1830 - 28 February 1913
09	Magdalene Giefer 1911 - __
32	Margaret Giefer 1902-1976
08	Nicholas Giefer (?) 23 July 1893 - 25 July 1919
33	Nicklous N. Giefer 1901-1988
08	Raphafl Wm. Giefer (?) 1917-1924
32	William Giefer 1899-1984
10	Frank Gitzen 1882-1956
11	Johann Peter Gitzen 29 June 1831 - 25 October 1914
11	Margaret Gitzen 11 July 1847 - 22 October 1928
15	Carl Gores 1896-1982
05	Leo F. Gores 12 June 1905 - 10 June 1907
06	Magdalena Gores 27 September 1865 - 1 November 1951
04	Margaret Gores (?) 1870-1944
04	Nicholas J. Gores (?) 1866-1926
06	Nicholas P. Gores 13 May 1860 - 9 March 1927
14	Pauline Mary Gores 1934-1935
15	Susan Gores 1896-1985
16	Albert M. Halfern 1898-1971
16	Michael Halfen 1894-1956
07	Emilie Hatzl 1872-1931
07	Frank P. Hatzl 1875-1934
09	Helena Lindenfelser Hauenstein 1871-1957
19	Anthony H. Heimann 1917-1983
19	Marcella A. Heimann 1920 - __
20	Erven Hennen 1916-1992
20	Lillian Hennen 1917-1986
02	Anna Maria Herschbach, born Fasbender
	25 December 1833 - 17 November 1901
01	George W. Herschbach 20 March 1905 - 2 December 1967
02	Johann Herschbach 8 May 1825 - 2 February 1909

02	John Herschbach 26 March 1869 - 20 January 1938
31	Anna M. Hoffmann 1901-1990
30	Betty L. Hoffmann 1940-1942
31	Henry M. Hoffmann 1894-1982
18	Katherine Hoffmann 2 June 1879 - 15 February 1946
18	Peter M. Hoffmann 30 December 1882 - 2 February 1960
15	Bonita P. Hogfoss 1931-1962
05	Alice J. Horn 1905-1973
11	Barbara Horn 1865-1954
05	John J. Horn 1894-1986
11	Joseph F. Horn 5 October 1865 - 7 August 1911
11	Marie Horn 1892-1969
14	Christ Horsch 1881-1960
18	Chas. (Carl) Humphries 1901-1988
18	Mariem (Madge) Humphries 1901-1929
14	James Patrick, son of Mr. & Mrs. Gerald Irrthum
	17 March - 19 March 1964
05	Emma Jensen 1921-1987
09	Regina Weber, wife of John Johnson
	8 September 1867 - 21 February 1906
02	son of Mr. & Mrs. Eugene Johnson - 1970 -
15	baby girl, daughter of Kenneth A. Kasel - 9 March 1965 -
15	infant daughter of Mr. & Mrs. Kenneth A. Kasel - 6 February 1966 -
19	Mary Kranz 1875 - 1942
20	Delores Kuhn 1918-1996
20	Edwin Kuhn 1916 - __
16	George Kuhn 1888-1919
18	Kenneth Kuhn 1946-1984
20	Philip Kuhn 1864-1935
16	Rose Kuhn 1894-1980
20	Susan Kuhn 1862-1933
13	Margaret Lange 1899-1966
01	Eva Langenfeld (?) 1873-1937
29	Siegfrid J. Letendre 1899-1988
29	Theresa C. Letendre 1903-1988
07	Alex Lindenfelser 18 July 1834 - 18 March 1921
02	Heinrich Lindenfelser 7 September 1865 - 16 July 1904
09	Joseph Lindenfelser 26 January 1864 - 20 August 1915
07	Katharina Lindenfelser 12 March 1841 - 16 June 1909
02	Susan Lindenfelser (?) 1860-1945
19	Benedict Louis, married Helene 28 November 1942
	31 January 1916 - 26 October 1983

19	Benedict J. Louis, TEC 4 United States Army World War 2
	1916-1983
19	Helen Louis, nee Leahy 27 March 1920 - __
	married Benedict 28 November 1942
01	Adam May 26 December 1899 - 1 February 1909
26	Andrew May 1896-1958
02	Carl May 26 February 1908 - 22 November 1908
02	Caspar May 6 July 1904 - 4 September 1904
32	Catherine May 1902-1991
02	Elizabeth May, born Kuhn 28 October 1860 - 4 March 1903
26	Frances May 1898-1989
26	Franklin 'Bud' May 1934-1989
10	Henry F. May (?) 11 December 1906 - 29 November 1931
01	Joseph May 14 June 1906 - 9 May 1917
30	Leo B. 'Spike' May 1910-1970
11	Margaret May (?) 25 May 1887 - 23 November 1944
01	Nicholas May 2 September 1894 - 17 May 1949
10	Peter May 9 August 1897 - 11 January 1991
11	Peter May (?) 8 September 1860 - 31 July 1934
26	Sharon May 1937-1993
32	William May 1905 - __
35	T. Mitch Mathews 1969-1994
09	Eva M. Mayer 22 August 1894 - 23 September 1914
09	Eva Maria Mayer (?) - no dates
09	Heinrich Mayer 4 July 1866 - 7 June 1907
08	Reinhardt H. Meis (?) 1865-1931
02	Jacob Mertes 28 September 1900 - 2 June 1906
09	Maria Mies 5 September 1869 - 30 September 1918
13	Marie V. Mies 20 June 1882 - 23 October 1928
13	Nikolas Mies 28 March 1862 - 24 April 1942
12	William P. Mies 1908-1987
	married Laverna M. (Freiermuth) 13 June 1935
21	baby boy Millard - 8 November 1951 -
32	Catharine Millard 1912 - __
	married Frank 19 February 1930
32	Frank Millard 1909-1978
	married Catharine 19 February 1930
30	Theresa L. May Moschkau 1914-1990
30	Glenn J. Mulvihill 1942-1994
27	Ann Marie Nicolai, daughter of Leo & Joyce - 23 January 1981 -
20	Appolonia Nicolai 1888-1979
28	Herbert Nicolai 1914-1981
28	Irene Nicolai 1919 - __
20	John C. Nicolai 1918-1983

20	John P. Nicolai 1883-1960
07	Katharina Nicolai, born Grode 22 May 1843 - 18 December 1929
07	Magdalena Nicolai (?) 1869-1953
07	Peter Nicolai 3 march 1833 - 20 November 1915
07	Sybilla Nicolai (?) 1867-1964
16	Anna Biebur 1896-1985
21	Clara M. Niebur 1890-1975
21	Clem A. Niebur 1886-1968
16	Earl Niebur 1939-1959
28	Flory Niebur 1920-1982 United States Army World War 2
16	John Niebur 1895-1955
28	Stella Niebur 1928 - __
10	Dianne M. Odette 1950-1970
25	John Pash 1873-1934
05	Otillia Pash 1887-1979
16	Anna Peine 1871-1945
16	John Peine 1865-1952
00	B?? Peters 7 December 1911 (?) - 10 May 1911
	- this stone was alone in the NE corner
09	Ferdinand Peters 1890-1947
09	Rosa S. Peters 1895-1936
15	M. Phyllis (Mathews) Peterson 1929 - __
15	Pamela T. Peterson 1958-1959
15	Russell J. Peterson 1925-1990, United States Navy World War 2
26	Johann Putz 29 August 1848 - 8 December 1918
26	Susanna Putz 24 April 1846 - 30 April 1926
22	Rachel Marie Raway (?) 30 August - 4 September 1987
27	Adolph Reinardy 1907-1991
27	Gary F. Reinardy 29 June 1957 - 7 December 1960
16	Helena M. Reinardy 1894-1972
16	Jacob M. Reinardy 1894-1959
27	Lorraine Reinardy 1918-1988
16	Melvin Jon, son of Mr. & Mrs. Jacob Reinardy
	6 April 1923 - 16 June 1924
11	?? Rischette 14 October 1913 - 14 July 1922
11	Nikolaus (?) Rischette 5 April 1886 - 6 February 1918
10	Robert (?) Rischette 29 January 1927 - 6 July 1927
29	Bernard J. Rother 1910 - __
31	Carl W. Rother 1912 - __
12	Catherine Rother 1888-1976
29	Cecelia C. Rother 1912-1965
19	Charles Rother (?) 28 December 1871 - 31 January 1949
13	Clara M. Rother 1912 - __

03	David Rother 1954-1967
13	Edward Rother 3 May 1838 - 19 December 1919
13	Helena Rother 19 April 1842 - 10 May 1914
21	Joseph Rother born & died 27 March 1922
19	Katherine Rother (?) 10 January 1878 - 7 August 1948
31	Louise C. Rother 1910-1992
21	Margaret Rother 8 February 1886 - 25 September 1959
03	Michael Rother 5 November 1950 - 20 December 1950
04	Mike Rother - 1952 -
12	Mildred M. Rother 1937-1943
12	Robert A. Rother 1878-1968
13	Robert V. Rother 1907-1994
21	Vincent Rother 21 August 1882 - 31 August 1937
06	John B. Schaack (?) 1868-1931
05	Joseph P. Schaack 1905-1970
06	Mary A. Schaack (?) 1876-1963
18	Henry Schaffer 2 November 1869 - 16 September 1942
18	Mary A. Schaffer 23 July 1874 - 1 December 1956
25	Jacob Scharpf 29 December 1878 - 13 November 1918
24	Adam Schiller 1899-1977
29	Christine H. Schiller 4 December 1911 - 13 November 1994
29	John Schiller 4 January 1904 - 5 January 1995
23	Margaretha Schiller 14 April 1872 - 3 May 1917
23	Mathias Schiller 24 April 1861 - 29 August 1942
20	Peter Schiller (?) 4 February 1864 - 30 April 1952
24	Susan Schiller 1899-1957
20	Theresa Schiller (?) 7 October 1877 - 5 August 1936
23	Pius Schmid, born in Bozen Tirol Am
	23 April 1848 - 18 March 1917
07	'Father' Schmitz (?) 25 October 1856 - 21 July 1954
07	'Mother' Schmitz (?) 8 July 1859 - 29 July 1913
07	Charles Schweich 1 September 1880 - 14 August 1932
19	Charles Schweich 1915-1995
07	Frances Schweich 17 January 1885 - 19 June 1960
07	Gertrude Schweich 13 October 1845 - 24 October 1922
07	John P. Schweich 24 January 1839 - 17 July 1906
19	Marcella Schweich 1927 - __
07	Peter M. Schweich 1887-1954
23	Cheryl Marie, daughter of Randy & Jackie Serres
	- 25 October 1979 -
23	Frances Serres 1928 - __
23	Gerald Serres 1929-1983
23	Mary E. Serres 1951-1985
23	Ronald M. Serres, son of Mr. & Mrs. Gerald Serres 1954-1969
05	Justine E. Schultz 1897-1972

05	Raymond J. Schultz 1896-1961
02	Mary Sieben (?) 1867-1952
02	William Sieben (?) 1861-1941
13	Lucille A. Siebenaler 1916-1993
13	Paul N. Siebenaler 1915-1992
15	Christina Simon 5 December 1864 - __
07	Eva Simon 16 December 1890 - 23 April 1984
07	Gregory P. Simon, Minnesota Cpl. Co. C 23 Infantry Regt.
	5 May 1928 - 16 November 1952
15	Julius Simon 27 May 1853 - 14 April 1924
07	Julius P. Simon 16 October 1892 - 7 April 1967
15	Mary Simon 17 July 1900 - __
10	Rose Weiler Smeltzer 1910-1969
34	Daniel J. Smith 10 April 1924 - 30 January 1991
07	James A. Smith 5 October 1947 - 1 September 1992
24	Jeffrey Smith, son of Charles & Linda
	14 December 1978 - 9 February 1979
07	Patrick James Smith, son of James & Mari
	17 March - 1 June 1972
20	Nicole Taarud 26 October 1970 - 25 November 1989
19	Nicole Taarud 26 October 1970 - 25 November 1989
29	John Tate 1912-1966
28	John A. Tate 1938-1962
29	Julia A. Tate 1914-1964
15	John Theis 24 October 1864 - 5 May 1926
15	Mary Theis 30 August 1867 - 14 June 1925
15	Nicholas Theis 24 October 1864 - 7 July 1924
28	Bradley Thurmes, son of Bud & Peggy, 1970-1983
14	Henry Thurmes 1896-1962
14	Henry Thurmes, Minnesota PFC Co. E 33 Engineers World War 1
	16 January 1896 - 28 August 1962
17	John M. Thurmes 1889-1958
17	John M. Thurmes 1889-1958
33	John M., son of Mr. & Mrs. Harold A. Thurmes
	July 1964 - November 1966
32	Kathryn Thurmes 1909 - __, married Math 17 September 1929
17	Lena Thurmes 1903-1963
32	Math Thurmes 1898-1983, married Kathryn 17 September 1929
14	Melvin J. Thurmes 3 August 1935 - 4 December 1935
14	Scott Anthony, son of Mr. & Mrs. Gerald Thurmes
	28 November 1966 - 15 January 1967
14	Susan Thurmes 1910 - __
15	Anna Tix 8 June 1882 - 23 March 1941
11	Anna Tix 20 February 1884 - 28 March 1915
04	Anna K. Tix 4 August 1848 - 2 February 1933

06	Anna M. Tix 1878-1973
04	Bernard Tix 4 September 1844 - 26 September 1937
22	Cecelia Tix 1915-1990
14	Dorothy E. Tix 1922-1985
16	Edward Tix 1912 - __
05	Florence M. Tix 1902-1973
12	Heinie A. Tix 1914-1951
13	John J. Tix 15 November 1875 - 18 March 1930
29	John M. Tix 1904-1985
18	John N. Tix 1904-1952
05	Joseph A. Tix 1912-1993
22	Joseph N. Tix 1898-1985
06	Katharina Tix 8 December 1840 - 10 June 1919
11	Katherine Tix 1899-1936
18	Katie Tix 3 September 1897 - 31 October 1918
14	Leo J. Tix 1917 - __
22	Marie C. Tix 1901-1971
26	Marlene Tix 1940-1987
29	Martha Tix 1903-1987
18	Mary Tix 1872-1957
15	Mathias Tix 26 October 1868 - 20 March 1926
22	Mathias Tix 1911-1996
12	Mathias J. Tix, PVT United States Army World War 2 21 May 1905 - 13 August 1978
18	Nick B. Tix 1870-1948
06	Nikolaus Tix 3 August 1839 - 18 August 1913
06	Peter P. Tix 1877-1949
11	Philip Tix 1873-1952
13	Rose M. Tix 1 December 1878 - 27 December 1943
13	Stephen John, son of Mr. & Mrs. Leo Tix 4 September - 5 September 1954
02	Adolph C. Turek 1882-1933
02	Adolph C. Turek 1882-1933
12	David A. Turek 21 January 1944 - 20 November 1966
13	Maria A. Turek 1923 - __
13	Rudolph C. Turek 1910 - __
13	Thomas J. Turek 1947-1948
02	Wilhelmina Turek 1886-1940
21	Leone J. VanGuilder 13 December - 29 December 1925
21	Marie G. VanGuilder (?) 1899-1947
13	Louis Weber (?) 1898-1918
19	Adam Weiler 4 November 1865 - 18 May 1901
11	Anna Weiler (?) 1885-1949
06	Anna M. Weiler 15 August 1845 - 22 January 1911

24	Bernard Weiler 1914-1987
07	Catherine Weiler (?) 1880-1963
19	Christ H. Weiler 1869-1950
06	Christoph Weiler 1 December 1838 - 19 July 1901
11	Frank Weiler (?) 1882-1935
24	Frank W. Weiler 1905 - __
07	Gertrude M. Weiler 1883-1958
24	Lorene Weiler 1919-1991
18	'Mother' Weiler (?) 1875-1942
04	Nicholas P. Weiler 1903-1969
04	Rose E. Weiler 1913-1933
24	Theresa Weiler 1907-1984
07	William B. Weiler 1875-1959
07	William H. Weiler 26 May 1923 - 26 December 1924
07	William M. Weiler (?) 1869-1950
15	Gertrude Wertzler 5 April 1847 - 25 October 1917
15	Johann Wertzler 11 June 1854 - 4 April 1912
17	Alexious Winter 1915-1986
17	Mildred Winter 1923-1977
24	Frank A. Wollmering (?) 1894-1951
24	Madeline Wollmering (?) 1894-1973
13	John Zeien 1885-1952
13	'Mother' Zeien (?), nee Anna Sieben 1888-1927

Hampton Township, Dakota County, Minnesota
T113N -R18W, section 8

Peters
burial

Row 27

Row 27

Row 26

Row 26

St. Mathias Catholic
Church Cemetery
Hampton, Minnesota

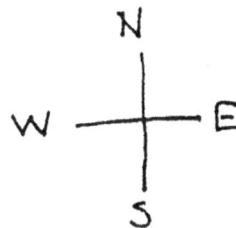

N

W ——|—— E

S

Row 1

Row 1

Church Grounds

St. MARY'S CATHOLIC CHURCH CEMETERY

Hampton township, Dakota county, Minnesota: T113N-R18W, section 11

This cemetery is located within the town of New Trier, Minnesota. The cemetery is upkept and in good shape. The church is still in use and has a sign that states the church was put on the register of historic places in 1980. I began numbering rows along the west edge. Row 1 is located almost under the pine trees that border the western edge. There are just a couple burials that comprise row 1. Rows 26, 27, and 28 are the circular rows that surround the statues. In the south central area of the cemetery there are very few burial stones. This cemetery also contains several large iron burial crosses. Unfortunately most of the burial crosses do no have any discernable information to identify the person buried. The good news is that this cemetery has a plastic covered permanent directory of the cemetery burials. The directory lists the name, year of death, block, and lot numbers. There is also a map of the cemetery. This was dated as May 1993. If you visit the cemetery I would recommend you use there map and information as it was compiled from the churches original records. I did not use there records to compile my information.

The Dakota county cemetery records compilation does not list a description for this cemetery, but it does show it on their map.   In the book, "History of Dakota County and the city of Hastings", by Rev. Edward D. Neill, in 1881, he writes: ... St. Mary's Catholic cemetery is situated near the church to which it belongs. (page 397 [lists this as] section 12). The first person buried here was Nicholas Riplinger Jr., who died 17 February 1857. The cemetery [in 1881] contains about four hundred graves (page 398).

Everyone is in alphabetical order. The number before each entry is the row number. There is a map at the back of this section.

This cemeteries burial monuments were transcribed during 1996.

03	Johann Achatz 15 March 1861 - 11 October 1906 (?)
22	Mathias Aghatz 5 August 1896 - 18 March 1917
06	Michael R. Angel 1959-1979
10	Anna M. S. Arendt 11 March 1833 - 24 June 1876
00	Ann Bast?? (rest broken off) 22 July ?? - 16 October 1890 or 1896 (?)
	- this partial stone was with some other partial stone near the statue area.
03	Peter Basting, born 2 September 1840 in Bartringen (?), Grossherzogthum, Luxemberg, died 15 June 1900
02	Christof P. Bauer 6 February 1903 - 16 April (?) 1903
18	John H. Bauer 1906-1978
05	Marie ?? Bauer (?) 27 June 1876 (?) - 22 December 1902
	- hard to read
18	Mary Bauer 17 October 1876 - 9 November 1947

18	Peter Bauer 30 June 1874 - 11 September 1932
18	Susan M. Bauer 1912-1975
20	Anna Maria Sayer, wife of Jolipius Bayer (?)
	28 February 1839 - ?? 1872
22	Johann Pius Bayer, Parish Priest of New Trier 1862-1872. Born
	16 April 1834 in the Archdiocese of Bamberg in
	Giechkrottendorf, of the Parish of Weismain in upper
	Franconia in Bavaria, Germany. Ordained a Priest
	9 November 1860, died of Small Pox at New Trier
	12 May 1872.
03	Andreas Becker 15 February 1867 - 20 July 1900
13	Elisabeth Becker 10 November 1801 - 28 March 1876
06	Anna Beissel 1870-1943
23	Anna Beissel 1907 - __
05	Anna M. Beissel 9 December 1900 - 27 October 1901
07	Anna M. Beissel, died 28 December 1897, age 80 years
25	Arthur M. Beissel, Sgt United States Army Korea
	8 May 1931 - 12 June 1995
25	Arthur M. Beissel 1931-1995, married Eileen M. 24 April 1957
06	Godfried Beissel 1867-1948
07	Helen Beissel 1902-1961
07	Johann Beissel 6 October 1803 - 11 February 1882
13	Johann J. Beissel 15 February 1833 - 26 November 1870
06	Johann M. Beissel 11 October 1895 - 31 January 1919
07	Joseph Beissel 1897-1983
24	Josephine Beissel 1911 - __
23	Nicholas Beissel 1897-1984
24	Peter Beissel 1899-1955
06	William G. Beissel 1896-1963
19	Catherine Beljong 12 July 1823 - 30 April 1923
04	Jacob Berg 1842-1919
04	Katherine Beissel, wife of Jacob Berg 1845-1884
23	Maria, daughter of C. & M. Bierscheid (?) - hard to read
	20 April 1870 - 23 April 1870
28	Sister M. Emilie Black, died (?) 21 November 1907
17	Clifford Blatz 30 May - 31 May 1930
22	Edward Blatz 1884-1964
22	Susanna Blatz 1887-1936
06	Amelia Braun 1897-1960
06	Michael Braun 1897-1990
23	Peter C. Braun 1889-1940
10	Peter Brochmann 29 ?? 1854 - ??? - hard to read
19	Margaretha Bruck 20 March 1832 - 8 July 1888
19	Michael Bruck 20 May 1832 - 8 January 1910
16	Anna M. Buchmann 1 January 1837 - 15 June 1902
16	Johann Buchmann 5 March 1871 - 7 July 1892

16	Jakob Buchmann 17 May 1823 - 16 January 1911
03	Jakob Buchmann - no dates
26	Lorraine Buss - no dates
27	Appolonia Conzemius 19 April 1881 - 27 January 1919
08	Clara Conzemius 1860-1931
22	Clara Conzemius 26 July 1830 - 30 July 1914
08	Henry Conzemius, born in Luxemburg, died 17 April 1924 age 76 years
08	J. P. Conzemius, born in Luxemburg, died 24 September 1922 age 65 years
27	John P. Conzemius 1899-1900
27	Marcus Conzemius 5 April 1872 - 21 January 1936
22	Peter Conzemius 11 April 1828 - 15 February 1908
03	Nikolaus Cordel, died 23 July 1870 (?), age 54 years (?)
13	J. P. Denn, born 15 April 1823 in Remagen, Rhein Preussen Deutschland, died 5 November 1897
06	Katharina Denn, wife of Peter Denn 14 January 1840 - 24 February 1910
28	Rudolph Deusterman, born in Vernich Bezirk Koln Rhein Provinz 12 February 1842 - died New Trier 12 March 1908
12	Elisabeth, wife of A. Dietsch 3 October 1816 - 4 May 1880
27	Alois A. Doffing 1907-1962
16	Anna K. Doffing 11 April 1859 - 25 May 1859
27	Anton Doffing 1868-1944
03	Augustine C. Doffing (?) 1943-1943
27	Catherine Doffing 1873-1962
03	Catherine L. Doffing (?) 1905-1964
27	Elizabeth A. Doffing 1883-1958
25	Frederick Doffing 1875-1950
27	Henry A. Doffing 1876-1959
03	Henry B. Doffing (?) 1897-1970
06	Jacob Doffing 2 November 1885 - 20 July 1910
15	Johann P., son of Peter & Maria Doffing 13 March 1883 - 29 January 1885
19	John Doffing 1916-1916
25	John P. Doffing 1873-1931
10	Johnie (?) Doffing 31 March 1859 - 16 December 1874
17	Joseph, child of Mathias & Margaretha Doffing 12 April 1880 - 10 September 1880 - worn and hard to read
06	Magdalena Doffing 19 July 1861 - 7 February 1933
11	Margaretha Doffing, born Hansen, died 24 November 1874 age 61 years
15	Maria Doffing 15 February 1856 - 24 September 1920
06	Marie O. Doffing 1883-1959

03	Marvin H. Doffing (?) 1927-1927
25	Mary S. Doffing 1876-1930
06	Mathias N. Doffing 3 September 1854 - 27 November 1901
06	Michael N. Doffing 1884-1949
03	Myron A. Doffing (?) 1928-1953
12	Nicolas Doffing 18 ?? 1862 - ?? 1879 (?) - worn and hard to read
13	Nicolaus Doffing 6 December 1809 - 22 March 1871
07	Nikolaus Doffing, died 28 December 1872 (?), age 24 years (?)
16	Paulus Doffing 2 December 1860 - 10 (?) December 1869
17	Peter, child of Mathias & Margaretha Doffing
	1 March 1864 - 30 ?? 1865 - worn and hard to read
15	Peter E. Doffing 23 September 1851 - 18 February 1910
03	Richard J. Doffing (?) 1930-1930
19	Rose Doffing 1899-1910
27	Rose C. Doffing 1909 - __
03	Stanley C. Doffing (?) 1938-1938
17	Theresia Doffing 17 April 1894 - 13 April 1895
19	Veronica Doffing 1913-1914
28	Jennifer Rose Dohmen - 3 July 1972 -
24	Susan Dondelinger 1852-1925
15	Emma, born Irrthum, wife of Jacob Donndelinger
	7 October 1843 - 21 April 1879
15	Jacob Donndelinger 6 December 1842 - 9 July 1896
15	Jeanette E. Donndelinger 1901-1994
15	Johann Donndelinger 4 January 1867 - 4 April 1867
15	John S. Donndelinger 1898-1954
15	Magdalena Donndelinger 20 September 1873 - 19 October 1874
15	Maria M. Donndelinger 15 April 1879 - 22 May 1879
15	Jacob Donolinger Co. F 7th Minnesota Infantry
03	Clemens Durr 14 February 1859 - 8 April 1893
22	Franziska Eck 11 October 1834 - 26 August 1908
23	Margaretha Eck 25 March 1825 - 1 April 1864
23	Peter Eck 17 January 1820 - 3 June 1878
22	Theresia Eck 28 September 1874 (?) - 20 February 1903
15	Anna M. Eischen 10 October 1864 - 26 October 1864
15	Johann Eischen 1 March 1839 - 2 August 1864
02	Peter J. Eischens 1905-1978
02	Susan M. Eischens 1903-1983
03	John Elsner 1864-1898
21	Anna Maria Elsen, wife of Paulus Endres
	15 August 1830 - 3 August 1871
18	Christina Endres 13 June 1862 - 22 June 1952
18	Franziskus X., son of Georg & Christina Endres
	13 June 1896 - 17 July 1896
18	Georg Endres 22 December 1858 - 25 December 1905

22	Leona C. Endres 2 May 1898 - 28 July 1899
21	Paulus Endres 16 May 1808 - 1 April 1891
22	Peter Endres 24 August 1861 - 5 April 1900
16	Franz Engel, born in Mensdorf, Grosserzogthum, Luxemburg 24 November 1827 - 11 April 1896
16	John Engel 3 April 1873 - 11 April 1889
16	Margaretha Engel, born in Mensdorf, Luxemburg 13 June 1836 - 8 August 1921
16	Nicholas Engel 19 April 1867 - 15 April 1868
16	Peter Engel 29 April 1865 - 10 April 1866
21	Elisabeth Feidt 1865-1925
21	Elizabeth Feidt 1890-1954
21	Jerome C. Feidt 1956-1984
21	Johann Feidt 3 December 1833 - 17 March 1923
21	John Feidt 1896-1978
23	Joseph Feidt 1924-1974, married Mary Rose 13 October 1948
21	Margaretha Huberty, wife of Johann Feidt 11 August 1836 - 5 February 1891
21	Maria Feidt (?) 2 March 1903 - 6 July 1903
23	Mary Rose Feidt 1927-1994, married Joseph 13 October 1948
21	Michael Feidt 1865-1942
21	Michael Feidt 3 November 1829 - 23 November 1903
25	Anna Maria Feipel, born (?) 26 July 1844 in Trier, Germany died (?) 13 December 1919
11	Anton Feipel, born in Godbringen, Grossh., Luxemburg died 3 November 1864, age 64 years
25	Helena Feipel, wife (?) of Johann Feipel 1828-1897
25	Johann Feipel, born (?) 17 April 1835 in Godbringen, Luxemburg died (?) 7 March 1918
11	Maria A. Feipel, born in Niederanven, Grossh., Luxemburg died 17 December 1877, age 72 years
03	Alex Feller 2 April 1896 - 3 October 1896
13	John Felton, died 18 September 1871, age 63 years
12	Clara L. Ficker 1892-1975
12	John Ficker 1869-1943
06	Magdalena Ficker 5 March 1880 - 6 February 1882
07	Maria Ficker 28 September 1848 - 12 September 1922
12	Mary Ficker 1862-1945
07	Mathias Ficker 9 February 1838 - 12 May 1909
23	Michael Ficker 1898-1976
23	Michael L. Ficker, Pvt. United States Army World War 1 1898-1976
06	Peter Ficker 20 May 1878 - 2 February 1882
23	Stanley J. Ficker, Cpl United States Army Korea 1930-1982
02	Theodore Ficker 1896-1986

17	Theodore J. Ficker 19 June 1926 - 13 November 1926
23	Theresa Ficker 1902-1984
02	Veronica Ficker 1893-1963
21	Catherine F. Fietz 28 April 1903 - 14 November 1974
20	Johanna Fietz 1841-1927
21	Marie Fietz (?) 1862-1934
21	Max Fietz (?) 1870-1956
19	just Fox 2 April 1904 - 9 August 1904
19	August N. Fox 15 May 1902 - 2 October 1908
19	'Father' Fox (?) 14 July 1874 - 27 January 1918
27	Ferdinand Fox 1871-1964
24	J. J. Fox 13 September 1819 - 3 November 1891
24	Joseph Fox 13 June (?) 1855 - 28 October 1884
24	Katharina Fox 26 May 1833 - 5 may 1913
19	Margaret Fox 7 February 1879 - 7 May 1965
27	Mary Fox 1876-1968
27	Bernice Freiermuth 1913-1918 'A car - train tragedy'
24	Brigitta Freiermuth, born Mies 28 December 1830 in Dolsndorf Preussen, Deutschland, died (?) 18 February 1911
03	Clarence Freiermuth 1909-1969
23	Clarence Freiermuth (?) 12 May (?) 1900 - 25 March 1906
24	Columbus Freiermuth, born (?) 24 June 1827 in Grosrederiching, Canton Rorbach Lotringen Frankreich, died (?) 9 March 1913
03	Columbus Freiermuth 1901-1985
27	George Freiermuth (?) 1858-1932
03	Goerge P. Freiermuth 16 July 1887 - 29 June 1968
03	Justine Freiermuth 1896-1989
27	Lillian Freiermuth 1916-1918 'A car - train tragedy'
27	Margaret Freiermuth (?) 1868-1931
03	Mary Freiermuth 1907-1987
03	Nick B. Freiermuth 1894-1977
03	Roy E. Freiermuth 1920-1961
27	Viola Freiermuth 1912-1918 'A car - train tragedy'
03	Walter J. Freiermuth 1911-1986
27	William C. Freiermuth 1889-1918
27	William C. Freiermuth 16 January 1889 - 14 July 1918
07	John Freilinger - no dates
07	Matt Freilinger - no dates
11	Joseph A., son of A. & M. A. Fuchs, died 28 August 1874 age 3 months
09	Nicolas Fuchs 3 June 1817 - 7 August 1879
01	Casper J. Geering, born in Schweiz 7 May 1832 died Cannon Falls 28 June 1882
17	Anna K., wife of Jacob Gergen 15 October 1852 - 27 August 1913

14	Arnold Gergen (?) - no dates
17	Bernard Gergen, married (?) Maria Schmitz 1855
	died 15 May 1880, age 50 years 2 months 21 days
17	Catharina, child of J. & A. Gergen
	5 March 1875 - 29 December 1881
07	Daniel J. Gergen (?) - August 1957 -
14	Elizabeth Gergen (?) - no dates
28	Genevieve Jean Gergen (?) 1 December - 13 December 1943
14	Gerhard Gergen 27 October 1866 - 26 April 1916
05	Helen Gergen 1913 - __
17	Jacob Gergen 3 march 1849 - 18 January 1930
17	Jacob Gergen (?), child of B. & A. Gergen
	13 August 1863 - 8 November 1865
06	Margaret Gergen (?) 1879-1962
14	Margaret Weber Gergen 1866-1939
17	Margaretha, child of J. & A. Gergen
	22 October 1873 - 26 August 1876
28	Mary Gergen (?) 1881-1968
14	Marie Gergen (?) - no dates
07	Marie A. Gergen 1892-1987
14	Mathias Gergen (?) - no dates
17	Mathias Gergen 15 May 1894 - 22 February 1895
28	Mathias Gergen (?) 1872-1936
28	Maxine Gergen (?) 1908-1929
06	Nicholas Gergen (?) 1876-1926
17	Nicolaus Gergen, husband (?) of Anna Gergen
	2 February 1805 - 20 July 1872
17	Peter Gergen (?), child of B. & A. Gergen
	16 March 1871 - 15 August 1872
17	Peter, child of J. & A. Gergen 26 May 1879 - 3 February 1880
07	Peter P. Gergen 1882-1937
05	Raymond Gergen 1906-1986
28	Rosella Gergen (?) 1912-1972
06	Veronica Gergen (?) 1913-1929
06	Veronica Gergen born & died 11 January 1909
04	Viola Gergen 1 August 1918 - 5 December 1918
17	Wilhelm Gergen (?), child of B. & A. Gergen
	18 April 1861 - 11 November 1865
18	'Father' Gerlach (?) 1855-1937
05	Hubert Gerlach (?) 1907-1931
05	Joseph Gerlach (?) 1913-1930
18	Katharina Gerlach 1857-1910
18	Magdalena Gerlach 1892-1910
11	Maria N. Gerlach 23 June 1875 (?) - 13 August 1876 (?)
	- hard to read
18	Martin Gerlach 1883-1911

05	Mary A. Gerlach (?) 1887-1924
05	William Gerlach (?) 1882-1940
21	Joseph Giefer 20 April 1837 - 30 November 1878
03	Theodor Gillen, died 28 December 1909, age 69 years
17	Ulbert Glatzel, died 19 October 1895, age 53 years
20	Anna Gonzemius 15 November 1847 - 7 March 1893
21	Cecilia Gonzemius 8 January 1865 - 3 November 1891
20	Franz Gonzemius, born in Medernach, Luxemburg died 18 May 1880, age 63 years
20	Theresia Gonzemius, born in Keispelt, Luxemburg died 29 January 1899, age 85 years
01	Leon H. Gooding 1911-1993, married Marie D. 30 December 1939
01	Marie D. Gooding 1909 - __, married Leon H. 30 December 1939
21	Nicolas Gotto, ?? Katharina Thein, died 6 April 1881, age 63 years
02	Beverly Lois Gotz 18 November 1926 - 7 April 1979
25	Antonius M. Gores 6 April 1903 - 30 March 1910
07	Cecelia Gores (?) 1912 - __
19	Christopher Gores 14 February 1870 - 17 December 1895
19	Elisabetha Gores (?) ?? 1861 - ??? 1878 - worn and hard to read
07	Emilia Gores (?) 1878-1947
25	Gertrude Gores 1890-1986
25	Hubert Gores 1899-1900
19	Johann Gores, born 20 October 1828 in Schonecken, Rhein Provenz, died 14 February 1909
19	Johann J. Gores ?? 1878 - ??? 1878 - worn and hard to read
28	Rev. John Nicholas Gores, ordained 8 June 1915 1885-1963
25	Joseph J. Gores 1901-1919
19	Joseph J. Gores 2 June 1857 - 17 June 1882
10	Katharina Gores (?) 8 April 1864 - 1 November 1876
19	Katharina S. Gores ?? 1873 - ??? 1876 - worn and hard to read
25	Katherine Gores 1859-1936
25	Margaretha M. Gores 1889-1911
25	Magdalen Gores, born Nicolai 30 June 1826 - 19 June 1916
10	Magdalena Gores (?) 28 December 1850 (?) - 28 November 1875
25	Magdalena Gores 7 December 1894 - 31 January 1896
16	Maria K. Gores, born Gores, died 18 December 1858, age 32 years
25	Martin Gores, born in Schoenecken, Rhein, Preussen 7 July 1823 - 30 January 1899
07	Martin Gores (?) 1882-1963
07	Mary Gores (?) 1884-1919
25	Nikolaus Gores 1858-1913
19	Veronicka Gores, born Weiler 14 February 1843 in Willesecken died (?) 21 March 1917
17	Elisabeth Graus (?) ?? 1864 - ??? 1865 - worn and hard to read
23	Anna Greten, wife of Peter Greten

	15 February 1830 - 1 August 1897
23	Maria Greten 1 January 1873 - 26 September 1890
23	Peter Greten 15 January 1828 - 16 October 1896
01	Conrad Gretin 6 January 1870 - 16 May 1897
25	Barbra Gretz 10 April 1830 - 21 January 1902
25	Nickolaus Gretz 17 August 1830 - 22 June 1903

21	Elisabeth, wife of Theodor Haas, born in Ellelbruck (?), Luxemburg
	15 August 1804 - 25 December 1895
21	Theodor Haas 15 August 1801 - 16 May 1883
06	A. P. Hammes 30 June 1882 - 10 May 1891
06	Anna Pia (?) Hammes (?) 20 June 1882 - 10 November 1891
02	Daniel Hartung 1924-1981, married Jean 27 October 1947
02	Jean Hartung 1924 - __, married Daniel 27 October 1947
05	Peter Heber, son of Mr. & Mrs. Gerald Heber - 17 November 1971 -
24	Amelia Heinlein 1899-1994
24	Andrew Heinlein 1875-1945
22	Catharine Heinlein (?) 25 June 1871 (?) - 22 May 1879
	- worn and hard to read
22	Johann Heinlein 12 February 1844 - 23 July 1929
24	Magdalene Heinlein 1873-1940
22	Margaretha Heinlein, born Bayer 21 May 1843 in Giegkrottendorf,
	Oberfranken, Bayern, died 19 December 1899 New Trier, Minn.
24	Philip Heinlein 1881-1953
24	Anna, wife of Michael Herber 15 October 1808 - 12 April 1889
24	Michael Herber 13 September 1801 - 3 July 1878
20	Margareth Hermes, age 73 years - no dates
20	Susanna Hermes 26 December 1816 - 2 January 1903
02	Anna Hoffman 1891-1963
05	Patricia Hoffman 1934-1993, married William 6 November 1954
02	Peter A. Hoffman 1886-1958
05	William Hoffman 1930-1984, married Patricia 6 November 1954
14	Heinrich Hoffmann 30 December 1881 - 12 April 1900
14	Heinrich M. Hoffmann 25 June 1827 - 11 December 1905
14	Katharina Meyer, wife of Heinrich M. Hoffmann
	6 August 1835 - 17 July 1870
21	Margaret G. Hoffmann (?) 9 March 1909 - __
06	Maria Hoffmann 4 May 1865 - 1 February 1885
21	Mathias Hoffmann (?) 12 October 1867 - 3 October 1944
05	Philip M., son of Heinrich & Franziska Hoffmann
	1 February 1890 - 5 July 1892
06	Theresia Hoffmann 10 January 1862 - 2 February 1889
21	Veronica Hoffmann (?) 26 October 1874 - 7 October 1938
20	Wilhelm Holtgrewe - dates are cemented over
07	Catharina Thinnes, wife of Johann Holzemer
	20 June 1860 - 17 June 1884

11	Katharina, daughter of Conrad & Susanna Holzemer 25 October 1872 - 19 September 1873
05	Katherine Hommertgen (?) 1874-1924
05	John N. Hommertgen (?) 1911-1931
05	Nicholas Hommertgen (?) 1867-1925
20	Andrew J. Horn 13 March 1872 - 28 October 1891
20	Eva M. Horn 20 January 1835 - 8 January 1914
20	Jacob Horn 10 November 1830 - 3 May 1899
24	Christian Horsch 11 November 1826 - 27 February 1904 (?)
03	Monica Schabert Hunter 1921 - __
22	Bertha Huss 4 July 1912 - 24 November 1977
22	Joseph M. Huss 1895-1952
19	Lorraine P. Huss 1910-1980
19	Raymond J. Huss 1904-1971
06	E. M. Irrthem 15 January 1911 - 29 November 1912
24	Anna Irrthum 1811-1879
24	Claudius Irrthum 1810-1893
06	Claudius Irrthum 1872-1962
06	Emma Irrthum 1912-1913
06	Emma Irrthum 1878-1948
24	John Irrthum 1844-1878
06	Raymond M. Irrthum, son of John P. & Gertrude 27 May - 1 July 1927
04	Johanna E. Jamma 20 December 1889 - 18 February 1930
22	Katharine Kasel, born (?) 30 December 1805 in Medernach Luxemburg, died (?) 24 December 1875
27	Margaretha Kasel 15 August 1840 - 6 January 1913
27	Peter Kasel 30 May 1834 - 29 April 1915
21	Margaret Keiser 1823-1879
23	Carolina Keller 11 January 1856 - 14 March 1940
23	Lena Keller 1877-1964
22	Lorenz Keller 20 September 1818 - 4 January 1885
22	Maria Th. Keller 10 December 1820 - 14 February 1901
23	Phillip Keller 1868-1954
16	Maria Katherine Kerst, born Girden (?) died 30 June 1869, age 75 years
27	Louis K. Kieffer 1906 - __
27	Peter J. Kieffer 1906 - __
04	Aloysius Kimmes (?) - 1924 -
04	Anna M. Kimmes (?) 1894-1981
08	Frances Kimmes 1917-1979
28	Jacob Kimmes 1915-1988
04	John Kimmes (?) - 1928 -

08	Leander Kimmes 1919-1980
03	Marie Kimmes 1907-1976
28	Mary J. Kimmes 1926 - __
04	Mathias Kimmes (?) 1890-1959
03	Mathias T. Kimmes 1901-1961
03	Norbert P. Kimmes 1933-1969
04	Theresa Kimmes (?) 1925-1926
15	Eva K. Werner, wife of Peter J. Klasen 7 February 1795 - 1 December 1870
15	Peter J. Klasen 14 June 1800 - 30 November 1885
23	Anna Klein 1849-1930
23	Anna Klein 1849-1930
23	Jacob Klein 9 October 1877 - 28 May 1911
06	James P. Klein 1880-1928
06	John G. Klein 1875-1934
06	John P. Klein 1841-1919
23	Mathias Klein 1844-1898
23	Mathias Klein 15 October 1844 - 9 June 1898
04	Franz Kneifel 18 August 1848 - 3 February 1919
03	Joseph J. Kneifel 9 October 1895 - 1 February 1903
04	Peter J. Kneifel 17 June 1891 - 15 October 1917
21	Catherine Konsbruck 1891-1973
21	Jacob Konsbruck 1880-1956
08	Jacob Konzbruck, born (?) 15 February 1838 in Waldbillig Grossh. Luxemburg, died 21 April 1903 Neu Trier, Minnesota
08	Magdalena Konzbruck, born Broos 13 December 1845 in Waldbillig Grossh., Luxemburg, died 25 October 1899 New Trier, Minn.
01	Lukac Koppel 1867-1948
23	Anna Margaretha, daughter of N. F. W. & A. M. Kranz 19 August 1868 - 6 April 1869
23	Anna Margaretha, daughter of N. F. W. & A. M. Kranz 19 August 1868 - 6 April 1869
25	Charles Kranz 4 April 1828 - 5 February 1904
25	John B. Kranz 4 October 1866 - 6 August 1925
25	Katharina Ebel, wife of Charles Kranz 25 July 1840 - 9 May 1887
25	Maggie Kranz 20 February 1897 - 5 March 1897
25	Mary A. Reinardy, wife of John B. Kranz 27 October 1868 - 14 October 1903
23	Nicolaus Kranz 20 September 1797 - 15 January 1879
23	Susanna, born Lutz, wife of Nicolaus Kranz died 20 May 1861, age 60 years
09	Georg Kuhn, born in (?) Leimersheim, Bayern 15 September 1826 - 16 October 1892
09	Katharina Kuhn, born in (?) Leimersheim, Bayern 9 January 1824 - 5 December 1877

25	Peter Kuhn 7 June 1856 - 11 April 1908
25	Susan E. Kranz, wife of Peter Kuhn
	1 August 1859 - 30 March 1903
05	Anna M., daughter of Jacob & Katharina Kummer
	23 March 1879 - 28 November 1881
08	Adolph E. Landsberger 1910-1989
24	Agatha Landsberger 2 September 1837 - 6 April 1924
27	Albert J. Landsberger (?) 1893-1919
20	Anna Landsberger 1865-1951
04	Anna, wife of Frank Landsberger 8 July 1871 - 12 January 1922
04	baby Claude Landsberger (?) 11 January - 8 December 1934
08	Emilie Landsberger 1908 - __
20	Eva Landsberger, born (?) 30 June 1816 in Konig Reich Bayern
	died (?) 29 April 1892
04	Frank Landsberger 1871-1942
25	Genovefa E. Landsberger 19 June 1909 - 3 February 1910
20	Georg Landsberger, born (?) 18 April 1828 in Konigreich, Bayern
	Died (?) 7 November 1908
04	George Landsberger 1936-1963
02	George Landsberger 1903-1988
20	Johann Leo Landsberger 28 June 1905 - 29 October 1906
08	Leo G. Landsberger 1901-1979
24	Ludwig Landsberger 30 January 1878 - 24 February 1882
20	M. Franziska Landsberger, born in (?) Konigreich, Bayern
	20 November 1829 - 17 May 1896
20	M. Rosa, daughter of F. & A. Landsberger
	26 February 1892 - 26 May 1892
09	Maria A. Landsberger 17 April 1870 - 19 November 1873
21	Mary Landsberger 1876-1955
25	Rosaline T. Landsberger 19 November 1907 - 8 February 1908
02	Rose Landsberger 1909 - __
04	Tony B. Landsberger 26 May 1968 - 30 October 1995
24	Wolfgang Landsberger 3 November 1825 - 12 October 1890
21	Gottfried Lansberger 1872-1906
04	Lena Landsburger 23 March 1858 - 19 December 1938
25	Margaret Langenfeld 1886-1956
23	Raymond G. Lather (?) 29 April 1920 - 31 October 1923
18	Anna M. Leifeld, born in (?) Brenken (?) Westtalen (?)
	26 February 1852 - 11 October 1925
21	Anton Leifeld 1875-1876
21	George Leifeld 1880-1881
18	Heinrich Franz Leifeld 15 June 1843 - 23 November 1905
08	Henry Leifeld (?) 1841-1926
21	Jacob Leifeld 1877-1881
08	Magdalena Leifeld (?) 1843-1928

21	Peter Leifeld 1874-1882
26	Jack P. Lenartz 1885-1965
26	Philip Lenartz 25 November 1853 - 23 February 1912
26	Susanna Lenartz 6 July 1854 - 1 February 1933
12	Heinrich Leven - dates were cemented over
12	Paulus Leven - dats were cemented over
03	Christian Linderfelser 15 April 1873 - 13 January 1894
03	Nicholas Lindenfelser 3 June 1876 - 22 June 1897
25	Barbara Lorentz 1873-1954
25	Charles Lorentz (?) 1877-1932
20	Gary Lorentz 1962-1978
25	Jacob M. Lorentz (?) 1898-1967
25	John Lorentz 1867-1964
25	Karl Lorentz 21 December 1821 - 14 February 1901
24	Kenneth Lorentz 1960-1982
25	Margaret Lorentz 24 June 1841 - 24 October 1916
26	Anna M. Lucius 1877-1945
24	Catharine Moes, wife of Michael Lucius
	25 July 1839 - 12 March 1912
22	Dominic Lucius 1860-1943
05	Dorothy M. Lucius 1919 - __
26	Edward J. Lucius 1870-1944
24	Elizabeth Lucius 3 August 1861 - 16 January 1877
24	Emma Lucius 1880-1944
20	Henrietta M. Lucius 11 March 1905 - 9 October 1905
05	Jacob E. Lucius 15 December 1911 - 29 October 1917
05	Jerome J. Lucius 1921-1992
05	Joseph Lucius 1882-1961
19	Marie L. Lucius 1898-1967
05	Mary Lucius 1889-1962
20	Mary S. Lucius 28 January 1867 - 24 June 1931
24	Michael Lucius 6 January 1830 - 20 September 1900
19	Michael W. Lucius 1898-1971
20	Peter Lucius 6 October 1866 - 8 September 1954
24	Theodore Lucius 1874-1965
24	Theresa Lucius 1883-1939
24	Theresa Lucius 11 April 1883 - 26 August 1939
25	Anna Maria Ludwig 27 February 1840 - 22 November 1901
27	Henry Ludwig (?) 1857-1945
27	Susan Ludwig (?) 1866-1946
22	Anna Maria, daughter of John & Barbara Mamer
	5 June 1889 - 5 September 1892
27	Arthur Mamer 28 July 1917 - 17 May 1926
25	Catherine Mamer 26 June 1849 - 12 October 1928
24	Heinrich, son of Theodor & Katherina Mamer

	6 September 1879 - 22 March 1885
24	Heinrich L., son of T. & K. Mamer
	5 July 1892 - 3 February 1893
24	Jacob, child of Theodor & Katharina Mamer
	4 December 1881 - 14 August 1890
25	Johanna Mamer 15 April 1814 - 28 March 1905
24	Joseph Mamer 11 November 1897 - 31 January 1901
25	Julia A. Mamer (?) 1890-1988
24	Rosie K., child of Theodor & Katharina Mamer
	29 August 1887 - 7 August 1890
24	Susanna, child of Theodor & Katharina Mamer
	22 September 1885 - 9 August 1890
25	Theodor Mamer 2 February 1845 - 25 December 1926
07	Katharina Doffing, wife of Johann Mangan 1853-1885
15	Lambert Marjan 10 April 1790 (?) - 26 August 1867
	- worn and hard to read
13	Anna, wife of Henry Marschal 1800-1882
13	Henry Marschal 1784-1868
27	John P. McCoy (?) 1902-1927
27	Robert J. McCoy 1923 - __, married Rosella M. 7 June 1944
27	Rosella M. McCoy 1920-1992, married Robert J. 7 June 1944
21	Catherine Thein Meyers 1860-1940
21	Frank N. Meyers 1872-1947
25	George A. Meyers 1933-1978
24	Joseph Michalke 27 October 1888 - 27 May 1894
24	Margaretha Lucius, wife of Joseph Michalke
	15 March 1862 - 9 March 1890
24	Michael Michalke 5 March 1890 - 6 August 1890
03	Casper Michels 19 (?) January 1846 - 9 March 1906
14	Amalia Mies 9 June 1820 - 16 March 1898
14	Christine Mies 17 May 1855 - 16 September 1869
14	Heinrich Mies 26 December 1849 - 16 June 1903
14	Kasper Mies 18 November 1852 - 5 June 1869
14	Peter Mies (?) 1857-1931
14	Wilhelm Mies, born in Dollendorf, Rhein-Preussen, Deutschland
	23 January 1823 - 23 December 1896
21	John B. Miller 1905-1965
22	Rita H. Miller - no dates
21	Susan A. Miller 1909 - __
25	Catherine Moes 1898-1977
03	Catherine A. Moes 1896-1984
20	Dominik Moes 4 March 1797 - 16 September 1865 (?)
20	Dominikus Moes 25 January 1866 - 3 August 1897
20	Elisabetha Ellringer, wife of Dominik Moes
	13 (?) November 1804 - 10 October (?) 1877 (?) - hard to read
03	Gilbert Moes 1932-1935

20	Johann Moes 25 November 1827 - 19 November 1903
03	John D. Moes 1895-1951
04	John J. Moes 1893-1985
05	Madeline Moes 1904-1991
04	Margaret M. Moes 1887-1963
20	Margaretha Moes 2 February 1835 - 25 September 1914
05	Peter Moes 1862-1932
25	Peter J. Moes 1898-1993
20	Raymond Moes 1918 - __
20	Regina Moes 1913-1992
05	Richard John, son of Peter J. Moes 1927-1928
05	Sophia, wife of Peter Mose 17 May 1868 - 8 May 1914
05	Willaim J. Moes 1930-1930
21	Arnold L. Molitor (?) 1888-1921
06	Fredrick Molitor (?) 12 November 1881 - 17 May 1894
21	Geo Molitor 24 November 1818 - 7 January 1913
21	Henry Molitor 1897-1898
21	Henry Molitor 1878-1878
22	John Molitor (?) 4 August 1852 - 8 November 1936
21	Kate Molitor 1881-1881
22	Katharine Molitor (?) 30 January 1857 - 27 September 1913
21	Maria, wife of Geo Molitor 8 May 1815 - 3 March 1871
06	'Mutter' (?) Molitor (?) 21 November 1843 - 21 January 1919
21	Nic Molitor 1845-1872
21	Rosy Molitor 1899-1899
06	Ruth K. Molitor 4 October 1922 - 6 May 1924
21	Valentine Molitor 1811-1877
19	Anna Muller 13 November 1852 - 16 March 1917
15	Anna Maria Muller, born Reinardy
	10 March 1830 - 2 March 1867
19	Johann N. Muller 7 January 1846 - 30 July 1908
10	Caspar Nahl, born in Schomehen (?) Rhein Preuszen (?)
	died 16 November 1880, age 53 years
21	Angela Nappin 1949-1970
21	Sharon Nappin 1970-1970
21	Todd Nappin 1969-1970
12	Anna Maria Ruys, wife of Hubert Nicolai, born in Bouchout, Belgen
	13 December 1833 - 20 February 1907
12	Hubert Nicolai, born in Schoenecken, Deutschland
	26 September 1831 - 25 January 1904
08	Marla Magdalen Nicolai - dates were cemented over
23	Agnes Niedere 25 August 1810 - 25 September 1872
23	Heinrich Niedere 9 January 1813 - 4 August 1871
18	Elizabeth Olsen 1886-1983

18	John Olsen 1891-1923
02	Marie M. Olson 1900-1975
02	Robert J. O'Rourke 1916-1987
02	Elizabeth Otto 1891-1978
02	Jonathan C. Otto 1983-1983
02	John Jerry Otto, Minnesota Pvt. 516 Sig ACFT WNG BN World War 2
	21 March 1922 - 23 August 1968
02	Nicholas Otto 1877-1966
07	Raymond Otto (?) 1906-1925
02	Raymond M. Otto 1923-1949
02	William J. Otto 1926-1975
02	William Joseph Otto, F1 United States Navy World War 2
	17 October 1926 - 29 October 1975
06	Peter Palm March 1838 - 17 June 1924
06	Raphael J. Palm 22 November 1916 - 16 December 1991
03	Anna Pasch 1875-1957
22	Anna K. Pasch, child of Johann & Katharina Pasch
	17 December 1881 - 15 January 1885
20	Catherine Pasch (?) 1862-1929
20	Gregory Pasch 23 July 1910 - 4 October 1932
20	Henry Pasch 1884-1969
20	John Pasch 17 November 1857 - 3 June 1909
22	Louis Pasch, child of Johann & Katharina Pasch
	22 April 1887 - 19 October 1887
22	Maria Pasch, child of Johann & Katharina Pasch
	17 October 1888 - 8 August 1890
20	Mary Pasch 1885-1949
03	Nick Pasch 1885-1959
19	Barbara Peiffer 1877-1948
19	Nicholas F. Peiffer 1874-1932
03	Alfonse Peine 1912-1929
02	baby Peine - 1940 -
24	Brian Joseph Peine, son of David & Joann
	13 June 1987 - 25 August 1987
03	Catherine Peine 1874-1946
03	Charles E. Peine 1871-1955
02	Clarence P. Peine 1914-1978
26	Dolores T. Peine 1930-1982
24	Elizabeth Peine 29 October 1839 - 16 February 1911
03	Ernest J. Peine 1900-1962
24	Henry C. Peine 1897-1978
26	Lawrence F. Peine 1957-1971
26	Lawrence J. Peine 1928 - __
24	Karl W. Peine 2 February 1835 - 25 June 1902
24	Margaret Peine 1898-1995

02	Veronica Peine 1917 - __
03	Anton Pichooto 13 June 1859 - 17 December 1907
18	Mary Bauer Polansky 1899-1943
23	Anna Rech 1874-1907
19	Anna Maria Rech, daughter of Nicolas & Maria Rech 7 May 1886 - 30 July 1892
23	John Rech - 1907 -
06	John M. Rech, child of Nicolas & Maria Rech 29 January 1888 - 12 November 1888
23	Josephine Rech 1905 - __
06	Leonard Rech, child of Nicolas & Maria Rech 5 October 1884 - 21 October 1884
20	Mary Rech 4 January 1863 - 13 September 1932
23	Max Rech 1862-1951
20	Nicholas Rech 1 November 1859 - 2 October 1928
25	Anna Reding (?) 1872-1929
25	Johann Reding 23 January 1822 - 2 July 1902
25	Maria Reding, born Giefer 23 April 1833 - 30 September 1911
27	Agnes Reinardy - no dates
24	Anna Reinardy 1874-1937
27	Barbara Reinardy 30 March 1861 - 26 August 1937
27	Domonic Reinardy - no dates
26	Emma Reinardy 1890-1966
05	Gertrude Reinardy 1911-1993
21	Herbert M. Reinardy 1916 - __
21	Jacob Reinardy 1878-1974
27	Jake Reinardy - no dates
24	Jakob Reinardy 11 January 1836 - 28 January 1910
26	John Reinardy 1891-1975
17	Joseph J. Reinardy 1903-1973
21	Kathleen Reinardy 1946-1947
17	Magdalena Reinardy 1904-1991
27	Margaret Reinardy - no dates
24	Maria Anna Reinardy 24 June 1833 - 25 May 1919
21	Mary Reinardy - 18 January 1950 -
21	Mary E. Reinardy 1884-1963
24	Math Reinardy 1871-1965
27	Michael Reinardy 8 April 1861 - 2 April 1919
05	Michael Reinardy - 1952 -
05	Nicholas Reinardy 1905-1988
23	John Wm. Resemius ?? 1900 - ??? 1901 (?) - hard to read
23	Mary A. Resemius ?? 1898 - ?? 1898 - hard to read
23	Wilhelm L. Resemius 27 July 1875 - 20 January 1914
07	Elisabeth Rischette, nee Zeien (?) 1851-1932

07	Wilhelm Rischette 1841-1914
07	Mathias Robert 7 March 1814 - 7 May 1869
07	Michael M. Robert 1903-1952
17	Susanna, born Hiltgen, wife of Mathias Robert
	14 February 1819 - 17 August 1887
18	Anna Rohr 20 October 1837 - 10 October 1906
18	Peter Rohr 29 January 1830 - 21 March 1917
05	Theresa Rohr 1842-1911
17	Donald Edward Rother 29 March 1928 - 15 January 1929
21	Eduard, son of Frank & Gertrude Rother
	17 July 1886 - 24 November 1888
24	Franz Rother 23 November 1809 - 15 April 1882
19	Hedwig, daughter of Eduard & Helena Rother
	15 October 1873 - 8 September 1890
24	Katharina, wife of Franz Rother 15 March 1817 - 21 March 1889
16	J. B. Sablohner, born Ulm 24 February 1802 - 17 August 1863
22	Anna Schaack - no dates
22	Charles Schaack 30 August 1863 - 21 July 1900
22	Johann Schaack 2 February 1823 - 13 May 1908
22	Magdlena Schaack 24 June 1833 - 3 May 1902
22	Mary Schaack 19 April 1871 - 28 January 1910
22	Nickolaus Schaack - no dates
19	Dorothy Schabert 1923 - __, married Edward J. 7 November 1946
19	Edward J. Schabert 1914-1971, married Dorothy 7 November 1946
07	Eugene Schabert (?) 1947-1950
03	George Schabert 1912-1958
05	Hildegard K. Schabert, nee Lucius 1919-1994
07	John Schabert (?) 1886-1948
19	Kevin E. Schabert, busband of Becky 1961-1994
03	Rita Schabert, daughter of Greg & Monica 1944-1945
05	Roger N. Schabert 3 June 1939 - 31 October 1939
07	Sophia Schabert (?) 1886-1962
19	Anna Maria, daughter of Adam & Elisabeth Schaefer
	23 August 1887 - 22 April 1890
19	Mary A. Schaefer 1863-1931
19	N. George, son of N. & M. A. Schaefer
	11 December 1887 - 17 February 1890
19	Nicolaus Schaefer 25 January 1859 - 25 May 1894
19	Adam Schaffer 1864-1952
28	Cynthia R. Schaffer 1940-1951
19	Elizabeth Schaffer 1864-1933
20	George Schaffer 5 February 1843 - 4 November 1904
19	J. Adam Schaffer 20 January 1820 - 27 January 1892
06	John F. Schaffer 1962-1980
28	John P. Schaffer (?) 1899-1957

19	Katharina Schaffer 17 July 1821 - 2 May 1911
28	Marie A. Schaffer (?) 1898-1987
28	Patricia Schaffer 1938-1955
20	Theresa Schaffer 9 June 1845 - 10 May 1921
02	Anna Scharfenberg 1886-1960
19	Anna M. Schiller 22 December 1830 - 7 January 1907
19	Antonius Schiller 11 May 1826 - 16 December 1905
27	Katherine H. Schiller 1906-1993
19	baby Zezia Schiller - 1909 -
19	Conrad, son of John & Margaret Schiltgen 29 June 1891 - 15 March 1892
25	Schmalen family - no names - no dates
05	Johann Schmitz 26 October 1899 - 17 June 1900
03	Katharina Schmitz 18 October 1828 - 15 November 1901
03	Michael Schroeder, born (?) 1866 Luxemburg died (?) 1882 Neu Trier
17	Ferdinand W. Schwartz 18 September 1911 - 24 December 1911
05	Frank, son of N. F. Schwartz 1887-1899
16	G. Margaretha, daughter of Nicholas & Barbara Schwartz 10 April 1859 - 15 February 1863
16	Gertrude, daughter of Nicholas & Barbara Schwartz 15 March 1854 - 2 February 1863
21	Bartholomaus, child of Johann & Katharina Schweich 12 January 1876 - 24 January 1882
20	Cecelia Schweich, child of J. P. & C. Schweich 17 January 1891 - 4 July 1891
27	F. N. W. Schweich 30 August 1867 - 7 April 1913
05	Gervase Schweich 1920-1921
21	John, child of Johann & Katharina Schweich 15 July 1877 - 27 January 1882
21	John, child of Johann & Katharina Schweich 7 March 1874 - 15 October 1874
27	Maria Schweich, born Siebenaler 12 February 1867 - 11 August 1912
20	Peter Schweich, child of J. P. & C. Schweich 25 February 1873 - 8 July 1885
05	Peter P. Schweich 1892-1968
21	Philipp, child of Johann & Katharina Schweich 27 February 1873 - 22 January 1882
05	Susan M. Schweich 1892-1956
17	Anna Serres 23 May 1837 - 5 March 1919
11	Clara M. Serres 1901-1974
16	Lambertus, child of M. & A. Serres 6 February 1865 - 2 October (?) 1865
17	Markus Serres 1897-1965
17	Markus Serres, born (?) 13 January 1831 in Schlindermanderscheid,

	Grossherzogthum, Luxemburg, died (?) 9 January 1903
16	Michael, child of M. & A. Serres
	27 July 1868 - 27 January (?) 1869
17	Michael Serres 22 January 1874 - 23 February 1947
16	Peter, child of M. & A. Serres 21 April 1877 - 19 January 1879
17	Veronica Serres 21 January 1874 - 28 January 1918
11	William F. Serres 1902-1966
21	George A., child of George & Theresia Shaffer
	12 April 1890 - 22 April 1890
21	Katie, child of George & Theresia Shaffer
	21 February 1868 - 28 August 1868
21	Peter, child of George & Theresia Shaffer
	5 June 1872 - 22 September 1872
21	Rosie, child of George & Theresia Shaffer
	20 May 1880 - 3 July 1880
22	Frances A. Shannon 1906 - __
22	William J. Shannon 1897-1977
23	Emma M. Sieben 1894-1970
07	Georg Sieben 24 August 1809 - 16 September 1883
23	John J. Sieben 1891-1938
02	Anton Siebenaler 1886-1973
02	Katherine Siebenaler 1882-1979
19	Katherine Siebenaler 1844-1944
23	Margaret Siebenaler 1875-1963
19	Maria Siebenaler, born Klasen
	10 August 1832 - 22 March 1871
19	Mathias Siebenaler 31 December 1838 - 21 November 1910
23	Nicholas Siebenaler 1880-1966
19	Anna M. Simmer 3 September 1833 - 14 December 1907
19	Johann Simmer 19 March 1832 - 31 January 1884
13	Magdalena Simmer 22 January 1870 - 23 May 1876 (?)
	- worn and hard to read
20	Alpheus E. Smithberger, PFC United States Marine Corps
	6 December 1908 - 24 December 1954
25	Arthur J. Smithberger 1905-1967
25	Elizabeth Smithberger 1906-1982
20	Magdalena Ebel, wife of B. Smithberger
	20 July 1830 - 29 May 1891
20	William C. Smithberger 1902-1929
08	Martha M. (Hoffman) Snyder 1916-1978
23	Christeen Staneart 1903-1981, married John A. 22 June 1925
23	John A. Staneart 1904-1966, married Christeen 22 June 1925
22	Anna K. Stein 1876-1962
17	Johann Stein 4 August 1878 - 7 July 1900
22	Magdalena Stein 1895-1981
17	Maria Molitor, wife of Nicholas Stein

	10 February 1857 - 10 June 1929
22	Mary M. Stein 1885-1949
22	Mathias Stein 1880-1943
17	Nicholas Stein 7 September 1844 - 5 September 1895
22	Philipp Stein 1883-1947
05	Barbara Stodola 1906-1984
04	Wilhelm Strassburger 1889-1891
20	Axel Stromquist 1894-1970
20	Lucy Stromquist 1891 - __
24	Elizabeth Stumf, born Lohr 22 November 1807 - 5 April 1889
25	Anna M. Stumpf 1839-1921
25	Joseph Stumpf 26 November 1835 - 9 May 1901
21	Elizabeth Thein Suttor 1853-1876
08	Marie Margaret Wienand Tague - 25 May 1917 -
25	Gertrude C. Taube 1900 - __
25	Henry A. Taube 1894-1951
22	Catherine A. Teuber 1906 - __
07	Katherina Teuber 18 December 1861 - 20 July 1909
12	Theresia Teuber 18 November 1862 - 2 December 1897
22	Vincent A. Teuber 1897-1965
11	Anna Catharina Thein 20 May 1869 - 20 March 1870 (?)
11	Anna Maria Thein 20 September 1872 - 21 September 1873
11	Eugene Thein, died 29 October 1874, age 45 years
21	John Thein 11 October 1854 - 18 January 1876
21	Josephine Thein 1858-1881
22	Katharina Thein, died 2 March 1884, age 40 years
21	Maria Thein, born Gonzemius
	7 December 1821 - 5 September 1900
11	Peter Thein 15 April 1868 - 20 June 1868
22	Peter Thein, died 17 June 1888, age 63 years
22	Katharena Theis 1869-1939
22	Margaret Theis 1829-1921
22	Nicholas Theis 1827-1896
22	Nicholas S. Theis 1861-1936
13	Maria Weimann, wife of Johann Therres, died 31 August 1871
	age 40 years
13	Catharina Tix, died 7 August 1871, age 64 years
02	Julius Tix 1908-1989
02	Marie Tix 1912-1958
11	Mathias Tix, died 11 November 1875, age 75 years
19	Maria VanBeeck, died 2 April 1879, age 42 years
01	B. W. Walker, born in Selma, Alabama 10 October 1832
	died 6 May 1872

10	Anna Maria, wife of F. J. Wallerius, born in Schoenecken, Rheinpreuszen 15 April 1831 - 28 April 1907
10	Franz Joseph Wallerius, born in Scheinnlan (?), Rheinpreuszin 6 April 1833 - 8 December 1880
16	Bernard Weber, born in Rippich (?) Canlon (?) Echlernach Luxemberg 15 October 1832 - 19 February 1889
16	Katharina Gretz, wife of B. Weber 20 September 1832 - 2 October 1896
23	Katherine Weber 13 November 1841 - 29 November 1906 (?)
23	Mathias Weber 4 February 1833 - 15 December 1904
07	Wilhelm Weber 28 May 1832 - 10 September 1890
16	Anna Weiland, died 3 May 1859, age 30 years
27	Delores M. Weiland 1918 - __
16	Johann Weiland 29 September 1820 - 23 July 1874
27	Katherine Weiland (?) 1871-1925
16	Margaretha Weiland, died 29 September 1895, age 71 years
27	Mathew Weiland (?) 1870-1969
27	Nicholas P. Weiland 1904-1988
19	Adam Weiler 1807 - 19 September 1866
06	Anna Weiler 8 March 1877 - 17 April 1890
19	Elisabeth, wife of Adam Weiler 1801 - 30 August 1883
06	Katharina Weiler 17 June 1883 - 22 April 1890
05	Nikolaus J. Weiler 21 June 1877 - 17 January 1925
05	Wilhelm Weiler 31 August 1833 - 4 March 1896
03	Jospeh B. Weinand 1921-1964
03	Louisa Weinand 1886-1930
03	Peter Weinand 1880-1939
20	Andreas Wiesen 23 June 1834 - 13 April 1898
20	Susanna Wiesen 15 August 1832 - 12 February 1915
03	Elizabeth Westbruck, nee Fipel, born in Luxemburg 13 April 1824 - 11 December 1915
03	Margaret Wick 28 July 1883 - 21 February 1926
17	Mary M. Williams 1887-1970
20	Maria Wilmes, wife of Nicolas Wilmes, born in Keispell, Grosserzogthum, Luxemburg, died 25 June 1892 age 68 years
20	Nicolas Wilmes, born in Keispell, Grosserzogthum, Luxemburg died 18 August 1876, age 52 years
13	Mary, wife of Frances I. Wise, born in Abbottsden (?), Adam County, Pensylvania 3 March 1834 - 8 January 1871
05	Mary Woodwick - 4 October 1954 -

Row 1 ⚹ burials near the pine trees.

Row 2

Row 2

St. Mary's Catholic Church Cemetery
New Trier , Minnesota

Hampton Township, Dakota County , Minnesota
T113 N-R18W   Section 11

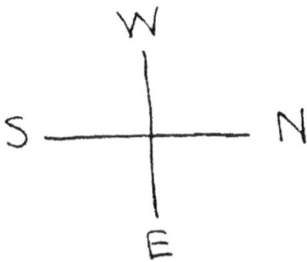

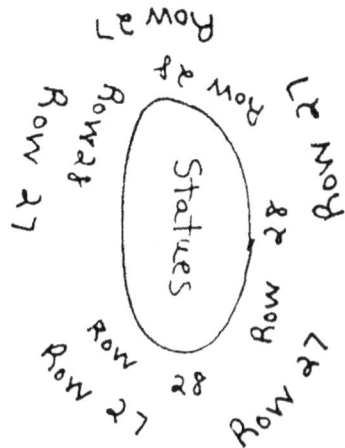

Le Moy
Row 27
Le Moy
Row 28
Row 28
Le Moy
Row 28
Statues
Row 27
Row 28
Row 27
Row 27

W
S —— N
E

Row 26

Directory Directory

Row 26

HILLCREST CEMETERY

Hampton township, Dakota county, Minnesota: T113N-R18W, section 20

This rural cemetery is upkept and in good shape. There is no church at this location. The cemetery burial rows are not in a straight line. The eastern most rows have sort of a curve from the northeast to the southwest. The rows are long. Between rows 5 and 6 there is a drive area. The far south end does not appear to have any burials.

The Dakota county cemetery records compilation lists this cemetery as Hillcrest German Baptist Cemetery, established 1857. 2 acres. Located Section 20, NE 1/4. Lewiston Blvd.

In "History of Dakota County and the city of Hastings" by Rev. Edward D. Neill, he wrote: ... The German Baptist cemetery is located on section 20, on land owned by the Otte brothers. August Otte, who died in 1857, was the first person buried here.

Everyone is in alphabetical order. The number before each entry is the row number. There is a map at the back of this section.

This cemeteries burial monuments were transcribed during 1996.

02	August F. Abendroth (?) 1814-1888
03	August L. Abendroth (?) 1850-1934
03	Bertha L. Abendroth (?) 1854-1886
05	Charlie Abendroth 1883-1959
02	Esther Abendroth (?) 1880-1972
03	Laura Abendroth (?) 1879-1926
05	Martha K. Abendroth 1881-1970

02	Caroline, wife of Conrad Becker
	27 March 1862 - 27 January 1946, age 83 years 10 months
02	Conrad Becker 24 December 1852 - 2 October 1914
	age 61 years 9 months 9 days
02	George T. Becker 1892-1980
02	Sophie Becker 1885-1966

08	Arthur E. Dahms 1878-1962
08	Ella Ruth Dahms -no dates
02	baby, child of J. & E.W. Dickman, died 11 July 1875
	age 1 year 2 months 10 days
02	Clara Dickman 28 February 1883 - 21 March 1887
03	Ellie Weste, wife of John Dickman, died 11 July 1880, age 30 years (?)
03	John Dickman, died 16 July 1900, age 60 years 2 months 28 days

09	Geraldine M. Drewry 1930-__
09	Stanley E. Drewry 1927-1977
08	Stanley E. Drewry TEC 5 United States Army World War 2
	31 May 1927 - 30 January 1977

04	A. George Engler 1921-1969
03	Ada, wife of Henry (?) Engler, died 22 January (?) 1892, age 25 years
04	Alvin Engler (?) 1887-1941
05	Anna D. Engler (?) 1893-1960
09	Anne H. Engler 1894-1986
05	Arlene M. Engler 1925-____, married Charles E. 4 June 1955
02	baby child of Jacob Engler
	10 March 1900 - 20 March 1900
02	Barbara Engler 1 June 1819 - 27 March 1882
05	Benjamin F. Engler (?) 1886-1960
02	Bernhard, son of Mr. & Mrs. Jacob Engler
	3 February 1898 - 19 April 1904
09	Bertha Engler 1866-1943
05	Catherine Engler 1856-1939
05	Charles Engler 1850-1927
05	Charles E. Enler 1924-1987, married Arlene M. 4 June 1955
08	Curtis G. Engler 1936-__
08	Della M. Engler 1905-1990
04	Dina Engler (?) 1853-1922
05	Emily G. Engler (?) 1890-1978
02	Galles (?) Engler 1 January 1800 - 12 August 1886
09	Henry Engler 1862-1939
08	Jacob Engler 1864-1939
04	Jane Engler 1920-__
02	Johannes Engler 17 February 1822 - 29 November 1893
04	John Engler (?) 1846-1926
03	Karl, son of J. & D. Engler 22 September 1881 - 26 September 1888
03	Leonard, son of J. & D. Engler
	6 October 1888 - 16 October 1888
07	Lizzie, wife of Jacob Engler
	18 January 1868 - 22 December 1915
08	Lizzie Engler 1868-1915
05	Lydia (no last name is close) Engler (?) or Legler (?) 1882-1950
02	Margaret Engler 30 June 1798 - 30 June 1885
02	Margaret Engler (?) 1890-1983
05	Ruth Engler 1924-1986
05	Thomas Lee Engler (?) -1965-
08	Walter J. Engler 1909-__
09	Wesley C. Engler 1895-1984
10	Jean S. Estes 1925-__
10	Leonard W. Estes 1918-1991

06	Bernice P. Fraley 1916-__
06	Donald R. Fraley 1918-1977
07	Donald R. Fraley, Pvt. United States Army World War 2 1918-1977
02	Augusta Fortenz (?) or could be Papenfus (?) 1856-1950
02	August Fortenz (?) or could be Papenfus (?) 1859-1944
02	Henry Fortenz (?) or could be Papenfus (?) 1862-1936
03	Clementie (?) Greip (?) 1856-1891
03	Effie Louise Hagan 1914-__
03	Eldon L. Hagan 1936-1983
03	Eldon McCune Hagan 1911-1983
05	Augusta Hedtke 1851-1939
05	Lydia Legler Hedtke 26 August 1859 - 23 November 1930
05	Selma Lydia Hedtke 11 December 1882 - 30 April 1921
	age 38 years 6 months 6 days
02	Anna M. Helmbrecht (?) 1891-1949
02	Charley Helmbrecht (?) 1861-1939
02	Henry W. Helmbrecht (?) 1893-1969
02	Mary D. Helmbrecht (?) 1867-1955
02	Rose E. Helmbrecht (?) 1903-1980
05	Amanda M. Heringer, nee Engler 2 March 1879 - 24 August 1911
10	Dorothy M. Hjelter 1926-__
10	Elizabeth M. Hjelter 30 July 1955 - 17 May 1979
10	Glen E. Hjelter 1927-1983
10	Glen Edward Hjelter, MML 3 United States Navy World War 2
	Korea 1927-1983
02	Arthur J. Hoffmann 12 February 1883 - 3 March 1901
05	Auguste Hoffman 25 June 1839 - 13 September 1907
05	Heinrich Hoffman 'Ehegatt Von Auguste Hoffman' (?)
	27 March 1827 - 9 August 1905
04	Herman Hoffman, died 16 August 1906, age 42 years
02	Cora Emma, daughter (?) of C. & R. (?) Hollins (?)
	3 October 1889 (?) - 18 December 1889 -hard to read
02	Casper A. Koch 1816-1893
05	Cathrine Otte Koch 1856-1940
02	Friedrich G. Koch 1844-1916
02	Sophia E. Koch 1852-1897
04	?ry Legler (?) ?-1941 -badly broken stone
04	Amanda Legler 1870-1941
03	John Legler (?) 1861-1943
03	Karl L. Legler 3 March 1900 - 29 July 1906
02	Leila E. Legler (?) 1895-1917

02	Luella V. Legler (?) 1893-1893
05	Lydia (no last name nearby) Legler (?) or Engler (?) 1882-1950
03	Martha Legler (?) 1870-1948
02	Meta R. Legler (?) 1898-1911
03	Miriam, daughter of Henry & Amanda Legler 25 January 1896 (?) - 26 January 1896 (?)
03	Rene F. Legler 16 June 1901 - 1 April (?) 1906
01	Sue Anita, daughter of D.R. & E.M. Legler July - December 1942
05	Catherine Lueben 22 December 1831 - 10 June 1910 age 78 years 5 months 18 days
08	Arden V. Lufi 27 January 1943 - 27 July 1955
08	Arnold B. Lufi 1913-__
05	baby boy Lufi (?) -22 February 1942-
05	baby girl Lufi (?) -28 November 1944-
05	Edna L. Lufi 1918-__
08	Gladys R. Lufi 1911-1979
04	Lydia L. Lufi 1890-1973
04	Marie K. Lufi 1911-1985
05	Nathan M. Lufi 1917-__
04	Oswald C. Lufi 1878-1941
08	Sarah Malmquist -15 August 1980-
03	Alvin M. Miller, M Sgt. United States Air Force Korea 1919-1993
10	Anna Dorothy, wife of Arthur Miller 1889-1918
10	Antonetta Miller 1884-1972
10	Arthur Miller 1884-1961
02	daughter of A.N. & M. Miller born & died 3 October 1888
09	Henrietta Miller 1862-1931
09	Henry Miller 1861-1942
08	Johanna Miller 31 May 1837 - 30 December 1905
01	Kate Miller (?) 1864-1941
02	Lillie Miller (?) 1889-1900
08	Peter Miller 21 August 1833 - 24 December 1919
02	Rosa M. Miller 30 March 1831 - 4 June 1903
03	Ruth C.A. Miller 3 May 1930 - 28 February 1976
01	William Miller (?) 1857-1935
02	Karl, son of I.F. (?) & ? M. Muller -28 July 1875- (?)
09	Albert C. Otte 1873-1935
05	Alberta M. Otte 25 November 1886 - 10 November 1906
08	Anna C. Otte 1885-1960
09	Anna S. Otte 1888-1969
06	August F. Otte 1877-1966
09	August O. Otte 1849-1931
02	August Otte 19 (?) January 1810 - 16 September 1869
02	Bertha Otte, daughter of W. & K. Otte, died 2 August 1885

	age 2 years 10 months 19 days
02	Caroline Peter, wife of Wm. Otte 18 June 1854 - 29 August 1875
08	Earl L. Otte 1903-1988
06	Edna C. Otte 1901-1973
06	Emma H. Otte 1882-1981
06	Floyd C. Otte 1901-1984
08	Gerald C. Otte 1913-1992
08	Helen L. Otte 1916-__
02	infant of J. & M. (?) Otte (?) 12 ?? 1880 - 12 ?? 1880
	-very hard to read
02	Johnie, ?? of W. & ? Otte (?), died 3 August 1880
	age 1 year 1 month (?) -very hard to read
03	Johnny, son of W. & C. Otte (?) 11 ?? 1885 - 18 July 1887 (?)
	-very hard to read
07	Lucille C. Otte 1905-1912
09	Mabel G. Otte 1885-1979
02	Mary Otte, daughter of I. & M. Otte
	23 June 1883 (?) - 19 May 1886
09	Mary A. Otte 1853-1918
07	Mary E. Otte 1920-1925
02	Mary Weber, wife of Wm. Otte, died 1 June (?) 1870 (?)
	age 22 years
02	Minnie Otte, daughter of W. & K. Otte
	10 March 1881 - 15 July 1885
07	Ruth B. Otte 1909-1943
09	Walter J. Otte 1888-1965
05	William Otte, died 16 May 1901, age 54 years 3 months 23 days
08	William W. Otte 1877-1963
02	Willie, infant son of W. & L. Otte (?)
	21 August 1875 - 6 September 1875
02	August Papenfus (?) or could be Fortenz (?) 1859-1944
02	Augusta Papenfus (?) or could be Fortenz (?) 1856-1950
02	Henry Papenfus (?) or could be Fortenz (?) 1862-1936
04	Orval F. Parish, husband of Marguerite Legler 1903-1936
04	David Paul 15 August - 18 August 1927
09	Anna M. Peter 1875-1958
08	Caroline Peter 31 June 1828 - 20 December 1902
09	Clifford L. Peter 1901-1987
09	Florence L. Peter 1910-1993
08	Jacob Peter 31 December 1851 - 7 December 1908
07	John P. Peter (?) -no dates
08	John P. Peter 10 July 1880 - 20 October 1904
09	Marvin L. Peter 2 January 1904 - 16 May 1933
08	Mary Engler, wife of Jacob Peter
	1 September 1859 - 17 March 1926

09	Ruth A. Peter 1911-__
09	William P. Peter 1872-1953
04	Marguerite Powers 1901-1976
08	Arthur E. Rich 1908-1989
08	Helen M. Rich 1916-__
03	David J. Schwendig 1911-1993
03	David J. Schwendig Jr. SP4 United States Army
	10 August 1945 - 3 May 1989
03	Mabel E. Schwendig 1915-1989
03	Rebecca J. 'Becky' Smith 1957-1973
02	Emma, wife of James Thompson, died 2 April 1876
	age 19 years 6 months 20 days
02	Ernestine Vacque 1825-1884
07	August H. Wille 1887-1970
08	baby Willie (?) -1921-
07	Edward A. Wille 1883-1973
07	Gertrude V. Wille 1890-1923
07	Pearl A. Wille 1890-1994
07	Herman C. Witte (?) 1858-1931
07	Margrete Witte (?) 1859-1912
02	Carrie, daughter of F. & C.K. (?) -couldn't read the surname
	died 31 August 1875 (?) age 11 (?)

Row 1 (shortrow)

Row 2 (full row)

Hillcrest Cemetery
Hampton Township T113N-R18v
Section 20

Row 5

Drive Area

Row 6

E

S

N

W

Row 10

Drive
Area

Lewiston Blvd.

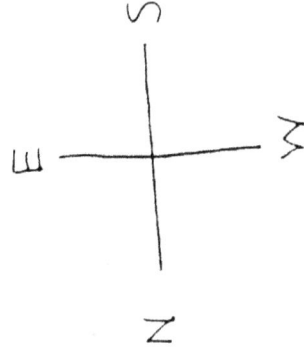

117

ZION CEMETERY

Hampton township, Dakota county, Minnesota: T113N - R18W, section 23

This cemetery is upkept and in good shape. There is no longer a church at this location. The gate has Zion Cemetery 1859-1963 listed. There are a couple of headstones that have disappeared into some lilacs. There are a couple of stones that are broken off and lying at ground level. There are indications that some of the old stones have been replaced. The rows of burials are short. I have numbered the rows 1-15. Row 1 begins on the east edge of the cemetery.

The Dakota county cemetery records compilation lists this cemetery as: Zion Evangelical Association Cemetery, established 1860. 2+ acres. Located Section 23, NE 1/4. Hogan Avenue between 250th St. and Highway 50.

In "History of Dakota County and the city of Hastings", by Rev. Edward D. Neill he wrote: ...The Evangelical Association cemetery is situated by the church whose name it bears (page 397 [lists as] section 23). The first person buried here was Mrs. Mary Ista, some time in 1860 (page 398).

Everyone is in alphabetical order. The number before each entry is the row number. There is a map at the back of this section.

This cemeteries burial monuments were transcribed during 1996.

05   Christoph Baguhn, born in Brenz, Mechlenburg, Schwirin
                25 July 1815 - 15 February 1883
05   Fredericka D. Baguhn, born in Postlin, Preussen
                10 February 1816 - 22 February 1894
08   Anna D. Becker, born in Bebera (?) Kr. Rothenburg (?), Kurhessen (?)
                1 April 183? - 17 January 1905
02   Annie E. Becker (?) 1867-1952
02   Ella M. Becker 1913-__
02   George W. Becker 1898-1983
02   Harry David Becker (?) -1888-
02   John H.G. Becker (?) 1860-1935
08   Johann Becker, born in Bebera Kr. (?) Rolhenburg (?), Kurhessen (?)
                15 April 1826 - 10 October 1885
08   Maria, daughter of J. & A.D. Becker
                9 January 1862 - 6 October 1866
08   William C. Becker (?) 1867-1915
14   Conrad Braun 20 January 1884 - 6 June 1885
14   Katherine E. Braun 3 April 1828 - 26 December 1916
06   ? Bunse (?), died 1867, age 58 (?) -hard to read
06   Etta (?) Bunse, died (?) 187?, age (?) 36 (?) -hard to read

10	Velma E. Christie 1904-1978
15	Alvina (?) L. Draeger 6 March 1891 - 3 August 1895
15	August Draeger 5 December 1816 - 21 February 1903
15	Wilhelmine Draeger, wife of August Draeger
	15 October 1815 - 13 November 1873
15	Annie L. Drager 1864-1946
15	Frank K.H. Drager 10 February 1888 - 10 August 1888
15	Fredrick Drager 1851-1935
13	Carl Dierke 23 March 1835 - 26 May 1916
09	Clarence E. Dierke 1909-1922
13	Fredericka Dierke 18 November 1848 - 7 June 1925
13	Gordon, son of Mr. & Mrs. J. Dierke 1903-1904
09	Harris C. Dierke 1874-1955
09	Hazel B. Dierke 1924-1993
09	Mangil W. Dierke 1914-__
09	Minnie E. Dierke 1887-1969
09	Wolwin C. Dierke 1904-1917
07	Bertha A. Freier (?) 1883-1941
07	Louis A. Freier (?) 1886-1959
10	Mary (?) Freier (?) 1864-1928
07	Ralph C. Freier -1913-
07	Roy W. Freier 1911-1926
10	William Freier (?) 1858-1907
06	Anna M. Gleim 1863-1881
06	Dorothy M. Gleim 1852-1853
06	infant Gleim 1876-1876
06	John H. Gleim 1868-1869
06	Katherine L. Gleim 1854-1857
06	Mary A. Gleim 1860-1880
11	Laura D. Gruber 19 July 1889 - 24 October 1991
11	Louis M. Gruber 1864-1949
11	Sarah H. Gruber 5 September 1868 - 6 February 1914
04	Britta Anna Alfreda Gustafson 1906-1994
04	Otto Alfred Gustafson 1902-1996
04	August Haverland 10 August 1822 - 5 June 1888
04	Elizabeth Haverland 27 June 1829 - __
04	Susanna E. Haverland 26 December 1869 - 25 March 1876
03	Friedrich W. Hermuth, died 27 July 1870, age 24 years
03	Wilhelm Hermuth, died 20 August 1867, age 57 years
03	Wilhelmine, wife of W. Hermuth, died 4 April 1878, age 67 years
03	Aron (?) J. Ista ? April 1865 - 8 January 1873

11	Augusta L. Ista 1868-1927
02	Bertha Ista 1870-1873
03	Charles G. Ista 1860-1948
03	Dorothea, wife of Georg Ista, born 21 July 1821 Postlin, Preussen
	died 13 April 1894 Dakota county Minnesota
04	Dorothea J. M. Ista 25 march 1830-__
10	Ferdinand G. Ista 1863-1954
10	Ferdinand T. Ista 1906-1918
03	George Ista 6 October 1855 (?) - ? January 1872 (?)
03	George Ista, born 20 September 1825 Postlin, Preussen
	died 15 October 1889 Dakota county Minnesota
04	J. Joachim Ista 16 April 1820 - 17 November 1896
02	Jacob Ista born & died 1863
10	Johann Ista, born February 182? , died 18 February 1879 (?)
02	Johann Ista 1858-1866
10	Maria Ista, born Preusen (?) 1821, died 17 February 1883
11	Mary L. Ista (?) -1928-
03	Sarah H. Ista 1862-1948
10	Elizabeth Kauffman 16 July 1871 (?) - 21April 1876
05	Heinrich Kauffman 14 February 1859 - 15 September 1900
05	Katharina Kauffman, born Becker
	26 August 1859 - 4 April 1894
10	John Kauffmann 26 October 1834 - 2 September 1911
10	Susanna Kauffmann 4 April 1834 - 14 November 1901
06	Helena Knoblauch 2 May 1831 - 2 July 1902
06	Xavier Knoblauch 22 September 1827 - 2 November 1898
01	Karl, son of Heinrich & Kath. Elisabeth Kurth
	23 January 1861 - 13 May 1864
12	baby Lockwood 1916-1916
01	Jeannie Lockwood 1888-1934
05	Albert G. Michael 23 August 1862 - 25 July 1882
12	Augusta Osman 1855-1891
12	Henry Osman 184?-1929
12	Otto Osman 1877-1878
12	Richard J. E. Osman, CPL United States Army World War 2
	1927-1984
12	Willie Osman 12 May 1891 - 4 November 1942
11	little Willie, son of ? & C. Otte 29 February 1861 - 21 July 1865
06	Anna M. Rech 1803-1880
02	Arthur R. Rettinger 1887-1887
02	Chester R. Rettinger 1899-1899

02	Emanuel Rettinger 1897-1898
11	Esther Rettinger 1899-1941
11	John Rettinger 1861-1943
09	Emphfrosine Seegert 28 December 1826 - 24 March 1906
09	Wilhelm Frederick Seegert 4 July 1832 - 20 February 1915
05	G.F. Schomacher 1 August 1808 - 10 December 1875
05	Charlotte, wife of G. Schumacher 9 February 1817 - 12 August 1894
08	baby Gustave Schwen 7 May - 20 August 1903
14	Lena Schwen 1837-1903
01	Freiedrich G. Tank 17 March 1828 - 17 July 1887
01	Henriette, wife of F.G. Tank 3 September 1828 - 18 December 1888
12	Caroline, daughter of Julius & Mary Wille 26 August 1893 - 29 September 1893
12	'Father' Wille (?) 1834-1879
12	Julius F. Wille 9 February 1859 - 6 January 1930
12	Mary Wille 9 March 1859 - 26 January 1923
12	'Mother' Wille (?) 1836-1922
02	Hermann, son of K. & Kath. Witthams 10 January 1871 - 28 August 1871
02	Catherine Witthans 1849-1928
02	Charles Witthans 1850-1929
02	Friedrich, son of Karl & K. Witthans 19 August 1868 - 15 December 1868

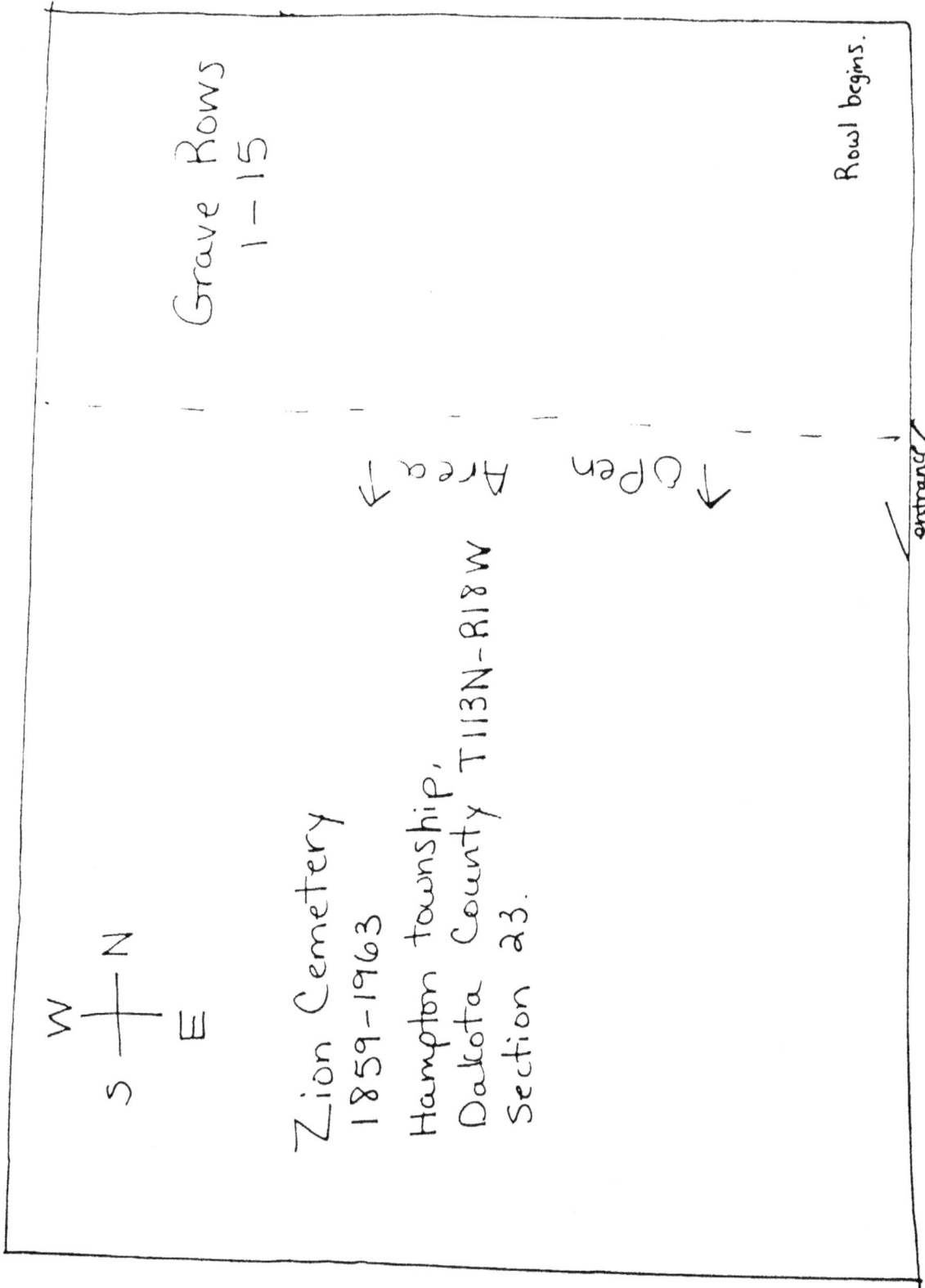

W
N
S
E

Zion Cemetery
1859-1963

Hampton township,
Dakota County T113N-R18W
Section 23.

Grave Rows
1 - 15

← Area 3

← Open ↑

entrance/
gate

Row I begins.

Highway 85

EMMANUEL EVANGELICAL CEMETERY

Castle Rock township, Dakota county, Minnesota T113N - R19W section 2

This cemetery is upkept and in good shape. The rows line up very well. There is a sign that reads: Emmanuel Church 1864-1957. Site of the first Session Minnesota Conference Evangelical Church -24 April 1868-. ... Here in 1864 they founded 'Eine Evangelische Gemeinde' - a Christian fellowship. ... and built upon this knoll in 1867 Emmanuel Church. ... in 1957 formed Faith Church. There is no longer a church at this location.

The Dakota county cemetery records compilation lists this cemetery as: Emmanuel German Evangelical Cemetery, established 1866. 3 acres. Located Section 2, NE 1/4. Blaine Ave.

Everyone is in alphabetical order. The number before each entry is the row number. There is a map at the back of this section.

These cemetery burial monuments were transcribed during 1996.

02	Sophia S. Baney	1871-1956
02	E. Bartel	-no dates
06	Alexander L.S. Becker (?)	17 December 1885 - 10 August 1888
02	Alvina A. Becker	1879-1966
07	Astrid T. Becker	1902-__
02	baby Becker	-no dates
02	Barbara Becker	16 March 1840 - 12 January 1912
07	Bertha L. Becker	1900-1996
08	Frances K. Becker	1908-1991
08	Harry M. Becker	1906-1992
06	Henry M. Becker	28 October 1856 - 8 March 1911
02	Jacob J. Becker	1881-1922
02	Jacob J. Becker	15 August 1834 - 29 August 1890
02	John G. Becker	1826-1903
07	Lewis A. Becker	1895-1981
02	Mary Becker	20 April 1837 - 20 August 1879
06	Mary A. Becker	19 April 1859 - 23 June 1945
02	Russell L. Becker	1910-__
02	Susanna Becker	1840-1911
02	Viola O. Becker	1921-__
02	Virgil J. Becker, son of Russell Becker	1944-1951
07	Wesley C. Becker	1888-1983
02	Charles Betzold (?)	1871-1959
09	Christian Betzold	6 October 1875 - 3 July 1902
05	Edwin R. Betzold (?)	1900-1941
02	Emily Betzold (?)	1881-1962

01	Henrietta Betzold, wife of Michael Betzold
	9 July 1841 - 26 September 1903
01	Henry B. Betzold (?) 1862-1947
02	Jacob Betzold 1921-1984
02	Lilian Betzold (?) 1915-1917
01	Michael Betzold 8 December 1831 - 16 August 1904
02	Miriam Betzold (?) 1914-1916
01	Regina (?) Mathilda (?), daughter of (?) ? & ? Betzold (?)
	died (?) ?? 1869 (?) -hard to read
05	Ruben A. Betzold (?) 1873-1923
01	William Betzold (?) 1887-1956
08	Ora S. Black 1911-1977
08	Russell S. Black 1911-1974
02	'Father' Bracht 14 September 1859 - 8 September 1908
06	Anna Marie Bromley 1879-1963
08	Lucile M. Bromley 1916-1967, married Nelson R. 2 March 1946
08	Nelson R. Bromley 1911-__, married Lucile M. 2 March 1946
06	Raymond N. Bromley 1877-1964
01	Nicholos Croft, died 20 February 1865, age 69 years & ? months
05	Adlai S. Duff 1892-1977
03	Barbara M. Duff 1930-1991
04	Bertha R. Duff (?) 1877-1963
03	Dale A. Duff 1928-__
07	Elizabeth Duff 1952-1953
04	Fred M. Duff (?) 1873-1938
04	James M. Duff (?) 1900-1933
05	Susanna M. Duff 1897-1985
08	Cheri L. Ervasti 1952-1981
06	Alice E. Falls (?) 1902-1968
06	Arthur B. Falls (?) 1899-1972
03	Beverly J. (Spavin) Findorff 1933-1992
06	A. Fischer 28 December 1832 - 21 September 1923
05	Maria, wife of Martin Gagstetter, died 5 April 1874
	age 22 years 4 months 21 days
03	Cleo G. Green 1910-1981
03	Arthur N. Green 1908-1977
06	Raymond W. Griebenow 1903-1979
07	Violet M. Haverland -no dates
11	Maria Stapf, child of Emanuel & Maria, wife of Heinerich Herr,
	28 February 1853 - 11 February 1871

03	Ariana Elizabeth Hoffman, daughter of Paul & Julie -23 January 1989-
07	Clifford Hoffman 1893-1963
05	Emelia Hoffman 1866-1917
05	Laura A. Hoffman 1890-1987
05	John Hoffman 1860-1950
07	Nina Hoffman 1902-1989
08	Delsia J. Jacobson 1924-1979
08	Milton J. Jacobson 1930-__
03	Caroline Juenke (?) 1864-1936
09	Crystal Lee Juenke -9 February 1983-
09	Fred W. Juenke 1895-1969
09	Grace H. Juenke 1898-1963
04	Heinrich C. Juenke 13 December 1823 - 10 January 1893
04	Henriette L. Juenke 8 July 1822 - 29 August 1888
09	baby (?) Pearl L. Juenke -no dates
03	William Juenke (?) 1852-1922
03	Wm. C. Kadel 1868-1947
09	Marcella R. Kauffman 1913-1996
06	Edna (Stapf) Keene 1921-1995
02	Christian Klaus 15 March 1812 - 19 September 1880
01	Christian L. Klaus (?) 1835-1915
01	Fredericka Klaus (?) 1833-1917
02	Fredrick Klaus 1840-1892
02	Karolina, wife of Christ Klaus 10 December (?) 1811 - 27 March 1876
01	Louisa M. Klaus 26 July 1871 - 25 October 1906
02	Marl (?) Klaus 29 February 1868 - ? July 1868 -hard to read
02	Rosa Klaus 25 September 1865 - 8 July 1868 -hard to read
04	Virginia M. Krier 15 September 1926-__
04	William E. Krier, Sgt. United States Army Air Corps
	World War 2 1924-1988
04	William E. Krier 5 June 1924 - 4 February 1988
03	Dora I. (Spavin) Krueger 1909-__
08	Charles Luedke 1859-1931
09	Clarence Luedke 1898-1958
09	Harvey C. Luedke 1895-1990
08	Julia Luedke 1862-1950
08	R. Luedke 3 August 1895 - 8 July 1897
09	Ruth N. Luedke 1909-__
01	Anna M. Manke 1876-1973
01	Laurence L. Manke 1903-1943
01	Louis W. Manke 31 October 1868 - 14 September 1910
10	Hanna M., daughter of ? & ? Miller

17 November 1867 - 26 August 1869

10	J.L.M. Miller 17 February 1814 - 23 February 1870
09	Edna Oldenburg 1900-1950
03	Anna Otte 1856-1936
03	Adolph Overby 1904-__
03	Margaret Overby 1909-1994
05	Helen Betzold Parsons 1881-1950
07	Hattie Peters 1890-1927
07	J. Henry Peters 1858-1940
07	Lena Peters 1875-1907
04	Caroline W. Pfenning (?) 1840-1924
04	Josephine Pfenning (?) 1877-1878
06	Bertha L. Poole 1888-1969
06	Forest E. Poole 1881-1971
06	Anna E. Schuler 1874-1950
03	George C. Schuler 1905-1938
09	Henry Schuler 25 July 1845 - 28 February 1912
06	Henry Albert Schuler 1904-1927
06	John Schuler 1867-1947
09	Susanna Schuller 8 June 1840 - 23 December 1929
07	Lena Miller Scott 1869-1921
10	Anna Miller Severin 1843-1902
03	Arthur E. Spavin 1901-1973
11	Albert M. Stapf 9 December 1871 - 8 March 1876
07	Albert S. Stapf 1890-1974
11	Ann M.R. Stapf 19 November 1865 - 17 March 1876
09	Anna Maria Stapf, died 1898
08	Anna Mary Stapf (?) 22 January 1875 - 22 February 1876
08	Anna W. Stapf 1857-1937
08	baby Stapf (?) born & died 17 December 1871
08	Catharina, wife of Jacob Stapf, died 28 November 1896
	age 41 years 7 months 13 days
11	Christian D. Stapf 5 September 1856 - 31 May 1889
08	Clara M. Stapf 1889-1967
07	Edythe M. Stapf 1887-1985
11	Emanuel Stapf 26 June 1824 - 21 June 1890
07	Gottlieb F. Stapf 2 November 1845 - 1 May 1876
06	Harvey L. Stapf 1917-1977
08	Jacob Stapf 1850-1929
08	Jacob F. Stapf 1885-1978
11	Jacob F. Stapf 13 May 1858 - 1 May 1863
08	Jessie A. Stapf 1914-1995
09	John Stapf, died 1870

08	John Stapf (?) 1873-1958
08	Katherine Stapf (?) 1875-1957
04	Larry Stapf -1948-
08	Leroy E. Stapf 1913-1996
03	Lillie M. Stapf 1894-1918
05	Lydia Stapf 1885-1977
05	Lydia S. Stapf 1885-1977
04	Mannie Stapf 1878-1973
03	Martin T. Stapf 1887-1981
07	Maynard Stapf 1924-1925
05	Ronald Marvin Stapf 17 February - 30 July 1962
07	Seybert S. Stapf (?) 1895-1989
04	Tillie Stapf 1882-1946
07	Vera F. Stapf (?) 1894-1987
05	Walter Stapf 1883-1970
05	Walter L. Stapf 1883-1970
11	Mina Steidle 17 June 1811 - 15 September 1890
03	Lizzie, wife of William Stiff
	11 January 1872 - 28 December 1893
08	Louis R. Teske 1886-1919
06	Beatrice Susan Williams 1912-1987
06	Roy E. Williams 1910-1994
05	J. Olive Worcester 1917-__
05	L. Henry Worcester 1881-1966
05	Mary Worcester 1891-1964
05	W. Dean Worcester 1925-__

I was not able to determine a surname for the following.

03	David A. ? 29 April - 30 April 1957

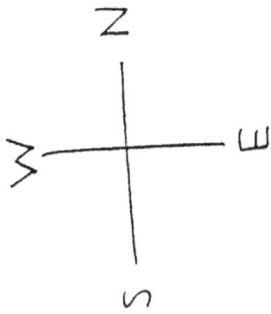

Row 1

N
W ─┼─ E
S

Row 9

Emmanuel Cemetery
Castle Rock Township, Dakota Co., Minn.
T113N - R19W   Section 2

Row 10

Row 11

Drive
Area

Gate

Highway 79 or Blaine Ave.

131

CASTLE ROCK TOWNSHIP
CASTLE ROCK VALLEY CEMETERY

Castle Rock township, Dakota county, Minnesota T113N - R19W section 21

This cemetery is upkept and in good shape. The central drive area leads to a large caste iron statue in the back central area of the cemetery. The statue is a life size soldier. The soldier is in memory of 'our soldier dead', dedicated 30 May 1913. The cemetery sign reads: Castle Rock Valley Cemetery, founded 1863.

In "History of Dakota County and the city of Hastings", by Rev. Edward D. Neill, written in 1881, he writes: At the annual town meeting held 7 April 1863, a committee was appointed to select a site for a public cemetery. ... The committee reported having selected six acres in the north-east corner of south-east quarter of section 21, which could be purchased for five dollars an acre. ... Upwards of a hundred internment's have been made. Previous to the establishment of the cemetery, the dead were buried in different parts of the town, on the farms of relatives on the deceased. A number of these bodies have been removed and placed in the public cemetery. (page 334).

Neill also writes: He [Joseph Harris] settled in the town in the spring of 1855, made his claim in the south-west quarter of section 17, but lived with his son on the north-east quarter of section 20 until he died 30 September 1869, in his eightieth year of his age. He was buried in the cemetery belonging to the town on the east side of section 21. (page 332).

The Dakota county cemetery records compilation lists this cemetery as: Castle Rock Valley Cemetery (formerly Rose Hill), established 1863. 6 acres. Located Section 21, NE 1/4 of SE 1/4. County Road 78.

Everyone is in alphabetical order. The number before each entry is the row number. There is a map at the back of this section.

These burial monuments were transcribed during 1996.

04	Alonic Aldrich 1825-1906
40	Hannah B. Aldrich, died 22 November 1901, age 78 years
40	Captain Edward Aldrich 17 February 1819 - 17 August 1903
	Co. F 8 Minnesota Vol.
04	Martha Aldrich 1854-1891
40	Willard E. Aldrich, died 1 May 1862, age 4 years 8 months
66	Dorothy Rose Alexander 1911-1986
24	Frances Witt Alexander 1907-1972
38	Milo Robert Alexander 7 September 1938 - 7 November 1938
46	Agnes Allen 1872-1959
02	Jefford J. Allery 1957-1974
33	Florence E. Alton 1883-1977

57	Catherine Angstman 26 June 1832 - 9 April 1925
57	Peter Angstman 28 February 1822 - 2 April 1899
06	Emma S. Atz 1855-1889
06	Lloyd A. Atz 1889-1969
40	Frank B., son of P. & C. Ayotte (?), died 2 May (?) 1869 　　　　age 1 month (?) 10 days -hard to read
20	Charles M. Badger 11 July 1843 - 27 January (?) 1863
21	Charles M., son of J. & E. Badger, died 27 January 1863 　　　　age 19 years 6 months 16 days
20	E.F. Badger 5 December 1814 - 7 July 1897
20	J. Badger 18 November 1815 - 20 March 1898
27	Carlton L. Ballard 1880-1965
27	John L. Ballard 1850-1931
27	Sarah A. Ballard 1855-1924
27	Verna P. Ballard 1889-1953
12	Ann R., wife of H.W. Barber, died 11 April 1859, age 23 years
03	Chas. T. Barkuloo 1868-1870
06	Harmanus Barkuloo, died 5 March 1873 　　　　age 68 years 8 months 15 days
06	Rebecca Ann, wife of H. Barkuloo, daughter of S. & H. Thorn 　　　　died 2 August 1885, age 75 years 1 month 28 days
03	S.M. Barkuloo 1848-1870
11	Eli T. Barnum, died 8 May 1882, age 77 years 8 months 14 days
11	Elizabeth, wife of E.T. Barnum, died 21 December 1888 　　　　age 85 years 5 months 12 days
24	George W. Batson 1860-1936
36	Grace E. Batson 1889-1930
36	Harland L. Batson 1884-1956
24	Hattie A. Batson 1885-1982
24	Katie E. Batson 1860-1916
36	Leroy Harland Batson, M. Sgt. United States Army World War 2 　　　　Korea 25 June 1921 - 9 January 1988
10	Bessie, daughter of F.E. (?) & E.J. Bean 　　　　February 1886 - December 1901
10	Henry M. Bean, died 6 June 1898, age 63 years
09	Horace Mann, son of H.M. & J.E. Bean, died 4 November 1864 　　　　age 8 years 2 months 15 days
10	Horace M. Bean (?), died 3 November 1864, age 3 years
10	I.E. Bean, died 19 March 1908, age 73 years
10	John L. Bean (?), died 3 October 1867, age 1 year 14 days
09	Jonnie L., son of H.M. & J.E. Bean, died 8 September 1868 　　　　age 1 month 9 days
61	Dietrich Becker 1829-1904
36	Edna M. Becker 1923-1934
36	Edward F. Becker 1887-1973

60	George D. Becker 1878-1940
61	Helen Becker 1882-1925
61	Katherine Becker 1851-1907
36	Threasa M. Becker 1898-1974
24	Estelle M. Betzold 1909-1995
24	Milton S. Betzold 1906-1959
03	Mary A. Blodgett 1851-1936
06	Selina Brackin, wife of Thompson Best 1829-1908
06	Thompson Best 1823-1902
01	Jean T. Bondhus 1924-__
01	Tom M. Bondhus 1923-1982
04	Binnie A. Boyd 1886-1908
04	Jessie A., wife of M.W. Boyd, died 7 November 1894, age 33 years
04	Mark W. Boyd 1861-1945
04	Mary Jane Boyd 1874-1968
34	Teckla Brunner 1842-1917
14	H. Bush 5 April 1838 - 26 April 1882
	Co. F 3rd Reg. Minnesota Vols.
13	Helen M. Bush 1854-1938
13	Hezekiah Bush 1838-1882
24	John A. Calaway, Major United States Air Force World War 2 Korea
	7 January 1920 - 23 June 1995
06	Gilbert R. Carlton, child of E.L. & C.L. Reed, died 8 September 1870
	age 2 months 24 days
44	Agnes Carmichael (?), died 1 July 1871, age 21 Years
44	Agnes Orr Carmichael 1827-1911
44	Belle Carmichael (?), died 22 March 1882, age 29 years
44	Charles Carmichael (?), died 25 September 1882, age 17 years
44	Laura Carmichael (?) 1887-1917
44	Niel Carmichael (?), died 20 January 1872, age 50 years
44	Ruth Carmichael (?) 1890-1977
44	Ruth Carmichael 1890-1977
44	Robert Carmichael 1854-1920 member of 39th & 40th Sessions
	Minnesota House of Representatives
44	Sarah Louise Carmichael 1858-1943
44	Walter Carmichael (?), died 2 July 1882, age 13 years
44	William Carmichael (?), died 23 August 1882, age 25 years
36	Garfield M. Casey 1907-1990
36	Kathryn J. Casey 1917-1989
61	Evelyn A. Challberg 1911-__
61	Henrietta Challberg 1880-1976
61	William C. Challberg 1872-1925
06	Etta Hendryx Chandler 1857-1922
11	Anson Chapel, died 8 November 1858, age 42 years
55	Clara E. Chapel (?) 1851-1914

55	Edwin J. Chapel (?) 1842-1924
11	Eli Chapel, died 24 August 1861, age 47 years
17	Alan J. Childs 1906-1967
16	Bertha Bodger Childs 1867-1951
10	Cornelia M. Childs 9 August 1828 - 19 January 1907
16	Deforest J. Childs 1864-1918
16	Deforest J. Childs 1864-1918
16	Effie Fish Childs 1868-1892
16	Effie I. Fish, wife of D.J. Childs, died 15 October 1892 age 24 years 6 months 8 days
16	Florence Childs 1902-1993
17	Marie H. Childs 1910-1973
17	Mira Childs 1891-1988
16	Ralph Childs 1901-1986
17	Richard D. Childs 1927-1994, married Lavonne D. 12 June 1948
10	Temple C. Childs 23 April 1828 - 17 February 1895
49	Olive D. Christenson 1905-1990
49	Otto J. Christenson 1902-1995
12	Jane Code 1831-1908
12	John Code 1820-1897
02	Krischelle Cassandra Coffing 25 July 1980 - 30 October 1980
65	Cecelia Cook 1886-1967
65	Irving Cook 1886-1978
08	Jurilla (?) C. Corman, daughter (?) of J.R. & S.M. Stevens (?) died 10 June 1869, age 30 years 6 months (?)
19	Mathew L. Craig 1890-1985
19	Vera Emily Craig 1893-1955
60	Andrew G. Damann 1879-1963
50	Ernest M. Damann 1899-1967
50	Ruth H. Damann 1899-1944
60	Sylvia Damann 1882-1952
61	William A. Damann 1905-1919
47	Jesse C. Davis 1886-1967
44	M. Davis -1875-
47	Pearl A. Davis 1886-1972
07	Alfred Day, died 13 July 1886, age 92 years
07	Alfred A. Day (?) 1834-1917
08	Allen J., son of Ditus & C.H. Day, died 29 December 1889 age 23 years 8 months 18 days
08	Clarrissa H., wife of Ditus Day, died 13 January 1889 age 58 years 5 months 3 days
16	Delton D. Day 1859-1934
08	Ditus Day 10 October 1817 - 14 February 1910
08	Ellen M. Day 1848-1926
16	Flora L. Day 1893-1951

08	Levi E. Day 1837-1938 Co. C 4th Minnesota Inf.
07	Lydia, wife of Alfred Day, died 1 June 1879, age 83 years
07	M. Louisa Day (?) 1838-1917
16	Mary E. Day 1858-1911
17	Nellie E. Day 1886-1953
17	Pearl M. Day 1889-1970
54	Adolph W. Demann 3 April 1881 - 19 March 1900
54	August Demann 1849-1938
54	August B. Demann 30 July 1889 - 8 August 1890
54	Emil R. Demann 27 February 1901 - 25 January 1904
54	Sophie Demann 1857-1949
61	Barbara Dircks 1954-1954
61	boy Dircks -1959-
61	Diane Dircks -1963-
61	Thomas Dircks 1955-1956
20	Kenneth E. Doebler 1911-1993
21	Emma Drucke 1877-1906
54	Clarence G. Dubbels 1911-1981
54	Esther A. Dubbels 1915-__
06	George E. Dubey (?) , died (?) 1872
06	Hannah, wife of Nicholas Dubey (?) died (?) 1909
06	Nicholas Dubey, died (?) 1870
06	Rose Belle Dubey (?), died (?) 1865
45	Amy, wife of Isaac Edick, died 24 September 1881, age 67 years
45	Isaac Edick, died 27 November 1883, age 77 years
50	Aaron H. Ehlers 1877-1957
23	Albert C. Ehlers (?) 1875-1932
23	Caroline Ehlers (?) 1882-1950
56	Christ Ehlers (?) 29 September 1845 - 18 February 1925
51	Christina A. Ehlers 1845-1909
50	Dora A. Ehlers 1874-1942
50	Effie Orr Ehlers 1881-1975
44	Elwyn Lewis Ehlers, RM United States Coast Guard World War 2 1922-1987
49	Esther M. Ehlers 1907-1994
47	Evelyn M. Ehlers 1902-1990
44	Frederick G. Ehlers (?) 1880-1946
51	Geo. Ehlers 1858-1927
50	Geo A. Ehlers 1884-1961
50	Gladys E. Ehlers 1911-1934
49	Harris K. Ehlers 1906-1969
64	Henry C. Ehlers 1877-1957
50	Henry J. Ehlers 1847-1939
50	Jessie R. Ehlers 1883-1954
51	John H. Ehlers 1849-1927

23	June M. Ehlers 1914-1993
65	Lavina L. Ehlers 1880-1966
65	Leslie H. Ehlers 1904-1971
56	Louise Ehlers (?) 5 December 1884 - 9 June 1885
44	Lydia A.M. Ehlers (?) 1887-1973
50	Lydia C. Ehlers 1873-1933
50	Mary A. Ehlers 1851-1937
64	Maude S. Ehlers 1877-1948
65	Mildred E. Ehlers 1909-1982
47	Milton C. Ehlers 1903-1981
23	Paul A. Ehlers 1913-1960
51	Ralph H. Ehlers 5 May 1908 - 6 November 1911
51	Shirley Mae Ehlers 31 March 1930 - 4 April 1930
56	Sophia Ehlers (?) 15 July 1848 - 2 June 1929
57	Walter K. Ehlers 5 February 1883 - 9 March 1927
65	William H. Ehlers 1872-1965
20	Karl Ellinger 1870-1924
20	Katherine Ellinger 1869-1945
41	John D. Ersfeld 1934-1988
40	Steven C. Ersfeld 20 July 1960 - 2 November 1974
48	Alice Falls 1870-1921
57	Alice D. Falls 1909-1992
57	Charles L. Falls 1902-1985
48	Imogene, wife of Wm. Falls, died 2 October 1889, age 59 years
47	Lana A. Falls 1905-1979
48	William Falls, died 18 January 1916, age 79 years
16	Amanda Fort 1818-1881
16	Sybrent Fort 1816-1896
06	John Franklin 1858-1882
62	William M. Fredricksen, S1 United States Navy World War 2 1925-1974
12	Beverly J. Gnos 14 June 1930 - 1 September 1990
12	Paul Joseph Gnos, A2C United States Air Force Korea 18 May 1932 - 12 July 1983
64	William H. Granger (?) 1856-1932
05	'Father' Grove (?) 1834-1874
06	Jerome Grove 21 January 1834 - 20 May 1874
05	'Mother' Grove (?) 1834-1919
32	Glenn Guildner 1925-1994
32	Glenn Guildner, M Sgt. United States Marine Corps World War 2 Korea 22 October 1925 - 17 August 1994
32	Marlys M. Guildner 1930-___
28	Carrie Haider, nee Sanders 1885-1965

59	Fred Hamann 1884-1948
59	Goldie H. Hamann (?) 1885-1957
59	Henry Hamann 1832-1896, served 4 years in Civil War
	3rd Minnesota Co. F
59	Mary Hamann 1847-1887
21	infant Georgie Hamm -no dates
05	Robert W. Hardman 1926-1996
05	Roma Lee Hardman 1927-__
08	Arthur P. Harnden 1859-1897
08	Esther Harnden (?) 16 January 1860 - 9 November 1883
08	Lucy (?), wife of Sam Harnden 7 April 1836 - 31 June 1878
08	Sam (?) Harnden (?) 15 November 1834 - 10 February 1887
43	Caroline M., daughter of D.A. & J. Harris, died 18 October 1855
	age 10 years
43	Clarissa, wife of Joseph Harris, died 22 April 1870
	age 41 years (?)
43	Elizabeth, daughter of D.A. & J. Harris, died 8 October 1855
43	Heodosha, wife of A. Harris, died 19 January 1863, age 38 years
43	Joseph Harris, died 29 September 1869, age 79 years
09	Mary A., wife of T. Hastings, died 23 June 1878
	age 72 years 7 months 24 days
42	Anna Heichert (?) 1853-1923
42	David Heichert (?) 1818-1880
43	Essie Myrtle, daughter of John E. Heichert (?) 1879-1882
42	John E. Heichert (?) 1852-1923
42	Mary Heichert (?) 1821-1879
06	Arodyne M., daughter of ? & ? Hendryx, died 6 September 1864
	age 2 years 5 months 10 days -broken stone and hard to read
05	Lucia Day Hendryx 1826-1888
05	S.V.R. Hendryx 1816-1872
02	Imogene B. Hertz 1910-__
02	Jakob Hertz 1899-1990
02	Jenny C. Hertz 1900-1968
53	Albert Hinz (?) 1873-1940
52	Cecelia C. Hinz (?) 1877-1954
52	Jurgen Hinz (?) 1845-1894
52	Rosa Hinz (?) 1852-1935
26	Adeline M. Hoff 1840-1926
26	Benjiman S. Hoff 1830-1915
18	Ellis W. Hoff 1851-1896
18	Lillian A. Hoff 1856-1925
31	George M. Holmberg 1894-1987
31	Sally B. Holmberg 1906-1984
26	Emma L. Anderson Holmes 1944-1983
35	Frank J. Hutton 1895-1978
34	Karen A. Hutton 1933-1971

35   Ruth E. Hutton 1899-1983

38   George E. Johnson 18 March 1921 - __
38   Morris A. Johnson 1 May 1911 - 17 January 1988
38   Russell A. Johnson 18 June 1910 - 21 April 1987

37   Charles H. Kamery 1863-1864
37   Dolly J. Kamery 1843-1866
37   Lizzie G. Kamery 1871-1878
37   Mary E., wife of P.J. Kamery 1841-__
37   Owen J. Kamery 1865-1867
37   P.J. Kamery 1831-1897
60   Ellen Damann Keilen, 26 June 1912 - 15 June 1993
                    VFW Aux. 7662
01   Calvin Kimber 7 November 1924 - __
54   Johanna F. Kimber 1887-1983
54   William J. Kimber 1884-1936
54   Abraham Kraft 1857-1950
55   Alvina Kraft 1896-1958
24   Amanda Kraft 1881-1881
58   Catherine Kraft 1875-1964
66   Clara Kraft 1886-1971
54   Clarence B. Kraft, Minnesota Pvt. 163 Dep. Brig. World War 1
                    5 September 1890 - 25 December 1946
58   Conrad Kraft 1870-1941
66   Edward Kraft 1880-1958
24   Emily Kraft 1876-1888
54   Emma Kraft 1871-1948
24   Henry Kraft 1831-1916
26   John Kraft 4 March 1854 - 24 September 1906
26   Margaret Kraft 20 November 1830 - 23 July 1909
24   Mary Kraft 1836-1923
25   Matthias, son of V. & M. Kraft, died 11 June 1884, age 21 years
26   Nicolaus Kraft 27 October 1857 - 11 April 1865
26   Susan Senftn (?) Kraft (?) 27 July 1827 - 15 June 1892
26   Valentine Kraft 28 August 1823 - 10 February 1890
19   Donna J. Kuhn 1950-1995, married Dennis R. 12 May 1973

45   John Lamb 23 August 1787 - 5 February 1873
02   Anna Lamp 1914-1987
02   Jorgen Lamp 1914-1979
42   Cora J. Woodworth, wife of L.N. Larson 1859-1882
02   Esther M. Lau 1913-1991
02   Fred C. Lau 1911-1995
55   Mary J. Lichtsinn 1937-1976
55   Martha A. Lieske 1895-1896

46	Eileen Lindsay 1901-1920
46	Elizabeth Lindsay 1868-1916
13	? G. Livingston 2 August 1833 - 30 October 1915
15	A.L. Livingston 1 October 1877 - 5 August 1900
14	Amos L. Livingston 1 October 1877 - 5 August 1900
14	baby Livingston (?) 27 September 1885 - 28 September 1885
13	C.A. Livingston 5 February 1836 - 7 January 1908
14	Calista A.M. Livingston 5 February 1838 - 7 January 1908
14	Charles Livingston 2 August 1833 - 30 October 1915
13	E.L. Livingston 9 July 1875 - 5 January 1882
14	Ernest L. Livingston 9 July 18785 - 5 January 1882
15	H.E. Livingston 25 September 1875 - 8 September 1898
14	Herbert E. Livingston 25 September 1879 - 8 September 1898
13	L.E. Livingston 18 August 1874 - 8 October 1912
14	Laura E. Livingston 19 August 1874 - 3 October 1912
32	Charles Lundberg (?) 1843-1917
32	Charlotte Lundberg (?) 1850-1922
32	John Albin Lundberg (?) 1877-1879
25	Andrew Markman Sr. 1845-1911
26	Andrew F. Markman Jr. 1875-1907
25	Augusta Markman 1851-1901
25	Emelia Lentz Markman 1851-1890
26	Ernest A. Markman 1879-1901
29	Mollie D. Markman 1880-1955
29	Joseph C. Markman 1876-1954
26	Adelaide Marsh 1888-1908
26	Annie M. Marsh 1868-1949
30	Helen D. Marshall 1910-1984
30	John F. Marshall 1887-1966
30	Mary E. Marshall 1890-1964
30	Vern C. Marshall 1911-1984
09	Frank E., son of J.N. & R.A. Martin, died 24 January 1869 age 2 months 5 days
14	Mindy May 1954-1983
64	Anna G. Michel (?) 1858-1951
61	Conrad Michel, born 4 May 1820 in Rheinpfalz, Germany died 11 September 1895 Farmington, Minnesota
60	Dorothea Michel (?) 1856-1931
60	Elizabeth Michel (?) 1821-1915
60	George Michel 1855-1922
64	Henry Michel (?) 1853-1931
60	Valentine Michel (?) 1849-1938
28	Lydia Moes, nee Sanders 1868-1948
10	Lizzie E., daughter of Wm. & M.J. More, died 11 April 1883 age 1 year 10 months

10	Mary J., wife of Wm. More, died 23 May 1898, age 56 years
16	Edith C. Morrill 8 June 1868 - 27 December 1899
56	Myra Stapf Muth 31 July 1914 - 4 January 1982
48	Jane Neasey 20 December 1844 - 4 October 1909
48	Thomas Neasey November 1829 - 19 February 1918
59	Franklyn Neeb 1910-1974
58	Clarice G. Nordvall 1897-1950
06	Charles B. Odell (?) 1858-1915
06	Sarah J. Odell (?) 1833-1907
06	Simeon G. Odell (?) 1811-1885
44	Caroline, wife of Henry Otte 1 May 1843 - 21 June 1885
	age 42 years 1 month 21 days
56	Caroline Otte 1871-1951
52	Carrie H. Otte 1865-1962
44	Charles Otte (?) 4 July 1882 - 17 May 1883
44	Charlie Otte, died 17 May 1883, age 10 months 13 days
53	Clarence W. Otte (?) 1890-1893
43	Essie Ruth Otte 1903-1981
44	'Father' Otte (?) 16 December 1836 - ??? 1914
56	Henry A. Otte 1868-1932
52	Herman G. Otte 1862-1931
43	Jeannie M. Heichert Otte 1875-1959
46	John C. Otte 1869-1899
53	Lila M. Otte (?) 1894-1909
44	Louisa Otte (?) 12 April 1866 - 13 July 1894
44	'Mother' Otte (?) 1 May 1843 - 21 June 1885
43	William E. Otte 1871-1955
15	Evelyn C. Ozmun 1914-__
15	Harvey R. Ozmun 1924-__
15	Thomas R. Ozmun 1962-1978
02	Edmund J. Pariseau 1906-1967
40	Alice G. Parker (?) 1853-1932
08	Jonathan Parker, died 16 January 1896, age 77 years
40	William L. Parker (?) 1846-1910
46	baby girl Perry -14 January 1981-
62	Charles Perry 1871-1936
63	Elizabeth Perry 1900-1930
62	Francis Perry 1873-1928
63	Geo. S. Perry 5 September 1842 - 15 June 1915
45	George W. Perry 1909-1982
45	George William Perry 1869-1944
63	Jeffery B. Perry 1954-1985
63	baby Ione Grace Perry -1936-

63	Mary E., wife of G.S. Perry, died 11 August 1886, age 37 years
63	Myrtle M. Perry 1911-1989
62	Nellie Perry 1877-1924
63	Orville F. Perry 1903-1989
63	Otis S. Perry 1875-1935
45	Phoebe Ann Perry 1863-1943
45	Ruth A. Perry 1917-1986
62	Alice J. Pettit 1903-1983
62	Johnny W. Pettit 1931-1931
62	Simon S. Pettit 1884-1963
23	Adam Pflaum (?) -no dates
38	Albertina Pflaum (?) 1874-1945
37	Donald W. Pflaum 1908-1988
39	Edith H.E. Pflaum 4 June 1918 - 5 December 1982
23	Emma Pflaum (?) -no dates
38	Frank Pflaum (?) 1870-1940
24	Henry Pflaum 1886-1967
24	Herbert Pflaum (?) -no dates
39	Howard D. Pflaum 20 December 1911 - 16 December 1971
24	Linde Pflaum (?) -no dates
23	Lize Pflaum (?) -no dates
38	Luella L. Pflaum 1914-__
24	Mary Pflaum 1879-1903
24	Mary A. Pflaum 9 November 1879 - 11 July 1903
37	Mildred A. Pflaum 1907-1981
24	Minnie Pflaum (?) -no dates
24	Myra Pflaum (?) -no dates
24	Peter Pflaum 28 June 1843 - 16 February 1900
23	Peter Pflaum 1843-1900
38	Russell Pflaum 1904-1981
23	Sarah Pflaum 1844-1926
24	Wil Pflaum (?) -no dates
01	Donovan D. Pietsch 23 August 1971 - 29 August 1974
09	Sibyl Childs, wife of Joseph Pike, died 27 February 1879 age 73 years 1 month 21 days
46	John Pilcher 1916-1996, married Lucille 23 May 1944
46	Lucille Pilcher 1916-__, married John 23 May 1944
21	Albert W. Radman 1875-1966
34	Anna Radman 1876-1961
21	Clara A. Radman 1884-1967
22	Clarence Albert Radman, United States Army 1917-1986
34	George Radman 1901-1953
34	Gustave Radman 1872-1951
21	Caroline Radmann 1835-1929
21	Christ Radmann 1834-1895

06	Caroline L., wife of Forest L. Reed, died 15 June 1876, age 43 years
06	Forest L. Reed 4 May 1830 - 25 November 1904
06	Mary Alis Reed, child of E.L. & C.L. Reed
	10 September 1872 - 12 August 1874
06	Mertie, child of E.L. & C.L. Reed
	8 March 1869 - 22 March 1874
06	Minnie, child of E.L. & C.L. Reed
	3 March 1859 (?) - 23 March 1869
52	Lillian Pearl Rhone, nee Trout 2 November 1884 - 15 April 1906
46	Anna D. Richel 17 June 1867 - 11 October 1965
46	Ben F. Richel 18 April 1865 - 20 December 1940
41	Caroline M., wife of Jesse Rice, died 25 August 1868
	age 38 years 5 months
41	Carrie M. (?), daughter of J. & C.M. Rice, died 12 September 1868
	age 1 month 12 days
41	Ella B., daughter of J. & C.M. Rice, died 27 November 1868
	age 17 years 7 months
41	Frank H., son of J. & C.M. Rice, died 16 August 1860
	age 7 months
41	James H., son of J. & C.M. Rice, died 21 October 1868
	age 2 years 3 months
06	Luther Rice (?) died (?) 1869
06	Mary, wife of Luther Rice (?), died (?) 1865
41	Minnie A., daughter of J. & C.M. Rice, died 15 August 1866
	age 11 years 7 months
19	Charles E.B. Rowell 1842-1898
19	Chase B. Rowell 1842-1898
20	Edna Mae Rowell (?) 1877-1928
18	Lester V. Rowell 1880-1881
20	Loren B.C. Rowell (?) 1870-1944
19	Sibyl Childs Rowell 1850-1934
01	Charlotte Rozelle 1918-1977
01	Raymond Rozelle 1913-__
46	Hazel B. Sachs 1912-__, married Juluis W. 20 May 1937
46	Juluis W. Sachs 1909-1993, married Hazel B. 20 May 1937
28	Barbara, wife of Henry E. Sanders
	14 September 1843 - 16 August 1911
28	Gustave H. Sanders 1869-1930
28	Henry E. Sanders 24 August 1837 - 4 February 1894
28	Louis A. Sanders 15 October 1876 - 27 February 1911
27	Patricia Ann Sanders 1932-1938
27	Petra Sanders 1904-1933
27	Richard C. Sanders 1907-1979
34	Augusta Schram 1867-1952
34	baby Schram -1921-

34	Gustave Schram 1858-1922
34	Ira Schram 1898-1922
66	Agnes P. Schultz 8 September 1912-__
66	Edward E. Schultz 14 October 1898 - 2 May 1972
66	Pearl W. Schultz 29 November 1918 - 15 January 1968
66	Robert J. Schultz 8 October 1904-__
02	Robert Schuman 1856-1931
04	J. Urban Sheffield 1872-1915
04	Marian T. Sheffield 9 April 1847 - 10 July 1892
04	Marion T. Sheffield 1847-1892
36	Berton Forest Shellenbarger (?) 1874-1939
60	Claude B. Shellenbarger 1903-1987
36	Harold E. Shellenbarger 1908-1932
55	Lois M. Shellenbarger 1916-__
60	Margaret K. Shellenbarger 1908-1959
55	Ralph W. Shellenbarger 1913-1969
36	Stella May Shellenbarger (?) 1881-1967
52	?, son of H.W. (?) & L.F. (?) Shumway, died 11 October 1881
	age 3 months 1 day -hard to read
62	Earl W. Shumway 1906-1925
62	Edward Shumway 1917-1983
53	Elbert C. Shumway 1871-1937
62	Gertrude Shumway 1881-1946
52	Henry Shumway 1834-1914
52	Jane E. Shumway 1842-1900
62	Walter B. Shumway 1866-1925
63	Warren Shumway 1910-1968
52	Warren H. Shumway 1869-1906
22	Albert Sievers 1876-1946
48	Anna Sievers 1844-1906
22	Christine Sievers 1875-1967
22	Floyd E. Sievers 1908-1992
48	Jacob Sievers 1841-1917
47	Lucia Sievers (?) 1884-1884
22	Marlys M. Sievers 1918-__
47	Sarah Sievers 1882-1971
04	Clarence, son of S.M. & C.A. Slaight, died February 1866
	age 3 months
04	Cornelia A., wife of S.M. Slaight, died 9 April 1877, age 36 years
04	S.M. Slaight, died 1 July 1872, age 44 years
64	Alice Smith 1880-1956
03	Catharine, wife of Thos. Smith, died 5 February 1875
	age 58 years 6 months 15 days
65	Dale Smith 4 July 1919 - __
64	Harvey Smith 1873-1966
65	Mildred Smith 20 February 1916 - 21 November 1982

60	Hildegard Becker Stanger 1886-1966
56	Emma Stapf 1879-1949
56	George Stapf 1878-1942
56	Harold L. Stapf 1902-1961
08	Allen Stevens (?) 1893-1902
08	Anna Stevens 1852-1950
08	Barney Stevens, died 12 January 1899, age 65 years 1 month 18 days
	C. F Minnesota Vol's
07	Emerishous Stevens 1887-1964
32	Flora Stevens (?) 1867-1920
32	Frances Stevens (?) 1878-1946
08	George B., son of B. & M. Stevens, died 2 June 1890
	age 32 years 3 months 8 days
32	George R. Stevens (?) 1894-1915
32	Gladys M. Stevens (?) 1903-1973
32	Helen Stevens (?) 1906-1917
32	James B. Stevens 1897-1984
07	James B. Stevens, died 8 April 1869, age 57 years
32	Louis Stevens (?) 1866-1952
32	M.L. Stevens 1872-1929
08	Mattie E., daughter of B. & M. Stevens, died 26 October 1864
	age 6 months 21 days
08	Mattie E., daughter of B. & M. Stevens, died 26 October 1864
	age 6 months 21 days
32	Minnie Marie Stevens 1915-1985
08	Ralph Stevens (?) 1885-1891
32	Ruth Stevens 1919-1958
07	Sally M., wife of J.B. Stevens, died 23 February 1875
	age 61 years 12 days
07	Verne Doyle Stevens 1891-1972
32	Virginia Stevens (?) 1918-1944
32	Wayne Stevens 1905-1982
08	William Stevens 1859-1924
02	Christine H. Strzyzewski, born Pohl 1934-1990
18	Frank H. Taylor 1864-1953
18	Lora M. Taylor 1869-1955
44	Ruth Taylor 1806-1879
19	Annis Teachout (?) 1861-1945
25	baby Teachout 1904-1904
18	Cordelia Teachout 1836-1927
19	Ella C. Teachout (?) 1857-1862
25	Freda Teachout 1905-1982
25	George H. Teachout (?) 1874-1960
18	John Teachout 1833-1905 Co. I Minnesota H Art.
26	Morris C. Teachout 1918-1994

26	Myrtle L. Teachout 1918-1979
19	Orena Teachout (?) 1868-1957
25	Retta M. Teachout (?) 1880-1921 'buried in California'
58	'Father' Towler (?) 1835-1919
58	Gertrude L. Towler (?) 1891-1919
58	Johanna M. Towler (?) 1865-1949
58	Joseph T. Towler (?) 1900-1906
58	'Mother' Towler (?) 1824-1905
59	Rosamond A. Towler (?) 1898-1949
58	Samuel T. Towler (?) 1858-1938
30	Albert H. Trout 1870-1941
31	Alberta Trout 1906-1906
31	Alice R. Trout 1898-1977
28	Amelia Trout 28 November 1809 - 24 May 1885
52	Carrie N., wife of C.H. Trout 31 August 1862 - 26 March (?) 1888
53	Charles H. Trout 1858-1940
30	Edna M. Trout 1904-1984
31	Gene L. Trout 1925-1980
28	Henry Trout 9 November 1833 - 19 December 1903
29	Henry Trout (?) 1874-1962
28	Johanna Trout 17 December 1837 - 19 March 1900
53	Julia Trout 1860-1948
30	Lawrence A. Trout 1904-1984
30	Maude R. Trout 1868-1941
31	Stella Trout 1902-1903
29	William Trout (?) 1876-1964
03	Winnie V. Tussey 1876-1899
45	Ann VanNess 22 August 1884 - 27 January 1897
45	William VanNess 15 May 1831 - 17 January 1914
21	Cyrus D. VanVliet 1838-1910
21	Emily M. VanVliet 1830-1905
21	Harlow VanVliet 1831-1901
21	Minerva VanVliet 1800-1882
34	baby Walker (?) -1919-
14	Emily Ward, died 13 March 1885, age 57 years 7 months
14	John L. Ward, died 3 September 1882, age 58 years 10 months
14	Wm. H. Ward, died 21 June 1884, age 21 years 8 months
30	Anne C. Whittier (?) 1914-1984
30	Henry P. Whittier (?) 1865-1933
30	Mabel G. Whittier (?) 1875-1916
30	Marie S. Whittier (?) 1844-1921
30	Philip P. Whittier Co. K Ohio Inf.
30	Stanley P. Whittier (?) 1912-1987
07	?, wife of R. Willard, died 15 December 1862, age 32 years

05   Esther Day Willard 1830-1862
15   Calista A. Winsor 1866-1947
43   Ella M., daughter of G. & ? Woodworth, died 17 September 1874
          age 17 years 1 month 2 days

I was not able top determine a surname for the following.

21   Amelia H., daughter of ??, died 1 February 1861, age 2 months 27 days

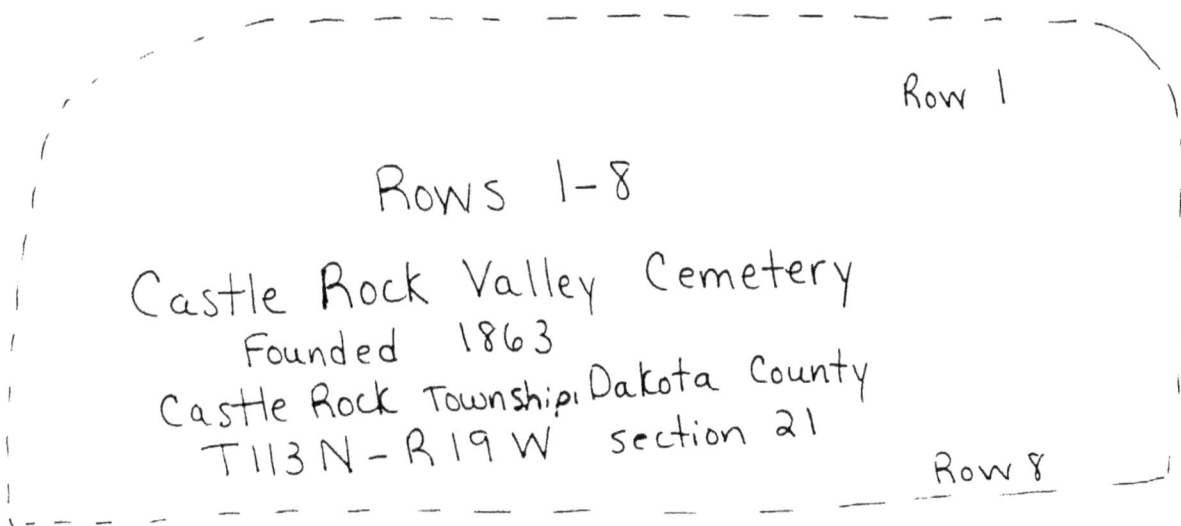

Rows 1-8

Castle Rock Valley Cemetery
Founded 1863
Castle Rock Township, Dakota County
T113N - R19W   section 21

Row 1

Row 8

Drive   Area

Row 9

Rows 9-39

Row 39

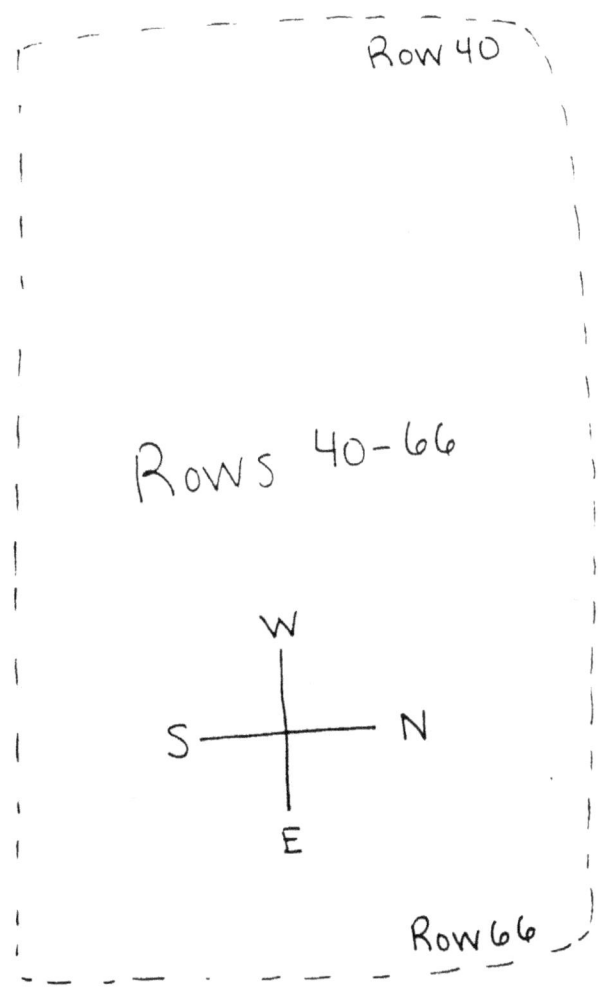

Row 40

Drive
Area

Rows 40-66

W
S —— N
E

Row 66

Drive area

Drive   Area

53N or Alverno Ave.

McNutt Cemetery ?

Castle Rock township, Dakota county, Minnesota: T113N - R19W, section 25

I was not able to get permission to view this cemetery. It is not accessible from the main roads. It must be accessed through private property. The 1899 Dakota county plat maps show the location of this cemetery.

The Dakota county cemetery records compilation lists this cemetery as: McNutt private cemetery, 1859. 1.875 acres. Located Section 25, NW 1/2. (Abandoned).

GREENWOOD CEMETERY
&
VERMILLION PRESBYTERIAN CHURCH CEMETERY

Eureka township, Dakota county, Minnesota: T113N - R20W, section 4

    This cemetery is in good shape and is upkept. It appears as though at some time in the past year or so someone has cut back some of the overgrowth of trees and shrubs.   Part of the north-east area had became covered by the overgrowth. I have labeled this area with a series of short rows numbered 3 -14. The area for this cemetery is good sized. Although in parts the burial stones are few and far in between. Rows 25-45 run from north to south crossing the old drive area on the west half of the cemetery. Row 46 is actually a family plot in the far north-west corner.

    Just east of the cemetery, outside the fence, is the area where the Vermillion Presbyterian Church once stood. I believe this church is the same on that is now on exhibit at the Dakota County Fairgrounds. There is a sign that reads: Vermillion Presbyterian Church 1856-1977.

    In "History of Dakota County and the city of Hastings", by Rev. Edward D. Neill, written in 1881, he lists: The Greenwood Cemetery Association was organized in May 1867, at the Vermillion Church ... Two acres of ground were purchased of Jacob VanDoren adjoining the Vermillion church on the west, and laid out and platted ... 3 June 1867. The object of the association is to furnish a burial place for the surrounding community without regard to sect, or religious denomination, and all the money received is expended in beautifying the grounds... A place is set aside for the burial of strangers and the poor. The first internment was that of Z.A. Bonham, age 79, a native of Virginia and a respected citizen of Lakeville. Quite a number of bodies have been removed from other locations and interned there. (page 379).

    The Dakota county cemetery records compilation lists this cemetery as: Vermillion Greenwood Cemetery, established 1867. 2 acres. Purchased 1867 and 2 more acres in 1876. (4 acres). Located Section 4, NW 1/4.

    Everyone is listed in alphabetical order. The number before each entry is the row number. There is a map at the back of this section.

    These cemetery burial monuments were transcribed during 1996.

19   Rachel Abel, died 15 September 1881, age 92 years
31   Charles D. Allard 1879-1944
31   Cora E. Allard 1901-1929
31   Janet Allard 1874-1963
18   Arthur Oswald Ash 1876-1919
18   C. Calista Ash 1876-1964
18   Ellen Mary Ash 1843-1917

18	Joseph Alwin Ash 1849-1936
18	Van John Ash 1883-1966
26	Emily Atwood, died 13 October 1883
	age 71 years (?) 1 month 25 days
26	Emily, daughter of A. & H. Atwood, died 25 February 1876
	age 7 years 6 months 22 days
26	Nellie M., daughter of ? & ? Atwood, died ??? 1878
	age 11 years 6 months 18 days -broken stone
25	William W. Atwood, died 8 May 1878, age 30 years 2 months
33	William, son of J. & M. Battin, died 5 November 1862
	age 18 years 26 days
39	Mahala C. Bean 1810-1874
39	Samuel Bean 1810-1891
26	Jedediah Bennet, died 23 February 1879
	age 76 years 9 months G.A.R. *
26	Verdu A. Bennett, died 15 April 1882
	age 59 years 1 month 5 days
43	Donald B. Berkey 1919-1989
43	Etta L. Berkey 1879-1951
43	Oscar F. Berkey 1875-1920
42	Laura E. Bixby (Mallery) 1916-1980
42	Robert D. Bixby 1914-__
16	Allen J. Bonham 1837-1891
16	Arthula A., wife of Allen J. Bonham 1847-1876
15	Cora Bonham 1875-1877
15	Cora S., child of E.W. & S.T. Bonham, died 8 February 1877
	age 1 year 11 months -hard to read
16	Ellen L. Bonham 1841-1911
15	Eugene W. Bonham 29 June 1835-14 April 1909
15	Mabel Bonham 1873-1877
15	Mabel (?) H., child of E.W. & S.T. Bonham, died 11 February 1877
	age 8 years 5 months -hard to read
16	Pearlie Bonham 1870-1877
15	Z.A. Bonham, died 26 June 1867, age 75 years
14	Arthur G. Borgen 1893-1985
14	Marion K. Borgen 1889-1974
32	Abigal, wife of Nathaniel Brimhall, died 19 May 1864, age 68 years
32	Nathaniel Brimhall, died 3 December 1865, age 73 years
19	Mary, wife of (?) ?? Bristol (?), died 7 February 1886
	age 76 years 4 days
19	Zekiah R. Bristol, died (?) 1 February 1864 (?), age 71 years
	-hard to read
27	Erma Brown 1907-1924
27	Fannie E. Brown 1875-1968
28	Frances Brown 1899-1993

27	Magnus Brown 1863-1948
28	Thomas Brown 1896-1987
27	William Brown 1894-1914
41	David Burton 1830-1928 Co. F 2nd Minnesota Cav. Civil War
40	David Lewis Burton 1878-1919
41	Elmira E. Burton 1831-1912
38	Charlotte S. Bruce 1842-1926
38	W.C. Bruce 1839-1920
35	baby Case -1962-
44	Barney Case 1909-1989
44	Florence M. Case 1916-1991
39	Burrell Chase 1900-1903
26	Clement C. Chase 1906-1961
25	Clement G. Chase 1881-1957
24	Elizabeth J. Chase (?) 1861-1913
24	Emeline L. Chase (?) 1819-1859
24	George M. Chase (?) 1833-1886 2nd Leit. Co. K. N.H. Vol.
24	Horace B. Chase (?) 1856-1929
39	John B. Chase 1864-1942
39	Lydia R. Chase 1869-1932
25	Margaret V. Chase 28 September 1910 - 26 August 1974
38	O.E. Chase 1862-1921
25	Sallie K. Chase 1874-1963
26	Vena Smith Chase 1909-1983
41	Albert Francie Cherry (?) 1900-1978
40	Catherine J., wife of James Cherry 1854-1907
40	James Cherry 1848-1944
40	Jeanette Cherry 26 March 1816 - 22 October 1890
19	Eugene, child of W.S. & S.E. Cobury (?), died 8 July 1862 age 11 months 16 days -hard to read
19	Isaac L., child of W.D. & S.E. Cobury (?), died 19 May 1864 age 11 months 27 days - hard to read
29	Aaron Collett (?), died 18 February 1858 age 2 years 6 months 18 days
29	Adnah Collett , died 1901
29	D. (?) Collett, died 31 March 1889 age 69 years 9 months 25 days
29	Emeline Collett (?), died 8 June 1865 age 3 years 10 months 18 days
39	Guy E. Collett 1875-1922
29	Mary G Collett (?), died 23 October 1885 age 19 years 11 months 17 days
39	Muriel Louise, wife of Guy E. Collett (?) 1882-1966
29	Sarah Collett 1824-1903
29	Susanna C. Collett, died 18 November 1856

	age 10 years 3 months 28 days
29	William Collett (?), died 19 November 1877
	age 10 years 3 months 28 days
28	Emma G., daughter of W.H. & G.E. Crist, died 30 May 1869, aged ?
	-broken stone
28	Ida Maud, daughter of ? & Alf (?) Crist, died 3 October 1875 (?)
	age 2 years ? months -broken stone and hard to read
28	William H. Crist, died 24 January 1864 (?)
	age 19 years 2 months -broken stone and hard to read
35	Allan F. Curry, United States Navy World War 2
	1 April 1925 - 14 March 1993
11	Andrew F. Curry 1870-1904
09	Ann E. Curry (?), died 1871, age 34 years
08	Eleanor Curry (?), died 1893, age 92 years
09	Isaac C. Curry (?), died 1908, age 77 years
08	James Curry (?), died 1864, age 67 years
12	John Vandoren Curry, died 25 January 1871
	age 46 years 7 months 21 days
08	John W. Curry (?), died 1886, age 38 years
34	Leona G. Curry 1901-1988
12	Mary Curry, died 14 May 1884, age 58 years 8 months 16 days
11	Nellie M. Curry 1876-1926
12	Sarah Ellen, daughter of John V. & Mary Curry, died 24 October 1864
	age 10 years 3 months 25 days
34	William H. Curry 1897-1972
09	Willie E. Curry (?), died 1862, age 4 months
17	Wm. Dewey 1899-1944
14	C.F. Donaldson 29 December 1849 - 28 April 1910
13	Eddie, son of R.S. & Eliz. Donaldson, died in infancy -no dates
13	Eliza, wife of R.S. Donaldson 27 September 1828 - 23 November 1893
14	infant son of Adis & Lucy Donaldson, died 18 March 1871, age 21 days
13	Col. Robert S. Donaldson 13 October 1828 - 13 September 1900
44	Charles H. Dunn 1902-__
37	David S. Dunn, Pvt. United States Army World War 1 1891-1984
36	'Father' Dunn (?) 1857-1929
44	Inga S. Dunn 1910-__
36	James S. Dunn 14 October 1887 - 24 September 1946
37	Joseph H. Dunn, Pvt. United States Navy World War 1 1896-1981
37	Mary S. Dunn 1858-1938
36	'Mother' Dunn (?) 1858-1938
36	W.J. Dunn 20 December 1886 - 8 May 1915
37	William Dunn 1857-1929
34	Edwin A. Ebeling, Pfc United States Army World War 2
	20 July 1923 - 30 October 1991

| 41 | Lewis F. Farmer 23 January 1861 - 14 May 1899 |
| 41 | Martha A. Farmer 1 August 1862 - 6 July 1911 |

21	Anna Gebhardt 1820-1910
21	John Gebhardt 1848-1871
42	Charles W. Gleason 1874-1942
42	Eva May Gleason 1866-1931
42	Gwendolyn Gleason 1899-1968
42	Lyman Gleason 1910-1929
37	Bishop Gordon 1836-1914
37	Bishop Gordon 1836-1914
37	Esther Gordon 1837-1904
37	Esther B. Hamben, wife of Bishop Gordon 1837-1904

09	Walter W., son of Mr. & Mrs. Geo. R. Hart
	2 July 1893 - 2 October 1894
23	James Hartland 1890-1891
24	D. Willis Hatfield 1859-1928
24	Maggie Annie Hatfield 1864-1935
07	Mrs. Pheobe Hatfield 20 February 1831 - 10 August 1926
	age 95 years 5 months 20 days
45	Lawrence Allin Hill 1934-1989
34	baby Holley -no dates
34	baby Holley -no dates
34	Maggie ? Holley 1897-1954
41	Rodney F. Holloway (?) 1914-1977
01	Elizabeth Ann Houts, died 17 December 1891
	age 69 years 5 months 23 days
01	John Houts, died 1 May 1870 , age 48 years 3 months 8 days
02	little Orrill, son of R.B. (?) & J.R. (?) Houts, died 27 July (?) 1871
	? months 21 days
02	Arthur, son of G.W. & S. Hull, died 23 April 1870, age 18 years

24	John E. Jelly (?) 1829-1908
24	Vemira Jelly (?) 1837-1864
26	R. Johnson (?), died 26 April 1877, age 67 years 6 months
	G.A.R. * -broken stone
34	Charles R., son of A.L. & Josse Jones (?), died 11 June 1878
	age 3 years ? months 7 days
34	Lorenz (?), child of C. & P. Jones, died 11 March 1862
	age 11 days (?)
34	Philena, wife of (?) Cha. Jones, died 11 December 1875 (?)
	-broken stone and part of stone is buried
34	Minie (?) E., child of C. & P. Jones, died 9 March 1866,
	age 10 months 4 days

40	A. Ralph Kelly 1883-1957
22	Edith M. Kelly (?) 1876-1896
40	Hannah M. Kelly 1886-1965
22	J.B. Kelly 1856-1908
22	Minnie C. Kelly 1857-1937
42	Myrtle E. Kelly 1919-__
42	Vern A. Kelly 1916-__
23	Ansel R. Kingsley 29 May 1823 - 3 January 1905
24	Cyrus M. Kingsley (?) 1831-1885, buried at Grants Pass, Oregon
23	Della Kingsley 1873-1955
23	John Kingsley 1861-1933
24	Lilly A. Kingsley (?) 1860-1920
23	Maria J., wife of A.R. Kingsley, died 15 January 1859 age 34 years 6 months 4 days
23	Rebecca A., wife of A.R. Kingsley, died 8 August 1892 age 71 years 10 days
24	Susan J. Kingsley (?) 1832-1901
40	Frank A. Koch (?) 1917-1966
02	Ann E. Record, wife of Ira B. Lattin, died 28 April (year missing)
02	Ira B. Lattin 11 July 1814 - 15 October 1886
28	Alice Elizabeth Livingston (?) 1877-1915
27	Ann M. Livingston 1815-1888
27	Ann McElrath Livingston, died 24 March 1888 age 72 years 9 months 6 days
27	Ann Vemira Livingston (?) 1881-1888
28	Ellen Elizabeth Livingston (?) 1852-1878
27	little Harold Livingston (?) -no dates
27	Jennie Livingston (?) 1857-1916
28	Leander Livingston 1849-1926
28	Leander Livingston (?) -no dates
28	Luella P. Livingston 1879-1908
28	Luella Livingston (?) -no dates
28	Nellie Livingston (?) -no dates
28	Mary Livingston (?) -no dates
27	Samuel Livingston 1815-1894
27	Vernard Roy Livingston (?) 1889-1908
22	James Lockwood 13 October 1830 - 4 April 1888
02	George I., son of R.J. & E.M. Lomsden (?), died 28 May 1864 age 1 year 9 months 21 days
27	James McElrath, died 19 October 1877 age 65 years 10 months 20 day
27	Mary McWilliam, wife of Archibald McElrath 8 January 1790 - 20 August 1873

38	Alfred L. Mallery, Cpl United States Army
	5 February 1890 - 23 October 1974
38	baby of J.H. & H.E. Mallery -1890-
29	Dan Mallery (?) 1883-1926
38	Ellen Bean Mallery 1850-1934
38	Esther I. Mallery 19 August 1906 - 24 April 1986
33	Ethel E. Mallery 1910-__
43	Francis A. Mallery 1886-1958
30	Garrick B. Mallery (?) 4 May 1825 - 22 October 1916
39	Garrick D. Mallery 1903-1989
29	John Wesley Mallery 1863-1950
29	Joseph Hinkle Mallery 2 October 1848 - 4 July 1926
29	Kitty Mallery (?) 1883-1973
33	Leigh A. Mallery 1906-1977
39	Lillian I. Mallery 1904-__
38	Lyman Mallery 1878-1947
43	Ora B. Mallery 1884-1969
38	Samuel Minor Mallery 1880-1940
29	Sarah A. Mallery 1868-1947
30	Susana Mallery (?) 28 February 1826 - 24 July 1915
30	Willie, son of G.B. & S. Mallery, died 24 June 1866
	age 6 years 5 months 14 days
08	Bernhard Johannes Meeg - Andersen 2 November - 5 November 1933
08	Johannes Meeg - Andersen 1906-1976
08	Lela Meeg - Andersen 1894-1986
24	Mary A., daughter of P. (?) & E. Miller, died 11 February 1869
	age 8 years 1 month 22 days
24	Peter G. Miller 19 January (?) 1829 - 17 May 1883
16	Henry J. Morris, died 21 August 1868, age 50 years 26 days
32	Frank A. Morton 14 October 1850 - 27 August 1928
32	Harriet A. Morton 15 April 1852 - 3 June 1899
32	Phinehas Morton, died 23 August 1874, age 68 years
32	Sarah E., wife of Phinehas Morton, died 9 March 1890, age 70 years
31	Walfred Nelson 1894-1926
27	Charles L. Newcomb 10 January 1850 - 10 October 1902
27	Mary A. Newcomb 3 September 1850 - 11 November 1901
11	A.C. Roy Niskern 4 January 1884 - 25 September 1898
11	Ada C. Niskern 1 October 1864 - 31 December 1896
02	Nelson Niskern, died 12 October 1871, age 24 years
02	Nicholas Niskern, died 10 March 1885, age 38 years
02	Peter Niskern -no dates
01	Petern Niskern, died 18 October 1880, age 60 years
07	Cora E. O'Connor 1891-1937
07	Cora E. O'Connor 5 September 1856 - 3 January 1929

07	Daniel O'Connnor 1 January 1847 - 26 May 1898
07	Ruth O'Connor 7 July 1897 - 4 June 1914
32	Anna M., daughter of ? & E. Ohlen (?), died 10 August 186?
	-hard to read
20	Samuel Osborn 11 December 1797 - 11 September 1872
34	Mary C. Parry 1837-1903
35	William A. Parry, Pvt. 4 Minnesota Regt. Civil War
	23 November 1842 - 3 April 1924
34	William A. Parry 1842-1924
44	Claryce J. Petrash 1920-__
44	Joseph V. Petrash 1918-1976
02	Oscar L., son of C. & S. Phelps, died 6 April 1862
	age 6 years 4 months 6 days
01	Eliza Ann, wife of Alfred Phillips, died 18 April 1874
	age 74 years 10 months 18 days
24	Helen, daughter of A.J. & N. (?) Phillips, died 1 September 1877
	age 12 years 10 months
01	Joseph Phillips, died 7 November 1877, age 80 years 5 months
01	Joseph D., son of A. & E. Phillips, died 8 January 1873
	age 1 year 2 months 26 days
01	Lucretia (?) Phillips, died 23 October 1879, age 82 years 4 months
23	Walter, son of A.J. & N. Phillips, died 20 May 1872
	age 1 year 1 month 11 days
34	baby Pool, son of James & Clara -no dates
34	baby Pool, son of James & Clara -no dates
37	Emma Pool 1861-1938
34	Emeline, wife of Jeremiah Pool, died 19 December 1863
	age 20 years 6 months 24 days
40	Ethel P. Pool 1899-1958
37	Frank Pool 1859-1918
23	Harold F. Pool 1889-1957
23	Hazel J. Pool 1891-1977
23	Helen Rae Pool 11 April 1920 - 19 January 1921
34	James, son of Wm. & M. (?) Pool, died 13 February 1867
	age 10 years 5 months 16 days
40	Jean A. Pool 1928-1967
35	John Pool 1810-1861
35	John W. Pool, died 19 October 1877, age 35 years 22 days
41	Laura E. Pool 1857-1939
35	Mary Pool 1811-1874
34	Mary G., daughter of Wm. & M. Pool, died 16 February 1863
	age 5 years 4 months 25 days
34	Nancy Pool 1807-1879
41	Robert Pool 1848-1913
35	Sarah, wife of John Pool 1815-1898

40	Wm. O. Pool 1889-1961
35	William Pool 1806-1878
41	Addie Belle, daughter of D. & E.E. Burton, wife of J.A. Post
	died 5 April 1887, age 22 years 5 months 2 days
24	Lilly Pychon 1811-1895
43	Allan B. Rayburn 1892-1965
43	Willetta B. Rayburn 1895-1947
05	Alphonso Record 1823-1885
05	Barahninar (?), daughter of ? & ? Record, died 17 October 1866
	age 2 years (?) -hard to read
04	Bertha J. Record 1850-1923
04	Charles E. Record 1868-1889
04	Edwin Record 1846-1923
03	George Anson Record 1819-1880 veteran *
05	Ira L., son of J.C. & E. Record, died 18 October 1866
	age 11 years 6 months 2 days
04	L.S. Record 1849-1927
01	Sarah Record 1790-1871
01	Thomas Record 1785-1866
05	Ann, wife of John Ryding, died 12 September 1865, age 41 years
05	John Ryding (?), died 8 February 1875, age 62 years
06	Albert L. Sayers 1873-1948
46	Gordon Lea Sayers 29 December 1904 - 10 April 1982
	son of Albert L. & Tune Gordon Sayers
	married Sylvia Alton 2 July 1932
46	Sylvia Alton Sayers 26 June 1910 -__, wife of Gordon Lea Sayers
	daughter of Patrick & Florence Lundberg Alton
	married Gordon Lea 2 July 1932
36	Tune Sayers 1871-1952
06	Eliza, wife of James Sayre 29 December 1803 - 19 June 1880
06	Fannie Louesa, wife of I.V. Sayre, died 8 January 1875, age 30 years
06	Isaac V. Sayre 27 October 1840 - 28 March 1876
06	James R. Sayre, born in N.J. 14 March 1800 - 16 October 1873
06	Mary Alice, daughter of I.V. & E.L. Sayre
	11 November 1871 - 28 April 1872
23	Vera E. Schachtel 1885-1967
22	baby Scofield, child of J.J. & P.M. Scofield 1905-1905
22	baby Scofield, child of J.J. & P.M. Scofield 1902-1902
22	Eliza, wife of S.C. Scofield, died 10 September 1859
	age 43 years 9 months
22	Elizabeth J., wife of S.C. Scofield, died 4 December 1907
	age 81 years 11 months 9 days
17	Huldah Marie Scofield (?) 1900-1982
22	J. Jesse Scofield 1865-1933

22	John E. Scofield (?), died 3 October 1872 (?)
	age 26 years 5 months 20 days
17	John Raymond Scofield (?) 1895-1972
22	Mary J. Scofield (?), died 26 September 1878
	age 18 years 2 months 11 days (?)
22	Percy M., wife of J.J. Scofield, died 10 September 1908
	age 42 years 9 months 23 days
22	Ralph C., son of J.J. & P.M. Scofield, died 24 February 1891
	age 1 year 5 months 3 days
22	Silas G. Scofield, died 15 February 1891
	age 74 years 2 months 11 days
17	Theodore R. Scofield (?) 1903-1981
22	Thomas M. (?) Scofield (?), died 22 April 1872
	age 28 years ? months 24 days
22	William W. Scofield (?), died 20 May (?) 1879
	age 16 years 8 months 16 days
30	Adam Seals 26 October 1891 - 16 December 1891
30	Gracie, daughter of H. & M.A. Shadinger, died 16 April 1875
	age 1 month 6 days
30	Isaac, child of H. & M.A. Shadinger, died 8 September 1860
	age 3 years 2 months 18 days
30	William D., child of H. & M.A. Shadinger, died 8 April 1864
27	M. Evalina, daughter of H.J. & M.G. Shaffanr (?), died 9 November 1868
	age 21 years 7 months
20	Sarah E. Smiley 2 July 1845 - 20 September 1884
10	Mary Curry Solseth 1904-1986
20	Andrew Stouffer 27 February 1822 - 14 November 1882
38	Roger B. Studenski, SSGT United States Air Force & United States Army
	24 January 1933 - 6 May 1989
37	Sumner C. Thurston, Sergeant of Co. C 4 Beg't Minnesota Vol's
	died 5 November 1863, age 26 years 6 months 8 days
16	Rhoda Tomson 12 July 1822 - 12 December 1909
14	little Abe, son of J.E. & Mary Turney, died 29 December 1882
	age 3 years
14	Joel E. Turney 1849-1901
09	Amy L. VanDoren 1888-1974
08	Archie T. VanDoren 1862-1953
08	Clara E. VanDoren 1860-1948
17	Isaac VanDoren 6 July 1811 - 13 April 1882
31	Clara C. Vining 1905-1931
34	Vivian Wade 1913-1914
16	Velzora F., wife of J.R. Weaver, died 11 August 1877, age 33 years
27	Albert W. Wild 1900-1965

27	James J. Wild 1898-1992
27	William G. Wild 1887-1979
27	Anna Wilde 1866-1955
27	David W. Wilde 1853-1937
28	Elizabeth Wilde, died 14 July 1900, age 83 years
28	Elizabeth Wilde 1817-1900
28	George Wilde 1801-1890
28	George Wilde 1 April 1801 - 20 May 1890
	age 89 years 4 months 19 days
28	George Wilde Jr. 1860-1883
28	George Wilde Jr. 7 January 1860 - 22 December 1883
	age 23 years 11 months 15 days
28	W.H. Wilde 1850-1881
28	W.H. Wilde 8 December 1849 - 20 May 1881
	age 31 years 5 months 12 days
30	Nancy J. Wilson, nee Mallery 27 May 1850 - 2 June 1940

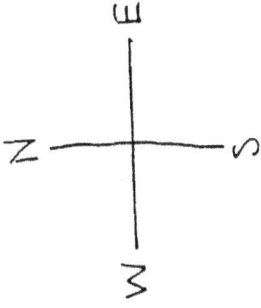

N — E — S — W

Greenwood Cemetery
Eureka Township, Dakota County, Minnesota
T113N-R20W   Section 4

Row 46

Rows 3 — 14

Rows 1 + 2

Rows 15 — 24

Rows 25 — 45

Rows 25 - 45

Drive Area

Gate

Vermillion Presbyterian Church 1856-1977
(this is only a lawn area in 1996)

225th Street or Highway 74A

165

ST. JOHN'S DANISH / FARMINGTON LUTHERAN CHURCH CEMETERY

Eureka township, Dakota county, Minnesota: T113N - R20W, section 14

This cemetery is in great shape. There is no church at this location. At the northern edge of the cemetery there is a sign that states: Farmington Lutheran Church Cemetery and St. John's Danish Lutheran Church 1903. The area is less than half used. I began with row 1 at the western edge.

The Dakota county cemetery records compilation lists this cemetery as: Farmington Lutheran Cemetery (St. John's Danish), established 1903. 2 acres. Located Section 14. 245th Street, West.

Everyone is listed in alphabetical order. The number before each entry is the row number. There is a map at the back of this section.

These burial monuments were transcribed during 1996.

03	Deborah M. Bixby	1955-1966
01	Christian Bjodstrup	1851-1937
01	Margaret Bjodstrup	1862-1941
07	Harold C. Boettcher	1904-1987
07	Rosella A. Boettcher	1909-1994
05	Chris Borup	1868-1937
06	Edna C. Borup	1896-1916
05	Laura Borup	1876-1941
01	Arnold A. Briesacher	1914-1986
01	Lorna M. Briesacher	1911-1961

07	Christine Casper	14 March 1835 - 19 August 1904
07	Holga Laurette Casper	4 February 1871 - 27 August 1891
07	Jens J. Casper	23 August 1846 - 5 July 1924
01	Rose K. Chesness	1936-1990
03	Harold J. Cruthers	1898-1961
03	Lauretta Cruthers	1909-1978

04	Helen A. Davidson	1914-__
04	L. Douglas Davidson	1912-1977
08	Anna (Hall) Dengler	1896-1971
04	Hendrina Doeling	1904-1984
04	Herbert Doeling	1893-1968
02	Ellen Dueholm	1843-1922

03	Anna Elling	1896-1976
04	Pastor Jerrold Elling	15 September 1917 - 1 January 1991
03	John Elling	1887-1968

04	Lyla Elling 26 May 1921 - 23 April 1975
03	Idan N. Elvestad, Cpl. United States Army World War 2 1919-1985
03	Idan N. Elvestad 1919-1985 married Patricia A. 12 April 1951
03	Nicholas James Elvestad, infant son of James & Diane -30 January 1994-
02	Helen C. Flaata 1909-__
02	Sigurd Flaata 1907-1992
03	H. Gehart 1898-1988
04	Ivan L. 'Sarge' Graham 21 April 1941 - 2 June 1992
03	Leonard E. Gustafson 1915-1996
03	Ruth N. Gustafson 1915-1986
08	David Graham Halvorson, EN1 United States Navy Korea 27 May 1932 - 14 September 1993
07	Hannah J. Hansen 1892-1975
07	Harry Hansen 1888-1976
07	Harvey C. Hansen 8 March 1899 - 7 February 1991
07	Mary C. Hansen 1874-1966
07	Rasmus Hansen 1865-1958
02	Clara M. Heath 1887-1970
08	Gary W. Heidmann 21 May 1952 - 8 June 1986
02	Edna A. Hoffman 1917-__
02	Grover H. Hoffman 1909-1986
03	Michael John Houk 21 September 1981 - 6 January 1982
03	Sarah Marie Houk -25 June 1983-
08	Hans N. Hauge (?), died 11 March 1922, age 69 years
09	Timothy Scott Iverson 6 February 1964 - 17 January 1993
06	Mildred R. Jacobson 1911-__ married Samuel J. 11 May 1930
06	Samuel J. Jacobson 1907-1977 married Mildred R. 11 May 1930
03	Emma M. Jennrich 12 May 1901-__
03	Frank Jennerich, United States Army World War 1 1 March 1892 - 10 October 1983
02	Anna S. Jensen 1859-1929
01	Carl Arthur Jensen 1891-1911
01	Carl E. Jensen 1914-1958
05	Dorothea Jensen 1829-1920
02	Hans J. Jensen 1881-1960
02	Harold Jensen 1910-1989
01	Jens P. Jensen, Minnesota Cpl. United States Army World War 2 20 July 1911 - 26 March 1955
02	Jens Jensen 1853-1922
01	Alice E. Johnson 1884-1970
03	Carl J. Johnson 1903-1987

01	Charles F. Johnson 1880-1958
01	Edith Johnson 1907-1988
01	Floyd Johnson 1906-1961
03	Mame B. Johnson 1903-1976
08	Elisuis Jorgensen 1870-1961
02	Lena Jensen 1879-1967
05	Peter Jensen 1829-1910
01	Roy Jensen 1908-1978
01	Thomas Edward Jensen 1896-1921
02	Linda (Swagger) Kreyer 1950-1992
02	Hans Larsen 1840-1913
02	Miss Larson 1834-1911
04	Esther M. Laursen 1924-1990
04	Harold Laursen 1920-__
04	Linda Laursen 1955-1979
06	baby boy Mallery -1960-
04	Eleanor Melson 1917-1985
04	Winfield Melson 1916-1990
07	Hans A. Mickelsen 1897-1981
02	Johanna Mickelsen 26 March 1840 - 3 April 1928
05	John Mickelsen 1882-1939
05	Karen Mickelsen 1877-1949
07	Kjerstine Mickelsen (?) 1865-1943
07	Mikael Mickelsen (?) 1869-1946
07	Olga S. Mickelsen 1900-1968
02	Soren Mickelsen 5 November 1833 - 18 April 1914
01	Donald V. Mickelson 1920-1926
01	baby Lloyd R. Mickelson -1921-
01	Sadie O. Mickelson 1895-1977
01	Soren N. Mickelson 1894-1975
05	Christina Miller 1855-1948
05	Ferdinand Miller 1865-1935
03	Howard C. Miller 1922-__ married Ingeborg 15 November 1947
03	Ingeborg Miller 1922-1995 married Howard C. 15 November 1947
03	Adella C. Nelson 1895-1979
05	Henry Nelson 1857-1916
05	Mary Nelson 1860-1946
06	Carl H. Nielsen 1913-1987
04	Chris Nielsen 1889-1953
04	Ellen Nielsen 1891-1990
06	Mildred R. Nielsen 1915-1984
01	Judith A. Noorlun 13 May 1946 - 30 October 1990

05	Jennifer Rae Olexa 30 March 1990 - 9 August 1994
03	Michelle Marie Olson 1968-1983
03	Duane Parker 1925-__
03	Jacob Parker (?) -25 October 1984-
03	Lucille Parker 1929-1979
03	Gladys A. Partlow 1931-1932
03	Lillian E. Partlow 29 December 1903 - 18 January 1990
03	Wallace V. Partlow 21 July 1902 - 8 July 1987
09	Minnie Pearson 1908-__
09	Norman W. Pearson 1896-1969
05	Alta Pedersen 1900-1976
05	Archie Pedersen 1898-1964
06	Delores E. Pedersen 1932-1989
05	Elisa Pedersen (?) 1867-1947
06	Florence Pedersen (?) 1892-1921
06	Josephine Pedersen (?) 1882-1972
05	Martha Pedersen 1904-__
05	Michael Pedersen -25 December 1961-
06	Richard Pedersen (?) 1887-1947
05	Robert Pedersen (?) 1857-1933
05	Stanley Pedersen 1894-1959
05	Thora Pedersen (?) 1889-1982
03	baby girl Perry -24 May 1956-
03	Marjorie Perry 1927-1992, married Roland 8 May 1947
03	Roland Perry 1921-1990, married Marjorie 8 May 1947
06	Carrie N. Petersen 1877-1915
06	Nels Petersen 1868-1958
07	Raymond N. Petersen 1900-1918
05	Elizabeth Kristine Peterson 8 April - 19 April 1983
09	Erik Peterson (?) -1992-
05	'Father' Peterson (?) 1860-1936
09	Hartwic C. Peterson 1908-1995
09	Jared Peterson (?) -1994-
05	Karen K. Peterson 1864-1927
05	'Mother' Peterson (?) 1864-1927
05	Peter Peterson 1860-1936
09	Rosena V. Peterson 1923-__
07	Donley A. Pettis 14 August 1912 - 12 November 1991 married Ruth C. 21 October 1937
07	Ruth C. Pettis, nee Hansen, 13 November 1916 -__ married Donley A. 21 October 1937
05	David J. Pilger 26 February 1944 - 20 August 1993
05	Matthew Scott Pilger, infant son of Stephen & Lisa -15 July 1991-
01	Robert L. Pinney 1933-1984

04	Soren Thomas Rasmussen 1878-1963
01	Glen Ronning 1929-1991
04	Carl O. Shirley 1889-1960
04	Gale Shirley 1931-1991 married Pearl 3 April 1954
04	Thilda C. Shirley 1896-1958
07	Clara A. Simonsen, wife of Henry 1897-1985
08	Elizabeth Simonsen (?) 1868-1942
07	Henry C. Simonsen, Sgt. United States Army World War 1 1892-1982
08	Martin C. Simonsen (?) 1862-1950
08	Robert Henry Simonsen, United States Navy 15 February 1930 - 25 January 1995
08	Vern C. Simonsen (?) 1899-1933
04	Lisbeth Sly 1950-1974, married Michael 27 January 1973
04	Michael Sly 1945-1974, married Lisbeth 27 January 1873
03	Henry Snesrud 1901-1981
03	Laurie D. Snesrud 1952-1994, married Duane 26 July 1975
02	Kristina Sorenson 1862-1938
01	Martin A. Sorenson 10 July 1885 - 12 October 1966
01	Nellie M. Sorenson 1900-1942
07	Edna H. Stroud 26 July 1911 - 6 November 1987
07	Ralph W. Stroud, United States Army World War 2 1909-1980
02	Madonna M. Swedin 1 August 1922 - 13 May 1992
01	Annie S. Thompson 1888-1980
01	Edwin T. Thompson 1886-1967
05	Herbert Ryno Thompson (?) 1885-1944
05	Laura E. Thompson (?) 1895-1984
02	Lawrence H. Thompson 1913-1981
02	Myrtle F. Thompson 1920-__
01	Ryno H. Thompson, United States Army World War 2 31 January 1917 - 14 March 1991
01	Sylvester E. Thompson, Minnesota PFC Army Air Forces World War 2 30 March 1915 - 20 December 1973
06	Hans M. Topp (?) 1909-1986
06	Laura C. Topp (?) 1918-1974
06	Richard L. Topp 1950-1965
06	Yvonne E. Topp (?) 1927-1981
09	'Father' Transburg 20 November 1968 - 25 April 1944
09	Foster Transburg 1913-1968
07	Inez L. Transburg 15 April 1905-__ married Peter V. 26 June 1934
09	Marion Transburg 1912-1993
09	'Mother' Transburg 10 October 1872 - 28 April 1927
09	P. David Transburg 26 January 1947 - 8 July 1981
09	Paul G. Transburg 9 May 1911 - 22 October 1971

07   Peter V. Transburg 28 October 1907 - 26 February 1994
                married Inez L. 26 June 1934

06   baby son Frederick Joseph VanCura -14 May 1972-
04   Carl Vang 1863-1943

01   Martin J. Walsh 1909-1957
01   Pearl V. Walsh 1915-1987
02   Anna U. Wiese 1888-1960
03   Beverly J. Wiese 1926-__
03   Ella M.C. Wiese 1918-1982
03   Norman E. Wiese 1921-1985
03   Ralph H. Wiese 1914-1980
02   William Wiese 1882-1961
04   Clarice A. Wiggins 1920-1991
04   Gerald W. Wiggins 1917-1969
02   Bernice P. Witter 1923-__
02   Harold H. Witter 1923-1995
02   Harold H. Witter, United States Navy
                18 September 1923 - 4 October 1995

There was one burial stone in row 9 that only stated 'Unknown'

_ _ _ _ _ _ _ _

Drive Area

_ _ _ _ _ _ _ _

Farmington Lutheran Church Cemetery
St. John's Danish Lutheran Church 1903
Eureka Township, Dakota County T113N - R20W
Section 14

_ _ _ _ _ _ _ _

Drive Area

_ _ _ _ _ _ _ _

Row 9

Row 8

Row 7

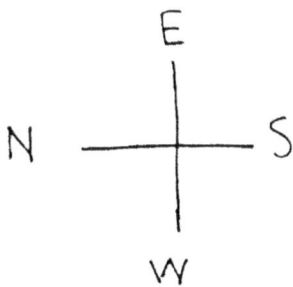

Row 6

Row 5

Row 4

Drive Area

_ _ _ _ _ _ _ _

Row 3

Row 2

Row 1 [173]

245th Street West

Gate

Gate

Gate

Eureka township, Dakota county, Minnesota: T113N - R20W, section 21

I was not able to locate the burial places that were listed by Rev. Neill in "History of Dakota County and the city of Hastings" (page 379). The 1874 Andreas Atlas of Minnesota, Dakota county, Eureka township, section 21 does show this cemetery. As I looked over the maps this stretch of road has changed. I regret that I was not able to determine what if anything exists of this old burial place.

Another bit of information that may be useful to future searchers is the old locations of the Christiana Post Offices. In "History of Dakota and Goodhue Counties", by Franklyn, written in 1910, he wrote the following about the postoffices: Christiana Post-office was established in 1859 at the house of Dominick Moes, section 19, with Magnus Sampson as postmaster, and Dominick Moes as deputy. In 1861 Mr. Sampson enlisted in the Army, when Silas C. Schofield was appointed postmaster in his stead, and the office was moved to his residence, where it remained fourteen years, when he resigned and Albert G. Oleson was appointed his successor. He removed the office to section 21, and opened a small store of general provisions, which he kept until 1879. The office was discontinued many years ago (page 416).

HIGHVIEW CHRISTIANIA

Eureka township, Dakota county, Minnesota: T113N - R20W, section 28

This cemetery is upkept and in good shape. There is a church at this location. It appears that the church is still in use. The name is Highview Christiania - ELCA.

When I numbered the rows for this cemetery I divided the cemetery in two parts. The divider is an old drive area. I began with row 1 in the north-west corner. The second section begins with row 21 in the south - east corner. The burial stones show some indication of patronymic naming.

The Dakota county cemetery records compilation lists this cemetery as: Christiania Free Church (Highview) Cemetery, established 1865. 2 acres. Section 28, SW 1/4. Highway 84.

In "History of Dakota and Goodhue Counties", by Franklyn, written in 1910, he wrote: ... Christiana Church. This church, which is officially known as the Norwegian-Danish Evangelical Lutheran church in Christiana settlement, was formally organized 28 March 1860, although it had been in existence before that time. (page 640).

Everyone is in alphabetical order. The number before each entry is the row number. There is a map at the back of this section.

These burial monuments were transcribed during 1996.

12	John N. Abrehamson 15 June 1827 - 2 May 1876
14	Alf, child of Torbjorn & Margit Alfson
	16 June 1867 - 1 November 1867
14	Aslak, child of Torbjorn & Margit Alfson
	17 April 186? - 2 July 1867
13	Sharon L. Alich 1 July 1940 - 21 December 1986
20	Rebekah Jean Almquuist 16 February - 19 February 1971
25	Joseph W. Anfinson 1900-1981
25	Olga M. Anfinson 1906-1984
18	Carl Anton 4 February 1865 - 1 October 1866
18	Carl Anton 8 January 1861 - 12 August 1863
18	Johannes Anton (?) 17 June 1874 - 14 December 1874
18	Karl Anton, died 12 May 1862, age 2 years (?) ? months 4 days
18	Karl Anton, died 1 October 1866 -rest is buried to deep to read
09	Anne Syverine Andersen 1855-1919
25	Adeline P. Anderson 1914-__
12	Adolph Anderson 1895-1963
09	Andrew Anderson 1851-1922
12	Andrew (?) Anderson (?) 8 May 1887 - ?? 1889 -hard to read
16	Arthur H. Anderson 1908-1990

09	Carl A. Anderson 1892-1957
14	Christian Anderson, nee Schjerva 1803-1871
16	Elmer Anderson 1883-1957
16	Evelyn E. Anderson 1912-1964
12	Gertrude M. Anderson 19 April 1910 - 2 June 1987
14	Guri Anderson, nee Eriksdatter 1802-1870
16	Ida Anderson 1885-1976
12	Ida Anderson 1886-1962
11	Johanna (?) Anderson 16 July 186? - 2 October 188? -hard to read
12	Joseph M. Anderson 14 October 1904 - 6 February 1983
12	Julius Anderson 1863-1950
07	Kittel Anderson 1845-1906
12	Maren Anderson 1871-1963
19	Olaus Anderson 1874-1932
19	Ole O. Anderson, died 9 January 1881, age 31 years 3 months
25	Raymond C. Anderson 1915-__
23	Arnold S. Arneson 1859-1938
23	Fred B. Arneson 1887-1976
22	Fred B. Arneson (?) 1887-1976
22	Harold B. Arneson (?)
23	Harold B. Arneson 1919-1962
22	Henry C. Arneson (?) 1880-1914
22	Henry C. Arneson (?) 2 October 1880 - 24 June 1914
22	Lillian H. Arneson (?) 1891-1970
23	Lillian H. Arneson 1891-1970
23	Susanne Arneson 1853-1912
22	only Augenson
25	Adella M. Barsness 1922-1969
09	Sophia Markuson Beam 1887-1968
28	Noel Edward Berg, TEC 4 United States Army World War 2 1918-1979
13	Gida, daughter of Bernt & Berthe Bendson, 24 July 1867 -rest buried
05	John Blocker 1857-1914
17	Mrs. Maren P. Blocker 2 June 1822 - 22 May 1909
05	Mina Blocker 1841-1918
17	Petter P. Blocker 10 February 1830 - 6 June 1916
18	Gordon H. Blohm 1914-__ married Myrtle A. 7 July 1941
18	Myrtle A. Blohm 1916-1990 married Gordon H. 7 July 1941
25	Aino M. Borfleth 26 March 1917-__
25	Leslie E. Bornfleth 1 January 1915 - 7 August 1992
19	Almer C. Borg 1897-1978
18	Aron J. Borg (?) 20 August 1858 - 4 January 1946
20	Arthur Borg 7 October 1891 - 12 October 1891
19	Elvira A. Borg 1894-1989
18	Emma W. Borg (?) 28 August 1858 - 8 June 1946

20	Juline Borg 30 April 1888 - ?? 1890
19	Maria Amanda Borg 1 January 1890 - 2 June 1906
01	Margit Brevig 1884-1910
12	Ole Arthur Bumer 28 July 1883 - 2 April 1901
12	Ole L. Bumer 7 October 1870 - 10 August 1880
13	Nekolai L. Bummer 1836-1908
15	Carl A. Carlson 1885-1964
15	George H. Carlson 20 July 1909 - 6 June 1937
15	Inga M. Carlson 1881-1969
28	A. Luella Christensen 1883-1971
07	Adolph Christensen 4 October 1881 - 15 October 1937
08	Albert Christensen 1857 - 19 July 1903
23	Alice V. Christensen 1887-1964
02	baby boy Christensen -11 June 194?- broken stone
04	Carrie Christensen 1872-1928
07	Christ Christensen (?) 1870-1938
07	Clara Christensen 1 August 1879 - 19 May 1962
28	Dena Christensen 1878-1950
07	Dena Amelia Christensen (?) 1875-1937
04	Dennis Christensen 1943-1991
23	Ella M. Christensen 1895-1976
28	Emma Caroline Christensen 1873-1948
04	Hans Christensen 1872-1954
03	Harry I. Christensen 1898-1972
10	Hogan Christensen 22 April 1824 - 4 October 1909
28	John J. (?) Christensen 1869-1941
04	Joseph Christensen 1910-1961
07	Juditha L. Christensen 1882-1972
07	Lars Christensen 12 August 1841 - 24 May 1905
07	Louisa Christensen 5 April 1842 - 25 March 1923
10	Marie, wife of Hogan Christensen 8 March 1840 - 12 December 1884
28	Marie M. Christensen (?) 13 December 1906 - 20 April 1991
04	Marjorie Christensen 1909-__
28	Monroe Christensen 26 August 1866 - 24 August 1925
03	Myrtle S. Christensen 1905-__
07	Olaf L. Christensen 1872-1961
23	Oscar W. Christensen 1876-1967
23	Peter M. Christensen 1880-1964
28	Sonja M. Christensen (?) 22 April 1940 - 9 October 1954
04	Terrance J. Christensen 1941-1986
28	Walter L. Christensen (?) 30 December 1903 - 13 February 1959
05	Gilbert Christenson 1884-1953
05	Ida Christenson 1879-1926
07	Idan Christenson 1875-1898
07	Olaf A. Christenson 1878-1903

25	Orville G. Christenson, SGT United States Air Force Korea 8 January 1926 - 28 January 1979
07	Maren Christenson 1847-1911
07	Martin Christenson 1849-1912
07	Halvor Christofersen 4 July 1840 - 5 February 1905
14	Maren Segellia Christoffersen 15 December 1816 - 3 September 1883
12	Gulbrand Christofferson 6 July 1823 - 7 November 1900
17	Gunder Christofferson 1832-1911
12	Louise Christofferson 10 March 1827 - 22 December 1914
17	Oline Christofferson 1826-1912
04	Alice M. Danielson 1929-1965
04	Pauline Brinda Danielson 1921-1994
07	Carolina, wife of Hans Davidson 1846-1921
07	baby Davidson (?) -no dates
07	Ernest C. Davidson 16 October 1920 - 28 March 1927
07	Hans Davidson 1848-1935
07	Orlen, son of A. Davidson - no dates
02	Carol Dian -1945-
04	Albert Dierking 1872-1958
04	Julia A. Dierking 1883-1958
21	Berdell H. Doub 1933-1991
22	Reynold Earl 1914-1979
18	Oscar Ellingboe 20 November 1917 - 27 November 1987
18	Veola Ellingboe 1929-__
11	Aase Marie Elstad 19 November 1819 - 20 December 1881
27	Alben S. Elstad 31 July 1906 - 6 May 1911
27	Alice E. Elstad 1899-1963
11	Alma L. Elstad 1919-__
27	Almer Elstad 1886-1962
09	Anna Elstad 1889-1957
27	Anna H. Elstad 1904-1992
11	Bill Elstad 1915-__
05	Edna H. Elstad 4 April 1913 - 5 June 1913
09	Edward Elstad 17 March 1841 - 12 April 1927
27	Elvin Elstad 1891-1973
11	Ingebor Elstad 22 April 1849 - 12 February 1947
11	Kenneth L. Elstad (?) 1913-1947
11	Kenneth L. Elstad 1913-1947
09	Leif H. Elstad 1892-1953
05	Ludwig O. Elstad 1892-1959
09	Maren Christine Elstad (?) 4 June 1854 - 9 April 1894
27	Marget Elstad 1864-1950
11	Martin Elstad 1884-1975
27	Murel W. Elstad 1894-1932

27	Olaf H. Elstad 1861-1934
11	Ole L. Elstad 18 February 1822 - 28 April 1898
05	Olivia J. Elstad 1894-1988
09	Otto E. Elstad 4 June 1883 - 4 November -rest buried to deep to read
27	Owen G. Elstad 1901-1989
27	Roy A. Elstad 1896-1972
11	Thyra M. Elstad 1887-1964
04	Anton Elvestad 1873-1953
05	Hans Martin Elvestad 5 December 1904 - 27 July 1911
04	Mina Elvestad 1880-1957
24	Carl A. Engelke 1916-1982
24	Genevieve Engelke 1917-__
16	Charley J. Erickson (?) 1894-1961
16	Phillip Erickson (?) 1861-1939
16	Ragnild Erickson (?) 1864-1945
25	Corrine J. Flaherty 1936-1980
08	John Forss 25 December 1840 - 19 January 1903
08	Betsy E. Forstrom 1853-1938
14	Edward S. Forstrom 1882-1939
14	Edward S. Forstrom 1879-1880
08	Ole Forstrom 1841-1897
14	Thomas Forstrom 1872-1873
05	Emelia Frederickson 1870-1961
03	Ida M. Frederickson 1896-1976
04	Margaret K. Frederickson 1900-1959
03	Martin Frederickson 1892-1974
05	Nels L. Frederickson 1860-1947
04	Ralph Loyal Frederickson, Minnesota PFC 8 Cav. Div. (Inf.) Korea PH 13 December 1931 - 6 September 1950
04	William Frederickson 1896-1978
05	Albert Fredrickson 1891-1971
04	Alfred Fredrickson 1887-1951
04	Axel Fredrickson 1894-1984
05	baby of William & Margaret Fredrickson -no dates
04	Carrie Fredrickson 1903-__
04	Clara Fredrickson 1896-1987
05	Dorothy J. Fredrickson 1906-1983
05	Edwin Fredrickson 1901-__
29	Eleanor J. Fredrickson 1914-__
05	'Father' Fredrickson 1863-1923
04	Fred E. Fredrickson 1891-__
03	Gary G. Fredrickson 1939-1961
29	Herman E. Fredrickson 1911-1991
05	Ida Fredrickson 1895-1985
05	Jens Fredrickson 1 April 1905 - 21 January 1919

03	Joseph Fredrickson 1899-1987
03	M. Elizabeth Fredrickson 1914-__
04	Minnie A. Fredrickson 1908-1955
28	Myrtle Fredrickson 1915-1986
04	Nels Fredrickson 1898-1969
03	Oscar E. Fredrickson 1881-1965
03	Otto Fredrickson 1903-1988
04	Russell A. Fredrickson 1925-1955
28	Soren Fredrickson 1906-1981
03	Vionnette M. Fredrickson 1939-1960
04	Debra May Gerardy 1957-1973
09	Alma C. Gilbertson 1894-1964
26	Julia Gilbertson 1899-1993
26	Laura Gilbertson 1896-1913
26	Lavina Gilbertson 1864-1938
26	Lewis Gilbertson 1857-1915
26	Walter Gilbertson 1899-1971
04	Kelly May, infant daughter of Keith & Kim Gilmore -18 October 1981-
29	Cynthia Wester Goodman 1952-1984
06	Conrad Grabe 1913-1918
06	Ellen Grabe 1889-1951
07	Elden Greger 24 July 1934 - 14 August 1992
07	Judith M. Greger 2 July 1936 - 15 May 1973
12	Laura Gulbrandsen 9 November 1867 - 11 January 1887
16	Anne Gunderson (?) 1865-1934
16	Emil Gunderson (?) 1864-1931
17	Olaf J. Gunderson 19 September 1884 - 14 January 1959
17	Paul J. Gunderson 10 March 1888 - 22 May 1969
14	Heidi Soberg Guerand (?) 1950-1990
24	Olaf W. Hallerud, Capt. United States Air Force
	9 April 1953 - 30 March 1989
29	Amy E. Halling 1896-1988 married Melford A. 31 July 1917
29	Melford A. Halling 1893-1993 married Amy E. 31 July 1917
06	Olaus O. Halling 1861-1947
06	Sophia Halling 1862-1938
09	Gilbert Halvorsen 1839-1919
09	Regine Halvorsen 16 September 1842 - 2 June 1898
11	John Halvorson, died 6 March 1896, age 60 years
09	Clara Hansen 18 June 1869 - 29 June 1890
09	Emma L. Hansen 22 April 1872 - 6 February 1889
24	Evelyn Hansen 1903-1984
10	Ana Sofie Hauge, born Tolstrup 10 March 1854 - 9 April 1886
10	Nels Hendricksen 1833-1895
12	Albert Hendriskson 1872-1950

13	Lovisa Hendrickson 1835-1914
10	Marthe Henriksen, born Davidson April 1810 - 31 January 1886
09	Theodora Hermandsen 29 November 1875 - 7 July 1890
28	Anne Maria Hermanson 6 February 1835 - rest is buried
28	Ole Hermanson 17 June 1834 - 4 April 1918
27	James A. Heuton 1940-1984
	'President Computer Video Productions, Inc.'
20	Kurt Thomas Hlady 24 May 1971 - 25 November 1973
20	Lorensie Hoffard 1887-1967
23	Charles Hottran 1862-1943
23	Ida Hottran 1865-1961
11	Anton ? Hulberg 29 May 1864 (?) - 6 January 1887 (?)
20	Charles Hulberg 4 February 1853 - 28 November 1922
20	Clarence Elmer Hulberg 16 October 1881 - 29 December 1902
14	Effie Selma Hulberg 8 July 1887 - 6 August 1887
11	Ida M. Hulberg 3 June 1874 - 28 June 1903
20	Martha Hulberg 6 January 1856 - 26 May 1906
08	Iver Iverson 24 January 1849 - 4 July 1933
09	Julia Iverson -no dates
09	Ole Iverson -no dates
08	Olia Iverson 10 September 1847 - 25 January 1930
19	Albert Johnson 1862-1915
19	Amanda Johnson 1875-1956
10	Anton Johnson 1873-1919
09	Bertha Marie, wife of R.L. Johnson 23 June 1854 - 30 September 1898
02	C. Emil Johnson 1866-1956
08	Caroline Johnson 1846-1932
24	Clarence O. Johnson (?) 1898-1979
20	E. Louise Johnson 1902-1973
22	Edan L. Johnson (?) 1887-1957
24	Gerhard J. Johnson (?) 1895-1988
22	Halvor L. Johnson (?) 1854-1932
25	Harry F. Johnson 1903-__
22	Helmer Emil Johnson, Minnesota Pvt. Co. D 54 Pioneer Inf. World War 1
	15 May 1893 - 13 September 1954
25	Ida O. Johnson 1905-__
17	Ingebor Johnson 24 October 1809 - 12 May 1860
22	Ingor Johnson (?) 1869-1949
10	Jane L. Johnson (?) 1854-1940
11	John A. Johnson 8 May 1870 - 11 February 1887
04	John A. Johnson 1903-1956
11	John L. Johnson 21 June 1843 - 8 June 1892
10	John L. Johnson (?) 1843-1892
11	Josef Johnson 28 February 1889 - 1 March 1889

10	Joseph Johnson (?) 1889-1889
19	Knute L. Johnson (?) 1854-1935
17	Lars Johnson 1807 - 6 November 1894
19	Lizzie Peterson, wife of John Johnson, died 8 May 1893
	age 61 years 3 months 2 days
22	Lloyd R. Johnson 1904-1969
24	Ludwig T. Johnson (?) 1889-1977
11	Luella Johnson 1879-1922
10	Luella Johnson (?) 1879-1922
19	Margit Johnson (?) 1862-1946
24	Nedvin Johnson (?) 1891-1978
08	Ole L. Johnson 1840-1899
09	Ole L. Johnson 6 January 1810 - 13 January 1899
09	Oley Johnson 1887-1903
09	Rolley L. Johnson 16 September 1850 - 5 March 1918
18	Allack Juvland 1858-1894
18	Aslak Juvland 1865-1946
18	Aslaug Juvland 1859-1866
04	baby boy Juvland -1928-
04	Carl Juvland (?) 1862-1946
18	Dorthia Juvland 1825-1900
04	Julia Juvland (?) 1877-1934
04	Linda Juvland 1945-1956
05	Loyal C. Juvland (?) 1906-1924
04	Marie E. Juvland (?) 1903-1930
18	Torger Juvland 1825-1907
07	Anne C. Kapaasen 5 June 1843 - 1 September 1906
10	Anne Marie Kapaasen 13 May 1829 - 3 ? June (?) 1884
07	Carl Kapaasen 1866-1940
07	Olava Kapaasen 1878-1978
07	Ingeborg Kaposen 1862-1929
10	John O. Kaposen 23 April 1830 - 20 September 1909
07	Ole Kaposen 1855-1911
14	Juline R. Kilen 1874-1952
19	Ambjor Knudtson, daughter of Juel & Inga Knudtson
	25 July 1851 - 1 November 1863
19	Mrs. Inga Knudtson, born Tideman Skrovigen
	6 April 1820 - 9 March 1893
17	Knudt Juel Knudtson, died 10 February 1912, age 58 years
10	Caroline 'Kari' Knudsen 18 August 1835 - 19 November 1919
17	Elias Knutsen 1876-1946
24	Genevieve L. Knutsen 1915-__
17	Hazel T. Knutsen 1907-1910
17	Mathilda Knutsen 1880-1967
24	Melford O. Knutsen 1916-__

15	Caroline E. Knutson 1918-1979
15	Charles J. Knutson 1941-1943
15	Milton S. Knutson 1910-1982
03	Anna S. Kopperud 1887-1968
03	Emil G. Kopperud 1884-1963
19	Juel Knudtson Kvale 10 December 1815 - 11 March 1889
10	Andrew Larson 1865-1948
26	Carl S., son of S. & C. Larson 16 April 1867 - 24 June 1914
19	Gunild Larson 4 May 1838 - 29 January 1915
19	Ingeborg Larson (?) 16 April 1867 - 20 December 1885
06	John Ed. Larson 1873-1949
26	John O. Larson 1862-1943
06	Laura C. Larson 1881-1910
19	Sigur Larson 11 September 1831 - 22 November 1892
15	Lars Leidal 1876-1896
16	Agnes I. Leidner 1915-__
16	Carl G. Leidner Sr. 1910-1955
15	Katherine A. Leidner 1909-1937
15	Marie Leidner 1885-1945
15	Otto E. Leidner 1880-1961
12	Sylvina Sundal Leske 1902-1975
11	Carl T. Lillemo 7 February 1877 - 12 March 1883
11	Hanna T. Lillemo 29 October 1878 - 17 February 1883
11	Ida T. Lillemo 29 December 1878 - 10 (?) March (?) 1883
11	Tilda T. Lillemo 1 February 1880 - 3 March 1883
23	Daniel M. Lucy, United States Army, 1938-1995
05	Charles A. Lundgren 1830-1916
05	Amelia M. McDonald 23 February 1906 - 24 April 1974
24	David Roy Madson 1953-1995
24	Nathaniel Madson, son of Renee & David 1979-1984
24	Renee B. Madson, wife of David 1957-1984
12	Albert Markisen -no dates
12	Christen Markisen -no dates
10	Carl Markuson 1857-1929
18	Chris Markuson 1884-1965
03	Hogan I. Markuson 1909-1988
09	Ingebor Markuson (?) 1856-1934
10	Isabel Markuson (?) 1912-1929
03	Martin A. Markuson 1921-1973
09	Martin C. Markuson (?) 1855-1929
18	Mary A. Markuson 1892-1936
10	Ragna Markuson 1885-1972
28	Ruth Martin 1893-1983
07	Hans C. Mattson 14 September 1875 - 29 December 1929

24	Alice Miller 1913-1983
24	William Miller 1910-1976
12	Augusta Mohn 3 May 1844 - 8 February 1936
05	Ella Mohn 29 September 1864 - 25 May 1926
16	Gladys E. Mohn 1924-__ married Wallace R. 1 November 1919
16	Hannah O. Mohn 1885-1945
07	Lars Mohn 20 April 1830 - 8 March 1906
05	Olaf Mohn 29 August 1865 - 30 August 1929
12	Ole Mohn 19 October 1834 - 16 December 1923
07	Olina Mohn 15 September 1832 - 20 December 1912
16	Oscar B. Mohn 1884-1953
16	Wallace R. Mohn 1919-1990 married Gladys E. 1 November 1946
06	Hanna Moller 1856-1931
06	Mons Moller 1846-1927
17	David Gene Myers 21 April 1961 - 23 November 1994
03	Helga A. Nelsen 1883-1957
02	Helga A. Nelsen 1883-1958
03	Hilmar N. Nelsen 1904-1985
03	Nels N. Nelsen 1909-1991
03	Palmer H. Nelsen, United States Navy World War 2
	25 June 1918 - 8 October 1994
02	Peter C. Nelsen 1882-1962
03	Petter C. Nelsen 1882-1962
11	Anton, son of H. & C. Nelson, died 1 May 1889, age 10 years
11	Hans Nelson, died 15 October 1895, age 43 years
04	Anton Nygaard 1890-1948
15	Edward, child of T. & R. Oleson, died 11 August 1872
	age 11 years (?) 17 days -hard to read
15	Marett (?), child of T. & R. Oleson, died ?? 1867 (?) -hard to read
12	Anton, child of K. (?) & ? Gustave (?) Olsen (?) -hard to read
12	Bertha, child of K. (?) & ? Gustave (?) Olsen (?) -hard to read
10	Pastor Nils Olsen 5 May 1815 - 14 October 1884
	age 69 years 5 months 9 days
10	Sarah Olsen 15 October 1810 - 4 May 1895
	age 84 years 7 months 11 days
12	Sybal, child of K. (?) & ? Gustave (?) Olsen (?) -hard to read
14	Albert C. Olson 1838-1918
12	Alfred Walter Olson 20 April 1889 - 24 April 1889
14	Anna C. Olson 1850-1928
12	Berte C. Olson 24 September 1819 - 19 June 1891
14	Clara A. Olson 4 July 1887 - 4 November 1887
14	Clara Mabel Olson (?), child of Mr. & Mrs. Warren I. Olson
	13 January (?) 1884 - 23 February 1884
06	Elizabeth Olson 1855-1918

07	Ellen Olson (?) 25 January 1861 - 2 November 1913
14	Emma S. Olson (Halling ?) 29 September 1876 - 4 December 1877
14	Gerhard E. Olson 1883-1929
11	Gilman Olson 1846-1926
12	Hans C. Olson 15 September 1821 - 16 April 1889
14	Helga Olson, born Juvland 5 January 1832 - 20 November 1874
08	Ida Duella Olson (?) 24 December 1888 - 3 September 1895
15	Johan David Olson 22 November 1860 - 3 July 1890
08	Joseph Olson (?) 13 March 1882 - 19 October 1895
14	Lota (?) Stella (?) Olson (?), child of Mr. & Mrs. Warren I. Olson
	11 June 1885 - 4 August 1885
03	Louis R. Olson 1916-1991
12	Maria Olson 1857-1927
12	Martin Olson 1845-1904
06	Ole Olson 1857-1915
07	Oscar J. Olson 1885-1972
14	Peder E. Olson (Halling ?) 14 July 1878 - 13 December 1873
06	Raghnild Kathrine Olson 22 March 1846 - 9 June 1911
03	Sadie E. Olson 1916-__
15	Steen Olson 20 March 1823 - 16 March 1901
13	W.I. Olson 1849-1901
03	Warren Levi Olson 1940-1994
15	Ingeborg T. Omnen 4 May 1852 - 8 April 1887
	age 34 years 11 months 4 days (?)
15	Carl T. Omnes, died 10 May 1871
	age 17 years 7 months 8 days -hard to read
15	Clara T. Omnes 2 January 1838 (?) - 13 May (?) 1878
15	Halvor T. Omnes, died 29 June 1871
	age 73 years 7 months 19 days -hard to read
15	Kari T. Omnes 12 march 1815 - 12 October 1882
	age 67 years 7 months
15	Hans T. Omnes, died 21 October 1874
	age 26 years 7 months 13 days - hard to read
11	Emma Osmundson 1882-1904
03	Helen Borg Oswaldson 1860-1932
17	Joahnnes Oswaldson - no dates
08	John Oswaldson 25 November 1824 - 2 April 1899
07	John J. Oswaldson 1856-1927
07	Knudt Oswaldson 1862-1902
08	Liv Oswaldson 3 June 1826 - 10 June 1909
07	Mary Oswaldson 1869-1926
07	Oswald Oswaldson 1852-1926
10	Tosten Knudsen Ovale 10 November 1823 - 9 May 1884
03	Olaf C. Overby 1885-1965
16	Rev. Ludvig Pedersen 1874-1938

16	Maria A. Pedersen 1880-1968
13	Anna, child of Nickolai & Olava Pederson
	28 November 1864 (?) - 20 September 1879
05	Carl Pederson (?) 1869-1951
18	Eline Pederson 1865-1882
06	Jens Pederson 1867-1950
05	Lina Pederson (?) 1872-1923
13	Lydia P., child of Nickolai & Oliva Pederson
	27 October 1877 - 26 September 1879
06	Nickoli Pederson 1840-1933
06	Olave Pederson 1841-1925
27	Dewey V. Petersen 1898-1977
27	Edna C. Petersen 1898-1992
15	Annie Peterson 1856-1944
21	Arden L. Peterson, Pvt. United States Army World War 2
	27 March 1923 - 10 April 1994
15	Christ Peterson 1860-1954
06	Christina Peterson 1889-1958
06	Eddie Peterson 1884-1971
15	Oscar Peterson 1894-1985
24	Peter J. Peterson 1905-1989
06	Raymond L. Peterson 1912-1989
04	Sophia Peterson 1872-1932
24	Thilda J. Peterson 1897-1980
04	Patrick Todd Poulton 1966-1993
26	Martin Qualey (?) 1896-1951
26	R.K. Qualey 1860-1953
26	Dolores M. 'Dody' Quinnell (?) 1922-1993
26	Leif N. Quinnell 1897-1979
26	Leroy S. Quinnell (?) 1917-1957
26	Marjorie O. Quinnell 30 March 1919 - 10 January 1931
26	Robert Wayne Quinnell 19 October 1927 - 15 June 1984
26	Richard L. Quinnell 1932-1980
26	Ruth A. Quinnell 1898-1983
14	Ane Kjerstine Rasmussen 9 April 1849 - 15 January 1930
13	Peter Rasmussen 1880-1948
14	Soren Rasmussen 12 May 1845 - 2 March 1934
12	Anna H. Roscoe, born in Danmark
	12 December 1871 - 4 October 1880
12	Hans P. Roscoe, born in Danmark
	11 December 1827 - 23 April 1882
12	Martin Roscoe 1860-1942
29	Delbert R. Rose 1898-1988
29	Joan Harriet Rose 11 June 1934 - 27 October 1986

29	Mary T. Rose 1907-__
24	Clara Roseland 1895-1957
04	Emma Roseland 1886-1983
04	Engel Roseland 1885-1977
24	Knute Roseland 1893-1986
14	Adolph B. Rue -1871- ,died 7 months old
14	Adolph J. Rue 1877-1886
14	Cornelia Ruh 1879-1903
18	Edwin P. Ruh 1867-1938
18	Ida C. Forstrom, wife of Edwin P. Ruh 1877-1905
14	Marith Ruh 1846-1914
14	Ole Ruh 1837-1926
19	Annie L. Sandness (?) 1895-1970
20	Clara Johnson Sandness 1901-1922
19	Joseph C. Sandness (?) 1895-1950
25	Donald Winston Schonning 1935-1989
25	Milton N. Schonning 1904-__
25	Rose F. Schonning 1907-1991
04	Knut Sekse 1888-1926
05	Oscar C. Sharwold 7 November 1884 - 3 May 1916
03	Dora Sherwold 1892-1980
03	Gertrude Sherwold 1898-1978
05	Hannah Sherwold 7 November 1854 - 9 July 1936
05	Knute K. Sherwold 25 February 1850 - 2 March 1927
09	Albert Shirley 4 August 1840 - 4 January 1921
08	Clara Shirley (?) 1882-1892
09	'Father' Shirley (?) 1834-1919
17	Joseph O. Shirley 1892-1982
09	'Mother' Shirley (?) 1837-1919
09	Nels A. Shirley 1885-1922
09	Ole O. Shirley (?) 1840-1922
09	Oscar Shirley 1879-1945
09	Thea N. Shirley (?) 1848-1932
14	John Herbert Sjoeberg 1 August (?) 1871 - ??? 1873 (?)
08	Halvor O. Sjolie 1835-1898
13	Pernille, wife of (?) ? Bersek (?) Syversen Sjolie
	died 17 ?? 1877 (?), age 51 years (?)
10	Johannes J. Skofstad 10 June 1824 (?) - 21 March (?) 1885
04	Josephine Caroline Skofstad 1869-1919
18	Marthe J. Skogstad (?) 1808 (?) - 8 January (?) 1863
23	Van C. Smith 1904-1977
13	Alice M. Soberg 1899-1987
13	George Soberg 1897-1968
14	Gladys M. Soberg 1923-__
13	Irving C. Soberg 15 August 1928 - 18 August 1929

13	Judith A. Soberg 28 June 1899 - 2 February 1991
13	Oline Soberg 1854-1941
14	Orlan E. Soberg 1927-1978
13	Palmer O. Soberg, Minnesota Sgt. United States Army World War 1 26 May 1892 - 6 July 1954
13	Paul J. Soberg 3 November 1890 - 9 March 1891
13	Peter Soberg 1848-1930
07	'Father' Sommervold (?) 1844-1913
18	Albert Sorenson 1845-1905
18	baby Sorenson -25 May 1939-
18	Marie B. Sorenson 1855-1930
18	Melvin C. Sorenson 1898-1980
18	Myrtle E. Sorenson 1910-__
15	Emelia Sorum 1843-1914
15	Ole E. Sorum 1855-1934
15	Bertha M. Steen (?) 1878-1952
29	Gertrude E. Steen 1935-1966
15	Guro Olson Steen 16 January 1831 - 5 March 1917
15	Lars W. Steen (?) 1863-1951
29	Sylvester O. Steen 1903-1970
29	Thilda Steen 1902-1989
05	Arthur Sigfred Stenerson 1907-1909
06	Edwin Oliver Stenerson (?) 7 September 1886 - 13 January 1904
05	'Father' Stenerson (?) 1863-1925
06	Maria Stenerson (?) 4 December 1852 - 8 May 1922
06	Oluf Stenerson (?) 26 August 1849 - 2 May 1925
05	Signe Stenerson (?) 1873-1920
08	Albertine Stevens, born Gulbrandsen 2 February 1837 - 7 February 1899
22	Edith June Stevens 1906-1962
08	Gilbert Stevens 1847-1907
16	Gustava Stevens (?) 1864-1952
08	Henrietta M. Richter Stevens 1908-1951
08	John Stevens 10 April 1839 - 15 January 1911
04	John Stevens - no dates
04	Joseph Stevens -no dates
07	Kari Stevens 1842-1926
08	Lena Stevens 1857-1939
07	Mattis Stevens 1814-1902
03	Melvin Stevens 1887-1962
16	Otto B. Stevens (?) 1860-1941
10	Embret Strate 1825-1905
10	Helvik Strate 1825-1904
10	Ole Strate 1855-1907
06	Anna Stratte 1886-1995
08	Marie H. Strand 1840-1928

08	Ole H. Strand 10 December 1838 - 29 September 1903
10	Hans Amundson Stuhoug 15 January 1804 - 20 January 1890
28	Fred A. Swedin 1910-1986
28	Lois C. Swedin 1915-1982
16	Lillie Ericson Swedine 1889-1986
14	Peter Swedine (?) 19 August 1822 - 6 April 1890
27	Carl C. Swenson 1907-1980
27	Evelyn M. Swenson 1910-__
10	Bertha Thompson (?) 1864-1935
10	Hadley Thompson (?) 1860-1933
18	Ingri G. Egge, wife of K. Thompson 1820-1863
08	Knudt Thompson 1822-1896
25	Lucille K. Thompson 1916-__
19	Mary Thompson 1849-1910
19	Ole Thompson 1861-1942
25	Ralph O. Thompson 1900-1987
25	Roger A. Thompson 1912-1984
14	Scneva K. Thompson 1819-1887
14	Thomas Thompson 1859-1872
14	Thomas K. Thompson 1851-1872
19	Belsey Thoreson 1825-1916
10	Carl Thoreson 1866-1944
10	Engebor Thoreson, nee Schjerva 1829-1912
11	Ingebor, wife of Stephen Thoreson
	16 January 1829 - 3 April 1912
19	Lena Thoreson 1872-1948
16	Margit Thoreson (Halling ?), died 18 November 1874, age 68 years
19	Ole Thoreson 1827-1913
16	Ole Thoreson (Halling ?), died 10 October 1866, age 68 years
19	Stephannus Thoreson 1868-1944
10	Stephen Thoreson 1830-1882
11	Stephen Thoreson 16 ?? 1830 - 22 September 1882
12	Petra Soberg Thorstensen 21 March 1884 - 11 April 1970
05	Andrew Gilbert Tonsager 1856-1939
05	Anna Bertha Tonsager 1871-1910
20	baby Raymond Tonsager -3 days 1927-
20	Frances Tonsager 1909-1995
10	Gustav Tonsager (?) 1894-1895
20	Luella Tonsager 1899-1927
20	Martin Tonsager 1899-1982
10	Ole Hendriksen Tonsager 21 July 1826 (?) - 6 June 1884 (?)
10	Paul Tonsager (?) 1840 - 1882
15	Annie Torbenson 1870-1938
15	Thomas Torbenson 1855-1924
28	James H. Tornio 1867-1981

28	Virgil L. Tornio 1934-1981
06	Christe Twedt 1850-1930
07	Christi Twedt 1850-1930
06	Enoch Olai Twedt 22 October 1890 - 2 April 1914
07	Hannah Twedt 1892-1969
07	Leander Twedt 1886-1975
06	Ole Twedt 1845-1903
07	Ole O. Twedt 1845-1903
11	Ole Olson Twedt 1812-1882
07	Adolph Twidt 1883-1927
07	Anna J. Twidt 1889-1935
09	Benny Ustad 28 June 1895 - 21 January 1896
09	Mrs. M. Ustad 14 December 1870 - 5 September 1895
29	Henry C. Wall 28 March 1913 - 26 September 1988
29	Margaret G. Wall 11 August 1915 - 28 August 1986
13	Cheryl Soberg Wesley 1946-1974
29	Bernice D. Wester 1925-__
29	Martin D. Wester 1922-__
06	Helga Wold 1887-1968
06	Palmer Wold 1898-1945
15	Edward, son of E. & H. Yahr 26 April 1888 - 25 August 1888
15	Hilda, wife of Emil Yahr 19 October 1860 - 14 August 1888

The following did not have a surname or I was unable to decipher what the surname was.

18	?, died 17 September 1867 (?), after 8 months (?) - hard to read
26	Alf 1892-1962 -no surname
17	?, Dovland (?), born 27 March 1858 - 20 May 1894 -hard to read
12	Josep W., 4 November 1873 - 11 November 1875
	-no surname and the stone was broken
12	Josep, 3 February 1876 - 18 July 1876
	-no surname and the stone was broken
18	Lillie Christina 1892-1924 -no surname
26	Melvin 1893-1952 -no surname

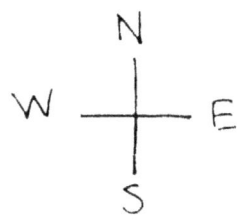

Highview
Christiania - ELCA
Church

Row 20

Row 1

Rows 1-20

Eureka Township
Dakota County
T113N - R20W
Section 28

Parking Lot

N
W —+— E
S

Old Drive area

Highview
enue

Row 29

Row 21

Rows 21-29

County Highway 84

EAST CHRISTIANA LUTHERAN CEMETERY

Eureka township, Dakota county, Minnesota: T113N - R20W, section 29

This cemetery is upkept and in good shape. There is no longer a church near this cemetery. The cemetery is on a slight hill. In the center of this area there are very few remaining headstones. The few that remain are laying flat, at ground level and in poor shape. Most have cracked and are difficult to read. The rest of the cemetery is in good shape. I have numbered the rows beginning with row 1 on the east edge.

The sign states Christiana Lutheran Church 1857-1950. A second sign states: Christiania Lutheran Church 1857-1957. ... In 1856, eight Norwegian immigrant families settled in this community. Later named Christiania. Others followed and in 1857 a congregation was organized. These pioneers built their first church on this site in 1867. This building was dismantled and rebuilt as the West Christiania Church in 1893. At which time a larger church was built here that was destroyed by fire in 1957. A new church to serve as a single unit of worship was dedicated at Eidswold in 1960. This united church may be located two or three miles west of this location, at the corner of Dakota county road 84 and Highway 46, just inside Scott county.

The Dakota county cemetery records compilation list this cemetery as: East Christiana Evangelical Cemetery, established 1866. 3 acres. Located Section 29, SE 1/4 . The 1896 plat map of Dakota county lists this as Norwegian Anglica Lutheran Church and cemetery.

In "History of Dakota and Goodhue Counties", by Franklyn, written in 1910, he wrote: ... Norwegian Synod. Professor Larson, of Decorah, Iowa made a missionary trip to the Norwegian settlement in Eureka in 1857 and effected a partial organization of a church and society which took the name of Christiana Synod Church. Regular ministerial work was begun in 1859 ... A church was erected in 1867 near the east line of section 29, on the south side of the main highway. A minister's house was built in 1879. The church purchased many years ago a farm of eighty acres (page 643).

Everyone is listed in alphabetical order. The number before each entry is the row number. There is a map at the back of this section.

These burial monuments were transcribed during 1996.

17	Aslak Aartveit 1828-1910
17	Engjer Aartveit 1833-1926
02	Olia Albertson (?) 1844-1925
17	Alexander Alexon (?) 1859-1931
04	Emma, wife of John Alexon 26 September 1871 - 11 May 1900
17	Jennie Alexon 1872-1946
17	Juliana Alexon 1877-1919
17	Martin Alexon 1874-1943

17	Rachel Alexon 1866-1936
06	Aslak Alfson 1871-1961
05	Margit Alfson, born Rismyr 1837-1915
06	Orlando M. Alfson 1899-1926
06	Sigurd M. Alfson 1903-1935
06	Sina Alfson 1872-1936
05	Tarbjorn Alfson, died 12 March 1894, age 63 years
18	Charles W. Alme 1885-1964
18	Hannah S. Alme 1886-1966
13	John Alme 1888-1952
16	Joseph O. Amundson 1861-1954
08	Julius A. Andersen 24 April 1880 - ?? 1882 -broken stone
07	Albert Anderson 1875 - 1949
14	Anna Miller Anderson 1887-1925
11	Anna Swedin Anderson 1886-1972
14	Charles F. Anderson 1877-1954
09	Christena Anderson 1884-1977
07	Gustav Anderson 1873-1941
09	Joseph Anderson 1882-1969
07	Julius A. Anderson 1880-1882
18	Leo C. Anderson 21 October 1917 - 1 August 1935
07	Martin K. Anderson, Minnesota MUS 2 C1 United States Army World War 1 22 April 1887 - 21 February 1945
09	Ole Anderson 1870-1953
03	Anfin Anfinson 1827-1906
03	Anna Anfinson 1821-1916
17	Gustave H. Austinson 1894-1929
08	Elmer A. Blocker 1887-1956
08	Gene Blocker 1898-1976
06	Melvin N. Borgen 1858-1977
06	Earl A. Carlson 1 July 1906 - 9 April 1995
01	John M. Chalmers 1923-1978
01	Jurdys T. Chalmers 1924 - __
02	Agnes E. Christensen (?) 1897-1955
02	Chris S. Christensen (?) 1886-1973
09	Ole Christianson 1836 - 30 December 1915
12	Elling Christopherson 1831-1894
12	Else K. Christopherson 1862-1879
12	Gunild M. Christopherson 1860-1879
01	Eileen Moore Clubb 1929-1968
15	Annie Dahl (?) 1880-1939
15	Annie Dahl 26 November 1880 - 14 July 1939
15	Carl Dahl (?) 1876-1912

15	Carl Dahl 27 May 1876 - 27 November 1912
09	Eugene E. Day 1926-1978
09	Rose A. Day 1927-__
08	John A. Eckdahl 1930-1995, married Donna C. 'Penny' 27 January 1951
09	Lizzie Elstad 1896-1949
09	Reuben O. Elstad 1887-1933
15	Maren Moscow Empey
15	Stella May Empey 20 March 1911 - 29 August 1911
15	Lester V. Erickson 1922-1979
03	Annie Evenson 1861-1945 -hard to read
05	Aslak Evenson 18 February 1819 - 9 January 1890
03	Ole Evenson 1852-1934 -hard to read
17	Anders G. Euren 1852-1905
13	Anne T. Euren 1823-1898
13	Gulbrand T. Euren 1821-1879
18	Albert L. Fanno, Pvt. United States Army
	18 November 1894 - 4 June 1974
18	Carl Fanno (?) 1883-1906
18	'Father' Fanno (?) 1858-1943
18	Henry O. Fanno Pvt. United States Army
	15 June 1892 - 20 February 1974
18	Ida Fanno (?) 1889-1910
18	Minnie Fanno (?) 1897-1984
18	'Mother' Fanno (?) 1858-1939
18	Nels Fanno (?) 1885-1937
06	Ida Lena Forstrom August - November 1895
15	Louise K. Fugle (?) 1868-1949
15	Minnie L. Fugle (?) 1900-1925
15	Mons A. Fugle (?) 1861-1925
15	Myrtle L. Fugle (?) 1898-1898
16	Gilbert Gilbertson 1855-1904
06	Clifford R. Groves 1924-1984
06	John Michael Groves 22 August - 27 August 1981
04	Joel W. Haglund 1930-1995, married Lois I. 25 November 1950
04	Lois I. Haglund 1931-__, married Joel W. 25 November 1950
14	Halbert M. Haldorsen 6 November 1866 - 20 May 1895
14	Hulda Malvene Haldorsen 29 September 1893 - 23 June 1896
14	Martin Halbert Haldorsen 18 September 1895 - 11 April 1901
12	?, daughter of Ole & Anne Haldorson
	17 February 1876 - 1 July 1877
18	Andrew Haldorson 12 December 1836 - 20 October 1912
12	Anne Haldorson 30 May 1839 - 24 October 1884

14	Halver Haldorson 16 December 1832 - 11 July 1897
18	Kjersti Haldorson 10 June 1825 - 27 December 1916
14	Mrs. Mary Haldorson 21 August 1835 - 28 February 1913
12	Mathilda Haldorson 14 October 1861 - 28 May 1906
12	Ole Haldorson 12 June 1839 - 12 June 1891
04	Aagaat Hammer 1861-1941
01	Albert Hammer 1902-1967
04	Alma Paulina Hammer 1858-1901
04	Edwin Oliver Hammer 1896-1916
01	Margaret M. Hammer 1905-1983
04	Paul Hammer 1859-1938
05	Carl C. Haug 1864-1939
05	Dina Haug 1862-1942
15	Marget Heiby 1817 - 15 August 1907
11	Ambjor Hougestol 1827-1870
13	Anund Hougestol 1790-1880
11	Ole A. Hougestol 1820-1911
07	Christen Hoffard 1845-1908
07	Ingborg Hoffard 30 April 1848 - 10 November 1886
07	child of Mr. & Mrs. Holland -18 April 1890-
15	Alma Holt 1896-1919
15	Gertrude Holt 1866-1944
06	J. Oliver Holt 19 May 1894 - 23 July 1894
15	Louis Holt 1893-1967
15	Mabel Holt 1906-1927
15	Martin Holt 1862-1933
06	Nels Holt 1830-1910
06	Olianna Holt 1829-1895
15	Vivian Holt 1910-1965
01	Earl G. Hovland 1905-1969
01	Ellen M. Hovland 1906-__
08	Andreas Husevold 1845-1920
08	Johann Quammen, wife of (?) Andreas (?) Husevold (?) 1844-1920
03	Swain Anderson Husevold 1839-1922
13	Bert (?) Johan son of Bjorn & Ingeborg Anundsen (?) Iamsgaard 14 June 1879 - 21 August 1879
17	Guy Iverson 1887-1921
03	Tillie Iverson 1879-1916
16	Anund Jamesgaard 1846-1917
16	Christe Jamesgaard 1849-1899
13	Andreas Jensen 10 June 1823 - 27 June 1877
13	Karen O. B. (?) Jensen 7 May 1822 - 19 ?? 1877
05	Clarence Johnson (?) 1896-1920
08	D.J. Johnson 1840-1909

05	Ernst Johnson (?) 1913-1939
03	Florence E. Johnson 1914-__, married Paul R. 20 April 1940
05	Ingeborg Johnson (?) 1871-1957
07	Johannes L. Johnson 16 August 1857 - 1 May 1888
04	John Michael Johnson 1951-1978
05	Lillian Johnson 1900-1980
05	Ludvick Johnson (?) 1908-1920
08	Marthine Johnson 1846-1923
04	Mary Dolores Johnson 1951-__
05	Maurice Johnson 1900-1978
03	Paul R. Johnson 1900-1978, married Florence 20 April 1940
05	Peter C. Johnson (?) 1872-1956
05	Rupert Johnson (?) 1898-1918
08	Petra Helena Joli, born Listad in Norge 27 November 1829 (?) died 16 September 1872
17	Jorgen Jorgenson (?) 1863-1935
17	Lawrence Jorgenson (?) 1902-1933
17	Mary Jorgenson (?) 1862-1924
08	Rev. A.T. Juvland 1868-1954
16	Agnes M. Kalheim (?) 1890-1919
16	Elizabeth Kalheim 1892-1893
16	Julianna Kalheim 1867-1949
16	Mildred S. Kalheim (?) 1894-1976
16	Nora Kalheim 1895-1896
16	Ole M. Kalheim 1864-1895
05	Agnes T. Kimber (?) 29 June 1901 - 18 February 1986
05	Fred J. Kimber (?) 3 July 1900 - 9 March 1979
06	Vern W. Kimber -25 July 1921-
05	Verna Mae Kimber 16 March 1930 - 11 December 1991
16	Albert Kokkin (?) 7 March 1884 - 15 February 1910
16	Anna Juline Kokkin (?) 20 July 1882 - 1 September 1899
16	Bennie Kokkin (?) 1 September 1879 - 25 December 1980
16	Bertha Marie Kokkin (?) 14 April 1846 - 5 July 1922
16	Ida Bertine Kokkin (?) 25 November 1886 - 5 September 1945
16	John Kokkin (?) 5 July 1836 - 16 October 1908
16	Maria Kokkin (?) 28 June 1874 - 11 June 1893
14	Lars Larson 1851-1920
04	Marie O. Larson 1902-1989
04	Martin O. Larson 1894-1947
10	Thelma K. Larson 1911-1993
06	Ellend Syverson Lee 25 March 1829 - 17 November 1887
06	Julian Severson Lee, died 12 May 1896, age 25 years
09	?, daughter of Halvor D. & Karen Leine 15 November - 20 November 1873

01	Carlton Edgar Leine, M Sgt. United States Army World War 2 1910-1978
04	Emma S. Leine 1877-1962
12	Ole Gorbjornse Leine 16 September 1804 - 28 April 1876
04	Oscar T. Leine 1878-1965
10	?gon (?) 4 July 1860 (?) - 2 September 1869 (?), child of O. & A. Lekne (?) - hard to read
10	Anne (?), child of O. & A. Lekne (?) ?? - 4 August 1865 (?) -hard to read
10	Olaus, child of O. & A. Lekne (?) 23 September 1872 - 5 October 1872 -hard to read
12	Metta, daughter of Ellend & Gunnild Siverson Lie 26 January 1868 - 1 February 1879
18	Anna R. Lillemo (?) 23 September 1837 - 20 June 1925
18	Lena P. Lillemo (?) 13 April 1875 - 16 June 1899
18	Oscar T. Lillemo (?) 30 August 1873 - 22 June 1922
18	Theodore N. Lillemo (?) 10 January 1846 - 23 March 1926
11	Elmo M. Lindberg 1896-1949
18	Hazel Lindham 1909-1923
18	Anton F. Lindhart 1873-1954
18	Sena C. Lindhart 1878-1968
14	Johan O. Lo 1816-1896
14	Marie Lo 1821-1892
14	Olof Peterson Lo 30 January 1859 - 29 October 1904
12	Andrew Loe 1851-1934
12	Anton Loe 1877-1941
15	Birget G. Loe 1837-1905
15	Gulbrand Loe 13 July 1845 - 9 June 1928
12	Hilda M. Loe 1884-1969
14	Iver Loe 1859-1948
15	Julia M. Loe 26 August 1879 - 29 October 1904
12	Theodore Loe 1888-1978
12	Tone Loe 1854-1940
08	Minnie Louise (not sure if this is a surname) 8 March 1888 - 20 December 1888
01	Helmer Markisen 1889-1968
01	Ida L. Markisen 1892-1928
04	Dorothy A. Martin 1921-__
04	Harold E. Martin 1917-1994
03	Albert C. Mattson 1883-1931
07	Clayton Mattson 1916-1989, married Marion 8 September 1943
07	Marion Mattson 1922-__, married Clayton 8 September 1943
14	Christ A. Mayer 28 May 1869 - 25 March 1898
18	Adolph J. Meyer 1898-1937
18	Clara Marie Meyer 1898-1935

16	Gilbert Michael 1904-1984
16	Viola Michael 1908-1995
03	Etta Miller 1881-1955
14	Hugo Miller 1895-1916
14	Ingar Berg Miller 1833-1906
14	Magnus Miller 1868-1946
14	Maria Miller 1868-1930
03	Oscar Miller 1880-1959
14	Pearl Miller 1908-1940
14	Pearl's baby Miller (?) 1929-1929
14	Raymond Miller 1909-1917
13	John J. Mo 1835-1882
13	Signe Olsdtie Mo 1 March 1839 - 14 January 1888
17	Anna M. (Snesrud) Mohn 30 May 1908 - 24 November 1992
17	Florence Luella Mohn 13 August 1906 - 25 December 1906
17	Fredricka Mohn (?) 1878-1956
17	Lauris Mohn (?) 1868-1944
17	Martin C. Mohn 26 August 1904 - 24 January 1988
17	Violet Mohn (?) 1915-1948
15	John J. Moscow 1874-1900
11	Johannes Moskau, died 7 May 1890, age 57 years
11	Serina J. Muskau 12 March 1866 - 27 April 1882
15	John J. Muskaw 1874-1900
15	Karen Muskaw 1825-1899
05	Andreas Nelson 26 February 1827 - 2 June 1892
05	Mary Nelson 1864-1952
05	Sever Nelson 1861-1945
12	Nicolai A. Nielson 29 December 1858 - 19 October 1884
05	Ingebor Nilson 1833-1910
12	Andreas O. Olberg (?) 1841-1918
12	Charlotte Olberg (?) 1864-1949
12	Halbert Osckar, son of Ole & Anne 12 June 1879 - 21 February (?) 1880
07	Anna Olsdater 1 ?? 1811 - 12 ?? 1892
	-with Johannes L. Johnson
11	Martha Olsdtr (Olson ?) 1800 - 13 November 1870
03	Anton Olson 1878-1940
01	Beatrice H. Olson 1909-1991
15	Clara Olson 1900-1988
03	Ellen Olson 1842-1917
11	Haldor Olson 1801 - 16 August 1871
01	Jean Olson 1906-1988
06	Johanna Olson 12 August 1875 - 11 November 1889
01	Lawrence Olson 1905-1972
15	Lewis O. Olson 1901-1983

06	Lisabeth Olson 10 March 1870 - 9 April 1889
03	Ole R. Olson 1877-1935
03	Robert Olson 1842-1929
17	Guro Ostenson 1860-1952
17	Halvor Ostenson 1850-1923
08	Adolph Ostlie 1894-1961
06	Dorothy A. Ostlie 1919-__
06	Harold H. Ostlie 1887-1933
06	James H. Ostlie 1919-1995
06	Lena M. Ostlie 1887-1972
08	Mabel Ostlie 1894-1975
08	Mardell Ostlie 1924-1986
05	Philip J. Ostlie 1953-1984
08	Russell Ostlie 1922-__
13	Knudt K. Ousby 18 January 1823 - 21 January 1876
13	? Holdensdater (?) Ousbye (?) 3 January 1821 - 19 October 1877
	-broken stone and hard to read
18	Bernt K. Ousbye 1850-1927
18	Johannah Ousbye 1876-1916
13	Knute K. Ousbye 1863-1931
13	only Paulson
03	Anna Paulson 29 September 1866 - 15 March 1901
03	Oline Paulson 1836-1912
03	Walter S. Paulson 7 May 1913 - 9 December 1913
15	Evelyn Petersen 1908-1989
15	Henry G. Petersen 1904-1987, married Sylvia M. 16 September 1936
15	Lavonne Petersen -1950-
15	Lavonne Petersen 1950-1950
15	Maurice Petersen 1902-1986
15	Sylvia M. Petersen 1919-__, married Henry G. 16 September 1936
05	Astrid G. Peterson 1923-1994, married Glenn E. 14 October 1948
05	Glenn E. Peterson 1927-__, married Astrid G. 14 October 1948
14	Julia Lo Peterson 25 November 1868 - 18 November 1955
03	Morris C. Peterson 1899-1958
14	Palmer Peterson 17 August 1900 - 28 June 1910
03	Rose A. Peterson 1902-1993
16	Clara M. Quammen (?) 1876-1895
16	Ingeborg L. Quammen (?) 1869-1892
16	Nils A. Quammen 1839-1915
16	Mrs. N.A. Quammen 1840-1920
02	Esther V. Roland 1913-__
02	Leonard D. Roland 1904-1989
03	Leonard L. Roland 1932-1936

01	Leonard O. Roland, F2 United States Navy
	16 August 1904 - 16 February 1989
05	Mabel Roland 1905-1985
05	Margit Roland 15 March 1840 - 28 January 1913
05	Ole O. Roland 14 June 1822 - 13 January 1892
04	Adeline E. Rouland 26 August 1911 - 29 March 1914
04	Agnethe Rouland 25 June 1877 - 11 March 1918
04	Olous O. Rouland 5 June 1867 - 18 November 1919
13	Emma Rozelle 1877-1951
13	Carrie Evenson, wife of P.H. Rue 1808-1879
13	P.H. Rue 1808-1897
04	Juline Ruh 1895-1934
04	Rudolph Ruh 1892-1966
11	Britna M. Sampson 1800 - 19 February 1889
11	Peder Samson 1816 - 22 February 1898
09	Andrew Sanderson 1870-1959
09	baby Sanderson -no dates
08	Belle Sanderson 1885-1984
09	'Mother' Sanderson 1833-1881
08	Ralph L. Sanderson 1914-__
09	Simon Sanderson 1868-1945
09	James Loren Schrepel 13 March 1945 - 24 May 1984
08	Loren C. Schrepel, United States Navy World War 2
	21 May 1909 - 22 June 1988
12	Anna Olson Seren 1855-1950
16	Anna Gilbertson Severson 1856-1934
01	Caroline Shirley 1874-1966
01	Clarence Gilman Shirley 1910-1966
01	Oscar Shirley 1907-1976
12	Eleanor A. Silverness 1924-1993
12	Sever E. Siverson 1857-1921
16	Agnetha Skille 18 January 1877 - 30 April 1925
16	Albert H. Skille 14 September 1860 - 24 January 1938
16	Hildore H. Skille 1907-1975
05	? Johanna S. Skjerdal, died 30 October 1893, age 69 years
	-hard to read
05	Lars Larson Skjerdal, died 24 October 1891, age 93 years
01	Mayme A. Sleette 1903-1987
01	Albert O. Slette 1899-1958
04	Christian O. Slette 1862-1940
04	Laura E. Slette 1890-1918
01	Louis O. Slette 1887-1932
04	Martha S. Slette 1857-1943
04	Martin J. Slette 1896-1915
17	Christiana Sorenson 1852-1912

17	Mary Sorenson 1891-1956
18	Dena Stephens 1885-1949
07	Clarences Sthordahl 6 May 1891 - 13 October 1891
13	Thorsten Thorstenson Sthordahl 18 October 1823 - 17 November 1879
13	Ole O. Storli 1835-1921
04	Anne Storlie 1870-1958
04	Bernice Storlie 1914-1958
05	Chester H. Storlie 1911-1971
05	Helen L. Storlie 1921-__
04	Olaf Storlie 1863-1935
13	Ole Storlie 1856-1880
13	Marget O. Storlie 29 September 1834 - 11 September 1894
04	Roy O. Storlie 1907-1921
17	Albertine Strand (?) 1863-1958
18	Alice Strand (?) 1918-1924
19	Andrew Strand (?) 1865-1933
17	Harold Strand 1892-1979
18	Mildred Strand (?) 1896-1951
05	Segre Amundson Stuhoug 1819-1902
13	Ole Svenson, died 26 April 1880, age 87 years
01	Albert Swedin 1924-__
11	Anna D. Swedin 1916-__
01	Jesse Albert Swedin 29 April 1955 - 30 January 1973
11	Leonard P. Swedin 1903-1979
11	Pete Swedin 25 December 1872 - 12 May 1926
01	Shirley Swedin 1929-1975
09	Sven Swenson 12 June 1860 - 1 July 1940
15	Arne T. Telle 1848-1919
17	Andrew Thompson 1831-1911
18	Barbro Thompson 1838-1897
18	Edward Thompson (?) 1881-1907
03	infant son of Mr. & Mrs. Ingmer Thompson -1949-
05	Inga Thompson 1913-1991
05	Ingmer Thompson 1898-1977
17	Knute A. Thompson 1863-1921
18	Laura Thompson (?) 1866-1896
04	Laura Thompson 1906-1995
03	Norman E. Thompson 1932-1957
18	Peter Thompson 1836-1917, 2nd Minnesota Battery Light Artillery
17	Randi Thompson 1833-__
04	Randi Thompson 1868-1944
18	Thilda M. Thompson (?) 1873-1963
04	Thomas Thompson 1858-1941
04	Walter Thompson 1902-1964

02   Anton Thorson 1868-1939
02   Mary Thorson 1867-1948
15   'Father' Torbenson (?) 1841-1910
15   Johnny Torbenson (?) 1882-1896
15   'Mother' Torbenson (?) 1848-1898
15   Sherman Torbenson (?) 1887-1967
16   Anund Torgerson 9 February 1823 - 19 November 1917
15   Ole Torgerson 1829-1920
14   Ole Torgerson 1829-1920
16   Sigri Torgerson 1 October 1821 - 14 June 1909
10   Knut, child of T. & A. Torgeson 25 December 1862 - 23 May 1867
            -hard to read
10   Svend, child of T. & A. Torgeson 2 June 1867 - 18 March 1871
            -hard to read
07   Anton Tollefson, Minnesota PFC 352 Infantry 88 Division World War 1
            4 October 1893 - 25 December 1951
07   Hage Tveito Tollefson 1860-1929
07   Osmund Tveito Tollefson 1844-1918
09   Bjorn Asmundsen Tveito 27 October 1832 - 12 March 1881

13   Anund Knudsen Vesaas 26 October 1810 - 7 September 1883
16   Olaf A. Vesaas 13 April 1848 - 4 February 1900
16   Knute A. Vessos 1846-1919
04   Alvin L. Vick 1912-1973
04   Evelyn M. Vick 1914-__
05   Lyder B. Vick 1880-1951

06   Andrew H. Weiby 1870-1941
06   Hans Weiby 1830-1900
18   Johan Weiby 19 October 1858 - 17 December 1937
18   Maren Weiby 20 January 1851 - 24 July 1922
06   Pauline Weiby 1836-1901
16   Agnes Cornelia Wessos (?) 1892-1899
16   Christopher Wessos (?) 1890-1901
16   Clara Olga Wessos (?) 1894-1895
16   Halvor A. Wessos (?) no date - 1899
16   Henry Newell Wessos (?) 1898-1899
16   Nettie Wessos (?) 1856-1930
16   Tina Etta Wessos (?) 1880-1900
04   Emma M. Wick 1887-1976
04   Victor C. Wick 1887-1978

I was not able to determine a surname for the following.

09   ?vra ? of ?or 23 January 1817 - September 1869
            -broken stone and hard to read

09   Ingeborg   March 1869 - April 1896 -broken stone and hard to read
09   Gunnil O., 5 March 1867 - 2 March 1879
          -broken stone and hard to read
10   Anon (rest buried), son of Tog (?) Tar (?) 18?? - 16 October ??
          -stone broken, buried, and hard to read
13   ? 21 May 1870 - ?9 July 1879
14   Herbert 1905-1939
14   only Maria
15   only Anna
16   only Ida B.
16   only Abert
16   only Bennie

Open area
with very
few stones

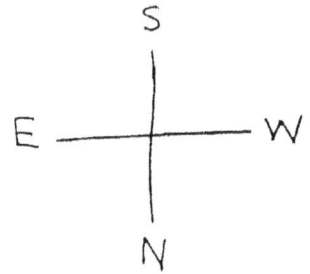

S
E —|— W
N

↕ Row 1
begins

↕ Row 18

Christiania Lutheran
Church

Eureka Township T113N-R20W
Section 29

Drive
Area

Drive
Area

County Highway 84 / 267th Street

Elliott's Hill Cemetery

Ravenna Township, Dakota County, Minnesota: T114N - R16W, section 16

This cemetery is in fair shape. There is no name posted on the cemetery grounds. The cemetery is situated within a rural area and appears to have minimal upkeep .

The Dakota county cemetery compilation lists this cemetery as: Elliott's Hill Cemetery. First burial August 18, 1855. 1 Acre. Located NW 1/4 of Section 16. Highway 54 South of 180th Street East.

Everyone is listed in alphabetical order. Row numbers are approximate at best. There is a map at the back of this section.

This cemeteries burial monuments were transcribed during the spring of 2001.

03	?, son of George and Alice Argetsinger, 2 August 1890 - 8 August 1891
03	Saban (?) Argetsinger (?), died 28 ? 1877 (?), age 26 days (?) - hard to read
03	Sarah L., wife of Hosman (?) Argetsinger, died 2 September 1865, aged 20 years 4 months 4 days (?)

02	Charles E. Blake, died 11 October 1871, age 11 months
02	George G. Blake 1854-1939
01	F.E. Blake 9 February 1852 - 6 June 1935
01	Frida, wife of F.E. Blake 14 January 1871 - 13 May 1913
02	George M. Blake, died 20 July 1903, age 83 years
02	Mary, wife of G.M. Blake 15 March 1828 - 13 November 1905
02	Adolph C. Bye 1892-1973
02	Conrad C. Bye 1884-1934
02	Gunder K. Bye 1853-1925
02	J. Arthur Bye (?) 1886-1911
02	Lena Bye 1862-1950

05	Christ Christianson 1839-1908
05	Dora Christianson 1849-1933
05	Lydia Christianson 1869-1870
02	Leon Clapp 1906-1940
03	Lugia Cole, mother of A.E. Knapp, born in Frutixburg (?) Canada 8 July 1800, died 27 January 1883
04	Emma Speakes Curtis 1871-1963
04	Julius M. Curtis 1866-1938

03	A.E. Day, died 18 February 1867, age 37 years 7 months 14 days

03   Abbie K. Day 25 December 1864 - 30 December 1889
02   Bessie Ella Day (?) 1912-1917
02   Elizabeth Black Day 1878-1948
03   Emeline T. Day 1833-1916
02   Evelyn Day 1908-1908
02   George C. Day 1874-1941
02   Irving E. Day 1872-1939
03   James H. Day 1827-1907
02   'Mother' Day (?) 1871-1920 'Albertina Bruber'

03   Adrien Egbert, died 15 March 1864, 16 years 4 months 12 days
03   P.G. Ellis 18 May 1805 - 22 June 1878
03   T. Ellis 29 October 1799 - 1 October 1882

02   Rachel M. Gelhar 20 October 1966 - 6 February 1967
04   Edythe Speakes Green 1880-1969

05   ??urs (?) Hunme ?? (?) - very worn stone
04   May E., wife of W.H. Hunter 25 July 1868 - 23 May 1900
02   Anna Hansen 1872-1935
02   Martha Hansen 1901-1904
02   Sigvart Hansen 1872-1943
02   Silas Hansen 1899-1973

01   John Johnson 5 July 1884 - 17 August 1909

03   Anna E. Knapp, wife of Henry C. Knapp, born in Essex County, New York
      7 December 1824 - 12 April 1886
03   Ella Jane, daughter of H.G. & A.E. Knapp, died 12 April 1871
      age 18 years 13 days
03   Henry C. Knapp, died 30 January 1865, age 45 years
03   Henry G., son of H.G. & A.E. Knapp, died 21 September 1866,
      age 17 years 3 months

02   Clayton, son of H.H. & L. Lovejoy 1906-1911
02   Daniel H. Lovejoy (?) 20 February 1866 (?) - 1 May 1874 (?)
02   Dorothy Lovejoy 1915-1957
02   Frances Lovejoy 1914-1957
02   Harriet J. Lovejoy 1842-1919
02   Henry Clay Lovejoy 1830-1909
02   Howard Lovejoy 1871-1946
02   Lena Lovejoy 1879-1943
02   Nettie Lovejoy (?) 18 July 1862 - 7 January 1865

03	Elisabeth Mavis 5 January 1879 (?) - 28 November 1881
03	Harriet (?) Mavis 1836-1910
03	Joseph Mavis 3 April 1863 - 29 August 1899
03	Sarah H. Mavis, died 9 July 1895, age 24 years
03	Simon (?) Mavis 1833-1905
04	Alexander Moizo 1852-1916
03	Arthur C. Nesbitt 1860-1929
03	Nannie Nesbitt 1858-1890
02	Carl S. Parten 1893-1982
02	Esther L. Parten 1903-1972
05	? Speakes ? - 1978
04	Carl E. Speakes 1882-1978
05	Corban Speakes 1826-1956
05	Corban Speakes, died 5 February 1856, age 30 years 5 months (?)
05	Eliza J. Speakes 1823-1901
05	George W. Speakes 1848-1933
05	Harry E. Speakes 1877-1945
05	Hester M. Speakes 1844-1965
05	Hester M., daughter of C. & E.J. Speakes, died 16 December 1865, age 21 years 4 months
05	Mary E. Speakes 1847-1939
05	Perry G. Speakes 1874-1970
03	Kate Nesbitt Taylor 1850-1923
02	Oscar Wathner 1867-1937
02	Sigvart Wathner 1870-1947
05	Eleanor, wife of - rest broken and to worn to read

Elliott's Hill Cemetery

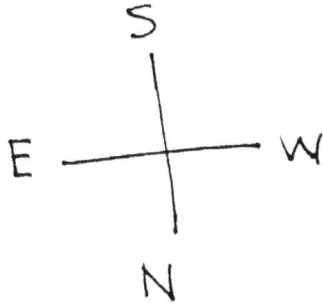

S
E —|— W
N

Private Home

gate

open | Row 1 → | Row 2 → | Row 3 → | Row 4 → | Row 5 →

Hwy 54

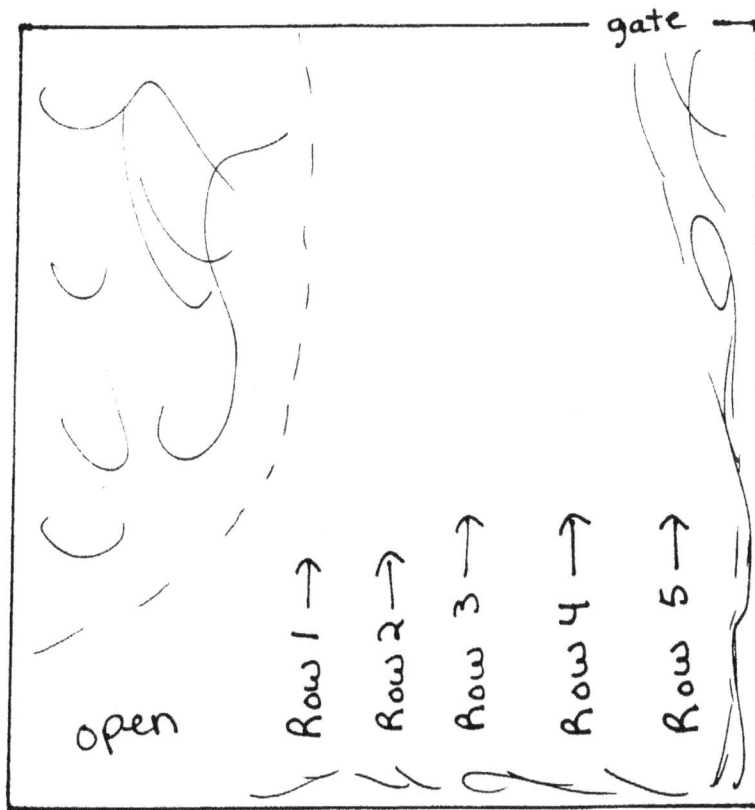

Ravenna Township
Dakota County, Minnesota
T114-R16W, section 16

213

Mounds (Catholic) Cemetery

Marshan Township, Dakota County, Minnesota: T114N - R17W, section 1

This cemetery was taken over by the forest many years ago. Currently the area is heavily overgrown and covered by many fallen trees. My understanding is that over the course of time many of the original burials have been removed and reintered in other cemeteries. As we walked through the area we noticed a couple holes that could have been left after a grave was removed. We did not confirm this. The remaining marked burials were toward the back of the cemeteries area and on either side of the central ridge in the cemetery. The area has not been maintained in a very long time.

The Dakota county cemetery compilation lists this cemetery as: Mounds Cemetery. Guardian Angels Church [Hastings], established 1857. 5 Acres. Located NW 1/4 of Section 1. Highway 91 east of Nicolai Avenue.

This cemeteries burial monuments were transcribed during the spring of 2001.

The burial monuments we located were:

Thomas Kaly, died 29 June 1857, age 35 years, Native of Ireland

Bridget, wife of John McNiff, died 13 May 1857, age 46 years (?)

John Shannon, died 11 June 1857, age 27 years, Native of Ireland,
    County of Rossea???
Mary Ann, daughter of D. & E. Sharry, died 8 ? 1861, age 1 year 11 months (?)
William Frank, son of F. & S. Sherry 22 September 1890 - 8 February 1891

Private
Home

S
E —┼— W
N

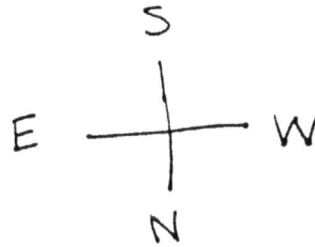

(remaining)
Burials

(remaining)
Burials

Mounds Cemetery

Marshan Township
    Dakota County, MN

T114N - R17W , sect. 1

160th Street

Hastings State Hospital/Asylum Cemetery - Hastings, Minnesota

Marshan Township, Dakota County, Minnesota: T114N - R17W, section 2

This Cemetery is located in the far southeast corner of the old Hastings State Hospital property. It can be difficult to access. I believe much of the surrounding property is now part of the 'Hastings Wildlife Management Area.' The 'road' we traveled on to get to the site went through a farm field and down an old soft field road with two foot deep ruts.

There was no sign identifying the site as a cemetery at the time of our visit. There was only one burial monument in the entire cemetery. This was for 'Fred Mass 1875-1949'.

In a Hastings Area Tourism Bureau publication titled 'Hastings Heritage Map,' there was a brief reference to the Hastings State Hospital. It read: 'The 1900 hospital included large brick buildings housing up to 900 patients. It was known as the Insane Asylum. On the complex's 460 acre farm patients produced garden and dairy products for the hospital. In 1979, it became the Minnesota Veterans Home.'

The Dakota county cemetery compilation lists this cemetery as: Hastings State Hospital Cemetery. Old section: 1st burial 16 July 1901. Last burial 17 September 1944. 671 graves. Graves face east. New Section: North side of old section. First burial 7 October 1944. Last burial 28 December 1964. 230 graves. Graves face north. (total 901 graves in cemetery). Located SE corner of NW ½ of Section 2. (Abandoned).

Hastings State Hospital Cemetery
Marshan Township, Dakota Co., MN.
T114 N - R17W, Section 2

open ?

← markers 17-24 →

← markers 17-24 →

← Rows 1-16 markers →
Newer section!

Rows 1-16 markers
older section?

W ─┼─ E
N
S

old

Drive area

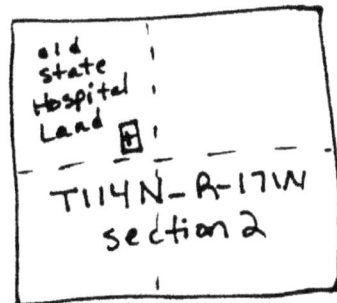

old
State
Hospital
Land

T114N - R-17W
section 2

William Lyon Cemetery

Marshan Township, Dakota County, Minnesota: T114N - R17W, section 6

This cemetery is in poor shape. There is no name posted on the cemetery grounds. The cemetery is situated in a rural area and appears to have no regular maintenance.

The Dakota county cemetery compilation lists this cemetery as: William Lyon Cemetery. Private. Started about 1870. 32' by 94' parcel. SE 1/4 of Section 6. 170th Street East, west of Highway 47. (Abandoned).

This cemeteries burial monuments were transcribed during the spring of 2001.

The remaining burial monuments were:

Geo. W. Lyon, died 24 June 1881, age 73 years 8 months
Jane Louisa, wife of Wm. Lyon, died 5 October 1882, age 60 years 6 months
William Lyon, died 28 April 1891, age 75 years 10 months

There was also a base of a burial monument with no other information.

William Lyon Cemetery

Marshan Township, Dakota County, MN.
T 114 N – R 17 W, section 6

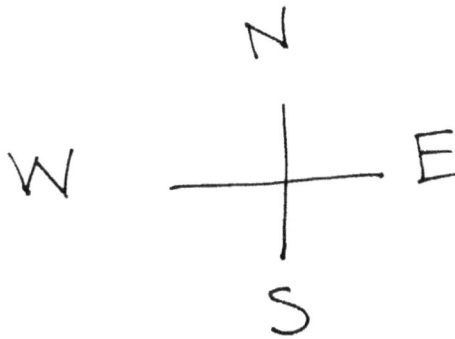

N
W —— E
S

Private Home

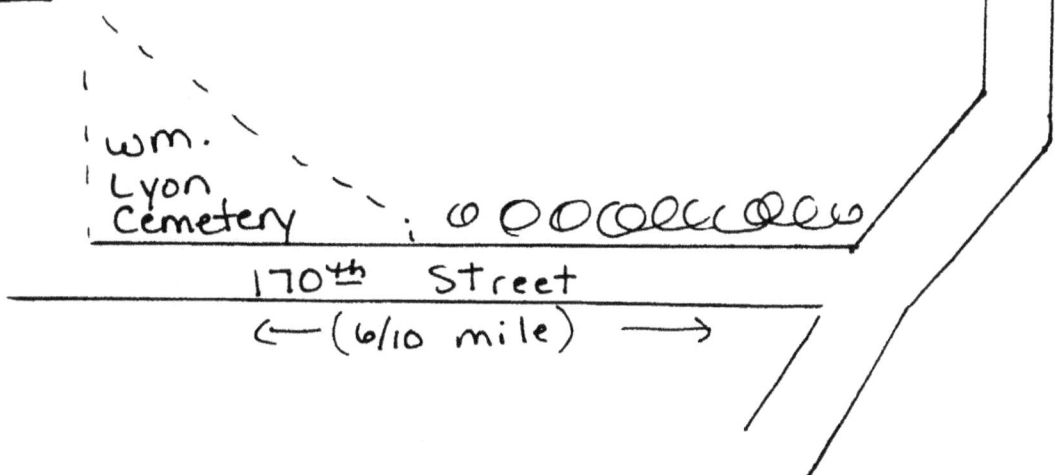

Wm. Lyon Cemetery

Jorgen Avenue Hwy 47

170th Street
← (6/10 mile) →

Bell Wood Cemetery

Marshan Township, Dakota County, Minnesota: T114N - R17W, section 22

This cemetery is upkept and in fair shape. The remaining burial monuments are very old. Most of the burials took place before 1900. There are several clusters of lilacs within this cemetery. It looks as though lilacs were planted around the trees that marked the burial rows. In a couple other places the lilacs were planted near burial monuments, which have now surrounded the burial monuments. My understanding is that this cemetery belonged to a Catholic mission church, which was part of Guardian Angels Catholic Church in Hastings, Minnesota. The mission church was closed around 1900 and the cemetery was closed at the same time.

In 'History of Dakota County and the City of Hastings, ...' By Rev. Edward D. Neill, written in 1881, he wrote ... 'Bellwood, on the east half of the north-east quarter and the east half of the south-quarter of section 28, was surveyed and platted, ... The Bellwood Catholic Church was built on land donated by the townsite company. The site, for want of encouragement, soon was abandoned.' ... ' The Collins brothers donated the land occupied by the Bellwood cemetery to Bishop T.L. Grace of St. Paul, for the use of Bellwood Catholic church as a cemetery. ... It contains five acres in the north-west quarter of section 22, ... There are now in the enclosure, four hundred and forty-five grave. The first one was that of Stephen Collins.' (page 424).

The Dakota County Cemetery Compilation lists this cemetery as: Bellwood Cemetery. Guardian Angels Catholic Church. Opened 9 May 1862. Platted July 1874. 5 Acres. Located NW 1/4 of Section 22. Highway 61 and 190th Street East.

Everyone is listed in alphabetical order. The number before each entry is an approximate row number. There is a map at the back of this section.

This cemeteries burial monuments were transcribed during May of 2000.

01 John Ahern, died 29 April 1869, age 37 years
08 Albert Arper 1868-1896
08 Francis Z. Arper 1828-1907
08 Margaret E. Arper 1871-1886
08 Mary E. Arper 1831-1907
08 Mary J. Arper 1852-1871
08 Mary Jane, daughter of F.Z. & Mary Arper, native of Trov (?) N.Y.,
    died 28 June 1870, age 18 years 14 days
08 Sarah E. Arper 1857-1861
02 Catherine, wife of Michael Atkinson, native of Parish of Forgney, County
    Westmeath, Ireland, died 13 March 1872, age 39 years
02 Michael Atkinson, born 11 November 1820 in Cloncullon, Parish Ballymore,

County Westmeath, Ireland, died 10 November 1879
03   H.G. Bailly, Co D 5th Minn. Inf.
03   Henry G. Bailly, 1st Lt. Co D 5 Minn. Inf., Civil War, A Founder of Hastings
       29 October 1828 - 7 January 1865
01   Edward Belamore (?), died 27 December 1886, age 73
01   Mary Belamore (?), wife of Edward, died 11 March 1883, age 69 (?) years

07   Leo Caneff - no dates
07   Thomas Caneff - no dates
08   James Carroll, his wife Kate and their children John & James - no dates
02   Mary Carroll, died 1 December 1869, age 38 years
       native of County Limerick, Ireland
09   Bridget Casserly 1835-1873
03   Rudolph, son of J. & F. Chiquet 14 May 1860 - 28 September 1874
05   Bridget, wife of Malaghy Collins, native of Kilkerrin, County Galway, Ireland,
       died 11 November 1861, age 63 years
06   Malaghy (?) Collins, died 22 September 1870, age 30 years
05   Peter Collins, native of Kilkerrin, County Galway, Ireland, who was killed in the
       battle of deep Bollom, Va. 11 August 1861, age 45 years
06   Peter S., son of Malaghy & Ellen Collins, died 18 January 1868,
       age 1 month (?) 23 days
05   Stephen Collins, native of Kilkerrin, County Galway, Ireland,
       died 31 November 1862, age 28 years
06   Bridget, daughter of Thos. & Rose Connelly, died 9 March 1872, age 16 years
05   Martin Connelley, native of the county of Roscomon (?), Ireland
       died 27 September 1880, age 74 years 10 months 12 days
05   Catherine, daughter of P.A. & Y.I. Conard 10 ? 1855 - 10 ? 187?,
       age ?0 years 8 months ? days

07   Ann Dean - no dates
07   Ellen M. Dean - no dates
07   Eugene Dean, born in Castle Gregory, County Kerry, Ireland in 1823,
       died 11 April 1893
07   Mary Ann Dean 27 July 1858 - 28 January 1889
02   William, son of E. & M. Delamore, died 30 June 1866, age 28 years 2 months
05   Ellen, wife of Patrick Devaney, died 25 March 1878, age 64 (?) years
05   Patrick Devaney, of the Parish of Bournia, County of Tipperary, Ireland,
       died 19 September 1877, age 69 years
08   Bridget Dordan, died 3 August 1886, age 65 years
03   John Dorigan, died 10 December 1879 - rest of stone missing
09   Daniel Driscoll, age 1 year - no dates
09   Daniel Driscoll, age 22 years 11 months 20 days - no dates
09   Ellen Driscoll, age 1 month - no dates
09   James Driscoll, age 15 months - no dates

09	Jane Driscoll, age 3 years 8 months - no dates
02	Michael Duffy 1821-1894
01	Margaret Dunn, died 14 March 1904, age 70 years
01	Patrick Dunn, died 6 December 1898, age 75 years

01	George H., son of J. & M. Fagan, age ? - rest buried to deep to read
03	Bridget Fagen, daughter of M. & C. Fagen, born 4 March 1862, died 13 October 1877, age 15 years 7 months 14 days
03	John, child of M. & C. Fagen 2 August 1865 - 4 August 1866, age 1 year 2 days
03	Mary Fagen, daughter of M. & C. Fagen 8 May 1863 - 3 September 1863 age 3 months
03	Thomas, child of M. & C. Fagen 13 August 1869 - 25 August 1869 age 12 days
07	Louis Faivre 3 February 1816 - 9 July 1867
01	Ann, daughter of Patrick & Bridget Fegen, died 16 September 1857, age 15 years
01	Bridget Fegen, wife of Patrick, died 10 August 1873, age 75 years
05	?ames Flahavan, died 30 September 1878, age 64 years native of Parish of Fo?, County Waterford (?)
05	Mary Flahavan (?), died 19 June 1875, age 60 years
06	Thomas F. Flynn, native of Canada (?), died 17 August 1870, age 31 years 9 months 8 (?) days

| 04 | Robert, son of M.P. & M. Goulson (?), died 1 October 1863, age 3 years 10 months 19 days |
| 05 | Bridget, wife of John Gready (?), died 29 May (?) 1872, age 34 (?) years |

06	James Higgins, son of Patrick & Anna Higgens, died 18 February 1868, age 8 days
06	Patrick Higgins, son of Patrick & Anna Higgens, died 31 August 1872, age 5 months
09	Daniel Holland 1826-1863
09	James Holland 1773-1868
05	Mary, wife of J. Hurley, died 6 August 1874, age 30 years 20 days
05	Peter Hurley, died 27 August 1874 - rest buried to deep to read

09	Ann McGrath, wife of John Judge 14 November 1818 - 17 April 1907
08	Bernard Judge 1840-1905
09	Bernard Judge 1881-1917
09	Eliza, ? of J. & A. Judge, died 19 November 1888, age 26 years
09	James, son of J. & A. Judge, died 19 December 1881, age 24 years
09	Jane Holland, wife of M. Judge, died 9 March 1889, age 33 years
08	John Judge 1873-1885

09	John Judge, died 7 December 1890, age 88 years
08	Margaret Judge 1850-1898
09	Michael, son of J. & A. Judge, died 26 July 1887, age 34 years
08	Michael J. Judge 1875-1908
09	Thomas I. Judge 1887-1928
11	Bridget Kane, died 11 February 1900, age 70 years, native of County Galway, Ireland
11	George Kane 1866-1890
11	John Kane, died 17 February 1901, age 40 years
11	William Kane, died 17 September 1879, age 16 years 9 months 1 day
02	Susan Ryan Kelly, wife of Daniel Ryan 1842-1927
01	Rosanna Keetley, wife of James, died 10 August 1869, age 50 years
04	Bridget, wife of John Lennon, died 25 November 1870, age 63 years
04	John Lennon, died 15 August 1872, age 70 years
04	Owen Lennon, died 5 November 1870, age 32 years
04	Patrick Lennon, died 29 January 1900, age 56 years
10	John T. Maher (?) - 1870 -
10	Maria Maher (?) 1835-1922
10	Mary B. Maher (?) 1878-1898
10	Thomas Maher (?) 1833-1922
10	Timothy Maher 1865-1868
10	Timothy J. Maher 1880-1881
06	Cornelius Mahoney, born in County Kerry (?), Ireland died 5 August 1877, age 43 years
02	Anastacia Maroney, died 7 March 1903, age 41 years
02	Mary Lamy, wife of Thomas Maroney, died 4 February 1904, age 79 years
02	Thomas Maroney, died 5 May 1894, age 78 years
09	Barney McGrath, died 5 March 1875, age 83 years
09	Mary, wife of Barney McGrath, died 21 November 1869, age 80 years
05	Nicholas & Mary McGree, died 1898
10	Bridget McKenna, died 26 November 1884, age 73 years native of County Wieklow (?), Ireland
04	Ellen McKenna, daughter of Thomas & Julia - rest is missing
06	John McLaughlin (?), died 13 October 1859, age 62 years
02	Daniel Molamphy, died 29 August 1882, age 72 years, native of Tipperary, Ireland
01	Thomas Morgan, died 9 March 1869, age 25 years
06	Jane, child of Michael & Mary Mullany, died 14 August 1862/67 (?), age 1 month
06	Mary, child of Michael & Mary Mullany, died 19 November 1864, age 11 months 13 days
09	Patrick (?) Murtgh (?), died 10 December 1868, age 77 years

native of County Longford, of Parish of Rectine (?), Ireland

09	Catherine, wife of John O'Brien 1830-1917
09	John O'Brien 1833-1870
09	John O'Brien 1861-1904
09	Mary O'Brien 1868-1923
09	Thomas O'Brien 1871-1872
09	Timothy O'Brien, died 7 January 1869, age 69 years
07	Mary O'Connor - no dates
03	John, son of Matt Orourke, died 16 ? 1857
03	?tin O'Shaughn? - rest buried to deep to read
03	J. Oshaughness? - rest buried to deep to read
03	Michael, son of ? & ? Oshaughness?, died 22 April 1861
10	Mary D., wife of Hugh Padden, died 27 April 1872, age 28 years
10	Mary, ? of Hugh Patton, died 5 August 1872, age 3 months 5 days
09	John Redigan, died 26 March 1868, age 53 years
02	Catharine Holly, widow of Dennis Ryan, died 29 May 1869, age 63 years
	native of Ros? Green, County Tipperary, Ireland
02	Daniel Ryan 1843-1884
05	'Father' Ryan (?) 1836-1897
02	John Ryan 28 May 1841 - 13 January 1920
07	Mary Ryan, mother of Mary Caneff 1829-1909
05	'Mother' Ryan (?) 1840-1872
05	Thomas M. Ryan (?) 1870-1890
03	Michael Scanlan, wife of Bridget, died 18 February 1884, age 55 years
	native of County Galway, Ireland
09	Daniel, son of D. & H. Sullivan, died 24 January 1874
09	James, son of D. & H. Sullivan, died 7 January 1874, age 4 years 6 months
09	Johnie, son of D. & H. Sullivan, died 21 September 1864
09	Mary, daughter of D. & H. Sullivan (?), died 11 January 1874
08	Charler Editor (?) Thorne (?) - no dates
08	Delia B. Thorne (?) - no dates
08	Emmet Thorne (?) - no dates
08	George Thorne (?) - no dates
08	Joseph Thorne (?) - no dates

Bell ♡ Wood Cemetery
Marshan Township, Dakota County, MN
T 114 N-R 17 W, Section 22

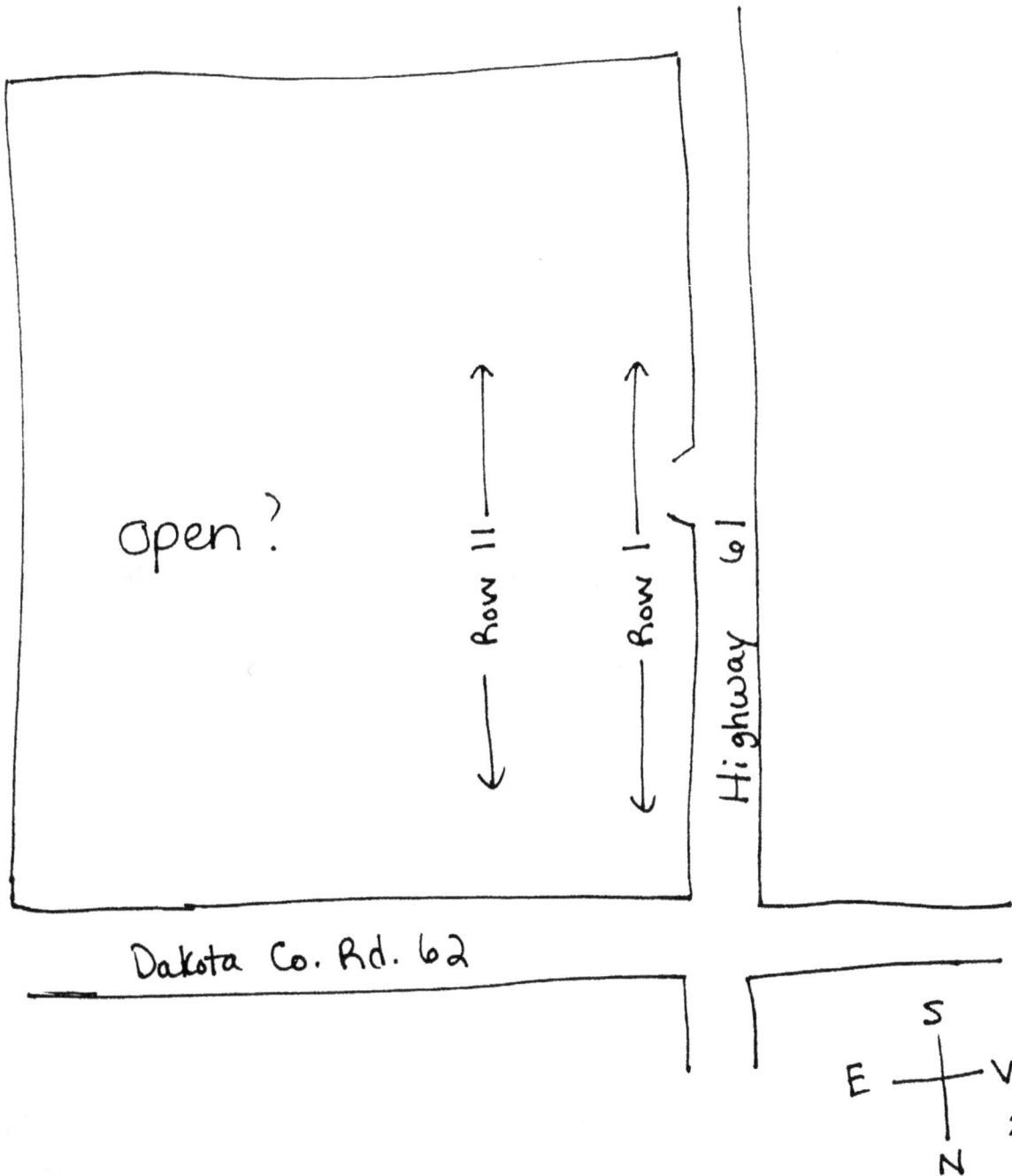

open ?

← Row II →

← Row I →

Highway 61

Dakota Co. Rd. 62

S
E ─┼─ W
N

233

Marsh Family Cemetery

Marshan Township, Dakota County, Minnesota: T114N - R17W, section 26

  This small family cemetery is no longer upkept and has become overgrown with trees, lilacs, and weeds. The cemetery is land locked in the southeast corner of a farm field which is located about one quarter of a mile east of Michael Avenue. I was told that this cemetery may have been started because one of the original burials was for a person who died from a quarantinable disease and they were not allowed to be buried in the local cemeteries.

  The Dakota county cemetery compilation lists this cemetery as: Marsh Burying Ground. Established about 1860. Michael Marsh Family. 2 acres. Approximately 11 graves. Located NW 1/4 of Section 26. Michael Avenue. Cemetery land locked on Irene Carroll property. (Abandoned).

  Everyone is listed in alphabetical order. There is a map at the back of this section.

  This cemeteries burial monuments were transcribed during May of 2000.

Mary Marsh, wife of M. Marsh, died 8 November 1865, age 39 years
Michael Marsh, born 11 March 1828 in Strasshoscheia (?) Luxemburg,
  died 4 September 1891
Nicholas Marsh, died 6 April 1860, age 33 years
Nikolaus, son of M. & M. Marsh 16 June 1856 - 23 January 1857
Rosina, daughter of M. & M. Marsh 24 August 1860 - 20 January 1864

Marsh Family Cemetery
Marshan Township, Dakota County, MN.
T114N-R17W, Section 26

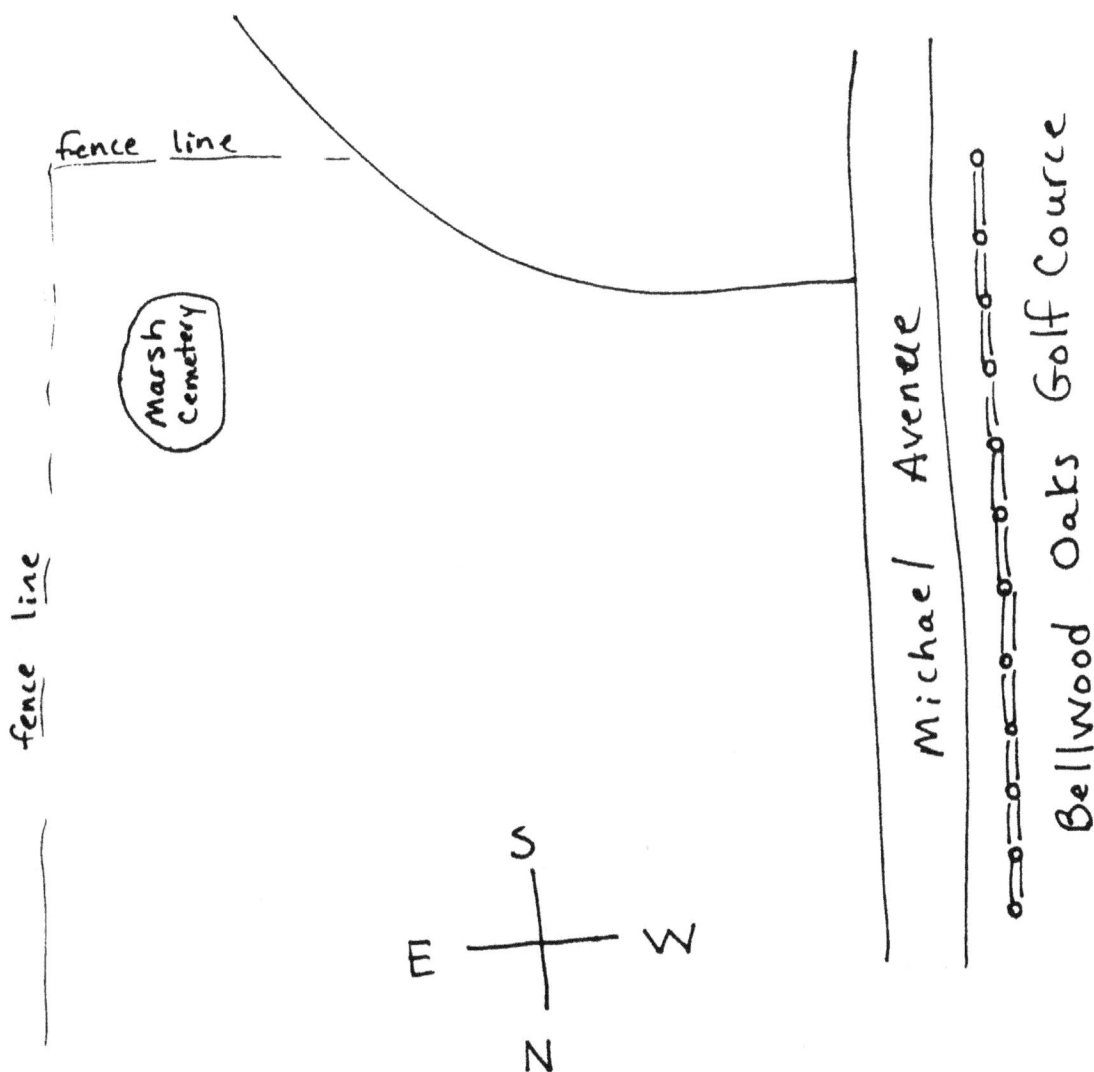

fence line

Marsh Cemetery

fence line

Michael Avenue

Bellwood Oaks Golf Course

```
      S
      |
E ----+---- W
      |
      N
```

St. AGATHA'S CATHOLIC CEMETERY

Vermillion township, Dakota county, Minnesota: T114N- R18W, section 8

This cemetery is located in rural Vermillion township. At the time I visited there was no visible sign stating the name of this cemetery. Other sources listed the cemetery as St. Agatha's Catholic Cemetery. There is no longer a church at this location. The cemetery is upkept and in good shape. Most of the burials are located in the northeast quarter, with a few in the southwest quarter. I began numbering the rows at the west edge. Rows 1 - 4 are in the southwest quarter. Rows 5 - 11 are in the northeast quarter. Row 5 begins directly east of the central drive area.

The Dakota county cemetery records compilation lists this cemetery as: St. Agatha's Catholic Cemetery. Surveyed in 1875. One and one half acres. Located NW 1/4 of Section 8. 170th St. E. West of Highway 52.

Everyone is listed in alphabetical order. The number before each entry is the row number. There is a map at the back of this section.

These cemetery burial monuments were transcribed during 1996.

09	Mary Adam, died 1933
10	Henry Backes 1851-1936
10	Mary Backes 1858-1937
05	Bridget Bennett (?), died in 1882
05	Edward Bennett 1829-1885
05	Ellen Bennett, died 1 October 1925
05	James Bennett (?), died in 1882
05	James Bennett, died in 1880, age 45 years
	Native of County Arma, Ireland
05	Mary Ann, wife of Edward Bennett 1851-1911
05	Maurice Bennett (?), died 19 July 1883
05	Peter Bennett, died in 1898, age 23 years
05	Peter P. Bennett 1874-1898
05	Sarah Bennett 1794-1885
06	'Father' Birk (?) 1874-1949
06	Marie Birk (?) 1907-1929
06	'Mother' Birk (?) 1878-1930
10	Rose E. Blackwell 6 July 1897 - 24 August 1985
02	Catherine F. Callaghan (?) 1870-1952
02	Ellen E. Callaghan (?) 1866-1954
02	Mary, wife of Wm. Callaghan, Native of County Limerick, Ireland
	died 24 October 1898, age 60 years
02	Mary Callaghan (?) 1838-1898

02	Nora A. Callaghan (?) 1872-1916
02	Patrick H. Callaghan (?) 1864-1916
02	William Callaghan (?) 1836-1924
02	William E. Callaghan (?) 1873-1958
07	Elmer F. Callahan (?) 1918-1966
07	Frank V. Callahan (?) 1883-1958
07	Jennie L. Callahan (?) 1886-1975
06	Elizabeth C. Casey (?) 1883-1939
10	Mary A. Clark 26 April 1854 - 4 February 1881
08	Elizabeth E. Condon (?) 1857-1921
08	Elizabeth E. Condon 1857-1921
09	Ellen Condon 1863-1924
08	James A. Condon 1913-1942, age 28 years
08	John F. Condon 1868-1945
08	Margaret Condon 1829-1921
08	Margaret Russell, wife of Michael Condon 1829-1921
08	Mary C. Condon 1870-1950
08	Michael Condon 1832-1890
08	Michael Condon 1869-1939
08	Michael Condon, born in County Limerick, Ireland
	died 19 August 1890, age 58 years
01	Michale J. Condon 1873-1933
08	Victoria Condon 1877-1971
09	William Condon 1863-1944
09	Patrick Crimmin, died 12 June 1901, age 76 years
10	Ralph deDominces 1908-1992
10	Tony deDominces 1913-1970
07	Anna Fahey Donaldson, died 1949
05	Ann Dordon 1861-1905
05	Ann Case, wife of Frank Dordan 1861-1905
05	Frank Dordan 1860-1938
05	John A. Dordan 1887-1918
	Co. A 362 Infantry - Killed in Action
06	John M. Dunlavy, Native of County Sligo, Ireland
	died 11 August 1881, age 46 years
07	Annie Evans 1882-1883
06	Anna Fahey (?) 1865-1945
06	Arthur Fahey (?) 1857-1938
07	baby Fahey - 1937 -
07	Dennis Fahey 1860-1944
07	Edward P. Fahey 1905-1972
07	John Joseph Fahey 1915-1915
07	John L. Fahey 1855-1940

07	Margaret Fahey 1858-1933
06	Mary Fahey (?) 1886-1887
06	Patrick Fahey, died 17 August 1860, age 42 years
07	Patrick J. Fahey 1895-1931
07	Rose C. Fahey 1888-1985
07	Sarah Fahey 1871-1908
07	Thomas E. Fahey 1889-1964
10	Leona M. Fennell 1922-1987
10	William J. Fennell 1903-1972
07	E. Marie Maloney Fisher 1899-1953
09	Austin Gillespie, Native of County Sligo, Ireland 1832-1916
09	Austin M. Gillespie (?) 1869-1947
09	baby Gillespie (?) - 1919 -
07	Catherine Gillespie 1871-1963
09	Ellen F. Gillespie (?) 1880-1919
07	Esther A. Gillespie 1915-1920
09	Frances Gillespie (?) 1907-1918
07	John H. Gillespie 1866-1936
07	John T. Gillespie 1893-1899
09	Joseph A. Gillespie (?) 1917-1937
11	Joseph E. Gillespie 1905-1969
09	baby Mary Gillespie (?) - 1914 -
09	Mary Gillespie, Native of County Sligo, Ireland 1836-1911
08	Clarence E. Herrley 1910-1979
08	Patricia M. Herrley 1904-1964
10	Chris Horsch 1920-1984
10	Delores Horsch 1922 - __
08	George P. King, died 1949
08	Gertrude King - no dates
09	James King, died 1935
09	Capt. John King, died 18 March 1886, age 49 years
09	Maria King, died 1934
07	Mary King, aged 80 years - no dates
07	Thomas King, Native of County Queens, Ireland 2 January 1825 - 28 April 1905
07	Mrs. Thomas King 1833-1912
09	William King, died 1888
09	Winifred King, died 1890
05	Catherine, wife of Martin Knaresbora died 15 September 1903, age 76 years
05	Martin Knaresboro, Native of County Kilkenny, Ireland died 11 February 1897, age 70 years

10	Barbara, wife of Edward Moore	1870-1945
09	Catherine Moore (?)	1859-1921
10	Edward Moore	1862-1914
08	Edward J. Moore	1892-1950
10	Grace Moore (?)	- 1907 -
08	Hannah Moore (?)	1854-1932
08	Johanna, wife of Michael Moore, born in County Limerick, Ireland 25 December 1819, died 30 March 1892	
08	Johanna Moore	1819-1892
08	baby John Moore (?)	- no dates
08	Mary C. Moore	1888-1952
08	Michael Moore	- 2 February 1901 -
08	Michael Moore, died 2 February 1901	
08	Michael P. Moore	1890-1951
08	Richard Moore (?)	1855-1919
08	Thomas Moore	1858-1929
09	William Moore (?)	1856-1919
08	William F. Moore	1893-1937
06	Margaret Murnane	1873-1910
06	Michael Murnane	1868-1939
05	Catherine O'Neil, wife of J. E. Murphy , died (?) 17 February 1897	
05	J. E. Murphy	1818-1897
05	Mary (?) Murphy, died 9 October 1895, age 3 years 6 months	
11	Michael Paul Neisen	12 May - 27 August 1989
10	Clarence Niesen	1925-1926
10	Henry Niesen	1924-1924
10	John C. Niesen (?)	1889-1970
10	Marie C. Niesen (?)	1892-1974
06	Rebecca O'Leary (?)	1855-1937
06	Thomas O'Leary, born in County Limerick, Ireland 27 March 1836 died 27 April 1903	
06	Thomas O'Leary (?)	1836-1903
06	Thomas O'Leary	1862-1936
07	Teresa Osman	1923-1949
05	Catherine Pilcher	1887-1967
05	Catherine M. Pilcher	1911-1913
08	Francis Pilcher	1908-1984
05	Joseph Pilcher	1873-1958
07	Annie Mary Raway	1838-1889
07	Clara C. Raway	1897-1897
07	George W. Raway	1898-1898
07	Henry Raway	1879-1879

07	J. H. J. Raway 1799-1881
07	John H. J. Raway, died 9 September 1881
	age 82 years 7 months 20 days
07	Joseph Raway 1879-1879
07	Leonard J. Raway 1884-1884
07	Mary K. Raway 1805-1887
04	Catherine Rice 1882-1949
03	James Rice 1 May 1876 - 30 June 1900
03	John Rice (?) 1869-1948
04	Joseph C. Rice 1918-1985
03	Katherine, wife of Peter Rice 1835 - 9 February 1880
03	Michael Rice (?) 1870-1905
03	Peter Rice 1830 - 5 November 1905
04	Thomas Rice 1865-1954
09	Helen E. Ries 1902-1989
09	Joe L. Ries 1904-1990
01	Louis Lawrence Ryan 5 March 1913 - 29 March 1914
06	Albert Schaffer 1910-1982
06	Frances Schaffer 1911-1987
11	Thomas W. Schaffer 1936-1985
08	Domonic L. Schmitz 1888-1949
08	Susanna Schmitz 1897-1955
07	Kathryn M. Sieben 1899-1974
07	William Sieben 1896-1975
01	Corp'l Absalon (?) Smith, Co. F Hatch's (?) Minnesota Cav. (?)
11	Harvey J. Swoboda 1916-1995
	married Bernice M. 9 August 1941
11	Harvey J. Swoboda, Sgt. United States Army World War 2
	6 March 1916 - 15 October 1995
08	Msgr. Vincent (Father Art), ordained 2 June 1951
	2 December 1925 - 4 May 1995
01	A. M. Wayman, Co. C 1st. Minnesota Batt'n Inf.
08	Edmund J. Wayman 1870-1949
08	Johanna Wayman 1873-1949
01	Mary E. Waymand, died 15 December 1872, age 57 years
10	John 'Jack' Welsh 1951-1975
10	John V. Welsh 1914-1983
11	Mary B. Wilson 18 December 1891 - 27 July 1979
11	William R. Wilson 1890-1938
11	William R. Wilson 1 November 1890 - 18 November 1938
08	Alfons A. Yzermans 1895-1976
08	Catherine F. Yzermans 1890-1971

No Graves ?

Rows 1-4

No Graves ?

St. Agatha's Catholic Cemetery ?
Dakota County
Vermillion Township
T114N - R18W
Section 8

Alter ?
With Cross

S
W
E
N

Drive
Area

Rows 5-11

Row 11

Row 5

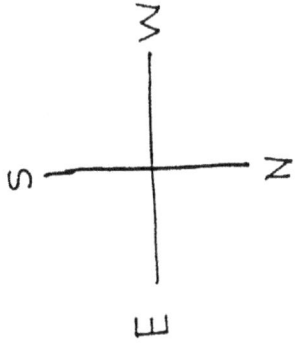

170th Street East

245

St. JOHN'S CATHOLIC CHURCH CEMETERY
or St. JOHN the BAPTIST CATHOLIC CHURCH CEMETERY

Vermillion township, Dakota county, Minnesota: T114N – R18W, section 22

This cemetery is located within the town of Vermillion, Minnesota. The cemetery is upkept and in good shape. There is a large statue area in the middle of rows 5, 6, and 7. I began numbering rows at the north edge. The burial plot sizes seem to vary from the west half to the east half. I ended up with rows 11 and 13 as short rows that started on the west and only continued about 2/3 of the way to the east edge.

The Dakota county cemetery records compilation lists this cemetery as: St. John's Catholic Cemetery. Started in 1882. About 3 acres. Located NW 1/4 of Section 22. 190th St. E.

Everyone is listed in alphabetical order. The number before each entry is the row number. There is a map at the back of this section.

These cemetery burial monuments were transcribed during 1996.

12	Wilhelm Bartels 1813 - 12 July 1886
18	Helen Bastien 1921- __
18	Stanley Bastien 1912 - 1981
16	Anton C. Bauer 1908 - __
20	Carl P. Bauer 1915 - __
	married Helen B 19 October 1943
03	Clara Bauer 1889 - 1973
18	Dorothy M. Bauer 1925 - __
16	Eva Bauer 1913 - 1995
20	Helen B. Bauer 1916 - __
	married Carl P. 19 October 1943
03	Jacob Bauer 1887 - 1968
18	Louis L. Bauer 1917 - 1978
09	Bernard Becker 1889 - 1939
09	Clara M. Becker 1897 - 1986
09	Elisabeth Becker 29 July 1861 - 24 July 1912
09	George Becker 9 November 1851 - 13 August 1938
09	George J. Becker 1895 - 1965
03	Larry Joseph, son of Mr. & Mrs. Laverne Becker
	3 March - 20 April 1970
10	Gottfried Beissel 1843 - 1892
10	Joseph J. Beissel 1875 - 1939
06	Katherine Beissel 1887 - 1959
09	Linda Annette, daughter of Mr. & Mrs. Donald Beissel - 12 July 1978 -
06	Louis Beissel 1879 - 1958
10	Mary Beissel 1847 - 1924

08	Johann Beying 11 April 1829 - 1 September 1908
08	Susanna Beying 14 June 1845 - 16 November 1934
10	Joseph Birk 1899 - 1979
	married Marie G. 19 October 1920
10	Marie G. Birk 1897 - 1977
	married Joseph 19 October 1920
10	William Birk 1931 - 1932
16	Stephen T. Braun 1954 - 1974
05	Elisabeth B. Kiemen, wife of John Breuer
	18 September 1869 - 21 July 1903
06	John Breuer 21 August 1826 - 24 November 1905
05	John L. Breuer 1870 - 1953
05	Magdalena Breuer 1884 - 1977
06	Sybilla Breuer 13 September 1829 - 30 August 1909
12	Anna E. Brochman 1908 - 1942
11	Appolonia Brochman (?) 1903 - 1924
11	Catherine Brochman (?) 8 January 1865 - 28 May 1931
16	Goerge J. Brochman 1910 - __
08	Jerome N. Brochman - 1934 -
02	John Brochman 1893 - 1967
11	John P. Brochman (?) 17 March 1862 - 14 December 1940
02	Kathrine Brochman 1896 - 1975
08	Marie R. Brochman 1906 - 1982
08	Marvin J. Brochman - 1931 -
16	Mathilda Brochman 1917 - 1972
08	Myron P. Brochman - 1931 -
08	Nicholas J. Brochman 1895 - 1974
04	Elisabeth Brochmann, born 25 February 1824 in Diekirch Grossh.,
	Luxemburg, died 25 May 1907
04	Johann Brochmann, born 22 August 1820 in Diekirch Grossn.,
	Luxemburg, died 30 August 1903
11	Peter Johann, son of J. P. & K. Brochmann
	24 November 1891 - 9 March 1892
03	Doris Jean Brown 22 April 1930 - 3 April 1940
03	Margaret Brown 1888 - 1939
03	Philip Brown 1920 - __
03	Theodore Brown 1880 - 1972
15	Anna M. Brummel 1905 - 1981
15	Joseph J. Brummel 1905 - 1972
20	M. Catherine Cauchy 1917 - 1990
20	Peter S. Cauchy 1916 - __
02	Anthony Chandler ? May 1915 (?) - 26 January 1916 (?)
02	baby Chandler (?) born & died 1921
02	Clara A. Chandler 1893 - 1971
17	Dorothy Chandler 1914 - __

02	Nicholas Chandler 1889 - 1971
02	Raymond J. Chandler 1918 - 1960
17	William Chandler 1914 - 1978
18	Elizabeth Cysiewski 1919 - 1983
	married Thomas A. 9 February 1946
18	Martha A. Cysiewski 1910 - 1979
18	Peter H. Cysiewski 1908 - 1982
18	Thomas A. Cysiewski 1914 - __
	married Elizabeth 9 February 1946

13	Viola Kieffer Dawson 1921 - 1986
18	Agnes Deutsch 1921 - __
18	Edward Deutsch 1915 - __
12	Elvira M. Doffing (?) 1918 - 1919
12	Irmina M. Doffing (?) 1925 - __
12	Maria Doffing (?) 1883 - 1958
12	Mathias Doffing (?) 1879 - 1947
12	Anna S. Dreis 1878 - 1954
15	Anthony H. Dreis 1909 - 1970
12	Barbara C. Dreis (?) 1906 - 1959
12	Daniel P. Dreis 1904-1969
07	Donald J. Dreis 1926 - 1960
03	Francis J. Dreis 1908-1981
13	Franz Dreis, born in Suren, Luxemburg 30 July 1840
	died 2 October 1885 (other German words which include the
	name Marla Brochman ?)
12	Henry F. Dreis 1876-1961
15	Iva M. Dreis 1916 - __
03	Jacob Dreis 1884-1963
03	John P. Dreis 1882-1955
03	Katharina Dreis 1879-1922
12	Leona J. Dreis 1915 - __
03	Margaret Dreis 1885-1964
07	Patricia M. Dreis 1932-1986
09	Anna Drewicke 21 June 1832 - 1 May 1913
10	Lawrence Drewicke 27 June 1874 - 13 August 1896
10	Lawrence Drewicke 23 August 1897 - 8 April 1899
09	Lorenz B. Drewicke 8 August 1823 - 10 April 1908
10	Lucy M. A. Drewicke 11 December 1871 - 12 July 1898

15	Johann B. Einsweiler 1 November 1870 - 1 January 1899
15	Joseph Einsweiler 1 November 1876 - 19 August 1896
15	Nickolaus Einsweiler 1834 - 22 May 1907

03	Barbara Fautsch 17 February 1874 - 30 August 1950
03	Nickolaus Fautsch 1 March 1864 - 25 March 1912

02	Catherine Feyen (?) 8 December 1864 - 28 August 1935
02	Eltina M. Feyen (?) 19 August 1908 - 5 October 1908
02	Leonellus R. Feyen (?) 19 August 1908 - 26 September 1908
02	Nicholaus Feyen (?) 1 March 1863 - 8 April 1936
02	Rosalia Feyen (?) 19 August 1895 - 8 March 1908
02	William N. Feyen 19 August 1908 - 2 October 1974
10	Anton Ficker 7 December 1832 - 13 January 1900
10	Elizabeth Ficker 6 January 1850 - 19 November 1896
03	Catherine Fox (?) 1863-1934
10	Henry C. Fox 1911-1920
10	Joseoh E. Fox 1913-1934
03	Nicholas Fox (?) 1860-1939
17	Arvie F. 'Bud' Frandrup 1926 - __
20	Charles B. Frandrup 18 July 1952 - 11 April 1992
	married Karen A. 14 September 1974
01	daughter of Art Frandrup - 30 July 1948 -
17	Dorothy J. Frandrup 1924 - 1991
20	Frank Frandrup 1924 - __
	married Loretta 16 October 1948
01	Fred J. Frandrup 1890-1961
01	Joseph, son of Arvie Frandrup - 27 September 1956 -
20	Loretta Frandrup 1927 - __
	married Frank 16 October 1948
01	Veronica Frandrup 1898 - 1987
13	Josephine Leuf, wife of Domminique Frantz
	6 April 1857 - 29 June 1895
15	Johann Frey 16 January 1827 - 22 March 1896
15	Katharina, wife of Johann Frey 8 May 1841 - 9 January 1892
08	Kathleen A. Frey 1901-1987
08	Margaret Frey 1878-1907
08	Margaretha Kasel, wife of M. W. Frey
	24 January 1878 - 17 September 1907
08	Mathias E. Frey 1904-1973
08	Mathias W. Frey 1873-1966
18	Cyrilla V. Friese 29 November 1927 - 25 February 1988
	married Reuben C. 7 October 1947
18	Reuben C. Friese 7 August 1923 - 14 September 1986
	married Cyrilla V. 7 October 1947
09	Elizabeth Fritscher 9 July 1942 - 27 March 1946
09	Helmuth Fritscher 1916 - __
09	Regina Fritscher 1917 - __
03	Apollonia Fuchs (?) 1820-1906
10	Catherine Fuchs 15 July 1874 - 22 December 1962
03	Elizabeth Fuchs (?) 1871-1942
05	John J. Fuchs 1899-1977
13	Math N. Fuchs 1900-1944

10	Peter J. Fuchs 22 August 1863 - 1 May 1914
03	Philip Fuchs (?) 1897-1938
03	William Fuchs (?) 1851-1929
05	Josephine P. Fusenig 1910-1984
05	Justine F. Fusenig 28 March 1880 - 11 August 1947
05	Nicholas J. Fusenig 1914-1977 U. S. Army
05	Nichols J. Fusenig 23 February 1873 - 6 March 1921
04	Alois M. Gergen 1901-1934
04	Anna Gergen, nee Wallerius 1869-1904
04	Anna K. Wallerius, wife of Jacob J. Gergen, and mother of Edmund,
	Johann, and Alois 2 November 1869 - 24 September 1904
18	Brian Michael Gergen - 12 August 1990 -
03	Edward J. Gergen 1899-1995
04	Jacob J. Gergen 1869-1940
03	Jacobus Gergen 3 March 1878 - 11 June 1905
12	Joan M. Gergen 1949-1974
16	John Peter Gergen 4 March 1946 - 8 August 1992
	married Kathleen L. Werner 21 May 1966
03	Julius N. Gergen 1905-1927
18	Mary E. Gergen 1959-1983
03	Mary K. Gergen 18 November 1875 - 18 December 1969
18	Michael F. Gergen 1958-1982
04	Victoria Lorentz - Gergen , nee Seffern 1865-1923
08	Mary Giefer (?) 1868-1956
08	Peter Giefer, son of Mary & Wilhelm Giefer
	26 August 1890 - 31 October 1896
08	William Giefer (?) 1862-1937
07	Aloys J. Girgen 1903-1967
	married Catherine A. 14 September 1932
07	Anna Girgen (?) 17 March 1863 - 4 February 1946
07	Catherine A. Girgen 1911-1995
	married Aloys J. 14 September 1932
02	Christina Girgen (?) 1869-1939
13	Johann Girgen 1 November 1836 - 24 January 1892
20	Leo F. Girgen 1928 - __
02	Louis John Girgen (?) 1864-1932
13	Margaretha Girgen 6 October 1830 - 13 February 1915
07	Peter Joseph Girgen (?) 10 May 1857 - 30 November 1928
13	Rosa Girgen 1862-1942
20	Ruth M. Girgen 1927 - __
06	Elizabeth Gitzen (?) 3 August 1875 - 17 August 1942
06	John Peter Gitzen (?) 2 October 1873 - 14 March 1952
08	Andrew C. Gross 1941-1996
08	Andrew P. Gross 1906-1944
03	Michael Grughten 1864-1929

07	Nicholas Haas 13 July 1878 - 19 October 1897
16	Angela Y. Halfern 12 March 1863 - 8 January 1925
16	Leonard J. Halfen 12 July 1866 - 17 March 1933
03	Peter John Harrington 1865-1992
06	Magdalena Heinen, nee Kerst, born in Muringen (?), Preussen
	13 December 1819 - 7 May 1901
01	Mary Heinen 1859 - 1930
01	Nicholas Heinen 1858-1935
06	Nicolaus Heinen, born in Huningen (?), Preussen
	20 January 1819 - 22 May 1879
06	Bertha Held 3 March 1844 - 4 December 1930
06	Christopher Held 1884-1945
06	Peter Held 6 July 1836 - 20 April 1901
05	Peter Held 1887 - 1964
05	Susanna Held 1880-1969
01	John Henkes 1818-1912
01	Lina Henkes 1860-1941
04	Appalonia Herschbach (?) 1865-1949
01	Marie Herschbach 1898-1960
04	Gertrude Hilger, nee Langenfeld 1895-1937
15	Adele M. Holzemer 1923 - __
09	Adelheid M. Holzemer (?) 1891-1925
02	Aloys Holzemer (?) 1898-1906
09	Ambrose C. Holzemer (?) 1923-1944
14	Anna Holzemer -no dates
15	Anna Holzemer 1 November 1846 - 12 November 1907
15	Anne K. Holzemer 1908 - __
10	August V. Holzemer (?) 1910-1940
18	Clemence Holzemer 1913-1982
14	Conrad Holzemer -no dates
15	Conrad Holzemer - died 1896
14	Conrad Holzemer 1843-1925
18	Conrad F. Holzemer 1909-1995
18	Eleanor R. Holzemer 1913-1996
10	Gertrude Holzemer (?) 1886-1967
15	David R. Holzemer 1948-1967
09	Helen H. Holzemer (?) 1906-1985
15	Helena Holzemer - died 1896
18	Henrietta Holzemer 1918 - __
15	Johann Holzemer - died 1896
09	John M. Holzemer (?) 1887-1986
14	Josephine Holzimer - no dates
02	Katherina Holzemer (?) 1859-1938
02	Katherine Holzemer (?) 1884-1909
14	Mathias Holzemer - no dates

02	Mathias M. Holzemer (?) 1882-1948

02   Mathias M. Holzemer (?) 1882-1948
15   Michael Holzemer - died 1896
02   Michael Holzemer (?) 1848-1933
09   Monica Holzemer (?) 1925-1926
15   Peter Holzemer - died 1896
15   Peter Holzemer 25 March 1841 - 14 July 1902
15   Richard J. Holzemer 1916-1993
15   Richard J. Holzemer, PFC United States Army World War 2
        1 May 1916 - 27 March 1993
14   Suzanna Holzemer 1848-1919
10   Theodore C. Holzemer (?) 1881-1962
15   Vincent F. Holzemer 1909-1972
07   Anna M. Holzmer (?) 1885-1937
07   John P. Holzmer (?) 1878-1965
01   Jacob Horn 1896-1975
15   Johanna Horsch 1906-1990
15   John F. Horsch 1906-1966
09   John P. Horsch (?) 1877-1939
09   Katherine Horsch (?) 1880-1950
18   Mary G. Horsch 1922 - __
18   Ray F. Horsch 1913-1990
14   Frank Hubley 1863-1942
20   Gary J. Hudak, United States Air Force
        12 March 1947 - 18 February 1989

14   Eugene S. Isenmann Jr., RM1 United States Navy Vietman
        9 December 1936 - 6 December 1989

15   son Jelinek - no dates
15   mother Jelnik - no dates
20   William W. Jacobson 1952-1987

05   Reverent Antony Kaesen, born in Cologne, Germany 25 November 1874
        - ordained - St. Paul Seminary 6 April 1901, Pastor of the
        Church of St. John the Baptist, Vermillion, Minnesota
        1911-1965, died 12 March 1965
16   Frank Karnick 1906-1974
16   Lois V. Karnick 1908-1976
15   Anna C. Kasel 1916 - __
17   Anthony J. Kasel 1910-1985
        married Dora K. 15 October 1935
01   Christ A. Kasel 1908-1971
02   Christoper Kasel (?) 1875-1960
17   Dora K. Kasel 1912 - __
        married Anthony J. 15 October 1935
10   Elizabeth Kasel 1912 - __

15	Frank D. Kasel 1952-1983
12	Hildegard E. Kasel 1915-1975
16	Jacob Kasel 1908-1990
08	John Kasel (?) 1871-1957
10	John L. Kasel 1901-1964
15	John R. Kasel 1950-1965
12	John W. Kasel 1911-1964
15	Joseph G. Kasel 1915-1979
02	Katherine Kasel (?) 1878-1915
02	Katherine Kasel 14 November 1878 - 13 December 1915
16	Leona Kasel 1910 - __
08	Margaret Kasel 1866-1953
17	Margaret Kasel 1905 - __
17	Marie Kasel 1903-1985
08	Mary J. Kasel (?) 1877-1925
01	Math A. Kasel 1894-1955
17	Mike M. Kasel 1914-1993
02	Peter C., son of Christopher & Katherine Kasel 4 September 1906 - 12 December 1907
08	Theodore Kasel 1864-1939
17	Veronica Kasel 1912- __
07	Nick Kaufman 1875-1933
09	Emma K. Kaufmann (?) 1875-1925
07	Johann Kaufmann 27 December 1840 - 27 May 1924
07	Maria Berens, wife of Johann Kaufmann 27 October 1840 - 23 December 1902
09	Peter H. Kaufmann (?) 1873-1916
17	Grace Kelly 1908-1982
17	William F. Kelly 1907-1975
09	Catherine Kerst (?) 1846-1924
09	Hubert Kerst (?) 1827-1884
09	Mary Kerst (?) - no dates
01	Mary Kerst 1879-1927
01	Michael Kerst 1868-1923
09	Nikolas Kerst 23 ? 1897 - 3 June 1900
13	Aloysius L. Kiefer 7 May 1916 - 4 September 1916
13	Katherine Kiefer (?) 1892-1939
13	Katherine Kiefer 1892-1939
13	Marcus Kiefer 1890-1976
13	Wilhelm J. Kiefer born & died 1920
17	Ambrose G. Kieffer, United States Army World War 2 22 February 1922 - 14 December 1986
13	Anna Kieffer 1895-1955
17	Catherine A. Kieffer 1947-1975
13	George Kieffer 1892-1971
17	Joseph W. Kieffer 1948-1988

17   Juliana L. Kieffer 1924-1984

19   Mary D. Kieffer 1955-1988

02   Anna M. Kiemen 1886-1912

02   Anna M. Kiemen 27 February 1886 - 22 November 1912

07   Nicholas Kiemen 23 August 1873 - 2 July 1903

02   Peter J. Kiemen 1879-1961

14   Barbara, child of Peter & Barbara Kirchens
          12 August 1886 - 23 October 1890

14   Joseph, child of Peter & Barbara Kirchens
          16 April 1888 - 4 February 1891

14   Maria, child of Peter & Barbara Kirchens
          20 October 1880 - 20 October 1890

17   Mark J. Kirchner 31 May 1974 - 23 September 1976

10   John M. Kirpach 1893-1958

10   Margaret M. Kirpach 1900-1994

07   Elizabeth Klein 1882-1942

07   John P. Klein 1878-1958

16   Anna M. Kleve - Boettcher (?) 1910-1996

06   Henry Kleve 1871-1958

16   Joseph A. Kleve 1904-1973

06   Julia Kleve 1877-1964

04   Ben Klotz   - no dates

04   Cristy Klotz   - no dates

04   Elizabeth Klotz   - no dates

10   Katharina Klotz 31 October 1890 - 21 October 1912

04   Lena Klotz   - no dates

04   Leo Klotz   - no dates

04   Leo, son of Peter & Lena Klotz
          8 November 1902 - 13 March (?) 1903

10   Maria K. Klotz 26 December 1848 - 24 November 1922

10   Nikolaus Klotz 18 December 1839 - 21 April 1908

04   Nikolaus R. Klotz 7 January 1870 - 16 September 1914

04   Peter Klotz - no dates

14   John J. Kostka 1900-1988
          married Marie G. 12 July 1921

14   Marie G. Kostka, nee Ries 1897-1991
          married John J. 12 July 1921

01   Robert, son of John & Marie Kostka
          14 May 1922 - 3 September 1930

08   Gilles Krausen, born in Frisingen Kanton. Esch an der Alzett
          Grossnerzogthum, Luxemburg
          7 November 1837 - 2 February 1899

08   Peter Krausen, born in Zu Frisingen Kanton Esch, an der Alzett
          Grossherzogthum, Luxemburg
          13 June 1835 - 28 March 1894

07   A. Magdalens Kummer (?) 1893-1914

11	Aurelie Kummer (?) - 24 September 1919 -
10	Helen M. Kummer 1923-1982
07	Jacob Kummer (?) 1845-1921
11	Jacob C. Kummer (?) 26 February 1875 - 30 January 1942
11	Josephine Kummer (?) 17 April 1882 - 25 October 1968
10	Martin G. Kummer 1917 - __
11	Theresa Kummer (?) - 27 September 1916 -

06	Aaron Langenfeld 20 June - 21 June 1977
01	Adam Langenfeld (?) 1859-1929
01	Angela Langenfeld (?) 1863-1933
16	Anna M. Langenfeld 1889-1974
17	August F. Langenfeld 11 August 1914 - 12 August 1915
04	Augustin Langenfeld 13 April 1819 - 19 December 1904
04	Elisabeth Langenfeld 27 January 1827 - 6 June 1911
16	Frank J. Langenfeld 1887-1978
14	Robert Langenfeld 1943-1944
14	Carleton Leaman 1917-1992
	married Julie 4 June 1940
14	Carlton T. Leaman TEC 5 United States Army World War 2
	26 March 1917 - 8 March 1992
14	Julie Leaman, nee Kieffer 1916 - __
	married Carleton 4 June 1940
01	Randy Annette Lees - 18 September 1975 -
03	Catherine Leifeld 1894-1972
10	Elizabeth Leifeld 1873-1957
11	Emma M. Leifeld 1885-1970
11	F. J. Leifeld 1882-1963
10	Frank H. Leifeld 1907-1993
10	Henry P. Leifeld 1869-1921
19	Joseph Leifeld 24 April 1925 - 16 September 1991
03	Louis Leifeld 1884-1967
16	Louisa Leifeld 1874-1942
11	Margaret E. Leifeld 1886-1965
10	Mary M. Leifeld 1903-1929
16	Nick Leifeld 1868-1926
10	William H. Leifeld 1908-1993
05	Jacob Leuf 20 September 1831 - 22 January 1909
05	Josephine Pohl, wife of Jacob Leuf, born 10 November 1830,
	married (?) 3 February 1855, died 14 February 1904
04	Anna Loesch, born Kummer
	1 September 1848 - 12 December 1918
03	Bertha C. Loesch (?) 1905-1986
05	'Father' Loesch (?) 9 August 1880 - 6 October 1949
04	George Loesch 1881-1942
19	Harold H. Loesch 1929-1983

03	John N. Loesch (?) 1889-1951
05	John W. Loesch 30 August 1930 - 17 November 1954
	enlisted in the United States Air Force 2 November 1948
04	Joseph Loesch 13 June 1850 - 3 February 1910
04	Joseph Loesch 1879-1947
05	'Mother' Loesch (?) 17 April 1886 - 25 December 1930
04	Eugenia Lorentz 1893-1926
14	Anthony Lucking 1892-1990
14	Barbara Lucking 1895-1982
08	Anschela Ludewig 1852 - no date listed
08	Michael Ludewig, died 3 April 1910, age 70 years
13	Anna K. Mamer 1883-1975
13	Dorothea Katherine Mamer 11 January 1919 - 28 August 1919
13	George H. Mamer 1879-1962
13	Jacob P. Mamer 5 January 1923 - 13 October 1923
11	Karl Marschal 2 February 1845 in Diekirch Groszherzogthum,
	Luxemburg, died 19 August 1899
11	Margaretha, born Huble, wife of Karl Marschal, 23 March 1849
	in Marshenk (?), Luxemburg, died 23 March 1885
14	Adeline Marschall 1898 - __
01	Anna Marschall 1839-1930
01	Anna Marschall 1894-1980
12	Anna Marschall (?) 1895-1980
01	Anna M. Marschall 1857-1938
14	Anton Marschall, born in Diekirch Grossherzogthum, Luxemburg
	17 June 1829 - 15 March 1894
15	Anton Marschall 6 October 1889 - 9 February 1977
02	Anton G. Marschall 1885-1968
12	Charles Marschall 1892-1964
12	Charles Marschall (?) 1893-1964
12	Charles N. Marschall (?) 1932-1978
14	Frances C. Marschall 6 January 1903 - 11 September 1982
14	Frances C. Marschall, nee Kasel 1903-1982
01	George K. Marschall 1854-1934
14	George P. Marschall 1893-1961
20	Gloria S. Marschall 1928 - __
05	Heinrich R. Marschall 20 June 1867 - 6 November 1901
05	Heinrich R. Marschall 1867-1910
14	Jos. P. Marschall 1893-1975
18	Joseph A. Marschall, S SGT United States Air Force Korea
	1930-1981
14	Joseph Peter Marschall, Pvt. United States Army World War 2
	16 August 1893 - 25 October 1975
14	Katharina Marschall, born Kasel 22 August 1867 - 1 May 1905
05	Magdalena Marschall 18 December 1898 - 18 March 1899

15	Margaret Marschall 6 March 1896 - 15 January 1980
01	Margaret Rosalia Marschall (?) 1895-1974
05	Maria A. Marschall 1874-1928
14	Maria M. Marschall 17 August 1828 - 18 May 1923
02	Mary Marschall 1886-1976
15	Mary Marschall 26 October 1891 - 10 April 1966
01	Peter Marschall 1837-1931
14	Peter Marschall 9 June 1860 - 18 November 1896
14	Lawrence A. Marshall 6 July 1921 - 15 May 1992
05	Maria A. Klotz, wife of Heinrich Marshall
	8 January 1874 - 12 March 1928
12	Marjorie Marshall 1921-1993
02	Mary Marshall (?) 1871-1959
01	Mary Magdalen Marshall (?) 1889-1961
02	Mathias Marshall (?) 1869-1923
02	Nicholas Marshall 28 September 1904 - 4 March 1991
02	Peter Marshall 19 July 1902 - __
07	George J. May (?) 1889-1953
07	Lillian A. May (?) 1912-1975
07	Mary May (?) 1893-1943
16	Merle McClintock 1922 - __
16	Rose McClintock 1927 - __
10	Anna M. Meyers 1894-1961
10	baby boy, son of Mr & Mrs. George A. Meyers - 17 October 1969 -
10	Herman J. Meyers 1891-1960
10	Judy Ann, daughter of Mr. & Mrs. George A. Meyers
	12 July - 28 July 1961
10	Mary, daughter of Mr. & Mrs. George A. Meyers - 24 November 1965 -
08	Nicholas Mollers, died 12 March 1877
	age 76 years 2 months 10 days
06	Josephine Mueller (?) 1850-1933
06	Michael Mueller (?) 1845-1921
18	Mark Donavon Murphy - 30 September 1994 -
20	Karen M. Murray, wife of Kenneth W. - married 30 May 1987
	daughter of Frank & Loretta Frandrup
	5 November 1962 - 29 September 1993
03	Alfred H. Neuman 1913 - __
12	Mary Rollinger Niederprim 1876-1955
14	'Mother' Niederprim (?) 1863-1919
16	Catherina Niesen 3 February 1854 - 27 July 1899
16	Christ Niesen 22 September 1848 - 8 March 1913
04	Katherine Niesen 1888-1966
08	Victor Pennell 1876-1921
04	Barbara F. Perlick 1901-1995

19	P. H. Philipp, died 14 January 1899, age 54 years
05	Clara Pohl 1879-1952
17	Ernest Pohl 1913-1979
05	Joseph R. Pohl 1874-1942
17	Lucille Pohl 1916 - __
08	Josephine Raway 1899-1965
08	Peter J. Raway 1899-1962
09	Aloys J. Reiter (?) 1900-1959
11	Henry John Reiter 6 June 1910 - __
11	John Reiter (?) 1862-1921
10	John H. Reiter 1896-1952
11	Katherine Reiter (?) 1869-1927
09	Margaret A. Reiter (?) 1895-1970
10	Martha E. Reiter 1900-1993
11	Nicholas Reiter 10 May 1827 - 31 July 1905
08	Catherine Reuter (?) 1888-1928
08	John J. Reuter (?) 1880-1961
08	John P. Reuter (?) 19 September 1854 - 5 February 1927
08	Mary Reuter (?) 29 November 1856 - 17 February 1942
15	Michael A. Reuter 1913 - 1994
15	Thersa R. Reuter 1918 - __
01	Adelheide Ries 1872-1960
01	Catharina Odelia Ries 1906-1995
20	Christian J. Ries 1920-1993
20	Eleanor E. Ries 1919-1995
09	Gregor Ries 1895-1978
14	John A. Ries 1911 - __
14	Lenora M. Ries 1911 - __
01	Mary Theresa Ries 26 October 1942 - 15 February 1943
01	Nicholas Ries 1873-1960
14	Robert A. Ries 26 March 1941 - 31 March 1965
01	Rose Scholastica Ries 1908 - __
09	Theresa Ries 1896-1975
11	J. August Rollinger 18 June 1863 - 10 November 1886
11	John Rollinger 6 May 1823 - 21 February 1910
12	John Rollinger 1865-1917
12	Katharina Rollinger, died 15 October 1886, age 56 years
11	Maria, wife of Johann Rollinger, born 10 April 1833 in Medernach Grossherzogthum, Luxemburg, died 9 May 1895
07	Albert Rother (?) 1898-1917
18	Albert Rother 1917-1994, married Ermelinda 23 September 1941
16	Andrew V. Rother 1914 - __
17	Anna Rother 1900-1989, married Nicholas 1 September 1925
02	Caecilia Rother 1899-1942
06	Caroline, daughter of H. & C. Rother

	25 August 1878 - 2 September 1900
06	Caroline Luef Rother 26 January 1854 - 7 April 1923
16	Catherine Rother 1894-1975
17	Deloris T. Rother 1928 - __
17	Emma C. Rother 6 April 1892 (?) - 4 July 1892 (?)
18	Ermelinda Rother 1917 - __, married Albert 23 September 1941
06	Henry Rother 1 February 1843 - 9 November 1923
06	Henry J. Rother 1 February 1886 - 24 September 1954
07	Johanna Rother (?) 1863-1934
06	John J. Rother 14 October 1891 - 16 May 1949
07	Katharina Rother (?) 1891-1901
18	Lawrence G. Rother 1924-1990
	married Rose M. 1 February 1947
18	Lawrence George Rother, S SGT United States Army World War 2
	16 March 1924 - 24 November 1990
16	Leonida Rother 1910 - __
17	Leroy G. Rother 1926 - __
16	Mary E. Rother 1914 - __
17	Nicholas Rother 1901-1984, married Anna 1 September 1925
18	Rose M. Rother 1926 - __
06	Victoria, daughter of H. & C. Rother
	28 September 1894 - 19 July 1901
07	Vincent Rother (?) 1861-1943
16	Vincent E. Rother 1908 - __
02	Vincent H. Rother 1879-1938
16	Vincent J. Rother 1888-1972
05	Phillip Saduske 1875-1960
19	Dennis Michael Sandkamp, son of Leo & Rita
	19 February 1964 - 8 October 1982
19	Thomas Alan, son of Mr. & Mrs. Leo F. Sandkamp
	28 April 1962 - 7 October 1964
01	Anna M. Schaal 1891-1976
09	Alfred W. Schanno 1904-1981
12	Antony Schanno 1881-1944
12	Catherine Schanno 1886-1944
09	Christine F. Schanno 1904 - __
02	Clarence C. Schanno (?) 1911-1976
14	Eduard Schanno 7 January 1906 - 23 February 1909
05	Ida J. Schanno 1890-1979
19	Irene H. Schanno 1914-1984
09	Jacob Schanno 11 May 1850 - 31 January 1931
05	Jacob P. Schanno 1882-1956
09	Katherine (?) Schanno (?), died 26 October 1890, age 42 years
19	Leo J. Schanno 1911-1996
09	Maria G. Schanno 20 April 1856 - 26 October 1913

02   Nicholas Schanno (?) 1874-1911
02   Susan B. Schanno (?) 1878-1962
09   Susan M. Schanno 1882-1957
09   William Schanno 1879-1950
19   Marion M. Schletty 1915-1994
19   William J. Schletty 1912-1985
12   Math Schlosser 1830-1895
04   Gertrude Langenfeld Schmitz 1869-1952
04   Agatha Schwartz 7 September 1871 - 5 June 1959
06   Cecilia M. Schwartz 1916 - __
05   Othmar N. Schwartz 1914-1963
04   Peter Schwartz 30 May 1880 - 22 February 1933
19   Lorraine R. Scully 1921 - __
19   Sylvester J. Scully 1913-1984
05   Anna M. Nahl, wife of Franz Seffern, born in Schonecke, Deutschland
         26 July 1829 - 6 August 1901
05   Franz Seffern, born in Hastings, Minnesota
         24 August 1859 - 15 September 1915
05   Franziskus Seffern, born in Rhein Provinz, Deutschland
         17 September 1825 - 20 November 1915
07   Amanda K. Severance - 1980 -
15   Rose C. Sherf 1876-1962
20   Helen Sieben, nee Letendre 1927-1992
         married Norbert 17 May 1947
20   Norbert Sieben 1923 - __, married Helen 17 May 1947
18   baby Siebenaler - 26 February 1946 -
18   Bernard W. Siebenaler 1921-1995
17   Emma M. Siebenaler 1922 - __
         married Willaim J. 24 February 1943
18   Evelyn A. Siebenaler 1924 - __
17   Joseph L. Siebenaler 1917-1985
17   Louise C. Siebenaler 1916 - __
18   Mary F. Siebenaler 1928 - __
18   Mathias L. Siebenaler 1923 - __
16   Sharon A. Siebenaler 1957-1974
17   William J. Siebenaler, TEC 4 United States Army World War 2
         5 October 1918 - 27 August 1984
17   William J. Siebenaler 1918-1984
         married Emma M. 24 February 1943
16   Margaretha Simmer (Niesen family ?)
         17 March 1820 - 19 September 1901
08   John J. Stelter 1942-1968
19   Paschel A. Stelter 1912-1987
19   Rose K. Stelter 1912-1988
14   Linda Rosanne, daughter of Mr. & Mrs. Corwin G. Staus
         28 June 1958 - 20 October 1964

18	Ambrose B. Stoffel 1914 - __
09	Anna Stoffel, born Wagner, died 15 February 1901, age 81 years
01	Annie L. Stoffel 1885-1974
02	Antony M. Stoffel 1917-1930
01	Bernard A. Stoffel 15 August 1925 (?) - 12 December 192? (?)
01	Cecelia A. Stoffel 1908-1993
13	Elisabeth Stoffel 15 September 1848 - 14 September 1888
12	Elizabeth Stoffel (?) 1864-1927
02	Florence R. Stoffel 1914 - __
09	Gerald Stoffel (?) 1936-1938
16	Hillary Stoffel - 1927 -
01	Irene L. Stoffel 21 September 1919 (?) - 21 February 1930
01	Jacob A. Stoffel 1876-1952
09	Johann Stoffel 1837 - 9 July (?) 1920
13	Johann N. Stoffel 28 May 1842 - 17 April 1908
02	John Joseph Stoffel (?) 1889-1925
13	Katharina Stoffel 15 January 1850 - 24 February 1925
02	Leona M. Stoffel (?) 1920-1921
04	Marcus Stoffel 1890-1972
02	Margaret Stoffel (?) 1891-1938
01	Maria Stoffel 1 January 1840 - 15 February 1928
01	Maria (?) A. Stoffel ? September 1910 - 9 February 1911
16	Marie Stoffel 1896-1981
08	Marie A. Stoffel 1908 - __
04	Mary Stoffel 1893-1987
12	Mechtilda Stoffel (?) 1902-1910
16	Michael Stoffel 1892-1962
01	Peter Stoffel 10 November 1834 - 20 March 1917
09	Peter Stoffel (?) 1935-1935
13	Peter N. Stoffel (?) - no dates
08	Peter R. Stoffel 1900-1983
16	Raphael Stoffel 1924-1925
02	Raymond P. Stoffel 1914-1976
01	Raymond P. Stoffel Jr., AA United States Navy Vietnam
	2 July 1949 - 19 October 1995
01	Raymond P. Stoffel 2 July 1949 - 19 October 1995
18	William A. Stoffel 1917-1991
17	Clara Studenmaier - no dates
04	Bertha Therres 1890-1972
04	Johann Therres 21 February 1826 - 8 May 1906
04	Johann Therres 1826-1906
04	Joseph Therres 1884-1954
04	Joseph C. Therres 1928-1977
04	Lena Therres 1873-1897
04	Magdalena Therres 25 August 1873 - 8 January 1897

04	Maria Therres 1881-1900
04	Maria Therres 10 August 1881 - 26 November 1900
04	Marie E. Therres 1843-1922
04	Marie P. Therres, born in Junker ? Rhein Provense Trier (?)
	28 October 1843 - 30 June 1920
04	Peter Therres 1877-1922
02	Anton Thurmes (?) 1878-1956
02	Ferdinand M. Thurmes (?) 1912-1982
02	Helen M. Thurmes (?) 1909-1948
07	Magdalena Thurmes (?) 1856-1929
07	Nicholas Thurmes (?) 1850-1932
02	Susan Thurmes (?) 1887-1962
08	Lori Ann Tix 6 December 1982 - 13 December 1982
18	Emmett P. Traynor 1911-1977
18	Shirley B. Traynor 1918 - __
19	Catherine C. Tutewohl 1918 - __
17	Dorothy F. Tutewohl 1908-1977
20	Dorothy T. Tutewohl 1923 - __, married Thomas F. 3 April 1948
17	Edward L. Tutewohl 1911-1975
19	Lorie Tutewohl - no dates
19	Mary Tutewohl - no dates
20	Thomas F. Tutewohl 1925-1987, married Dorothy T. 3 April 1948
19	Vincent H. Tutewohl 1914-1984
18	Alfred J. Wagner 1899-1982
16	Aloys Wagner 1907-1983
05	Anna Maria Wagner 4 May 1832 - 6 June 1908
21	Bernard A. Wagner 1911-1996
	married Lily M. 16 September 1939
04	Christopher Wagner 1871-1944
12	Domnic Nicholas Wagner 6 June 1892 - 12 March 1894
12	Emma Mary Wagner 17 September 1882 - 30 December 1889
04	'Father' Wagner (?) 1872-1935
15	Frances Wagner 1911-1979
12	Helena Christina Wagner 31 December 1895 - 11 June 1896
04	Johanna Josephine Wagner, nee Leuf
	31 January 1859 - 19 October 1949
04	Joseph Anton Wagner 6 February 1863 - 25 February 1915
17	Joseph N. Wagner 1921-1986
21	Lily M. Wagner 1915 - __, married Bernard A. 16 September 1939
01	Margaretha Wagner 17 March 1855 - 12 February 1920
12	Mary Anne Wagner 18 June 1887 - 31 July 1887
01	Michael Wagner 5 October 1853 - 13 April 1915
04	'Mother' Wagner (?) 1875-1920
05	Nicholas Wagner, born in Hostert Grossh. Luxemburg
	28 February 1828 - 13 April 1902

15	Othmar Wagner 1909-1979
16	Susan Wagner 1908-1990
17	Theresa M. Wagner 1922-1977
11	?? Wallering (?) 22 October 1892 - 25 November 1892 - hard to read
11	?? Wallering (?) ??? - 26 ? 1897 (?) - hard to read
14	George P. Weiland (?) 1910-1935
14	John Weiland (?) 1873-1935
14	John P. Weiland 1904-1924
14	Mary Weiland (?) 1870-1956
16	Anthony Werner 1913 - __
12	Beverly Werner 6 June 1962 - 14 December 1962
12	Catherine Werner (?) 1856-1955
14	Christ Werner 1895-1991
12	Josephine Werner (?) 1899-1975
07	John N. Werner 1884-1965
03	John W. Werner 1883-1968
06	Justina Werner (?) 1857-1945
07	Mary A. Werner 1889-1987
03	Mary A. Werner 1893-1983
16	Mary K. Werner 1923 - __
06	Nicholas Werner (?) 1853-1937
16	Nicholas G. Werner 1952-1970
01	Nikolaus Werner 17 October 1887 - 15 December 1918
14	Rose Werner 1905 - __
16	Stacy Leigh Werner 10 August - 22 October 1984
12	William Werner (?) 1855-1939
09	Al Wiederhold 1898-1973
06	Frank Wiederhold 1896-1966
03	John Wiederhold (?) 1861-1942
10	Joseph Wiederhold 2 December 1856 - 4 May 1906
03	Joseph C., son of Johann & Theresia Wiederhold 2 April 1899 - 10 June 1913
10	Louise, daughter of Joseph & Margaretha Wiederhold 11 January 1890 - 15 April 1891
09	Magdalen Wiederhold 1906-1986
10	Margaretha Meisch, wife of Joseph Wiederhold 6 December 1866 - 1 May 1892
03	Theresa Wiederhold (?) 1872-1960
12	Nora M. Wise 1916-1969
12	Eugene H. Wollmering 1923-1927
03	Henry Wollmering (?) 1865-1954
03	Henry Wollmering 18 October 1905 - 18 February 1906
03	Henry F. Wollmering 19 April 1908 - 15 December 1910
20	Henry J. Wollmering 1917 - __
04	John Wollmering 4 July 1858 - 5 March 1922

10	John Wollmering 1896-1988
03	Joseph A. Wollmering (?) 1900-1938
12	Joseph C. Wollmering 1934-1936
03	Margaretha Wollmering (?) 1874-1953
04	Peter Wollmering 1902-1983, married Theresa 5 October 1932
04	Ramona M., daughter of Peter & Theresa Wollmering
	- 28 April 1940 -
20	Rose C. Wollmering 1915 - __
04	Susan Wollmering 1856-1948
04	Theresa Wollmering 1904 - __, married Peter 5 October 1932
10	Veronica Wollmering 1901-1980
08	Anna Zeien 1862-1944
08	Joseph Zeien 30 September 1858 - 26 October 1915
08	Wilhelm Zeien 8 August 1886 - 29 August 1886
08	William Zeien 1886-1886
08	William N. Zeien, PVT United States Army World War 2
	1901-1980

The following were unreadable or I could not get a surname.

12	Elizabeth 1901-1901 - no surname - with Math Schlosser
12	Joseph 1904-1905 - no surname - with Math Schlosser
12	Peter 1888-1892 - no surname - with Math Schlosser
17	6 September 1890 (?) - ? April 1892 (?)
	can't read name - very hard to read
18	?? 1892 - ? October 1893
	can't read name - very hard to read

St. John's Catholic Cemetery
(or St. John the Baptist Catholic Cemetery?)
Vermillion, Dakota County, MN.
T114N–R18W, Section 22

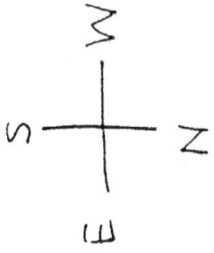

Row 7
Row 6
Row 5

Statues

Drive
Area

No
Marked
Burials

Row 7
Row 6
Row 5

Row 1

Row

CORINTHIAN CEMETERY

Empire Township, Dakota County, Minnesota: T114N-R19W, section 29

This cemetery is upkept and in good shape. This cemetery is located along the northeast edge of Farmington. The area that comprises the cemetery is actually two cemeteries. The western side of the area is Corinthian Cemetery and the northeast side is St. Michael's Catholic Cemetery. I have listed the cemeteries separately.

I began numbering with row 1 along the east edge of Corinthian cemetery. At the time I began numbering the old fence line could still be detected by a couple of fence posts and the changing of fencing style along the north edge of the cemeteries. The cemetery gate was dedicated to the memory of H.W. Hosmer - Corinthian Cemetery 1872.

In 'History of Dakota County and the city of Hastings, ...' By Rev. Edward D. Neill, written in 1881, he wrote ... In 1872, the freemasons of this place talked strongly of purchasing land for a cemetery for the use of the members of their order, but some dissatisfaction arose among them, and the measures were never carried out. The citizens, however, in the same year organized an association for the fitting up of a cemetery for general use, and bought five acres of land, ... About eighty internments have been made. (page 363).

The Dakota county cemetery records compilation lists this cemetery as: Corinthian Cemetery, established 1872. 5 acres. Located Section 29, SW1/4 (west side).

Everyone is listed in alphabetical order. The number before each entry is the row number. There is a map at the back of this section.

These cemetery burial monuments were transcribed during 1996.

34   Chandler (?), son of (?) H. and A. (?) A??ler (?)
                died (?) 12 March (?) 1878, age 1 month (?) - very hard to read
42   Anna L.P. Abell, wife of Erasmus Darwin Abell
                6 March 1820 - 26 February 1911
42   Erasmus Darwin Abell 26 January 1817 - 2 October 1899
37   ? Ackley (?), died 24 January (?) 1873,
                age 27 years 9 months 24 days - hard to read
24   Vern Adkins 1921-1976
45   Elaine M. Akin 1 August 1920 - 19 August 1992
                married Lamar H. 26 March 1942
30   Gerrit F. Akin, died 18 April 1934
45   Lamar H. Akin 12 June 1918 - 8 February 1997
                married Elaine M. 26 March 1942
30   Nellie Akin, died 20 April 1945

01	Melinda Alden 2 April 1943 - 20 February 1973
08	George J. Alexander 1872-1945
08	Lydia B. Alexander 1872-1943
07	Myrle G. Alexander 1899-1962
07	Myrle G. Alexander 22 August 1899 - 20 June 1962
	MN Sfc 1 ORD Depot Co WW1
07	Vera Mae Alexander 27 September 1895 - 26 May 1975
07	Vera R. Alexander 1901-1967
41	Carroll C. Allen 1874-1938
41	Gladys Louise Allen 10 July 1893 - 13 August 1901
41	Mae E. Allen 1875-1964
31	David H. Allgor 1896-1972
32	Henry Allgor 1852-1940
32	Margaret Allgor 1864-1938
31	Ruth E. Allgor 1899-1987
22	Maggie, wife of J.A. Almquist 11 June 1854 - 14 November 1888
33	Grace M. Alton 1871-1922
09	Beverly A. Ames 1932-1933
10	Chester C. Ames 1907-1994
	married Ruby B. 3 July 1928
10	Ruby B. Ames, nee Reisinger 1910-1996
	married Chester C. 3 July 1928
19	Dorothy Atley Amidon 1811-1904
38	Emma S. Amidon 1857-1928
38	Hattie E. Amidon 1866-1902
38	William W. Amidon 1851-1932
26	Leo Amundson 1898-1991
26	Thelma Amundson 1905-____
38	Ethel P. Anderson 1889-1968
38	Oscar Anderson 31 August 1876 - 24 June 1955
	Cpl US Army Sp Am War
38	Phillip Anderson 1908-1921
02	Theodore Anderson, died 24 October 1912
44	Bradly A. Angen 1962-1990
02	Enoch Arneson 10 March 1931 - 5 June 1932
24	Eloise J. Asher 1913-1991
24	Loran K. Asher 1912-1974
28	Robert Averill 1925-1989
28	Wilford Averill 1913-1990
41	Marion, wife of W.C.B. (?), died 15 May 1879, 19 years 6 months
	- hard to read
26	Frances C.B. Guiteau Babcock 1794-1882
24	Helen Backes 1910-1988
01	Pamela M. Backes 1977-1996
24	Raymond Backes 1901-1975

40	Josephine V. Bailey, died 17 April 1877, age 36 years 29 days
30	Anna A. Baker 1869-1945
29	Arnold A. Baker 1906-1962
22	Edna, daughter of A.J. and O.H. Baker
	died 11 April 1889 (?), age 7 years
22	Guy, son of A.J. and O.H. Baker 1879-1897
30	Thomas E. Baker 1875-1936
10	Fannie P. Balch (?) 1857-1933
10	George S. Balch (?) 1851-1932
42	Birdie Ballard (?) - no dates
42	Flora, wife of Peter W. Ballard - no dates
42	Florence B. Ballard, age 20 years - buried at the east side of
	foster fathers and mothers monument
42	J. Ballard, husband of Mary A. Ballard - no dates
42	Mary A., wife of J. Ballard - no dates
42	Peter W., son of J. Ballard - no dates
24	Caroline Barbey 1903-____
24	Emil Barbay 1898-1975
33	Alexander A. Barclay 1842-1905
21	Harmon F., son of H.W. and E.E. Barkuloo
	12 August 1876 - 8 June 1883
21	Harmon W. Barkuloo, died 8 October 1876, age 35 years 4 months
23	baby girl Barlage - 1960 -
35	LeRoy J. Barlage 1914-1986 Sgt US Army WW2
35	LeRoy J. Barlage 1914-1986
	married Mary O. 26 June 1948
35	Mary O. Barlage 1918-1995
	married LeRoy J. 26 June 1948
19	Charley R. Barnum 5 April 1878 - 7 November 1891
18	Frona V. Barnum ? - 1940 (?) buried
19	Milton T. Barnum 1833-1912
19	Rachel C. Barnum 1839-1918
32	baby Bartelds - 1930 -
32	John A. Bartelds 1903-1989
32	Lucille E. Bartelds 1900-1973
31	Selma E. Bartelds 11 January 1912 - ____
03	Lewis Bartz Sr. 1903-1980
16	Harriet, wife of Rev. John B. Batson 1840-1927
16	Rev. John B. Batson 1836-1919
16	Jud L. Batson 1875-1948
03	Bliss H. Becker 1889-1964
03	Edwin Anthony Becker 18 November 1893 - 25 February 1958
	MN Pvt 163 Depot Brigade WW1
11	Emma A. Becker 30 December 1865 - 2 August 1965
03	Gena M. Becker 1902-1991
17	George Becker 1797-1886

11	Harry F. Becker 30 August 1900 - 6 July 1917
03	Luella A. Becker 5 July 1900 - 22 May 1980
11	Oliver N. Becker 19 May 1861 - 20 June 1923
13	Alfred H. Beenken 1918-1991
13	Shirley N. Beenken 1927-1993
16	Ann Selena Bell 1855-1920
17	baby Bell (?) - 1915 -
17	baby Bell (?) - 1914 -
17	C. Maybelle Bell (?) 1887-1961
25	Doris R. Bell 1914-1979
03	Esther P. Bell 1910-1974
17	Frank P. Bell (?) 1883-1954
03	George F. Bell 1916-1980
03	George F. Bell 1944-1957
11	Henry J. Bell 1878-1934
16	James Bell 1844-1915
11	Mary Jane Bell 1871-1942
25	Wayne M. Bell 1910-1974
01	Arthur W. Belter 1907-1986
	married Verona M. 20 February 1930
01	Verona M. Belter 1912-_____
	married Arthur W. 20 February 1930
15	Clara Wescott Thomas Bemis 1849-1926
02	Lila M. Benham 1903-1982
02	Lowell Benham 1902-1970
26	Clarence A. Benjamin 1912-1964
26	Mary L. Benjamin 1916-_____
35	Anna S. Berry 1919-_____
35	Howard D. Berry 1915-1986
38	Carrie I., Wife of Nelson Best 1865-1939
26	David C. Best (?) 1875-1950
26	Ida M. Best (?) 1879-1982
13	Gary R. Bester 1948-1980
20	Jennie Sachs Bester 1895-1983
08	Ardis L. Bethke 1913-1987
06	Emmons M. Betzold 1903-1982
08	Fred A. Bethke 1902-1975
21	George F. Betzold 1860-1945
06	George M. Betzold 1902-1979
21	Katherine A. Betzold 1859-1948
05	Lee Ann, infant daughter of Mr. and Mrs. Geo A. Betzold
	11-12 August 1954
20	Lewis C. Betzold 7 August 1888 - 26 March 1908
21	Lewis C. Betzold 1888-1908
08	Louisa M. Betzold 1871-1956
06	Mabel M. Betzold 1903-1982

06	Martha H. Betzold 1886-1959
06	Melvin O. Betzold 1917-1966
08	Samuel M. Betzold 1864-1961
07	E. Grant Birdsall 1871-1947
06	Eleanor A. Birdsall 1 March 1912 - 18 June 1992
07	Eva F. Birdsall 1871-1950
43	Forest Birdsall 1892-1972
	married Margaret 20 November 1910
06	Harvey V. Birdsall 18 August 1908 - 12 May 1984
17	J. Ralph Birdsall 1895-1976
17	L. Ruth Birdsall 1903-____
43	Margaret Birdsall 1893-1965
	married Forest 20 November 1910
17	Retha O. Birdsall 1904-1928
30	Hazel Bisek 1911-1985
30	Joe Bisek 1909-____
30	Russell F. Duff (?) or Bisek (?) 1907-1938
13	Murdice L. Bjerke 1923-1984
33	Lois Alice Bliss 1875-1921
45	Nilo John Blomquist 7 December 1908 - 13 December 1987
41	Chas. P. Blunt 1862-1931
41	Minnie Bell McConnell, wife of Chas. P. Blunt
	23 January 1867 - 30 May 1899
24	Reuben O. Boehlke 1904-1975
23	Steven Robert Bohart - September 1957 -
42	Phoebe Jane Boland - rest of the stone buried to deep to read
42	Ralph, son of J. and P. Boland, died ? June 1883, age 1 month 1 day
42	Richard Boland, died 14 October 1882, age 1 year 8 months 24 days
42	William C. Boland 1884-1954
40	Luella Bonham 12 February 1870 - 23 January 1894
04	Donald W. Boyd 1903-1962
04	Olive B. Boyd 1906-1985
23	Hattie L. Boyer 1873-1966
39	A.B.W. Bracket (?) 1851-1904
39	Carlton Brackett (?) - 1870 -
39	C.L.B. Brackett (?) 1868-1921
39	D.M.B. Brackett (?) 1881-1924
39	E.H.B. Brackett (?) 1846-1907
39	E.L.B. Brackett (?) 1836-1918
39	Frank Brackett (?) - 1873 -
39	G.M.C.B. Brackett (?) 1833-1878
39	M.E.B. Brackett (?) 1847-1926
39	'Mother' Brackett (?) 1812-1891
39	W.M.B. Brackett (?) 1843-1927
12	Alice H. Bradford (?) 1875-1884
12	Bennie Bradford 1885-1886

12	Cynthia M. Bradford 1850-1929
12	Eva A. Bradford 1881-1956
12	Fanny P. Bradford 1879-1956
12	'Father' Bradford (?) 1832-1896
12	Frank H. Bradford 1887-1961
12	Henry B. Bradford 1878-1963
12	'Mother' Bradford (?) 1834-1911
12	Pliny F. Bradford 1850-1908
39	Zoie Fluke Bradford 1876-1931
06	Emma A. Briesacher 1879-1967
06	Fred C. Briesacher 1873-1952
05	Leila A. Briesacher 1912-1993
05	Walter E. Briesacher 1903-1954
06	Jennie Briggs 1893-1954
39	Arthur Francis, son of C.A. and J.J. Brooks
	died 10 December 1874, age 1 year 5 months 12 days
39	Cynthia, wife (?) of J.J. Brooks (?), died 20 October 1873
	age 27 years 8 months 23 days
07	Anna Mae Brown 3 June 1903 - 21 November 1969
12	Jennie (?) Brown 1866 - 1930
12	John J., son of Samuel and Betsy Brown
	17 August 1865 - 14 April 1878, age 12 years 7 months 27 days
07	Orley V. Brown 13 July 1898 - 22 October 1954
	2d. Lieutenant Infantry WW1
12	Robert J. Brown 1863-1919
12	Samuel J. Brown 10 January 1823 - 19 August 1896, age 73 years
39	Abigail Brownell 2 March 1813 - 15 April 1874
08	Elmer A. Brosseth 1910-1971
08	Grace V. Brosseth 1909-____
08	Margaret M. Brosseth 1870-1942
35	Cheryl L. Brule 1957-1996
35	Stephanie Brule 1975-1992
23	Lynn Brummund - 29 July 1964 -
15	Nina L. Bullard 1873 - 1909
23	baby boy Bung - August 1950 -
40	Laverna M. Bung 1903-1991
40	Lyle E. Bung 1902-1993
28	David Waverly Burton 6 December 1891 - 15 February 1959
	MN Pvt Co C 41 Infantry WW1
28	Forest W. Burton (?) 23 August 1859 - 14 September 1940
28	Lydia Gerrie Burton 3 August 1906 - 31 August 1990
28	Rachel G. Burton (?) 6 June 1858 - 27 February 1943
28	son of Mr. and Mrs. D.W. Burton - 8 May 1937 -
43	Benjamin F. Cable 1866-1942
39	George S. Cable 1837-1902 ; 161 N.Y. Vol. Inf.

39	Ira L. Cable 1877-1957
39	James H. Cable 1870-1958
43	Nettie A. Cable 1875-1952
39	Telina M. Cable 1844-1925
39	Walter, son of G.S. and T.M. Cable (?) died 8 January (?) 1873, age 10 months
19	Clara Edna Cadwell 1894-1973
19	Claude E. Cadwell 1892-1983
19	Mary Jane, daughter of Mr. and Mrs. Claude E. Cadwell 9 September 1921 - 6 April 1923
03	Audley R. Canfield 1873-1966
33	Clarence L. Canfield 1879-1935
03	Mary E. Canfield 1877-1972
23	Herman Carlson 1876-1962
23	Erin Westley Carroll - 7 July 1977 -
41	Harriet Staplin Carter, mother of Wm. and Wallace Stapliistie 1894-1914 born in Jefferson Co. NY, died April 1899, age 85 years
38	Anna E. Case 1874-1962
38	Zadie Nellie Case (?) 1901-1924
38	Zeph Case 1899-1980
38	Ziph A. Case 1855-1917
40	Audrey L. Chader 1923-1929
40	Dorothy D. Chader 1895-1929
36	Bernie E. Christenson 1920-____ married Walter G. 31 August 1941
36	Walter G. Christenson 1919-____ married Bernice E. 31 August 1941
07	James S. Christie 1915-1986
39	Jane, wife of Lewis Christie 1830-1900
14	Overton E. Christie 1894 - 1914
06	Ralph S. Christie 1904-1951
14	Robert R. Christie 1888-1896
12	Florence Chrystal 23 August 1856 - 12 July 1929
12	John Chrystal 26 December 1825 - 7 July 1901
12	Mary Didpie, wife of John Chrystal 1818-1903
29	Harry J. Clark 1869-1938
02	Marguerite J. Church 1920-1971
02	Otis T. Church 1917-1989
11	Caroline Clay (?) 1869-1919
26	Earl C. Clay 1898-1964 married Martha G. 13 June 1929
11	Hamilton Clay (?) 1865-1951
26	Hamilton J. Clay 1895 - 14 December 1978
26	Harriet L. Clay 1901 - 13 December 1978
01	Inez Clay 1882-1970
04	Mack W. Clay 1891-1958
26	Martha G. Clay 1907-1987 married Earl C. 13 June 1929

04	Nellie A. Clay 1897-1979
02	Roger N. Clay 9 May 1928 - 2 July 1971
03	Wayne William Clay 5 September 1921 - 20 July 1971
	MN Cpl US Marine Corps WW2
16	Helen Clemens 1888-1972
16	Peter Clemens 1876-1954
40	Edith A. Clements 1855-1932
09	Eileen G. Clements 1892-1962
09	Joseph R. Clements 1889-1962
10	Josephine Clements 1913-1937
37	A.A. ? S. Cleveland 22 April 1805 (?) - 3 February 1882 (?)
37	Andrew J. Cleveland 28 October 1854 - 17 April 1882
24	Herbert C. Clute 1917-1983 Pvt. US Army WW2
22	Philinda, wife of Horatio C. Colcord 1 July 1841 - 7 May 1879
42	Mary E., wife of L.A. Colson, daughter of Jacob W. Works
	30 September 1845 - 15 May 1886
39	Hulda Conley 1863-1932
36	George Fred Connell 14 November 1874 - 5 May 1963
	N.Y. Cpl Btry B5 Regt Arty Spanish Am. War
36	Lottie I. Connell 25 July 1881 - 30 August 1965
02	Earl A. Cook 1903-1977
04	Forest H. Cook 1894-1978
28	George Cook (?) 1856-1944
36	Irene Rice Cook 1816-1906
36	John Jackson Cook 1817-1880
04	Laura I. Cook 1891-1985
28	Lena Cook (?) 1863-1941
36	Louisa Cook 1853-1931
02	Marion J. Cook 1904-1996
36	William Cook 1846-1928 Pvt Co F(?) 1st Minn Heavy Artillery
35	Marvin R. 'Butch' Cordes 1943-1986
17	Martha J. Coryell 9 May 1857 - 19 March 1942
37	George Coulter (?) 22 ? 1838 (?) - 5 February (?) 1884 (?)
22	Ethel M. Cox 1904-1960
22	Raymond J. Cox 1896-1994
14	Mina Cowell (?) 1862-1926
14	Walter Cowell 1902-1956
14	Wm. Cowell 1858-1948
14	Mrs. Wm. Cowell 1865-1908
21	J.M.D. Craft 1832-1915 Co A 99 Ind Vol Inf
21	Louese M. Craft 1834-1934
21	Mattie M. Craft 1837-1878
39	Catharine F., wife of Rev. Ben. J. Crist 1 March 1836 - 12 April 1862
39	infant son Eddy Crist - no dates -
42	A.C., wife of C.H. Crocker, daughter of J.W. Works
	24 May 1841 - 23 August 1889

17	Grace W. Crooks July 1874 - June 1932
17	John Crooks July 1876 - January 1933
16	Anna M. Curry 1874-1942
16	Charles W. Curry 1851-1916 - buried in Roselawn
16	Jane Barkuloo Curry 1847-1927
16	Rebecca E. Curry 1877-1908
16	Willis C. Curry 1884-1938
42	baby Curtis 1907-1907
42	Carrie Curtis 1878-1952
42	Evadine Curtis 1910-____
42	Frank H. Curtis 1869-1940
42	Frank H. Curtis 1900-1911
30	George Curtis 26 December 1843 Clinton, N.Y. - 20 December 1928 Farmington, MN.
42	Ralph Curtis 1903-1981
37	Karl O. Dahlager 1909-1994
37	Muriel E. Dahlager 1908-____
34	Mary Daine 8 May 1803 - 4 January 1880
40	Kate Darling 1860-1923
34	Caroline K. Day 1825-1910
34	Edwin L. Day 1856-1900
11	George Day 1870-1965
34	Lee Day 1850-1872
11	Lucy Whittier Day 1871-1951
17	Grace Dekine (?) 1890-1948 (?)
17	Minnie B. Dekleine 1877-1965
17	Richard Dekleine 1879-1946
17	John Dekline (?) 1890-1947 (?)
13	Fred Carl DeMann 1909-1983
13	Mildred Bell DeMann 1913-____
15	Charles Dement 1889-____
15	Zella Dement 1884-1969
38	Hattie Demuth 1902-1978
01	Ella Deuth 1893-1982
01	George Deuth 1889-1970
01	George J. Deuth 21 October 1925 - 19 February 1979
02	Henry A. Deuth 17 May 1916 - 9 December 1978 Tec 5 US Army WW2
08	Albert 'Al' Diesen 1914-____
07	Dallas W. Diesen 1937-1946
08	Viola 'Vi' Diesen 1917-1990
35	Esther L. Dilley 1910-1989 married Merrel D. 9 October 1934
35	Merrel D. Dilley 1909-1986 married Esther L. 9 October 1934
40	Henrietta C. Dodge 1846-1938
40	Inez McG. Dodge 1884-1971

40	Levi Parker Dodge 1839-1893
40	Myra W. Dodge 1865-1929
39	Ruth E. Dodge 1902-1967
40	W.M. Dodge 1866-1945
39	Warren M. Dodge 1901-1971
24	Fred H. Doehling 1908-1993 married Lillian C. 28 April 1934
04	Leonard H. Doehling 14 May 1958 - 27 May 1960
24	Lillian L. Doehling 1910-____ married Fred H. 28 April 1934
12	Mary C. Dome 13 August 1861 - 12 October 1929
42	Ellen R. Donaldson 1856-1914
20	J.M. Donaldson 4 December 1815 - 11 January 1877
20	Joseph Donaldson 3 October 1849 - 31 August 1924
42	Mary Montgomery (Donaldson) 1907-1986
02	Lance P. Doran 25 July 1962 - 9 April 1979
23	Grace I. Dowers 1871-1957
13	Marie Dubbels 1890-1979
13	Paul Dubbels 1884-1987
34	James Duff (?) 1836-1926
34	Nellie Duff (?) 1847-1921
30	Russell F. Duff (?) or Bisek (?) 1907-1938
15	John E. Duffey 1892-1918
15	John P. Duffey 1866-1956
13	Barbara J. Dugas 1955-1983
34	Clara Day Egle 1846-1911
23	Kenneth Duane Ellingson - 17 October 1956 -
39	Gertrude W. Elsner 1898-1978
36	Adone Empey 1888-1976
34	Alexander Empey 31 July 1862 - 2 June 1949
22	Alyn J. Empey 22 April 1928 - 30 May 1991
	A2C US Air Force Korea
22	Calvin G. Empey 11 November 1924 - 23 November 1924
22	Clifford W. Empey 1895-1957
30	George A. Empey 24 January 1905 - 14 January 1991
22	Gretchen G. Empey 1895-1988
34	Mrs. George (Mae) Empey 24 July 1897 - 14 October 1965
30	Helen May Hall Empey 1905-1947
36	Irving Empey 1886-1976
39	Margaret Empey 27 October 1862 - 7 March 1904
34	May Empey 20 August 1870 - 17 May 1935
34	Merrill Empey 31 May 1899 - 5 September 1906
22	Steven Empey 27 May 1946 - 20 April 1993
29	Genevieve Engelman 8 January 1921 - 16 March 1997
29	Robin Engelman 18 October 1951 - 9 November 1995
23	Swan Engh 1870-1935
35	Christine Englert 1918-____

02	Christine M. Englert 10 June 1972 - 10 November 1972
35	Louis H. Englert 1916-____
34	Martha Ennis, died 23 March 1879, age 61 years 7 days
06	Benjamin A. Erickson 1894-1953
25	Chester H. Erickson 1915-1964
25	Irene A. Erickson 1914-1997
06	Ora M. Erickson 1897-1960
04	Oscar W. Erickson 1886-1963
01	Patricia A. Erickson 1937-1974
04	Rose A. Erickson 1888-1972
06	Edward Esmay 1885-1963
06	Ellsworth L. Esmay 1909-1964
06	Hattie Esmay 1886-1952
38	Christian Etter 25 May 1860 - 1 May 1914
38	Evelyn A. Etter 5 May 1892 - 28 June 1969
38	Minnie Etter 3 August 1868 - 8 December 1938
38	Rudolph C. Etter 19 April 1905 - 28 April 1905
39	Alice Knowles Eustis 1852-1882
06	Gladys Everote 1887-1966
06	Peter Everote 1887-1954
21	G.W. Fager, died (?) 3 December 1874, age 51 years 3 months 18 days
42	Gracia M. Field, died 12 October 1877, age 21 years 2 months
42	Rhoda S. Field, died 20 March 1889, age 59 years 10 months 22 days
25	Ann Feiner 1913-____
24	Charles A. Filkins 1935-1990
	married Ruth Ann 2 July 1966
15	Alex Lee Fischer - 28 February 1988 -
15	Carri Jo Fischer, nee Sacks 11 November 1958 - 12 April 1988
40	George E. Fischer 1875-1912
15	Ephriam Fish 21 September 1806 - 15 January 1894
15	Hiram L., son of Ephraim and Meriba Fish
	died 20 February 1860, age 21 years 8 months 22 days
15	Meriba, wife of Ephriam Fish
	died 3 October 1886, age 76 years 9 days
41	G.M. Fjetland 1880-1921
41	Nellie M. Fjetland 1876-1971
14	Mary Jane Fletcher 1860-1944
14	Wilbert J. Fletcher 1858-1949
45	Khalifa Bayyinah Flowers 1977-1993
39	baby Fluke - 1870 -
39	Della M., wife of LeRoy P. Fluke, 1841-1907
39	Harry L. Fluke 1865-1873
39	LeRoy P. Fluke 1838-1916 Co C 27 Ohio Vol. Inf.
39	Pearl L. Fluke 1868-1883
35	Albin N. Foss 1913-1983

35	Delta L. Foss 1920-1982
26	Nile C. Foss 1939-1996
	married Janice M. 13 August 1966
26	Sharon L. Foss 1940-1965
01	Edwin Fredrickson 1919-____
01	Helen Fredrickson 1920-____
37	Harriet E. Freer 1908-1987
37	John W. Freer 1902-1988
28	Grace A. Froemming (?) 1899-1966
28	Harry B. Froemming (?) 1900-1991
01	Ellen Deuth Funari 1929-1995
45	Cynthia A. Gerald 1959-1988
01	Ginger Gerald 5 April 1960 - 26 July 1973
05	Esther L. Gerardy 1914-1974
05	Jean Gerardy 1950-1952
22	Alfred C. Gibbs 1922-1930
01	Edwin F. Gibbs 1913-____
01	Fannie F. Gibbs 1920-____
22	Florence Baby Gibbs 1924-1927
06	Annie Gilbertson 1886-1973
02	David Gilbertson 1960-1979
06	George Gilbertson 1884-1970
02	Patty Gilbertson 1934-1993
02	Ronald Gilbertson 1934-1996
39	Abigail (?) J. Giles (?), died 25 November 1873
	age 88 years 11 months 19 days
39	David D. Giles (died ?) 25 July 1879 age 52 years 6 months 5 days
40	Eva M. Giles - no dates -
38	Florence E. Giles 10 September 1911- 22 August 1987
40	Florence O. Giles - no dates -
39	Harry H. Giles 1893-1973
40	Henry D. Giles 1859-1931
40	Katherine Giles 1865-1954
39	Lenora L., wife of H.N. Giles, died 6 January 1883
	age 23 years 2 months 24 days
39	Mabel E. Giles 1890-1975
40	Mary E. Giles 1869-1889
02	Reginald E. Giles 1963-1981
40	'Father' and 'Mother' Gilkey - no dates -
40	Oliver A. Gilkey, died 10 September 1871
	age 18 years 1 month 25 days
38	Gilman 1826-1913 'Remembrance - P. Gilman'
15	Blanche Meeker Gilman 1868-1910
38	Minnie J. Gilman 1847-1917
12	Mary E. Gleim - no dates -

26	Frank Glewwe 1924-1989
26	Herman L. Glewwe 1884-1969
26	Luella Glewwe 1890-1969
32	Beth A. Godby 1889-1984
32	Lewis A. Godby 1888-1978
45	John H. Goerss 1915-1988
45	Lorraine M. Goerss 1919-____
16	Ritie Underwood Goodsell 1846-1910
27	Ann M. Gordner 1913-____
02	Clarence Gordner 1907-1971
	married Virginia 24 February 1932
28	Maria M. Gordner 1885-1978
27	Raymond S. Gordner 1912-1987
28	Stanley Gordner 1882-1962
02	Virginia Gordner 1907-____
	married Clarence 24 February 1932
31	Harry F. Gould 1880-1950 twin brother of Carrie Snyder
06	Eugene E. Graham 1940-1965
05	Chester W. Graham 1908-1994
06	Clara Graham 1875-1956
05	R. Corinne Graham 1914-____
06	Wallace Graham 1877-1953
06	Greta Mae Grant - no dates -
06	Wallace S. Grant - no dates -
15	Addie Greco 1874-1948
15	Viola Greco 1901-1914
15	Wm. J. Greco 1868-1953
31	Clarence L. Griebenow 1905-1984 Tec 4 US Army WW2
38	C.R. Griebie 1845-1910
31	F.H. Griebie 30 March 1864 - 12 December 1926
28	Fred H. Griebie 8 January 1837- 28 October 1911
31	Fred R. Griebie 1905-1984
31	Gladys Griebie 5 December 1887 - 17 January 1966
31	Grace Moor, wife of F.H. Griebie
	1 November 1869 - 25 July 1926
31	Isabel Griebie 1906-_____
19	Louise, wife of H. Gross 28 November 1830 - 21 May 1888
19	Warren H. (?), son of Wm. and M.E. (?) Gross (?)
	died 27 October (?) 1871, 4 months 2 days - worn and hard to read
01	Glenn S. Grove 1903-1969
01	Jessie M. Grove 1905-1993
01	Orville M. Gudim 20 May 1920 - 9 November 1983
	Tec 4 US Army WW2
26	Kendrick N. Guiteau 1821-1918
45	Angeline B. Haack 1956-1996

married Terrance E. 26 May 1979
24   Jacob Haasnoot 1909-1997
24   Maria Haasnoot 1910-____
26   Florence Haefs 1900-1986
26   Phil H. Haefs 1929-1978
26   Phil W. Haefs 1887-1961
01   Ellen Hagen 1907-1980
02   Harriet E. Hagen 1907-1995
01   Herman Hagen 1909-1995
01   Herman O. Hagen 1909-1995   US navy WW2
02   Marvin L. Hagen 1907-1970
41   Hall - Syckes   - no names or dates
24   Bertha A. Hall 1915-____
33   Charles L. Hall 1893-1985
32   Jesse J. Hall 1891-1990
33   Marie Hall 1897-1973
24   Walter R. Hall 1907-1987
25   Jennie Hallanger 1892-1964
25   Thomas Hallanger 1888-1966
43   Elliott W. Halstead 1923-1982 Cpl US Army WW2
24   Louis O. Halvorson 1892-1972
24   Lucille G. Halvorson 1893-1978
38   Annie Laurie, wife of John S. Hamaker 1865-1901
            born at Towanda, PA., died at Farmington, MN.
21   'Father' Hamann (?) 1824-1905
21   Frank Hamann (?) 1855-1936
21   Henry H. Hamann (?) 1865-1921
21   'Mother' Hamann (?) 1828-1889
21   Peter Hamann (?) 1861-1922
21   Salome M. Hamann (?) 1842-1894
21   William Hamann (?) 1867-1886
02   Ardell W. Hansen 1900-1982
02   Mary L. Hansen 1913-1986
02   Kenneth H. Hanson 1911-1994
02   Ruth K. Hanson 1904-1970
43   Frances D. Harmer - no dates -
23   Jon Russell Harstad - 29 October 1980 -
43   Effie J. Hunter, wife of L.M. Harrington
            died 31 January 1895, age 31 years
43   Maranda A. Harrington (?) 1834-1918
43   Mary Ann Seward, wife of David G. Harrington
            26 August 1839 - 24 September 1906
43   Mary Luedke Harrington 1879-1941
43   Nellie M. Harrington (?) 1869-1951
43   William Harrington (?) 1829-1920
43   Alice L. Harris 1891-1984

31	Deanne L. Harris 1917-1965
43	Emma (?) Harris, child of Orinda (?) and M. Harris
	9 February 1887 - 9 August 1887
43	Eugene Harris 1913-1980
32	Gladys A. Harris 1890-1967
43	Grace E. Harris (?) 23 May 1887 - 20 March 1950
32	H. Lee Harris 1880-1957
43	Hattie J., child of Orinda (?) H. and M. Harris
	6 February 1888 - 28 October 1888
43	Hilda Harris 1914-1983
43	J. Logan Harris 1890-1957
43	James M. Harris (?) 28 March 1879 - 3 May 1965
43	Monroe Harris 1845-1923 Co I 140th Ill. Volunteer
43	Orinda Harris 1856-1908
43	Russell J. Harris 5 August 1922 - 13 May 1945
	MN Pfc 306 Infantry WW2
05	Violet R. Harter - 1978 -
33	Harriet Baker Haskell 1808-1911
07	Bessie Hauge 1906-1982
37	Alfred M. Haugh 1900-1974
37	Grace Haugh 1896-1974
24	Edna E. Hayden 1919-____
24	Raymond L. Hayden 1916-____
41	Charles I. Hayes 7 February 1841 - 12 May 1929
41	Mary J. Hayes 3 November 1843 - 8 August 1913
41	Albert E. Haynes 1873-1952
41	baby Haynes (?) 31 October 1912 - 27 December 1912
41	Nanna B. Haynes 1878-1967
41	Nellie J. (?), daughter of C.I. and M.J. Haynes
	died 11 August 1887 (?), age 12 years (?) 5 months 26 days (?)
41	C.B. Headley 20 march 1810- 25 June 1885
41	Jennie V., wife of S.C. Headley, died 25 September 1882
03	Margaret Hegstrom 3 September 1944 - 5 May 1977
01	Lynette Marie Heikes January 1966 - August 1971
23	Tim H. Heikes - 16 May 1977 -
44	Celina Grace Heikkila 13 March 1997 - 30 March 1997
45	Timothy Dean Heikkila 27 July 1967 - 11 June 1985
23	baby Henderson - 1945 -
35	Dorothy S. Henderson 1933-1979
25	Leonard 'Red' Henderson 1906-1963
25	Lulu E. Henderson 1905-1988
01	Elizabeth Henry 1916-____
26	Frank E. Henry 1871-1964
01	Gerhard Henry 1912-1993
26	Leora D. Henry 1871-1957
01	Suzanne Renee Henry 1959-1981

15	Harry B. Hicks - no dates - age 2 years 8 months 9 days
22	Claudia Higgins 1884-1968
22	Margaret Higgins 1886-1935
22	Maria Higgins 1860-1988
22	William Higgins 1849-1921
06	Agnes Hill 1892-1976
02	Charles L. Hill 1895-1978
24	Gertrude E. Hill 1901-1976
35	Harold T. Hill 1 April 1916 - 28 July 1983
35	Irene I. Hill 12 June 1918 - 2 August 1987
06	John Hill 1883-1954
24	Milo L. Hill 1898-1977
02	Sherman W. Hill 10 May 1953 - 31 March 1994
14	Florence V. Hines 1900-1977
11	Herman Hinz 1885-1923
11	Meta Hinz 1885-1963
01	Avis G. Hoeppner 1904-1987
26	Cora M. Hoeppner 1905-____
26	Otto C. Hoeppner 1899-1963
01	Werner F. Hoeppner 1897-1973
11	Anna M. Hoffman 1868-1929
11	Christian Hoffman 1865-1941
11	Clara C. Hoffman 25 June 1890 - 21 December 1969
04	Dietrich L. Hoffman (?) 1891-1989
06	Emelia K. Hoffman (?) 1867-1954
12	George Hoffman, came to Dakota County 1855
	31 December 1833 - 11 October 1917
06	George W. Hoffman (?) 1863-1950
08	Glen C. Hoffman 1924-1945, buried in Liege, Belgium
08	Henrietta Hoffman 1897-1991
04	Lydia I. Hoffman (?) 1895-1957
08	Milton E. Hoffman 1894-1985
12	Susanna, wife of George Hoffman 23 April 1835 - 10 September 1916
08	Virgil G. Hoffman 1919-1940
44	Edward H. Holm 1902-1989
44	Verna A. Holm 1904-1989
37	Etta L. Holmes 1884-1944
37	Gabriel John Holmes (? - Closest Surname)
	30 September 1973 - 26 June 1978
37	Jamie LeRoy Holmes (? - Closest Surname)
	24 August 1976 - 26 June 1978
36	Marjorie D. Holmes (? - Closest Surname) 1908-1914
36	Mary Holmes (? - Closest Surname) 1916-1928
17	Nelson M. Holmes 22 September 1845 - 2 December 1870
	Pvt Co F 7 Regt Minn Inf Civil War
37	Thomas W. Holmes 1882-1973

06	Roy L. Holt 1908-1951
45	Ethel A. Holten 1915-____
45	Goodwin Holten 1904-1992
24	Elizabeth Holtgrave 1907-____
24	John Holtgrave 1899-1986
34	Coral I. Homola 1882-1978
34	Addie B. Hosmer (?) 1869-1871
32	Alice M. Hosmer (?) 1874-1961
32	Amanda M., wife of Hobart N. Hosmer 1837-1921
34	Chester L. Hosmer (?) 1834-1881
34	Chester L. Hosmer, died 6 September 1881
	age 57 years 2 months 17 days
32	Ella B. Hosmer (?) 1882-____
34	Emma J. Hosmer (?) 1858-1866
32	Eunice S. Hosmer (?) 1883-1930
32	Frank H. Hosmer (?) 1866-1951
34	Frank L. Hosmer (?) 1856-1866
32	Fred C. Hosmer (?) 1862-1921
32	Grace L. Hosmer (?) 1872-1955
34	Harriet A. Hosmer 1833-1905
32	Herbert W. Hosmer (?) 1870-1962
32	Hobart N. Hosmer 1833-1909 Co C Minn Vol Inf
34	Irving E. Hosmer (?) 1871-1873
32	Leavitt S. Hosmer (?) 1872-1935
32	Maynard R. Hosmer (?) 1878-1944
41	Lida, wife of J.E. Houston, died 27 July 1882
	age 27 years 9 months 24 days
42	Ernest S. Houts 12 January 1863 - 22 August 1885
08	Edgar Hurd 6 April 1876 - 28 December 1962
08	Margurete Hurd 19 December 1870 - 22 May 1956
20	Agnes L., daughter of H. and C. Huyck 8 - 27 December 1910
21	Amanda Huyck 1840-1921
21	Clara Huyck 1882-1968
21	Harry Huyck 1881-1973
21	Randolph Huyck 1842-1919
08	Marion I. Peterson Hyland 1897-1975
45	Albert F. Ideker 1905-1996
45	Alma L. Ideker 1907-____
16	Esther C. Idso 1886-1953
45	Florence Ingerson 1903-____ married Francis 15 July 1926
45	Francis Ingerson 1899-1986 married Florence 15 July 1926
24	Johannes Ippell 1906-1987
18	baby boy, son of E.L. and C.G. Irving - no dates -
19	'Father' Irving (?) - no dates -
19	'Mother' Irving (?) - no dates -

05	Albern Ista 1896-1981
26	Augusta W. Ista 1889-1973
28	Bertha Ista 1864-1948
05	Cora Ista 1899-1992
26	Edwin A. Ista 1889-1964
05	Fern E. Ista 1889-1985
05	George F. Ista 1890-1963
28	Herman Ista 1859-1945
09	Ethel Ives 1913-1956
20	Frank Ives 1860-1940
23	Fred C. Ives 1886-1950
10	Ira A. Ives 1890-1978
41	Jesse Ives Sr. 26 December 1824 - 28 January 1867
41	Jesse Ives Jr. 13 May 1852 - 18 August 1873
23	John Ives 1888-1956
24	Leona E. Ives 1898-1992
24	Levi Ives 1894-1972
41	Martha Amidon, wife of Jesse Ives 21 June 1825 - 6 May 1886
10	Millie J. Ives 1889-1975
09	Richard Ives 1931-1934
02	Clara Jacobs 1900-1993
02	Peter Jacobs 1890-1972
44	Jarrett Willis Jacobson 29 October 1987 - 23 February 1993
13	Joel Lloyd Jacobson, son of Leroy and Jane 29 October - 23 November 1987
15	Mrs. D.C. Jay, died 29 September 1900, age 36 years
22	S. Jenkins 1818-1896
22	S. Jenkins, died 11 May 1888, age 71 years 11 months 12 days
06	Christen Jensen 1893-1955
06	Clara Jensen 1934-1960
03	Dorothy E. Jensen 10 September 1913 - _____
06	Elizabeth Jensen 1899-1972
33	Erna B. Jensen 1902-1996
34	Frieda S. Jensen 1878-1935
34	George J. Jensen 1906-1926
02	Harland O. Jensen 1913-1975
33	Harriet Jensen - 1924 -
34	Ida S. Jensen 1899-1899
11	J. Theodore Jensen 1889-1920
34	Jens S. Jensen 1846-1906
34	Jess H. Jensen 1871-1926
03	John E. Jensen 8 January 1904 - 31 January 1975
33	Kamella Jensen 1891-1943
33	Lars P. Jensen 1892-1947
11	Lorena R. Jensen 1893-1993

34	Martha A. Jensen 1896-1896
11	Merle T. Jensen 6 June 1912 - 11 November 1969
	MN S Sgt 491 Bomb Gp AAF WW2
33	Nels C. Jensen 1885-1948
03	Sharon M. Jensen 24 October 1936 - 30 June 1990
33	William F. Jensen 1903-1958
10	Alice C. Johnson 1918-1969
28	Andrew Johnson 1888-1943
26	Andrew A. Johnson 1879-1953
44	David Johnson 19 August 1977 - 7 September 1996
26	Elosina C. Johnson 1886-1967
36	George (Ernie) Johnson 1925-1995
28	George E. Johnson 1927-1928
36	George Ernest Johnson 1925-1995
	CWO US Air Force WW2 Vietnam
34	Harold Johnson - 1938 -
26	Helen A. Johnson 1889-1967
34	infant boy Johnson - 1941 -
16	J.A. Elmer Johnson 1912-1913
25	Lillie J. Johnson 1885-1974
26	Louis R. Johnson 1883-1965
01	Roger J. Johnson 1910-1972
26	Wendell G. Johnson 1923-1981
21	William, son of H.T. and H.L. Johnson
	died 22 May 1886, age 19 years 7 months
33	Arnold K. Jones 1904-1971
33	Edna H. Jones 1909-1976
01	Joe Jones 1921-1979
01	Joe Paul Jones 1944-1971
22	John Scott Jones - May 1953 -
40	Marie Jorgensen 1894-1976
40	Morris Jorgensen 7 May 1898 - 18 November 1968
40	Otto Jorgensen 1893-1964
10	Mary A. Josephson 27 March 1931 - 26 October 1995
	married Willard L. 6 August 1955
14	Lucy Maria, wife of Roswell Judson
	29 November 1817 - 16 April 1891
14	Roswell Judson 19 October 1806 - 21 April 1891
14	Stella M. Judson 1886-1965
24	Gordon H. Kath 24 October 1931 - 21 November 1991
24	Gordon H. Kath 24 October 1931 - 21 November 1991
	Sgt US Army Korea
24	Kyle M. Kath - 27 April 1992 -
12	Benoni C. Kelley 23 November 1818 - 29 December 1885
12	Mary P. Kelley 14 February 1826 - 30 September 1910

33	Carrie E. Kenney (?) 1863-1933
33	Martin W. Kenney (?) 1864-1944
11	Esther Kent (?) 1867-1933
06	Lawrence Klingberg 1880-1954
06	Mathilda Klingberg 1884-1978
02	Elbert (Al) Kindseth 1911-1978
02	Theodora (Mikie) Kindseth 1915-____
27	Marie Averill King 1917-1945
13	Roldon F. Kingman 15 January 1912 - 27 April 1992 US Merchant Marine WW2
26	George M. Kingrey 1885-1957
26	Grace W. Kingrey 1894-1981
36	Ula M. Kissel 1898-1979
26	Gladys V. Klahr 1911-1989
30	Annie Klatt 1876-1959
30	E.C. Klatt 1863-1931
42	Esther L. Klatt 1906-1994
42	Harlow H. Klatt 1901-1981
42	Mabel M. Klatt 1908-1976
23	baby boy Klaus - 12 November 1961 -
26	E. Beryl Klaus 1914-1986
38	George Henry Klaus 1868-1949
10	Henry P. Klaus 1866-1948
38	Ida M. Klaus 1875-1934
26	Lloyd R. Klaus 1909-____
10	Maud P. Klaus 1880-1929
38	Phillip W. Klaus 1873-1940
25	Theresa E. Klaus 1885-1966
38	Wilhelmina Kloepping Klaus 1877-1960
38	F. Kloepping 27 May 1845 - 2 September 1902
38	Johanna Kloepping 1852-1921
37	Ethel M. Klotzbeacher 1917-____
37	Jake R. Klotzbeacher 1912-____
40	Sarah Knight, daughter of K. and A.M. Record died 11 July 1876 (?), age 11 months 15 days (?)
39	Harry L. Knowles 4 April - 19 August 1881
39	Jane Marie Knowles 1825-1917
39	Joseph Knowles 1812-1876
39	Winslow L. Knowles 1850-1924
08	Amelia M. Knoblauch (?), died 3 September 1960
08	Frank A. Knoblauch, died 4 March 1944
08	Susanna L. Knoblauch 1898-1982
23	Karl Koch 1862-1951
30	Gertrude Kopeske 1879-1960
13	Martin Korsman 1922-1981
13	Martin J. Korsman 1922-1981 US Army WW2

33	Glenn T. Kraft 1902-1920
21	John G. Kraft 1865-1933
21	Katherine B. Kraft 1873-1947
08	Mary A. Kral (?) 1899-1985
08	Robert H. Kral (?) 1883-1964
13	James Alan Krech 27 June 1958 - 18 January 1981
21	Frank H. Kregel 1838-1912
19	Frank H. Kregel 1873-1946
21	Rachel A. Kregel 1844-1919
21	Schuyler H. Kregel (?) 22 March 1888 - 4 March 1889
19	Jens Kristian 1899-1988 (Topp ?)
04	Elsie I. Krubsack 1903-1958
04	Ernest J. Krubsack 1908-1979
16	Emanuel Kuchera 1883-1962
16	Ethel Kuchera 1897-1922
15	Marvin N. Kuchera (?) 1915-1979
16	Scott Anthony Kuchera (?), son of Roger and Jeanne 1969-1986
15	Verna E. Kuchera 1914-1939
07	Jeffrey Gene, son of Mr. and Mrs. Eugene Kuhlman
	3 December 1955 - 7 January 1956
33	August Kulstad (?) 1878-1943
40	Henrietta D. Kulstad 1894-1968
33	Stella M. Kulstad (?) 1885-1929
35	Frances E. Lagerquist 1913-____
35	Gordon E. Lagerquist 1907-1983
26	Charles A. Lanner 1875-1953
26	Mathilda C. Lanner 1879-1971
22	John W. Lansing 18 August 1873 - 17 September 1892
01	David Lapham 1951-1980
13	Adeline I. Larsen 1921-____ married Lewis C. 11 September 1940
04	Albert J. Larsen 1875-1958 married Augusta K. 27 September 1902
04	Augusta K. Larsen 1880-1958 married Albert J. 27 September 1902
24	Edna M. Larsen 22 September 1911 - 2 May 1974
32	Hans Marcus Larsen 1886-1964
13	Lewis C. Larsen 1911-1980 married Adeline I. 11 September 1940
03	Martin O. Larsen 26 July 1909 - 18 November 1971
14	Nancy Larsen 1942-1984
32	Signe Larsen 1887-1966
30	Caroline M. Larson (?) 1869-1940
30	Clifford G. Larson (?) 1892-1918
	Killed in Action Co C 130 Inf
23	Earl L. Larson 1893-1963
38	Elmer A. Larson 1889-1917
29	baby Esther Larson (?) - 1896 -
41	Esther E. Larson 23 August 1898 - 21 April 1993

23	James R. Larson 1943-1965
41	Joe Larson 16 June 1874 - 2 June 1955
41	Hansena Larson 24 February 1874 - 14 October 1929
25	Hattie J. Larson 1881-1967
41	Lee Larson 31 March 1859 - 14 August 1952
30	Louis N. Larson 1850-1935
29	Myrtle L. Larson (?) 1897-1903
23	Otto W. Larson 12 September 1936-____
	Iowa Pvt 138 Inf 35 Div
30	Pearl E. Larson (?) 1894-1915
03	Barbara Mae Lawler 1942-1996
15	Alice D. Lawrence (?) 1896-____
15	Bela M. Lawrence (?) - 1891 -
15	Bela Malcom Lawrence (?) 1857-1925
15	Laura E.H. Lawrence (?) 1853-1935
15	Mark D. Lawrence (?) - 1887 -
15	Ruth A. Lawrence (?) - 1866 -
24	Caroline Legare 1918-1987 married Clifford 27 December 1939
24	Clifford Legare 1913-____ married Caroline 27 December 1939
30	Myrtle I. Lehr 1900-1972
30	William Lehr 1894-1948
43	Florence Myrtle Watson Lenmark, wife of 63 years to Ivar Lenmark
	12 May 1899 - 16 April 1995
29	Arthur A. Leroy 1895-1971
30	Henry Leroy 1930-1944
30	Louise Leroy 1904-1936
29	Lucille J. Leroy 1913-1975
28	Charles Sumner Lewis 1874-1947
28	Violet Chapel Lewis, wife of Charles S. 1874-1940
01	Arne Lien 1911-1984 married Theresa 21 February 1942
01	Theresa Lien 1909-____ married Arne 21 February 1942
03	Lotta Frances Tucker Lightwood 21 January 1921 - 19 May 1989
33	Walter P. Lilly 1817-1896
42	Vernon Larry Lindberg 23 July 1937 - 24 September 1991
	Sfc US Army
02	Bernard A. Lindblad 1915-1983
28	Alan Lindgren 1936-1991
36	Bert Lintner (?) 1880-1913
33	Beatrice E. Lintner 1883-1956
36	Harriet M., wife of T.H. Lintner 12 November 1852 - 10 January 1900
36	Harriott M. Lintner 1852-1900
36	Theodore H. Lintner 1852-1932
33	William M. Lintner 1887-1966
15	Andrew Lipe, died 23 August 1907, age 25 years 5 months 13 days
16	George Lister, died 24 December 1891, age 68 years
16	Mary Ann, wife of George Lister

12 October 1832 - 20 July 1909

44	Sharon A. Livingood	1955-1986
01	Albert Lomas	1895-1973
01	Lois (Lolly) Lomas	1934-1993 married Dale 29 March 1957
01	Martha Lomas	1894-____
01	Charlie A. Lord	1888-1968
01	Mamie E. Lord	1897-1990
02	Marjorie J. Lorenzen	1920-____
02	Paul C. Lorenzen	1909-1971
30	Bert Louk	1889-1940
04	Hilda J. Lovegren	1921-1975
02	Christoph H. Luebke	1903-1989
02	Lydia C. Luebke	1904-1992
43	Carl Luedke (?)	1830-1923
01	Dorothy Luedke	1910-1994 married Raymond 9 August 1930
35	Earl C. Luedke	1897-1983
28	Ethel V. Luedke (?)	1901-1955
35	Hazel E. Luedke	1901-____
28	Mathilda Luedke (?)	1873-1958
01	Raymond Luedke	1906-1982 married Dorothy 9 August 1930
28	Robert Luedke (?)	1862-1945
43	Wilhelmine Luedke	1835-1914
44	Arlene L. Lund	1936-1994 married Harold O. 8 October 1955
08	Esther M. Lundgren	1883-1973
08	Eugene H. Lundgren	1917-1945
08	Henry Lundgren	1884-1963
07	Jean Ann Lundgren	1945-1946
06	Maxine G. Malley	- no dates -
32	George D. Mandell	1880-1978 married Sarah L. 18 December 1902
32	Sarah L. Mandell	1882-1978 married George D. 18 December 1902
13	Sophie L. Manke	1908-____
13	Walter F. Manke	1912-1979
33	Eliza Haskell Manton	1847-1913
33	John S. Manton	1853-1931
35	Earl R. Mapes	1927-1988 Cpl WW2, married ? 22 May 1948
45	Harriet E. Marcell	1909-1990
45	Vernard K. Marcell	1906-1994
38	Lala J. Martin	1879-1912
38	Lewis P. Martin	1864-1927
38	Porter Martin	1827-1915
38	Richard A. Martin	1867-1944
38	Sarah A. Martin	1832-1926
34	Florence Mattson	1912-____ married Harold 4 February 1931
34	Harold Mattson	1907-____ married Florence 4 February 1931
25	Jesse A. McAlister	1885-1975

25	Pheobe L. McAlister 1888-1983
04	Jane L. McBride 1865-1957
21	Artie, son of Rev. A. and Mrs. McCausland 1891-1897
08	Clara B. McClintock 1899-1958
08	Jessie O. McClintock 1897-1970
08	Russell M. McClintock 19 August 1918 - 12 November 1944
	MN Tech Sgt US Marine Corps
39	Alice B. McCluskey 12 August 1878 - 1 June 1924
14	Allan W. McCluskey 28 April 1887 - 22 July 1890
39	Asa G. McCluskey 17 October 1876 - 25 November 1953
29	Esther McCluskey 1903-1985
14	Ettie McCluskey (?) 1865-1919
41	G.W. McCluskey 1874-1955
38	Hannah McCluskey 29 June 1835 - 19 March 1931
38	Hannah Bailey McCluskey 18 June 1895 - 9 May 1916
14	Kenneth McCluskey (?) 1906-1918
29	Raymon McCluskey 1900-1972
41	Rose McCluskey 1877-1959
38	Wm. T. McCluskey 10 January 1835 - 30 January 1909
14	Clara McConaghie 1873-1940
13	Mary McConaghie 1884-1968
14	Maurice McConaghie 1911-1921
13	Ross T. McConaghie 1903-1934
21	Anna McConnahey, died 2 August 1892, age 63 years
04	Fern Gavin McDaniel 1900-1959
04	Samuel P. McDaniel 1894-1987
24	Vyrl J. (Mac) McDermott 1936-1971
14	F. Belle McDonald 1877-1952
14	William J. McDonald 1910-1928
43	Frances O. McGeough 1909-1986
43	Iona M. McGeough 1918-1991
17	James McGuiggan 29 December 1853 - 15 August 1900
28	Earl N. McKay (?) 1892-1944, 311th Btry T.A.
28	Elza L. McKay (?) 1891-1983
29	John W. McKay 1865-1947
44	Robert C. McKay 1930-1989 Pfc US Army
44	Doris L. McKee 1910-1988
12	Florence McKenna - 7 January 1899 - age 3 months
12	Hannah D. McKenna 1859-1935
12	James McKenna 1854-1923
12	John McKenna 1895-1934
01	Laurie McKeon 1970-1979
01	Marilyn McKeon 1947-1979
15	Martha H. McKinnon 1918-1983
30	Alanson B. McKown 20 March 1869 - 8 June 1948
30	Susan H. McKown 21 May 1870 - 11 March 1930

25	Etta M. McNamara 1895-1960
04	Emma H. McNew 1879-1972
04	Mert F. McNew 1868-1965
21	Frank J. Mead 1839-1908
21	Mary Rowley Mead 1844-1910
15	G.N. Meeker 1876-1954
14	May Shaw Meeker 1872-1960
14	Merrill C. Meeker 1872-1907
04	Duane J. Meine 1948-1983
16	Nellie S. Mondonsa (?) 1868-1931
16	Robert R. Mendonsa (?) 1866-1935
42	Myrtie A. Merrill, child of L.F. and M.A. Merrill died 10 July 1879, age 2 years 8 months
42	Percy L. Merrill, child of L.F. and M.A. Merrill died 24 July 1879, age 6 years 10 months
42	Ronald L. Merrill, child L.F. and M.A. Merrill died 26 August 1879, age 20 years 8 months
28	Alby Merritt 1874-1954
28	Ethel Merritt 1887-1960
11	Dietrich C. Michel (?) 1877-1963
11	Dora J. Michel (?) 1876-1928
33	Gertrud L. Michel 19 March 1879 - 29 October 1964
43	Hazel Mick 1906-____ married Maynard 14 April 1924
43	Maynard Mick 1901-1980 married Hazel 14 April 1924
09	Augusta Miller 15 August 1879 - 28 November 1967
37	B.F. Miller 7 November 1837 - 3 November 1910
10	F.J. Miller 17 March 1875 - 3 January 1932
08	Flossie Miller, died (?) 29 March (?) 1881 - ? - stone broken and hard to read
10	Fred Paul Miller (?) 9 January 1903 - 12 July 1928
19	Kristian Miller 1953-1982 (Topp ?)
37	Martha J., wife of B.F. Miller 14 December 1844 - 14 February 1876
13	Spencer T. Miller 1953-1981
02	Doreen Mary Mills 5 January 1962 - 27 April 1971
45	Joyce E. Mills 1942-1996 married Thomas J. 19 January 1963
44	Stephen C. Mills 10 March 1969 - 28 February 1995
45	Diane L. Milstead, nee Heise 1953-1996 married William A. 7 August 1982
14	Paul Mitchell 1889-1889
14	Susie Mitchell 1892-1892
45	Myron H. Mohn 1921-1996
29	Albert H. Moll 1863-1940
23	David Edmund Mongeau 8 - 10 February 1954
26	Emma C. Mongeau 1890-____
26	Zepheire G. Mongeau 1890-1963
30	Anna Montgomery 1887-1971

42	Mary Montgomery (Donaldson) 1907-1986
30	Melvin Montgomery 1881-1942
42	Otis Montgomery 1908-1988 US 841 Avn. Engineers
29	Russell Montgomery 1910-1986
39	Harriet S., daughter of J.W. and M.L. Moore
	24 August 1895 - 19 January 1898
39	Mary Elizabeth Moore 1828-1897
30	Mary D. Morgan 1880-1940
24	Clifford D. Morrisson 1915-1982 Cpl US Army WW2
10	Delbert G. Morse 1863-1932
09	Irvin A. Morse 1907-1983
10	Mary E. Morse 1874-1947
09	Ruth L. Morse 1912-1993
23	Max Motley 1895-1965
04	Anton Motzko 1904-1988
04	Bessie Motzko 1906-1960
45	Betty J. Murphy 1932-1988 married Gilmore 22 December 1956
34	Emaline Murray 1843-1901
13	Darwin W. Muzzy 1933-1984 married Ann 7 January 1952
39	Ida V. Myers 1893-1989
39	James W. Myers 1881-1968
16	Catherine H. Nason 8 December 1887 - 8 October 1973
16	Christena, daughter of G. and M.A. Lister, wife of Pembroke Nason
	died 18 March 1893, age 34 years
16	Florence S., daughter of Pembroke and Christena Nason
	died 14 October 1893, age 9 years 6 months
16	Frederick Morley, son of L. and M. Nason
	10 January 1869 - 8 February 1902
16	George L. Nason 25 May 1886 - 14 December 1949
	MN 1st Lt Engr Off Tng School WW1
16	Lemuel Nason 4 February 1826 - 18 May 1904
16	Martha Ferguson, wife of L. Nason
	14 September 1829 - 16 November 1906
16	Pembroke Nason 1852-1924
16	Pembroke Somerset, son of L. and M. Nason
	15 May 1852 - 31 May 1924
24	Alice U. Nelson 1886-1975
09	Andrew G. Nelson (?) 1866-1950
06	Annie M. Nelson 1882-1950
09	Carl J.F. Nelson (?) 1898-1976
10	Charles Nelson (?) 1863-1933
26	Christ Nelson 1900-1993
05	Craig A. Nelson 1960-1963
24	David A. Nelson - 23 April 1989 -
05	George L. Nelson 1907-1974

09	Helma J. Nelson (?) 1866-1953
01	Leslie N. Nelson 1930-1973
10	Nancy Nelson (?) 1878-1975
06	Peter Nelson 1876-1954
24	Raymond F. Nelson 1890-1985
06	Robert Nelson 1944-1955
05	Roberta C. Nelson 1918-1978
23	William L. Nelson 12 November 1908 - 19 December 1967
23	Travis Raymond Newman 14 December 1982 - 7 March 1983
40	H. Louise Warweg Nichols 11 February 1886 - 19 November 1979
36	Medith D. Nicholson 1920-____
18	William 'Billy' Nixon - Co A 1st Minn Vol Infty. Born in Liverpool, England 4 March 1845 - Came to St. Paul, Minn in 1855 - To Farmington in 1868 - died 24 December 1915. (This Monument Stone has a copper / brass plate that tells more about his military history)
09	Marion E. Nogle 1915-1930
30	Selma Nordberg 1877-1937
12	Emma M. Nordling 1899-1983
17	Franklin P. Norris - no dates -
17	Geo. A. Norris, died 2 May 1883, age 25 years
17	Lizzie A., wife of W.H. Norris, died 8 October 1880, age 25 years
17	Mary A., wife of C.F. Norris, died 5 May 1885, age 53 years
17	Theoline Norris - no dates -
39	Adella M. Norton 1868-1944
10	Alfred C. Norton 1861-1937
39	Arthur P. Norton 1864-1942
39	Emery W. Norton 1870-1941
39	Helen Norton (?) 1903-1903
39	Jane Norton 1842-1904
10	Octavia M. Norton 1876-1966
39	Pearl Norton 1908-____
39	Ralph Norton 1898-1980
39	Ramsom Norton 27 December 1835 - 18 August 1897
40	Edith Clements O'Brien 1883-1936
13	Della M. Olson 1903-____ married Herman G. 9 November 1929
24	Helen I. Olson 1918-____ married Leonard M. 25 November 1950
13	Herman G. Olson 1901-____ married Della M. 9 November 1929
24	Leonard M. Olson 1910-1993 married Helen I. 25 November 1950
24	Leonard Martin Olson 29 April 1910 - 25 June 1993 Sgt US Army WW2
08	Mary Olson 1870-1955
13	Norman C. Olson 1916-1984
08	Ole Olson 1867-1945
08	William A. Olson 1896-1955

22	Lilliam M. Ristow O'Malley 9 December 1916 - 9 October 1960
03	Chester Orndorff 1910-1960
03	Viola Orndorff 1910-1990
37	only Ostrom - no names or dates - older stone
23	Brent Duane, son of Duane and Marjorie Ott 23 March - 7 April 1977
22	Beret Anna Otterstad 15 September 1862 - 24 October 1926
23	Douglas Otte 6 February 1965 - 22 February 1967
09	Charles C. Otto 1915-1953
09	Viola Otto - no dates
07	LeRoy Vernon Page 28 November 1929 - 15 January 1997 Private First Class, 75th Field Artillery Battalion US Army Wounded in action in Korea, awarded the Purple Heart. Active service from 10 September 1953 - 9 June 1954 married Marie P. 27 November 1957
07	Marie R. Page 20 November 1934 - 28 December 1995 Marie Ruth Kral, daughter of Robert and Mary (Voita) Kral of Farmington, Minnesota. Married LeRoy Vern Page, son of James and Eleanor (Anfinson) Page of Northfield, Minn on 27 November 1957
13	Michael J. Page 29 January 1947 - 15 August 1980
18	Betty M. Partington 13 January 1928 - 28 December 1928
18	Donald A. Partington (?) 1955 - 3 June 1963 - died in plane crash
18	Edward G. Partington (?) 1962 - 3 June 1963 - died in plane crash
02	Helen M. Partington 1926-1972
19	Mary Lomas Partington 1888-1973
18	Myrtle M. Partington (?) 1931 - 3 June 1963 - died in plane crash
18	Robert G. Partington (?) 1957 - 3 June 1963 - died in plane crash
18	William G. Partington (?) 1918 - 3 June 1963 - died in plane crash
19	William S. Partington 1886-1960
10	'Father' Partlow (?) 1868-1936
10	'Mother' Partlow (?) 1870-1951
28	Jessie Griebie Paulette 1886-1972
28	Robert Justice Paulette 1886-1941 WW Capt Co C 513th Eng WW
30	Eddie E. Payne 1879-1944
17	Floyd E. Payne 1906-1964
17	Gerald Payne 1931-1931
17	Jennie A. Payne 1901-1977
30	Mary L. Payne 1883-1973
04	Andrew Pelach 1886-1957
03	Andrew Pelach 1913-1966 married Ione 31 July 1937
04	Anna Pelach 1891-1975
22	baby Pelach - no dates -
03	Ione Pelach 1919-1976 married Andrew 31 July 1937

35	John Pelach 1916-1979
35	Ruth Pelach 1919-____
19	A. Susan Penwell 1884-1963
18	Charles A. Penwell 1910-1913
19	Clarence J. Penwell 1884-1958
21	Harry Penwell - 1888 -
21	Ida C. Penwell 1859-1945
21	James Penwell 1857-1936
39	Lorley R. Perra 1908-1964
18	baby Perry - 8 September 1945 -
09	James A. Perry 1882-1969
09	Myrtle A. Perry 1899-1974
34	Edward Peters 1898-1974
17	Elizabeth A. Peters 1865-1930
34	Mildred P. Peters 1898-1991
43	Richard Peters, died 4 September 1891, age 64 years
43	Sarah E. Peters, died 22 July 1894, age 58 years
17	William D. Peters 1862-1922
06	Alice M. Petersen 1911-1954
06	Reuben P. Petersen 1906-1982
08	Godfrey Peterson 1886-1951
06	Naomi A. Peterson 1903-1988
14	Wesley Peterson 1962-1981
13	Gordon Pfahning 1930-1980
13	Gordon L. Pfahning AN US Navy 1930-1980
36	baby boy Phillips - March 1958 -
17	Dorothy McGuiggan Phillips 1893-1944
36	Elizabeth E. Phillips 1919-____
34	Frank W. Phillips 1879-1950
34	Mabel J. Phillips 1882-1947
36	Theodore L. Phillips 1914-1990
06	Anna S. Pietsch 1891-____
11	August F. Pietsch 1845-1918
11	Gustave W. Pietsch (?) 1877-1955
11	Ida H. Pietsch (?) 1883-1961
06	Louis F. Pietsch 1879-1950
06	Russell G. Pietsch 19 May 1922 - 12 July 1969
	OK ADRC US Army WW2
11	Theresa C. Pietsch 1848-1931
08	Mary Jane Pilcher, wife of J.E. Pilcher 1879-1944
12	Adin K. Pitcher (?) 1884 (?)-1908
12	Alice L. Pitcher (?) 1849-1934
12	David S. Pitcher (?) 1887 (?)-1917
12	Dwight D. Pitcher (?) 1835-1913
12	Lucy F. Pitcher (?) 1814-1890
08	Barbara Jean Pontliana, nee Wescott

10 September 1957 - 16 March 1990
01	Esther C. Prebish 1920-1986
08	James E. Price 1868-1958
23	Randy Priem - 55 -
45	Milford W. Pulja 1934-1996

35	Clarence Quie 1903-1995
35	Linda B. Quie 1940-1991
35	Sylvia Quie 1910-____
01	Myra E. Quinnell 1911-1993
01	Oliver E. Quinnell 1904-1996

30	Laura E. Randall July 1883 - January 1938
30	Roscoe D. Randall September 1879 - May 1947
30	Roscoe D. Randall 20 October 1879 - 14 May 1947
	Pvt 29 Iowa Inf Sp Am War
42	James Rankin 1848-1875
42	James Rankin, died 21 December 1875, age 27 years 6 months 24 days
42	Margaret Rankin 1860-1943
42	Mary Rankin 1822-1879
42	Mary, wife of Robert Rankin 6 July 1822 - 27 July 1879
42	Mary J. Rankin 1846-1910
42	Robert Rankin 1819-1881
42	Robert Rankin 15 August 1819 - 28 April 1881
33	Isaac L. Rarick 1886-1956
33	Nettie V. Rarick 1884-1969
17	Dora J. Rasmussen 1885-1959
17	Peter Rasmussen 1888-1979
17	Rasmus Rasmussen 1892-1966
29	Katherine B. Rech 1887-1980
29	William Rech 1886-1961
12	Wilma K. Rech 15 - 23 January 1930
40	Adelia M. Record 1826-1901
08	Elizabeth S. Record 1878-1948
08	George H. Record 1875-1949
40	Knight Record 1832-1922
07	Mildred S. Record 1913-1944
15	Alexander Records (?) 1846-1916
15	Alice Records (?) 1857-1930
15	Edythe Records (?) 1894-1931
15	Florence A. Records (?) 1896-1988
21	Gerald C. Regan 1942-1982
21	Otto R., son of R and C. Rehmenklau 17 August 1880 - 29 January 1881
01	Martin W. Reinke 1902-1973
07	baby boy Reisinger - 16 December 1945 -
08	Ellen E. Reisinger 1911-1990 married Ralph W. 3 August 1929

10	Glen Reisinger 1867-1953
10	Maggie Reisinger 1871-1938
08	Ralph W. Reisinger 1906-1958 married Ellen E. 3 August 1929
24	Harold Rice 1933-1986 married Marjorie 13 September 1952
13	Nancy E. Richards 1938-1982
40	Albra Ricker 31 July 1827 - 17 October 1892
40	Edward H. Ricker 3 April 1858 - 9 January 1886
08	Esther E. Ricker (?) 1898-1945
08	Katherine S. Ricker (?) 1867-1969
08	Walter S. Ricker (?) 1861-1938
22	Mary E. Ristow 30 May 1893 - 4 March 1972
22	Wilbur Ristow 1919-1920
22	William Ristow 1917-1918
22	William A. Ristow 25 November 1882 - 10 August 1955
14	Lea Robaur 1872-1911
24	Cliff Roberts 1920-____
24	Vera Roberts 1907-____
02	Carol J. Robertson 1944-1973
02	Ernest M. Robertson 1908-1981
02	Violet Robertson 1918-____
35	Ethel Roche 1907-____
35	Harold Roche 1902-1981
39	John W. Roche 1864-1961
39	Mary L. Roche 1865-1933
33	Robert F. Rodger 1878-1905
32	Charles L. Rodgers 1882-1949
33	Elizabeth M. Rodgers 1851-1944
32	Frances W. Rodgers 1884-1967
33	James Rodgers 1840-1918
32	James Rodgers 1890-1977
33	Nancy B. Rodgers 1880-1962
33	Walter S. Rodgers 1875-1963
29	baby Rolfing - 1947 -
30	Mary M. Rolfing 1882-1966
02	Ralph Rolfing 1906-1988
02	Ruth Rolfing 1912-____
30	Wellington Rolfing 1877-1955
17	Augusta Roots 1847-1925
17	George Roots 1891-1910
17	Wm. Roots, died 1907
35	Joyce Roschen 1933-1985 married Kenneth 24 November 1951
35	Kenneth Roschen 1929-1987 married Joyce 24 November 1951
35	Kenneth E. Roschen 6 march 1929 - 27 June 1987
	Cpl US Army Korea
33	Pearl Rosenwald 1897-1922
17	Grace Roshon (Wallace ?) 1893-1933

25	Glenn N. Rowell 1929-1992
26	Lloyd G. Rowell 1898-1984
26	Nettie E. Rowell 1902-1966
21	Abigail W., wife of N.B. Rowley 2 June 1819 - 21 July 1890
21	Nelson B. Rowley 15 March 1810 - 10 May 1893
44	Melody Anne Rud 1953-1985
22	Harold Wayne Rushton 1 February 1923 - 11 October 1924

15	Dorothy Sachs 1 July 1910-____ married Gerald 19 September 1931
15	Gerald Sachs 24 July 1908 - 28 February 1989
	married Dorothy 19 September 1931
21	Jennie (?), wife of J.S. Sachs (?) 1874-1914
21	John Sachs 1866-1939
35	Lawrence O. Sahagian 27 July 1915 - 18 May 1978
	T Sgt US Army WW2
07	Alila St. John 1937-1947
08	D. Elizabeth St. John 1875-1941
30	Ednard E. St. John (?) 15 April 1862 - 10 February 1930 (?)
08	G. Lloyd St. John 1873-1952
07	Gloria St. John 1938-1947
02	Lloyd A. St. John 1909-1967
02	Margaret St. John 1917-1992
08	Mathilda S. St. John 1916-1993
08	William R. St. John 1910-____
44	Genevieve B. Sandberg 1926-1988
	married Kenneth W. 2 August 1952
19	Adeline, wife of I.R. Sanderson 2 June 1822 - 6 November 1891
19	I.R. Sanderson 29 March (?) 1818 - 26 March 1907
32	James Richard Sanford 1904-1942
32	Luverne Jane Sanford 1880-1967
35	Clarence Sather 1899-1988 married Karine J. 30 July 1924
35	Karine J. Sather 1900-1987 married Clarence 30 July 1924
24	Jack D. Satriano 1913-1975
14	Ben Saures (?) 1830 (?) - 6 (?) August (?) 1850 (?)
	- stone worn and hard to read
09	baby Schaar - 20 June 1942 -
13	Allan A. Schauer 1911-____
13	Bernie A. Schauer 1918-1995
23	Roger A. Schauer 1939-1968
33	Levi E. Schertz (?) 1867-1946
33	Maggie Schertz (?) 1873-1965
25	August Schindeldecker 1892-1962
25	Mary Schindeldecker 1900-1983
23	Anna T. Schjeldahl 1887-1962
23	Mildred H. Schjeldahl 1911-1965
23	Ole C. Schjeldahl 1880-1954

06	Ernest John Schmidtke 1893-1949
06	Sandra June Schmidtke 1944-1948
05	Angelic Marie Schnell 3 - 5 July 1980
29	Eleanor Marie Schonning (?) 1931-1983
30	Kenneth David Schonning (?) 1938-1949
30	Palmer Herbert Schonning (?) 1901-1993
30	Ora Esther Schonning (?) 1904-1995
26	Agnes G. Schuler 1889-1974
26	Jacob Schuler 1878-1957
28	Josephine K. Schuler 1879-1950
28	William M. Schuler 1870-1940
02	Alyce M. Schulz 2 March 1907 - 20 March 1985
02	Clarence E. Schulz 16 March 1904 - 11 April 1968
01	Dorothy Marie Schulz 1906-1996
21	Edward G.F. Schulz (?) 1874-1959
21	Mary K. Schulz (?) 1877-1942
21	Mildred Schulz (?) 1902-1919
21	Milton Schulz (?) 1902-1902
01	Roland F. (Sonny) Schulz 1912-1978
23	Erwin W. Schutt 1901-1968
23	Roger R. Schutt 1939-1965
23	Verna M. Schutt 1903-1975
15	Agnes Seals 1858-1914
15	George Seals 1862-1919
15	Jeannette M. Seals 1887-1913
17	Nancy Seeley 1829-1928
17	Nathan Seeley 1820-1908
11	Axel J. Sejrup 25 April 1890 - 29 April 1955
	MN Pvt 163 Depot Brigade WW1
11	Dennis E. Sejrup 1954-1971
11	Marie Sejrup 1896-1937
18	Edward E. Selk (?) 1879-1942
19	Elizabeth Selk (?) 1874-1930
19	'Father' Selk (?) 1839-1913
19	Idella M. Selk (?) 1881-1911
19	Jimmy, son of I. (?) and E. Selk, died 17 January (?) 1875 (?)
	age 3 months 10 days - worn and hard to read
19	'Mother' Selk (?) 1841-1906
01	George Senrick 1901-1980
01	Lydia Senrick 1903-1983
22	Charlotte Sprute Severson 1900-1977
22	Monroe Hartley Severson 1899-1977
22	J.I. Seward 1861-1924
26	Sally Shadrick 1957-1978
11	Caroline E., wife of P.L. Share 1824-1914
11	Elizabeth, daughter of P.L. and C.E. Share 1859-1912

11	Mary, daughter of P.L. and C.E. Share 1861-1950
24	Earl S. Shellenbarger 1910-1988
24	Grace M. Shellenbarger 1912-____
45	Roy G. Shelton Jr. 15 October 1965 - 29 June 1993
03	Roland C. Shirley 1909-1993
04	Ruth E. Shirley 1916-____
41	George H. Siebold (?) 1857-1926
41	John George Siebold 20 March 1892 - 6 June 1960
	MN CBM USNR WW1 and WW2
41	Lena Siebold (?) 1860-1938
41	Lillian M. Siebold 4 May 1894 - 9 July 1988
41	Phyllis Siebold (?) 1915-1924
11	Caroline W. Sieckert (?) 1855-1934
11	Frederick W. Sieckert (?) 1848-1917
22	Lloyd Sieckert 4 January 1892 - 15 September 1978
	Pvt US Army WW1
22	Mary M. Sieckert 1867-1924
38	Annie M., wife of John F. Sikora 1863-1937
02	Donald W. Skallerud 1924-1972 WW2 Vet US Navy
17	Catherine Slack, died 9 February 1879, age 72 years
16	Carrie M., daughter of N.E. and M.S. Slack - no dates -
	aged 3 years 6 months 18 days
17	George Slack, died 27 December 1873, age 31 years
16	N. Ezra Slack, died 12 May 1873, age 36 years 3 months 7 days
17	Robert Slack, died 13 December 1887, age 91 years
33	Eleanor S. Slater, wife of Robinson 1899-____
21	Adelbert Charles Smith (?) 1918-1967
34	Anna L. Smith (?) 13 May 1861 - 1 October 1922
34	C.H. Smith 18 October 1830 - 28 November 1910
16	Caleb Smith 2 March 1831 - 30 July 1903
21	Dana Elizabeth Smith (?) 1919-1991
13	Duard Smith 1914-1980
32	Edna M. Smith 1898-1942
31	Eleanor Smith 1932-1970
40	Ellen E. Smith 1843-1931
40	Elsie J. Smith 1870-1952
34	Henry J., son of C.H. and Nancy S. Smith
	8 January 1861 - 15 November 1906
42	Jennie, wife of D.C. Smith 1848-1889
16	Martha D., wife of Caleb Smith 11 December 1831 - 30 January (?) 1892
45	Maryann Moriarity Smith 7 July 1944 - 2 May 1996
42	Milford Lee Smith 1867-1878
34	Nancy S. Smith 13 May 1835 - 11 January 1921
32	Okley J. Smith 1898-1963
13	Retha Smith 1913-____
20	Richard Gordon Smith (?) 1948-1983

31	Russell Thomas Smith 17 February 1930 - 21 March 1930
40	Sylvester Smith 1837-1922
32	Carrie E. Snyder 1880-1964
32	Francis G. Snyder 1912-1975
32	Hazel Smith Snyder 1913-1968
32	Roscoe F. Snyder 1876-1946
32	William E. Snyder 1874-1944
35	C. Oscar Soderlund 1915-1990 married H. Jeanne 3 December 1949
35	Carl Oscar Soderlund 28 February 1915 - 4 February 1990
	Sgt US Army WW2
33	Charles W. Sorn (?) 1869-1920
33	Christiana Sorn 1844-1929
33	Julia O. Sorn (?) 1873-1950
33	William Sorn 4 March 1843 - 20 April 1924
34	Allen F. Spangenberg 1903-1948
34	LuWana B. Spangenberg - 1922 -
34	Mary A. Spangenberg 1874-1963
34	Viola C. Spangenberg - 1897 -
17	Elizabeth B. Sparks 1868-1939
39	Caroline Knowles Spaulding 1855-1948
15	Herbert G. (?) Spearin, died 23 August 1887, age 23 years
15	Julia B. Spearin (?) 1833-1914
15	Simon B. (?) Spearin, died 27 February 1892, age 65 years
33	Charles C. Spottswood 1823-1910
33	Charles P. Spottswood 1863-1913
33	Nancy J. Spottswood 1830-1883
33	William C. Spottswood 1858-1932
22	Amelia, daughter of August H. and Anna C. Sprute
	5 April 1898 - 18 March 1975
22	Anna Charlotte Sprute, nee Beins, wife of August H. Sprute
	4 November 1865 - 4 March 1944
22	August H. Sprute, son of Fredrick and Sophia Sprute
	29 March 1864 - 31 August 1929
23	baby Sprute - 2 June 1956 -
22	Caroline L. Sprute 1879-1960
22	Eddie Sprute (?) 8 April - 25 October 1918
22	Emil E.L. Sprute 1910-1983
24	Ernest W. Sprute 1906-1974
22	'Father' Sprute (?) 1819-1894
22	Fred Sprute, son of Fredrick and Sophia Sprute
	22 December 1853 - 15 December 1926
22	Fredrick A., son of A.H. and Anna C. Sprute 1895-1914
22	Freidrich Sprute 11 September 1824 - 30 July 1906
24	Helen A. Sprute 1906-1981
22	infants of A.H. and Anna C. Sprute
22	'Mother' Sprute (?) 1844-1919

22	Sophia Sprute 11 September 1824 - 6 September 1911
02	Ruby P. Staats 1894-1984
02	William P. Staats 1884-1970
35	Glenyce M. Stahnke 1920-1986
35	Leslie W. Stahnke 1916-1989
03	Alfred G. Stapf 1908-1983 Pfc US Army WW2
04	Alfred G. Stapf 1908-1983
08	Lewis J. Stapf 1880-1965
08	Lillian D. Stapf 1883-1970
08	Merrill L. Stapf 1911-1941
04	Ruth M. Stapf 1916-____
28	Stella C. Johnson Stapf 1897-1975
41	Harriet Staplin Carter, mother of Wm. and Wallace Staplin born in Jefferson Co. NY, died April 1899, age 85 years
41	Wallace Staplin, born at Niagara Falls, NY October 1934
02	Benora Staupe 1896-1970
02	Helmer Staupe 1890-1977
05	Marcia Kay Staupe 1948-1965
45	Gene R. (Spec) Steadman 20 March 1931 - 4 August 1994 married Sandra L. 30 June 1977
26	John Steefes 1886-1978
26	Mary E. Steefes 1883-1979
30	Ada L. Steele 1863-1931
33	Bertha Jensen Steele 1901-1929
30	James Steele 1855-1937
27	James E. Steele 26 October 1920 - 19 June 1988 Pvt US Army WW2
02	Margie Steele 1905-____
27	Myra E. Steel 12 December 1900 - 19 June 1988
02	Percy Steele 1901-1980
01	Shane R. Steeves 1969-1971
28	Dora N. Stelle - 1949 -
28	Georg W. Stelle - 1940 -
02	Clarence Stempfley 1911-1969
33	John C. Stempfley 1885-1971
33	John J. Stempfley 1905-1923
33	Rose A. Stempfley 1884-1982
38	William Stewart, died 4 March 1882, age 42 years 3 months 17 days
23	John L. Stofer 1882-1956
26	Lillian R. Strand 1915-____
26	Roy B. Strand 1907-1960
23	Lauren M. Summers 22 July 1983 - 21 May 1984
28	Clara D. Swanson 1884-1983
27	Ellen C. Swanson 1909-1965
35	Fred W. Swanson 31 December 1910 - 17 July 1990 married Willametta 12 May 1940

28	Garfield V. Swanson 1884-1953
27	Merl F. Swanson 1915-1995
35	Willameta T. Swanson, nee Burritt 9 October 1918-____
	married Fred W. 12 May 1940
37	Albert Sweet, born in Wells (?), Minn (?) ?? 1856 (?)
	died 7 June 1873
11	Alonzo R. Taft 1851-1932
23	baby girl Taft - 26 September 1962
11	Earle B. Taft 1884-1947
10	Glenn D. Taft 1888-1967
10	Irene H. Taft 1909-____
11	Isabella C. Taft 1851-1934
12	Jessie E. Taft 1881-1960
10	James F. Tapp 1919-1996
10	Mary D. Tapp 1917-____
44	Gray Edwin Tate 19 June 1938 - 3 June 1993
23	Lance D. Tharaldson 17 November 1970 - 5 June 1972
24	Maureen Thill 1937-1996 married Charles 27 October 1956
40	Alva C. Thomas 1873-1937
40	Ardee C. Thomas 1883-1956
32	Bertha Thomas 1900-1991
31	Calvin L. Thomas 1900-1980
31	Catherine A. Thomas 1908-1991
08	Ella G. Thomas 1870-1946
32	Ellen N. Thomas 1871-1945
32	Everett A. Thomas 1896-1949
32	Fred A. Thomas 1867-1927
40	Virgil V. Thomas 25 January 1833 - 22 July 1900
03	Emma B. Thompson 1903-1991
30	Harley G. Thornton 27 August 1896 - 30 September 1949
	MN Pvt QMC WW1
30	Mildred I. Thornton (?) 1905-1983
32	W.W. Tibbetts 1883-1930
22	Frieda F. Tillges 1888-1962
22	Nick Tillges 1880-1958
10	Harvey Tingley 1886-1958
10	Ida A. Tingley 1893-1961
10	Robert H. Tingley 1924-1935
19	Cornelius Tipler 1860-1910
19	Mary Ann, wife of Cornelius Tipler 1833-1895
23	baby girl Tonsager - 15 July 1966 -
02	Palmer Tonsager 1907-1981
02	Velma Tonsager 1911-____
19	Amanda B. Topp (?) 1894-1953
18	baby Topp 1947-1947

18	Dennis Topp (?) 1933-1936
18	Idella Topp (?) 1920-1920
19	Jens Kristian Topp (?) 1899-1988
19	Kristian Miller Topp (?) 1953-1982
18	Morris Topp (?) 1932-1932
04	Pearl Traux 1914-____
22	J.K. Troll 1885-1916 (?)
34	Gordon Trout 1906-1973
34	Gordon S. Trout 1906-1973 SK3 US Navy WW2
34	Harriet Trout 1912-____
33	Louise Trout 1882-1938
34	Sandra Trout 1948-1961
13	Frank W. Tubb 1913-____
13	Geraldine B. Tubb 1914-1983
03	Hazel K. Tucker 1891-1969
04	Robert J. Tucker 17 January 1919 - 5 October 1989
	Lt 5th AF WW2
03	William H. Tucker 1884-1967
25	John Turnquist 1899-1965
24	Melvin Turnquist 1929-1975
25	Millie Turnquist 1906-____
22	Karl Tutewohl 12 September 1847 - 7 December 1892
24	Victor Tymoshuk 1952-1988

02	Chris Uhl - Christiane Hannelore (born) 13 April 1954 in Germany
	- daughter of Nikolaus and Irmgard Uh, died 2 July 1974, age 20
02	Irmgard Uhl - Irmgard Minna Junghanis 14 August 1926 in Germany
	- married to Kikolaus Uhl 10 July 1948, died 4 January 1972
	age 45
16	Alfred Spreckley Underwood 1846-1921
17	Blanche Wilmot Underwood 23 September 1879 - 30 March 1899
16	D. Underwood 23 September 1812 - 27 January 1899
17	D. Francis Underwood 1873-1890
17	Ernest W. Underwood 12 January 1881 - 23 November 1894
17	Hannah Underwood 9 January 1818 - 20 September 1905
16	Maria, wife of D. (?) Underwood, died 3 March 1888
	age 69 years 11 months
16	Ruth Ada Underwood 1852-1924
17	Sarah Underwood (?) 10 April 1856 - 11 April 1920
17	Spreckley Underwood 10 April 1827 - 21 June 1910
16	Susan, wife of F. (?) Underwood, died 13 May 1881
	age 71 years 9 months 4 days

03	Ida Vall 1893-1962
02	Floyd F. Vanderford 1923-1976
27	Alfred W. Vanderlick 1896-1960

27	Margery H. Vanderlick 1899-1972
01	Amanda VanGuilder 1901-____
17	Earl H. VanGuilder 1896-1899
02	George L. VanGuilder Sr. 27 January 1913 - 30 March 1972
02	Lillian VanGuilder 25 October 1916 - 9 September 1993
01	Ray I. VanGuilder 1897-1970
16	Edna VanValkenburg (Closest Surname ?) 1881-1886
16	Gerald VanValkenburg (Closest Surname ?) 1897-1898
16	Luella VanValkenburg (?) 1871-1872
16	Warren A. VanValkenburg (Closest Surname ?) 1900-1902
16	Wynne VanValkenburg (?) 1874-1911
01	Della Varey 1906-1990
01	Edwin J. Varey 21 April 1926 - 17 February 1976 US Army
01	James Varey 1896-1979
21	Francis Vaughn, died 25 February 1879, age 33 years 7 months
21	Mary E., wife of Francis Vaughn 10 November 1848 - 7 January 1900
43	Harrington Verna 1904-1905
03	George L. Vieths 1893-1961
03	Olga M. Vieths 1897-1982
35	Florence I. Vincent 1915-____
35	Kenneth E. Vincent 1917-1991
28	David J. Volden (?) 1933-1952
41	Albert J. Wachter 1906-____
41	Carl H. Wachter 1911-1984
35	Deborah Ann Wachter - Johnson 1953-1985
41	Esther K. Wachter 1915-1964
41	Hazel O. Wachter 1914-1980
01	Roberta C. Walsh 1910-____
01	Thomas G. Walsh 1908-1984
10	Bernice Lorraine Wanha 23 November 1919 - 5 November 1989
43	? (buried) Warner 1879-1944
43	Elizabeth Warner 1887-1933
43	Jos. A. Warner - no dates - Co C 52 Mass. Inf
22	Alma S. Warweg 9 November 1889 - 19 September 1899
10	Caroline J. Warweg (?) 1858-1931
03	Claire M. Warweg 1921-1974
40	Clara Warweg 1862-1950
04	Edna E. Warweg 1901-1993
03	Edna E. Warweg, nee Larson 17 July 1901 - 10 January 1993
	born in Marine MN on St Croix
04	Fred P. Warweg 1885-1960
05	Geo H. Warweg 1884-1957
04	Henry G. Warweg 1922-1964
10	Louis P. Warweg (?) 1851-1921
03	Louis P. Warweg 28 July 1891 - 28 June 1965

	CM3 US Navy WW1
04	Louis Phillip Warweg 1891-1965
22	Louise J. Warweg 14 April 1892 - 30 May 1892
04	Mary F. Warweg 1887-1969
40	Phillip H. Warweg 1854-1918
43	Frank Watson 1858-1935
42	Hatty Watson 1863-1929
43	Jennie Watson 1867-1959
42	Mary Watson 1825-1906
43	Rinnie Belle, daughter of F.M. and J. Watson
	died 16 June 1902, age 6 years
42	Wm. H. Watson 1824-1898
24	Donna M. Weflen 1926-1980
24	Palmer M. Weflen 1923-1995
24	Palmer Marvin Weflen 27 February 1923 - 20 April 1995
	US Navy WW2
24	Lori Ann Wegner 1962-1986
01	Emily E. Weierke 1890-1970
01	Paul C. Weierke 1887-1979
32	Rose Tibbetts Weimern 1893-1960
39	Mary Ruth Moore Welch 1856-1912
10	Ariel Wellman, died 29 May 1872, age 75 years
10	Lucy Wellman, died 31 January 1881, age 83 years
34	Addie C. Wells 1874-1958
34	Artie, child of Geo. and Flora Wells, March 1869 - July 1869
34	baby girl, child of Geo. and Flora Wells - 1876 -
34	baby son of Clifford and Addie Wells - 8 April 1900 -
34	Clifford I. Wells 1870-1948
34	Flora Daine Wells 15 November 1846 - 28 February 1926
34	George W. Wells 16 December 1840 - 15 February 1908
	Co F 5th NY Calvalry
34	Willie Wells, child of Geo. and Flora Wells
	4 March 1867 - November 1868
23	baby girl Wenthold - 1949 -
14	Amanda H. Wescott, died 17 November 1888, age 59 years
14	Frank H. Wescott, died 28 September 1893, age 4 weeks
15	James Wescott 22 October 1823 - 4 May 1910
14	Jane E. Cockbain, wife of W.H. Wescott
	7 January 1869 - 1 September 1893
05	Lucille Wescott 1906-1987
14	Mary A. Wescott 1867-1954
08	Ora A. Wescott 1892-1946
05	Walter G. Wescott 1902-1957
14	Wells H. Wescott 1863-1931
14	Wells J. Wescott 1898-1920
35	Donna L. Westenberg 1940-1985

43	Blanche M. Wetterlin 1880-1960
43	Carrie Wetterlin 1852-1933
43	Charles Wetterlin 1847-1934
43	Frank O. Wetterlin 1881-1946
43	Junior T. Wetterlin 1914-1916
43	Mable Wetterlin (?) - no dates -
43	Mildred F. Wetterlin 1916-1932
23	Lois Ann Wetterlund 20 July - 11 November 1964
13	Windy Wetterlund 1915-1978
43	Winnifred Wheeler 1889-1898
40	John White ?? Age 21 years 5 months 17 days - broken stone
12	Addie B. Whittier, died 3 November 1891, age 34 years
12	Albert Whittier 17 April 1828 - 25 August 1901
11	Albert A. Whittier 1884-1962
12	Asa M.P. Whittier 16 June 1814 - 4 January 1899
24	Bernice Whittier 1908-_____
28	Charles B. Whittier 1872-1960 married Edith V. 7 December 1893
28	Donald B. Whittier 1905-1991 married Marguerite E. 17 June 1928
28	Edith V. Whittier 1873-1964 married Charles B. 7 December 1893
42	Ella L. Whittier 1876-1846
12	Emily M. Whittier, wife of Asa M.P. Whittier
	25 March 1820 - 29 September 1897
42	Emma Jane Whittier 1854-1929
11	Frank A. Whittier 1860-1925
42	George Henry Whittier 21 July 1842 - 4 March 1901
	Co I 2nd Minn Calvalry
41	infant son of M. and S.C. Whittier, died 4 April 1858
11	L. Grace Whittier 1888-1970
12	Lettice, wife of Giebord (?) Whittier (?)
	died 2 October 1853 (?), age 66 years 1 month - hard to read
42	Lloyd A. Whittier 1876-1949
12	Lucy A., wife of Albert Whittier 13 November 1827 - 14 January 1884
24	M.G. (Mid) Whittier 1903-1975
11	Margaret Whittier, nee Cameron 1860-1960
28	Marguerite E. Whittier 1905-1997 married Donald B. 17 June 1928
41	Myra Bell, child of M. and S.C. Whittier
	died 3 August 1859, age 4 months 10 days
11	Myra H. Whittier 1893-1988
12	Polly, wife of E.P. Whittier , died 29 January (?) 1872 - rest buried
12	Richard Whittier, died 21 October 1878, age 88 years
41	Sophia C., wife of M. Whittier, died 14 March 1873, age 53 years
11	Walter F. Whittier 1886-1919 - Co B 131 Inf Nantes France
33	Gustave A. Wiechman 1911-1924
35	Angeline Wille 1914-_____
28	Anna E. Wille 1883-1972
28	Charles A. Wille 1880-1956

28	Fred W. Wille (?) 1890-1977
26	Henry A. Wille 1892-1964 married Verney R. 21 November 1918
35	Henry G. Wille 1907-1981
28	Linda M. Wille (?) 1894-1949
26	Verney R. Wille 1896-1995 married Henry A. 21 November 1918
24	Marc A. Williams 8 November 1971 - 9 November 1984
36	Charles Whitcher 1844-1927
36	Helen M. Witcher 1823-1913
36	Sarah Witcher 1847-1923
36	Sylvester C. Witcher 1821-1904
22	Virginia M. Wolke 29 August 1915 - 29 August 1915
22	Vivian M. Wolke 29 August 1915 - 3 October 1915
37	Budette Z. Wood 1893-1985 Pvt US Army WW1
37	Olive M. Wood 1901-1990
42	Frankie, daughter of M.E. and P. Woodard died 6 January 1876, age 17 years 6 months 20 days
40	baby Woodruff 7 May 1906 - 21 September 1906
40	Franklin J. Woodruff 1836-1923 Corporal Co C Bracketts Battalion MN Cavalry
40	George W. Woodruff 1875-1960
40	Mary L. Woodruff 1890-1964
40	'Mother' Woodruff 4 October 1844- 26 October 1926
42	Hannah R., daughter of J.W. Works 29 September 1833 - 6 August 1915
42	James W. Works 13 December 1847 - 18 October 1884
42	Jacob W. Works 18 May 1809 - 30 December 1885
42	Mary H., wife of J.W. Works 5 March 1810 - 2 April 1896
41	Frank S. Wright 1881-1940
12	Helen W. Wright, died (?) 23 April 1941, age 82 years
40	John Wright, died (?) 25 July 1931, age 80 years 1 day
40	Lucy M., wife of John Wright, died 2 March 1897 age 39 years 9 months 21 days
40	Mildred Eunice, daughter of J. and L.M. Wright died 22 October 1896, age 9 years 7 months 6 days
41	Nancy J. Wright 1847-1926
40	Ora May Wright 10 November 1892 - 13 November 1892
27	Lena L. Yennie 1871-1961
30	Amy F. Young 1896-1984
30	Amy F. Young 25 August 1896 - 24 February 1984
21	Harvey Young 1818-1891
21	Pamela Young 1818-1894
30	Ward D. Young 1896-1972
30	Ward D. Young 8 August 1896 - 15 May 1972 MN Cpl US Army WW1
15	Arvid E. Youngkrantz 1911-1994

15   Mary Ann A. Youngkrantz, nee Wescott 1911-1997 (? recent burial)

11   Mildred Zellmer 1912-_____   married Roy 27 February 1936
11   Roy Zellmer Sr. 1911-1996   married Mildred 27 February 1936
12   Frank Zitzke 1860-1915

I was not able to determine surnames for the following:

18   Percy L. died 17 August 1860, age 2 years (?) ? months 1 day
           son of ? and E.H. ??ing (probably Irving ?)
           - hard to read - stone on side and partially buried
21   3 person stone between Penwell and Smith - stone very worn
37   ?? age 55 years 16 days - rest of stone broken off
           - between Sweet and Haugh
41   Earl ?, died ? 1872 (?) - difficult to read

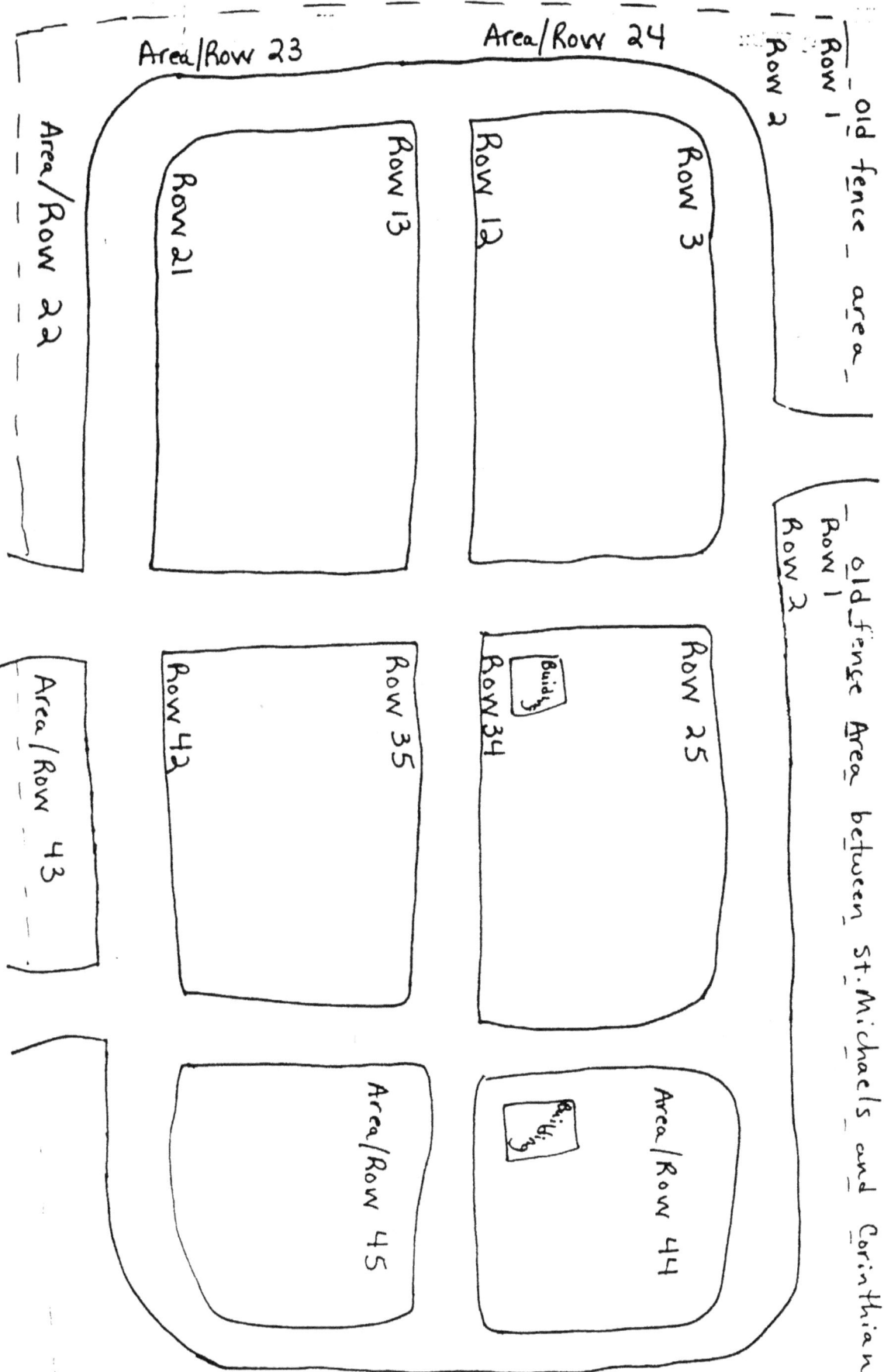

St. Michaels Catholic Cemetery

Old fence - area

Row 1
Row 2

Area/Row 23

Area/Row 24

Row 1
Row 2

Old fence Area between St. Michaels and Corinthian

Area/Row 22

Row 21

Row 13

Row 12

Row 3

Row 42

Row 35

Row 34

Building

Row 25

Area/Row 43

Area/Row 45

Area/Row 44

Building

Corinthian
Cemetery

Empire Township
114-R19W
Section 29

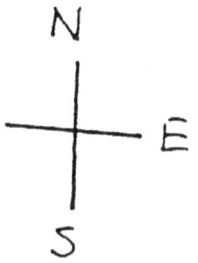

N
E
S

313

St. Michael's Catholic Cemetery

Empire Township, Dakota County, Minnesota: T114N-R19W, section 29

This cemetery is upkept and in good shape. This cemetery is located along the northeast edge of Farmington. The area that comprises the cemetery is actually two cemeteries. The northeast side of the area is St. Michael's' Catholic Cemetery and the Western side is the Corinthian Cemetery. I have listed the cemeteries separately.

I began numbering with row 1 along the east edge of St. Michael's Catholic Cemetery. Row 22 ends at the west edge of this cemetery. There is evidence of an old fence and poles along the drive area. It appears that several four foot pine trees were planted in place of the fence. The burials that are listed as row 10 are part of children's burial area near the southeast area of the cemetery.

The Dakota county cemetery records compilation lists this cemetery as: St. Michael's Catholic Cemetery, established 1877 - church. 2 acres. Located Section 29, SW1/4. (East Side).

Everyone is listed in alphabetical order. The number before each entry is the row number. There is a map at the back of this section.

These cemetery burial monuments were transcribed during 1996.

10	daughter of Mr. and Mrs. Fred C. Adelmann - 17 May 1958 -
10	Maria E., daughter of Mr. and Mrs. Fred C. Adelmann 5 - 7 February 1962
10	boy Akin - 16 May 1959 -
09	Dennis C. Akin 1941-1983 RD2 US Navy
11	Ethel Akin 1896-1984
11	Jerome Akin 1895-1985
09	Jesse D. Akin 1895-1967
03	Lisa Dale Akin - no dates -
09	Marcella A. Akin 20 July 1920 - 20 July 1989
09	Valerie M. Akin 1897-1954
03	Lynn Marie Alexander 19 April 1967 - 16 April 1991
20	Agnes Ives Alich (?) 1901-1918
08	Anna M. Alich 1906-____
19	Pvt. Carl J. Alich 1910-1945 Co C 9th TRN BN 3rd TRN REGT
19	Clarence J. Alich 1918-1981 married Evelyn L. 22 September 1938
20	Emil Alich 1869-1938
19	Evelyn L. Alich 1915-____ married Clarence J. 22 September 1938
20	'Father' Alich (?) 1869-1938
08	Glenn R. Alich 1941-1953
03	Julia A. Alich 1914-____ married Paul J. 21 September 1932
20	Karl Charles Alich (?) 1877-1946
20	Millie L. Alich (?) 1877-1936

20	'Mother' Alich (?) 1879-1966
03	Paul J. Alich 1904-1989 married Julia A. 21 September 1932
20	Pauline Alich 1879-1966
08	Robert J. Alich 1902-1970
01	Robert L. Alich 1933-1996
19	Frances M. Angus 1906-____
19	Raymond H. Angus 1903-1984
20	Colleen Marie Applegate 30 May 1963 - 23 March 1984
23	Carroll L. Auge 24 February 1913 - ____
23	Marie L. Auge 17 February 1914 - ____
19	Catherine L. Ayotte 1901-1978
19	Fred D. Ayotte 1903-1971
20	Margaret Ayotte 1870-1951
20	Merritt Ayotte 1856-1932
07	Bardon E. Bakke 1888-1967
07	R. Jean Bakke 1892-1976
04	Bernice F. Ballard 13 February 1902 - 20 February 1993
04	Ralph J. Ballard 13 January 1899 - 10 March 1988 US Navy WW1
16	Elizabeth M. Baltes 1879-1942
29	Iona R. Baltes 1909-____
16	Joseph N. Baltes 1882-1964
29	Lisle J. Baltes 1907-1984
15	twin boys John and Paul Baltes - 20 January 1952 -
18	Florence Barlage 1908-1976 married Leo 1945
17	Henry Barlage 1854-1939
18	Leo Barlage 1900-1978 married Florence 1945
17	Paulina Barlage 1874-1953
09	John Bauer - 25 December 1955 -
09	Kirk Patrick Bauer - 23 October 1972 -
19	Barbara Becker 23 August 1894 - 25 April 1984
19	Hildegard Becker 1917-____
19	Peter Becker 1909-1994
22	Alpheus S. Beeney 1899-1986
22	Ramona M. Beeney 1903-1994
01	Elsie J. Belden 1905-1992
22	Allen C. Benolkin 25 August 1939 - 20 January 1940
22	Calvin Benolkin 5 November 1941 - 26 May 1994
22	Charles T. Benolkin 1 May 1917 - 28 November 1994
15	J.J. Bennett 2 September 1871 - 16 February 1937
15	Terrance J. Bennett 20 July 1878 - 29 March 1922
07	Bessie Berres 1890-1966
07	George W. Berres 1919-1983 Tec 4 US Army WW2
07	Valeria M. Berres 1918-1995
07	William Berres 1878-1965
19	Edward D. Bettinger 18 December 1923 - 3 January 1951

Washington Sgt 68 Armd Infantry BN WW2 BSM - PH

20   'Father' Bettinger (?) 1856-1915
15   Joseph J. Bettinger 12 December 1894 - 29 February 1972
         MN Pfc US Army WW1
19   Kenneth C. Bettinger 4 May 1927 - 14 July 1951
         MN Pvt 38 Armd Inf BN 7 Armd Div
20   'Mother' Bettinger (?) 1859-1913
20   Raymond J. Bettinger   August 1925 - July 1938
19   Richard C. Bettinger   October 1930 - January 1951
19   Raymond Charles Beyer 29 November 1948 - 9 April 1984
         SP4 US Army Vietnam
20   Richard G. Beyer 1913-____
20   Rose P. Beyer 1913-____
12   A. Lulu Blake 1873-1957
03   Clair J. Blake 1917-1991
12   Frank R. Blake 1873-1921
12   Richard S. Blake 1914-1980 RT2 US Navy WW2
07   Alden Bohm 1901-1965
07   Louise Bohm 1901-1959
03   Joseph C. Boley 7 February 1913 - 2 August 1990
         S Sgt US Army WW2
04   Alfred J. Bolster 1911-1980
04   Isabel M. Bolster 1908-1996
06   Alfred E. Bradley 1892-1963
06   Dianne Bradley 1953-1960
06   Mary E. Bradley 1887-1961
05   Anton Brand 1901-1972
05   Elizabeth Brand 1906-1992
16   Frances M. Brossard (?) 1891-1974
16   Jane Brossard (?) 1861-1939
16   Paul V. Brossard (?) 1896-1973
16   Wm. Adolph Brossard (?) 1858-1947
04   Joseph B. Brost 1903-1993
04   Phil C. Brost 1909-____
24   Ethelwyn C. Brunette 10 April 1917 - ____
24   Gerald P. Brunnette 10 December 1955 - 22 September 1971
24   Joseph E. Brunette 14 April 1912 - 28 April 1963
         WI Pfc US Marine Corps WW2
17   Edna A. Buberl, nee Schletty   1904-1992
16   Julia Buckley (?) 1880-1938
16   Mary Buckley (?) 1843-1935
16   Michael Buckley (?) 1840-1913
22   Nina M. Bucklin 1920-1924

09   Martin C. Campion (?) 1867-1952
09   Mary C. Campion (?) 1878-1952

06   Emmet F. Carey 1892-1982
04   Kenneth C. Carey 1925-1984
06   Marie A. Carey 1893-1969
31   Ann P. Carlson 1900-1982
31   Carl M. Carlson 1897-1978
20   Charles E. Caron 1898-1983
20   Dorothy L. Caron 1900-1990
20   Richard Whittier Caron 1929-1937
12   Kathleen S. Carr 14 December 1942 - 30 January 1997
14   Mildred A. Carr 1918-1978
14   Russell O. Carr 1916-1984
03   Carl T. Case 1907-____
05   Humphrey A. Case 1897-1964
05   Margaret M. Case 1901-1993
03   Mildred K. Case 1906-1996
09   Margaret T. Case 1882-1961
20   'Mother' Casey (?) 1874-1918
09   Patrick H. Casey 1873-1951
04   Ernest Christen 1899-1988
04   Madeline Christen 1905-1992
19   Daniel Churchill 1 January 1945 - 1 January 1995
                married Patty 6 April 1990
20   Anna Clark (?) 1882-1936
20   Bertrum Clark (?) 1878-1954
20   Nora Clay 1889-1921
17   Arnold H. Clobes 1928-1982
09   Arthur C. Cook 11 June 1893 - 13 January 1948
                MN Wagoner Hq TRP 91 Div WW1
21   Arthur D. Cook 1941-1979
13   Barbara Cook 1889-1977
22   Benedict A. Cook 18 September 1935 - 3 September 1991
                Pfc US Army Korea
04   Bertram L. Cook 1891-1965
22   Calvin C. Cook 1925-1939
13   Joseph Cook 1889-1941
04   Mary L. Cook 1891-1971
22   Rose C. Cook 1899-1972
15   Adeline C. Cordes 1923-1980
15   Anna Mae Cordes 1931-1984
15   Marvin F. Cordes 1923-1990
08   Dorothy Corrigan 1916-____
08   James F. Corrigan 1904-1980
03   John J. Corrigan 1906-1989
03   Margaret McAndrews Corrigan 1912-1994

15   Harriet Daily 1921-____

15	Lawrence F. Daily 1919-1978
13	Andela M. Deary 1908-1991
14	Edward B. Deary 1859-1936
14	Edward J. Deary 1904-1959
14	Katherine B. Deary 1880-1966
14	Margaret M. Deary 1906-1932
18	Catherine Deegan 1875-1957
18	Francis J. Deegan 15 February 1915 - 10 April 1990
	S Sgt US Army WW2
17	Irene Churchill Deegan 26 February 1912 - ____
18	James Deegan 1868-1951
17	James Edward Deegan 6 May 1910 - 15 July 1995
	M Sgt US Army WW2 Purple Heart
17	John F. Deegan 7 March 1948 - 29 March 1948
17	John Paul Deegan 19 May 1935 - 22 May 1935
18	Mary A. Deegan 1904 - ____
17	Wilfred J. Deegan 13 March 1906 - 2 September 1913
06	Catherine Deibler 1886-1963
06	John N. Deibler 1888-1969
13	Benita Devney 1898-1990
12	Edward J. Devney 28 August 1875 - 27 April 1902
12	'Father' Devney (?) 1850-1929
13	John A. Devney 1885-1951
12	Margaret C. Devney 1895-1984
12	Michael H. Devney 1887-1983
12	'Mother' Devney (?) 1854-1935
12	Suzanne Blake deLongpre 1913-____
16	Katherine Doffing 1918-____
16	Melvin Doffing 1913-____
15	Peter Doffing 1886-1973
15	Wilhelmina Doffing 1886-1970
26	Daniel Doyle 1895-1985
01	Daniel C. Doyle 1916-____ married Pearl L. 30 August 1939
26	Margaret Doyle 1885-1975
01	Pearl L. Doyle 1918-____ married Daniel C. 30 August 1939
30	Jan Duchek 4 February 1924 - 31 March 1970
19	Bruce L. Duff 1910-1972
19	Winnifred B. Duff 1911-1995
18	Gustav Edfast 1896-1941
03	Kenneth N. Ekness 19 December 1917 - 18 January 1990
	Pfc US Army WW2
13	August Elsner (?) 1899-1925
14	August R. Elsner 1871-1952
13	Henry G. Elsner 1905-1962
13	John B. Elsner 17 September 1896 - 9 April 1955

MN Pfc 46 Co Trans Corps WW1
14   Regina Elsner 1868-1911
14   Regina Elsner 11 June 1868 - 2 January 1911
07   Albert J. Emond 1901-1969
26   Clara O. Emond 1909-1975
26   Joseph S. Emond 1905-1976
07   Vivian L. Emond 1900-1980

31   James Fahey 31 March 1872 - 27 April 1955
03   Michelle M. Fasbender 25 August 1983 - 7 June 1989
05   Agnes T. Feely 1914-____
05   Donald T. Feely 1912-1979
14   Ellen Feely 1881-1964
09   Edward C. Feely 1894-1952
11   Hazel M. Feely 1895-1944
09   Pearl A. Feely 1897-1988
14   Thomas J. Feely 1880-1960
11   William F. Feely 1883-1957
09   Hugh Forsaith Field 1882-1953
09   Frank W. Finnegan 1876-1945
09   Nellie Finnegan 1887-1976
09   Thomas Finnegan 1916-1990
13   Alfred F. Fischer 1 February 1905 - 16 November 1994
17   George E. Fischer 15 March 1917 - 12 November 1977
           Sgt US Army WW2
18   James H. Fischer 1948-1966
07   John Volden Fischer 1956-1957
13   Mary Daly Fischer 4 May 1913 - 15 April 1993
07   Sue Ann Fischer 1954-1975
09   Elizabeth Flach (?) 1907-1991
09   George J. Flach (?) 1908-1957
07   George E. Flynn Sr. 1893-1977
06   Joseph Flynn 30 March - 2 April 1962
06   Mary Flynn 14 - 15 October 1959
07   Myra S. Flynn 1901-1995
17   Clarence Foster 1886-1972
17   Jeanette Foster 1921-1997
17   Maude Foster 1892-1959
07   John W. Frame 1901-1971
13   Patricia Ann Frame 1934-1945
07   Rose M. Frame 1901-1963
03   baby girl Frandrup - 9 April 1989 -
02   Ervin H. Frandrup 1920-1994
04   Frank B. Frandrup 1892-1970
21   'Father' Franske (?) 22 April 1855 - 22 November 1911
21   'Mother' Franske (?) 28 August 1854 - 3 October 1921

07	James M. Fread 1913-1996
07	Louise K. Berres Fread 1920-1994
05	David Alyn Fredrickson 1960-1981
03	Katie Jane Fritz 26 December 1982 - 27 June 1989
02	Michael Fritz 1953-1991 married ? 10 July 1982
06	Arlene M. Gannon 1917-1970
13	Elizabeth L. Gannon 1873-1952
06	Joseph T. Gannon 1914-____
	Ordained Priest 1975 by Pope Paul VI Rome
08	Julia Gannon 1886-1978
13	Lloyd P. Gannon 1905-1928
13	Patrick J. Gannon 1870-1919
08	William Gannon 1881-1956
17	Sylvia J. Garr 1932-1979
04	Patrick John Garvey 1957-1966
04	Timothy Hyland Garvey 1947-1971
15	John C. Gephart 1920-____
15	M. Eileen Gephart 1917-____
05	Ernest M. Gerster 1895-1979
05	Esther M. Gerster 1905-____
08	Earl C. Granger 1892-1968 Pvt WW1 90 Spruce Sqd ASAP
08	Edith Granger 1893-1951
08	Fred J. Granger (?) 1893-1958
08	Martha M. Granger (?) 1891-1952
08	Michael W. Granger 1918-1988
29	John Grove 1903-1982
29	Fred (Jerry) Grove 1932-1972
01	Glen 'Sonny' Grove 1 January 1924 - 17 February 1994
	married Harriet M. 1 June 1946
01	Glen T. Grove 1 January 1924 - 17 February 1994 US Army WW2
18	Lucas Calles Grundman 4 June 1974 - 26 October 1996
05	Brian Michael Haan 11 February - 14 May 1976
05	Justin A. Haan - 7 November 1989 -
22	Allen James Haffner - 1945 -
03	Mary Ellen Haffner 1923-1992 married Howard E. 6 February 1945
23	Florence A. Hall 1891-1981
23	George C. Hall 1886-1947
19	Rowena A. Hanson 21 August 1909 - 2 March 1997
02	Anne P. Hartley 1920-1991
16	Diane Barbara Heinen 1931-1933
16	Elizabeth A. Heinen 1898-1915
13	Gertrude Heinen 1891-1977
15	J.V. Heinen 1903-1931
16	Joseph Heinen 2 March 1867 - 25 March 1935

15	John S. Heinen 1896-1961
16	Mary E. Heinen 1904-1918
13	Nicholas Heinen 1888-1970
16	Sarah A. Heinen 28 October 1867 - 8 July 1929
15	Virginia Heinen 1900-1981
25	Francis J. Henneberry 1907-1985
25	Helen E. Henneberry 1917-1975
25	James M. Henneberry 1956-1972
25	Thomas J. Henneberry 1949-1976
08	Albert C. Bermann (?) 1884-1956
08	Marie L. Hermann (?) 1892-1992
07	Frank Hince 1894-1987
07	Lena Hince 1894-1989
03	Margaret A. Hince 1928-1992 married William B. 13 September 1950
01	Donna M. Huebner, nee Thelen 1959-1995
	married John B. 17 October 1980
31	David R. Hulsing 1940-1980
14	Albert L. Humphrey 1867-1945
14	Mary Anne Hunter 1924-1982
04	Catherine A. Hyland 1884-1979
04	Grace L. Hyland 1890-1971
30	Joseph F. Hyland 1893-1971
04	Maude R. Hyland 1877-1974
14	Bernard Jensen 1962-1964
22	Elizabeth Johnston, died 20 December 1935
22	Harry Johnston, died 7 July 1936
13	Margiana D. Jones 1907-1994
20	Raymond A. Kalscheuer 1895-1983
20	Salona E. Kalscheuer 1895-1982
06	Clarence A. Kamen 1918-____
06	Pauline C. Kamen 1894-1982
06	Rosalia R. Kamen 1926-1959
06	Theodore J. Kamen 1889-1982
13	baby girl Kaufenberg - 29 June 1964 -
30	Patrick J. Ketelboeter 3 March 1967 - 4 October 1988 FA US Navy
14	Mary Kimber (?) 1859-1919
14	Matilda Kimber (?) 1885-1956
14	William Kimber (?) 1853-1921
06	Jeannette L. Klahr 1898-1989
06	William Klahr 1904-1962
22	baby Klement - 28 January 1937 -
22	baby girl Klement - 1967 -
06	Lawrence C. Klement 1911-____
06	Mary J. Klement 1912-____

04	Patty Jo Spaniol Kleve 1939-1978
04	Sarah M. Kleve 1899-1985
04	William H. Kleve 1898-1979
03	Gregory C. Klotter 14 March 1974 - 13 November 1991
24	Christopher Klotz 1886-1963
25	Cora C. Klotz 1914-____ married Gregory C. 7 February 1940
25	Gregory C. Klotz 1904-1974 married Cora C. 7 February 1940
31	Jacob Klotz 1866-1949
24	Katharina Klotz 1891-1981
23	Mary Klotz 1887-1972
23	Michael Klotz 1884-1946
31	Michael R. Klotz 1911-1958
07	Dana Andre Knott 1951-1961
18	Dorothy Koehnen 1918-1918
01	Sandra Kolstad 1950-1996 married Roger 13 September 1982
03	Roman Charles Kotz 1 April 1941 - 29 September 1992
	Pfc US Army
17	Bette M. Kubista 1919-1985 married Roman S. 11 November 1937
17	Roman S. Kubista 1910-____ married Bette M. 11 November 1937
05	Donald W. Kulstad 1909-1972
05	Mary A. Kulstad 1908-1980
10	Kevin Joseph Kurowski 28 April - 27 August 1970
05	John H. Kurrasch 1887-1968
05	Martha M. Kurrasch 1896-1973
12	Anna Agnes Langer (?) 1862-1927
12	August Langer (?) 1850-1942
11	August Langer 12 July 1890 - 15 September 1966
	MN Pvt Co H 160 Infantry WW1
12	Frank Langer 1862-1929
11	George Langer 1884-1952
12	Jeanette Langer (?) 1897-1984
22	John Langer 1855-1919
11	Joseph Langer 23 February 1894 - 19 February 1964
	MN Pvt 10 Co 161 Depot Brigade WW1
12	Julius Langer 1872-1931
22	Mary Langer 1851-1916
12	Matilda Langer 1860-1944
01	Deon Joy Larson 13 May 1935 - 28 February 1993
02	Emmett W. Larson 1916-____
01	Jeanelle E. Walker Larson 5 June 1961 - 18 June 1996
02	Marie M. Larson 1919-____
10	Annette Lennox - 1961 -
01	Helen R. Lennox 20 October 1919 - 20 January 1994
	Y2 US Navy WW2
24	Steven Little 29 September 1953 - 3 September 1996

07	George J. Loesch 29 July 1919 - 24 November 1988
	Fpc US Army WW2
07	Mary T. Loesch 1883-1969
07	Mathew M. Loesch 1884-1958
19	Melba T. Logan 1915-____
19	William J. Logan 1920-1990
19	William J. Logan 1 September 1920 - 22 January 1990
	Sgt US Army Air Corps WW2
11	Zenobia A. Losinski 1906-1946
05	Genevieve E. Lubke 1912-1984
05	Oscar J. Lubke 1906-1968
08	George Ludescher 1898-1986
08	Rose Ludescher 1901-1962
30	Michael A. Lynch 1948-1988
14	Anna A. MacPhee 1874-1933
14	Daniel J. MacPhee 1870-1937
13	LeRoy E. MacPhee 8 April 1896 - 14 March 1972
	MN Pfc US Army WW1
13	Rose E. MacPhee 1900-1976
13	Roy E. MacPhee 1896-1972
13	Mary McGinn Mahoney 1898-1966
31	Vincent J. Majerus 5 June 1914 - 9 April 1980
19	Catherine Markey 1881-1934
19	Thomas Markey 1877-1946
12	Anna Martin 1867-1941
11	Elmer A. Martin 1898-1954 Major A.U.S. WW2
12	Julius Martin 1861-1943
11	Kathryn Martin 1900-1971
12	Pfc Robert D. Martin - Corps of Engineers Co B 271 St Engr BN
	27 March 1945 Vicinity of Speyer Germany
05	Doris Mauer 1929-1978
10	Lisa Jane Mazurkiewic 1962-1962
12	Fred L. McAndrew (?) 1892-1978
12	Mary A. McAndrew (?) 1899-1992
13	John J McBrien 13 April 1912 - ____ married Ruth E. 29 May 1939
13	Ruth E. McBain 25 June 1910 - 5 January 1996
	married John J. 29 May 1939
01	Florence C. McCarthy 22 August 1918 - 7 April 1992
30	F. Berkey McClusky 1910-1980
29	George B. McCluskey 1904-1983
29	Mary (Walsh) McCluskey 1908-____
30	Mayme C. McCluskey 1910-____
12	Evelyn C. McDermott (?) 1896-1964
12	Patrick T. McDermott (?) 4 September - 5 September 1967
12	Robert V. McDermott (?) 1892-1967

16	Ambrose McDonald 1912-1915
09	John J. McDonald 1879-1952
13	Anne E. McGinn 1902-1989 married Sylvester B. 25 August 1932
11	Arthur J. McGinn 1900-1972
14	Bernard D. McGinn (?) 1876-1932
11	Beryl M. McGinn 1899-1959
07	Cecilia Casey McGinn (?) 1905-1985
07	Gregg McGinn 1911-1984
07	John Patrick McGinn (?) 1907-1986
14	Margaret L. McGinn (?) 1872-1957
13	Sylvester B. McGinn 1904-1972 married Anne E. 25 August 1932
14	Thomas E. McGinn (?) 1898-1937
11	William B. McGinn 1923-1923
09	Ellen McGovern 1875-1966
09	Joan Mary McGovern January - April 1955
09	John McGovern 1872-1954
08	John B. McGovern 1907-1989
01	Leonard V. McGovern 14 September 1915 - 24 June 1994
	US Coast Guard
08	M. Helen McGovern 1906-1978
09	Thomas P. McGovern 5 June 1912 - 10 July 1947
	MN 1 Sgt Engineers WW2
13	baby sister McGrath (?) - 24 July 1928 -
14	'Father' McGrath (?) 1830-1923
13	baby Forciea McGrath (?) - 1950 -
13	Harry McGrath (?) 1889-1982
13	James McGrath (?) 1883-1965
14	Kathryn McGrath (?) 1881-1923
13	Margaret McGrath (?) 1886-1957
13	Mary Ellen McGrath (?) 1889-1965
14	'Mother' McGrath (?) 1849-1930
14	Patrick McGrath (?) 1877-1955
13	Thomas Byron McGrath (?) 1875-1928
04	Marie F. McGuire 1899-1992
04	Paul E. McGuire 1924-1993
04	Paul Edward McGuire 1924-1993 S Sgt US Army WW2
04	Timothy McGuire 9 March 1894 - 16 September 1978
	Cpl US Army WW1
04	Timothy F. McGuire 1894-1978
16	Estelle Hyland McHugh 1887-1936
15	Hazel M. McHugh 1894-1975
15	Henry J. McHugh 1892-1957
16	James H. McHugh 1919-1938
16	William B. McHugh 1886-1966 veteran *
24	Avon E. McKague 1907-1996
24	George W. McKague 1946-1964

24	Winifred E. McKague 1912-1990
07	Anna K. Mester 1916-1986
07	Frank J. Mester 1913-____
07	Roger F. Mester 1951-1968
31	Julius L. Methner 1897-1962
03	Ronald G. Meyers 20 October 1969 - 2 February 1991
24	Ryan Dennis Michaelis 18 October 1981 - 12 July 1996
19	Doug Millard 1959-1987
12	Edward S. Minnick 1904-1984
12	Edward P. Minnick 1866-1941
12	Mary E. Minnick 1883-1946
12	Nelda A. Minnick 1904-1988
18	Dominic Moes 1857-1929
07	Anna Molitor 1881-1953
07	Hubert Molitor 1873-1954
06	John Molitor 1876-1944
12	Joseph P. Molitor 1878-1941
12	Katherine Molitor 1885-1954
06	Mary Molitor 1886-1972
08	Peter Molitor 1870-1951
10	Brandon Joh Moore 21 January - 22 January 1981
12	Father David Moran 1881-1944 - Pastor - Humanitarian - Legionnaire
03	Andrew M. Mogenson - 1 August 1996 -
08	Erna Mroz 1910-1983
04	Anna Mulligan 1896-1981
04	Leon Mulligan 1895-1963
13	Eva M. Mulvhill 1906-1976
13	Wm. J. Mulvhill 1896-1983
07	Anne V. Murphy 1896-1981
07	Raymond T. Murphy 1890-1964
22	Robert J. Murray 1925-1928
06	George Mussman 1896-1980
06	George F. Mussman 1896-1980 Pfc US marine Corps WW1
06	Rose Mussman 1897-1985
13	Pearl E. Myervold 1906-1976
10	Ann Marie Narum - 24 April 1966 -
15	Edith May Neilan (?) 1890-1946
15	George Hugh Neilan (?) 1889-1962
30	Evelyn T. Neilen 4 June 1906 - 28 December 1988
11	Henrietta Nelson, nee Langer 1889-1955
09	Emma L. Nonopatski 1912-____
18	Elizabeth O'Connor 1882-1943
18	Michael O'Connor 1869-1961
17	Elizabeth M. Olson 1920-____

17	Enoch E. Olson 1914-1974
19	Mary A. Olson 1933-1992
14	Catherine J. O'Meara 1864-1931
14	Irwim (Mike) O'Meara 1895-1965
06	Marcella O'Meara 1910-1991
14	Thomas J. O'Meara 1862-1940
06	Thomas L. O'Meara 1902-1960
05	Clara J. Oster 1893-1973
04	Daniel Oster 1911-1987
13	Hannah Oster 1870-1959
05	Ishmael P. Oster 1893-1986
04	Lucilla Oster 1913-____
13	Peter Oster 1867-1945
02	Emilinne L. Oxborough 1916-1995
28	Claude Pearson 1886-1972
28	Mary Pearson 1900-1983
08	Edward F. Pechacek 1913-1984
08	Elizabeth M. Pechacek 1914-1983
03	Ferro Pellicci 1900-1985
16	Nicholas J. Pellicci, son of John and Lori - 23 April 1992 -
03	Norma Pellicci 1918-1993
02	Thomas T. Peters 8 December 1963 - 23 July 1990
06	Margaret M. Pietsch 1910-1989
06	Marvin L. Pietsch 1910-1974
08	Joseph J. Rademacher 1945-1963
06	Audrey Ann Raidt 1930-1967
06	Steven R. Raidt, husband of Deborah 1952-1978
10	Ann Raymond - 10 July 1981 -
05	Bernard A. Record 1913-1971
06	Anna F. Reichow 1877-1948
06	Edward F. Reichow 1878-1954
14	Dora Reinardy 1897-1961
14	Jacob Reinardy 1893-1962
09	Emma C. Reisinger 1897-1985
04	Harold (Jug) Reisinger 1919-1976
09	Rex T. Reisinger 1898-1948
01	Kristine M. Rezac 14 April 1968 - 29 March 1995
05	Charles Riegert 1903-1973
05	Ida Riegert 1909-1964
18	James Ristow 1939-1943
17	James Harold Ristow 1939-1943
18	Robert W. Ristow 1914-1968
18	Robert W. Ristow 16 August 1914 - 24 June 1968
	CM1 US Navy

18	Vivian M. Ristow 1914-1974
22	baby Roach 28 April - 28 April 1924
21	Irene Roach 1917-1926
22	John A. Roach 26 November 1965 - 18 February 1996
22	Lois A. Roach 1928-1994
21	Nellie Roach 20 March 1898 - 13 February 1967
14	Barbara Rollmann 5 July 1891 - 4 November 1973
14	John Rollmann 6 August 1889 - 25 July 1986
08	Agnes M. Rosen 1880-1956
08	August F. Rosen 1876-1960
08	Lloyd F. Rosen 1905-1976
08	Ruth D. Rosen 1908-1982
13	Ann M. Rother, born Rollmann 26 October 1913 - 27 October 1995
05	Edward Rother 1910-____ married Marjorie 4 September 1937
29	Henry E. Rother 1903-1993
05	Marjorie Rother 1915-1966 married Edward 4 September 1937
29	Mary K. Rother 1919-1985
19	Pat Rother 1955-1987
08	Catherine Rotty 1897-1956
02	Gordon E. Rotty 1931-1987
02	Gordon Edward Rotty 1931-1987 Sgt US Army Korea
08	Vincent Rotty 1893-1965
05	Clara Ruddle 1894-1971
05	Edward Ruddle 1894-1982
03	Kermit Ruona 1909-1987
21	Myrna Rush 1919-1925
16	Anna B. Ruzicka 1908-1986
16	Joseph J. Ruzicka 1904-1973
22	baby Ryan - 1942 -
20	John H. Ryan 1910-1980
15	Katherne Ryan 1912-1985
20	Marie A. Ryan 1911-1966
14	Emma L. Sauber 1899-1972
14	Irene S. Sauber 1898-1992
09	John E. Sauber 1895-1957
09	John Edward Sauber 5 October 1895 - 3 October 1957
	MN Pvt Co H 110 Infantry WW1
14	Katherine Sauber 1865-1944
14	Matt Sauber 1862-1950
09	Nelena Sauber 1899-1966
14	William M. Sauber 1890-1932
14	William M. Sauber - 3 June 1932 - MN Mech 321 Inf 81 Div
11	Francis J. Scanlon 1891-1987
12	James Scanlon (?) 1866-1933
11	Margaret E. Scanlon (?) 1918-1988

12	Nellie Scanlon (?) 1874-1925
11	Nellie M. Scanlon 1895-1987
05	Albert H. Schiller 1911-1964
05	Anton J. Schiller 1899-1995
05	Josephine M. Schiller 1898-1967
10	Gordy Lee Schmitz, son of Steve and Barb
	19 July 1983 - 4 November 1983
08	Adolph M. Schneider 1877-1962
08	Alvin F. Schneider 27 October 1914 - 29 March 1996
18	Bob Schneider 1928-1985 married Lauretta 24 May 1952
09	Helen C. Schneider 1900-1958
08	Helena J. Schneider 1883-1962
09	James M. Schneider 14 October 1892 - 29 August 1955
	MN Pvt Med Det 161 Depot Brig WW1
10	Mary Rose Schneider 8 - 11 October 1972
20	Juanita C. Schoenle 30 January 1908 - 30 December 1976
20	Leo I. Schoenle 1 February 1907 - 22 April 1976
06	Blandina C. Schroeder (?) 1913-1967
06	Elizabeth Schroeder (?) 1883-1970
06	Ethel L. Schroeder (?) 1916-____
06	Francis E. Schroeder (?) 1914-____
06	Vincent J. Schroeder (?) 1885-1965
09	Clara J. Searle 1888-1954
09	Donald Searle (?) 1912-1955
21	Roy Searle Jr. 1918-1918
09	Roy T. Searle 1889-1967
18	Mary C. Seurer 19 May 1913 - 4 January 1990 Tec 5 US Army WW2
09	Exzilda Shankey 1894-1981
21	Gladys M., daughter of John and Evilda Shankey
	22 October 1926 - 20 October 1930
09	John Shankey 1884-1959
16	Adelaide M. Shirley 1891-1983
10	girl Shirley - 1 January 1958 -
10	girl Shirley - 22 July 1961 -
16	Rudolph G. Shirley 1892-1979
23	Joseph H. Siegler 15 July 1894 - 4 December 1963
	MN Pvt Co C 55 Infantry WW1
23	Nettie M. Siegler 7 November 1896 - 19 March 1990
23	Ralph Joseph 24 July 1927 - 28 April 1950
	MN HA2 USNR WW2
11	Elizabeth A. Smith 1890-1979
11	Roy A. Smith 1886-1963
18	Adolph E. Smithberger 1908-1987
15	Anna C. Smithberger 1906-1976
04	Anna M. Smithberger 1873-1967
15	Bernard Smithberger 1898-1973

04	Charles B. Smithberger 1867-1958
16	Frank J. Smithberger 1874-1939
16	Josephine E. Smithberger 1875-1970
03	Donald R. Stang 1936-1988
10	Paul Martin Stapleton 4 August 1975 - 6 June 1976
07	Anna G. Stegmaier 1889-1985
07	John N. Stegmaier 1884-1974
18	Julia Stegmaier 1920-1996
18	Robert Stegmaier 1917-1996
16	Gregg W. Steigauf 1966-1979
16	Michael Stifter 1954-1981
03	Janice L. Stock 1936-1994 married Wayne H. 17 September 1955
03	Wayne H. Stock 1934-1986 married Janice L. 17 September 1955
18	Bernard C. Stoneberg 1933-1971
17	Bert Stoneberg 1894-1977
17	Bruce Arnold Stoneberg 3 February - 11 February 1948
18	Margaret L. Stoneberg 1898-1966
06	Daniel J. Sullivan 1892-1948
06	Josephine C. Sullivan 1890-1959
07	Eugene Robert Swanson 15 April 1924 - 25 July 1964
	MN S1 USNR WW2
06	Bertha Sypal 1892-1978
06	Edward Sypal 1886-1962
11	Mildred L. Terante 1910-1954
01	Donald J. Thelen 3 December 1927 - 22 April 1991
	S2 US Navy WW2
01	Donald J. Thelen 1927-1991 married Genevieve E. 10 January 1948
04	Leo Thelen 1894-____
04	Margaret Thelen 1895-1973
04	Agnes F. Theurer 1885-1960
04	John L. Theurer 1886-1972
01	Barbara A. (Kaufenberg) Thomas 29 July 1900 - 7 September 1995
	husband - Roman Thomas 1900-1934 buried in New Market
04	Mabel C. Thurmes 1900-1978
04	Nick Thurmes 1885-1946
04	Peter M. Thurmes 1883-1958
15	Esther A. Tierney 1883-1981
15	Dillon P. Tierney 1882-1971
16	Mary A. Tierney 17 September 1843 - 14 January 1924
16	Phillip Tierney 1876-1940
16	Thos Tierney 15 January 1832 - 12 May 1913
18	Alvina 'Vi' Tobias 1911-1987 married Merril 27 April 1935
18	Merril Tobias 1911-____ married Alvina 'Vi' Tobias 27 April 1935
10	Adam Christopher Trevis 3 May - 22 October 1971
09	John L. Turek 1885-1951

09	Rose M. Turek 1886-1959
13	Richard Tussing 1932-1984
22	Agnes Tutewohl 1872-1934
06	Albert Tutewohl 1902-1996
21	Alois Tutewohl 4 September 1850 - 13 February 1917
21	Angeline D. Tutewohl 1913-_____
09	Anna Tutewohl (?) 1884-1984
22	Appolonia Tutewohl 3 May 1838 - 15 May 1912
07	Arnold L. Tutewohl 1911-1982
19	Bertha A. Tutewohl 1879-1918
09	Edward Tutewohl (?) 1881-1954
21	George E. Tutewohl 1908-1987
22	John Tutewohl 1868-1947
22	Joseph Tutewohl 14 February 1811 - 14 November 1889
11	Joseph C. Tutewohl 1918-1989
06	Joseph L. Tutewohl 1896-1984
20	Joseph M. Tutewohl 25 December 1912 - 14 March 1913 (?)
06	Laurence Tutewohl 1908-1994
09	Louis Tutewohl February 1883 - February 1961
09	Louise Tutewohl June 1885 - June 1951
11	Margaret C. Tutewohl 1921-_____
06	Margaret C. Tutewohl 1894-1964
20	Marie Tutewohl, died 26 September 1910, age 6 weeks
06	May Tutewohl 1914-_____
07	Pearl E. Tutewohl 1918-_____
21	Rosa Tutewohl 1850-1919
20	Annie S. Ulvi 1907-1989
20	Henry M. Ulvi 1898-1981
19	Richard J. Ulvi 1931-1936
18	Nancy L. Vogel 1953-1986
25	Agnes Wagner 1912-1990
02	Dallas M. Wagner 11 July 1925 - 30 May 1995
25	Ralph Wagner 1908-1981
16	Agnes Walker 1894-1944
16	Anthony Walker 1898-1960
02	Michael Walter 1968-1994
11	Ida V. Watters, nee Langer 1894-1972
03	Margaret J. Wear 1913-_____
03	Raphael R. Wear 1912-1990
05	Wendy M. Wear 1959-1977
01	Clarence L. Weatherly 2 May 1942 - 8 October 1991 Sgt US Army
01	Donald C. Weatherly 5 January 1937 - 3 January 1995 Pfc US Army
02	Everell L. Weatherly 1912-_____

02	Louise M. Weatherly 1916-_____
26	Francis Weber 1908-1986
26	Mildred Weber 1912-1981
01	Lance B. Weierke 23 August 1968 - 2 May 1990 SR4 US Air Force
02	Lance B. Weierke 1968-1990
21	Shirley J. Weierke 1935-1980
26	Mary F. Weiler 1940-1995 married Robert P. 17 September 1960
16	Anton Weisbrich 10 May 1842 - 19 June 1915
08	Charles Weisbrich 1909-1965
15	Charles A. Weisbrich 1875-1939
08	Charles N. Weisbrich 1909-1965
08	Clarence E. Weisbrich 1912-1991
08	James Weisbrich 1950-1951
08	Lillian M. Weisbrich 1916-1976
16	Mathilda Weisbrich 20 July 1844 - 14 November 1914
08	Mary Weisbrich 1913-1985
15	Mary E. Weisbrich 1882-1957
18	Cecelia Deegan Welsch 1911-_____
17	Della M. Wessman 1906-1992
05	Mary C. White 1892-1967
05	William G. White 1887-1969
30	David L. Whittier (?) 1935-1966
11	Jeanette M. Whittier 1906-1988
11	Leslie B. Whittier 1902-1956
18	Louise A. Wiederhold (?) 1900-1939
18	Luverne Wiederhold (?) 1926-1931
17	Magdalena Wiederhold (?) 1875-1966
17	Raymond A. Wiederhold (?) 1917-1930
17	Valentine Wiederhold (?) 1872-1933
22	baby boy Williams - May 1931 -
22	Irene M. Williams, nee Oster 1904-1989
10	Thomas Wingert 7 June - 17 November 1945
08	Mary J. Weisbrich Wolkow 1913-1985
18	Ralph Wolters 4 May 1941 - 13 February 1996
15	Worrell, son of Peter L. Jr. - 2 December 1980 -
03	Lyell E. Yetzer 1934-1986 married Rita J. 25 August 1952
08	Harvey A. Yost 1878-1956
08	Mary Yost 1878-1953
10	Lynn Michelle Youngkrantz March 1958 - June 1958
08	Alvina L. Zieman 1918-1987
08	Anthony R. Zieman 1908-1994
16	Phyllis Zweber 1928-1981

I was not able to determine a surname for the following:

20   Casandra Ann   2 March 1987 - 28 August 1987
         - closest surnames are Ulvi and Caron

St. Michaels Cemetery

Row 1

Empire Township
T114 N-R19W
Section 29

Row 3

Row 10 Area

Row 4

Storage Building

Row 9

Statue

Parking Area

Row 11

Row 23

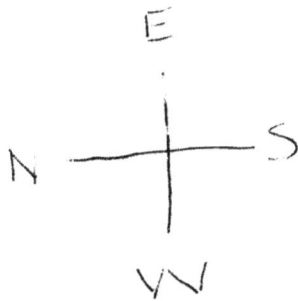

Row 22

old Fence Area - Small Pines

Corinthian Cemetery - Tar Drive area

Row 31

old Fence Area - Small Pines

HIGHLAND CEMETERY

Lakeville township, Dakota county, Minnesota: T114N - R20W, section 1

   This cemetery is very old and in poor shape. The vast majority of the burials took place before 1890. We visited the cemetery in late August 1996. At that time it appeared that the cemetery had not been mowed since earlier in the summer. Much of the area had tall grass and weeds. There were several areas on the grounds where small trees or sumac began to grow. This past summer (1996) the path of Dodd Boulevard was changed so that the northern quarter stretch that went through section 2 and connected up with 160th street was closed. The new part of Dodd Boulevard now connects up with Pilot Knob Road. This is just a little north of the Highland Cemetery. I am not sure if this construction or the heavy truck traffic or just the soil is the cause, but parts of the cemetery appear to be showing evidence of shifting or sliding down the hill. As I wrote down burial information for the western rows I began to notice gaps in the soil at what appeared to be the east edge of some of the burials. These gaps were about a foot in length and a couple inches wide. Some were deep. They did not appear to be rodent holes.

   I began numbering rows at the west edge. Row 1 is just two burials at the west edge. Row 2 begins with more of a noticeable row. Row 14 is an area at the east central edge of the cemetery. As we left the cemetery we came across a burial stone that was south of the drive area and along the south central edge of the cemetery. This was: Emma, daughter of Frank & Mathilda Langer 8 May 1883 - 5 November 1883. I do not know if this is the actual burial place or if the stone just ended up there. When I transcribed the burial stone information in this cemetery I noticed that G and C were very hard to discern with the lettering style used on the monuments.

   The Dakota county cemetery records compilation lists this cemetery as: Highland (Hyland) Cemetery. (Formerly St. Joseph's Catholic Cemetery). Platted 1868. 4 acres. Located NW 1/4 of Section 1. Highway 31 south of Highway 9.

   In the book "History of Dakota County and the city of Hastings" by Rev. Edward D. Neill, written in 1881, he wrote: ... Four acres of land were surveyed and platted in 1868, ... and called St. Joseph's cemetery. This land is situated in the north-west quarter of section 1. The first internment was a daughter of Thomas Murray, and there are now about one hundred and fifty bodies buried there ... The storm of 1881 did great damage to many of the monuments in the yard (page 417).

   In "Over The Years 1961-1978", compiled by the Dakota County Historical Society, they wrote: ...After considerable discussion as to where to locate the church, Thomas Hyland gave St. Joseph's parish seven acres of land between Rosemount and Lakeville for a church and cemetery. A big wind destroyed the Hyland (St. Joseph's) Church in the early 1880's and it was replaced by a new church built in Rosemount. Contract for the present St. Joseph's Church at Rosemount was in March 1924 and the corner stone laid 22 June 1924 (page 136).

Another reference to the Hyland cemetery can be found in "Over The Years 1961-1978" ... Burial Records Compiled for Hyland Cemetery... One of the very worthy historical projects being carried on in Dakota county is the compilation of burial records for those interred in Hyland Cemetery at Rosemount, and the restoration of the cemetery grounds to a presentable state. This work is being carried on personally by Gerald (Jerry) G. Mattson of Rosemount, who is being commended for his efforts. In a letter from Mattson, he said he had finished compiling burial records this spring (1977 ?) and he now has a record of 254 of the burials in the cemetery. During his research, Mattson wrote that he had decided to expand the history of the cemetery on which he is working, to include a general history of the area and a history of St. Joseph's parish to the year 1880 when the original church was destroyed (page 416).

Everyone is listed in alphabetical order. The number before each entry is the row number. There is a map at the back of this section.

These cemetery burial monuments were transcribed during 1996.

13	Katie Bally 9 May 1859 - 22 June 1881
14	Bridget, wife of Maurice Bamberry 4 February 1856 - 5 October 1882
14	Maggie, daughter of Maurice and Bridget Bamberry 1 November 1880 - 15 June 1890 (?)
14	Mary, daughter of Maurice and Bridget Bamberry 10 July 1881 - 7 January 1883
14	Maurice Bamberry (?) 1839-1920
14	Richard, son of Maurice and Bridget Bamberry 2 April 1878 - 30 April 1878
14	Richard, son of M. and B. Bamberry, died 10 ? 1879, age ?
10	Bridget Burke, wife of E. Brennan, native of Co Sligo, Parish of Kiloglass, Ireland, died 11 March 1880, age 50 years
10	Mary, daughter of George and Mary Brown died 10 November 1872, age 2 years 5 months
03	Catherine Burns, died 20 October 1876, age 85 years
05	'Father' C/Garvey (?) 1840-1874
05	'Mother' C/Garvey (?) 1845-1917
05	Patrick C/Garvey, native of Hedford Co Galway Ireland died 13 December 1874, age 34 years
06	Agnes Casey, died 27 August 1868, age 18 years
05	Ellen Casey 1802-1880
05	George Casey, son of Ellen Casey - no dates
06	Hanora, wife of Michael Casey, native of Co Cork Ireland died 10 August 1872, age 65 years
06	Henry Casey, died 15 July 1867, age 55 years
11	James Casey (?) 1881-1902
02	James Henry Casey 1841-1913

02	Margaret Ann Casey 1851-1897
06	Mary, wife of Henry Casey, died 11 September 1875, age 61 years
11	Mary, wife of Patrick Casey, native of Co Mayo Ireland died 31 May 1879, age 50 years
05	Michael Casey, son of Ellen Casey - no dates
11	'Mother' Casey (?) 1854-1888
13	Mrs. Bridget Collins, wife of James Collins 12 May 1862 - 3 January 1906
13	Nellie C. Collins 25 August 1894 - 26 October 1918
07	Bridget, wife of Michael Costello, native of Co Mayo Ireland died 27 October 1881, age 60 years
07	Maria, wife of Michael Costello, died 26 July 1871, age 25 years (?)
13	Isabel McBreen, wife of John Daly, died 30 October 1889, age 71 years
13	John Daly, died 28 August 1881, age 74 years
13	Mary McCarthy, wife of Patrick Daly, died 6 February 1892, age 36 years
04	Marcella Deavitt, died 30 October 1916
04	Ann Devitt, born 11 June 1849 Co Clare Ireland died 5 May 1910
04	Patrick Devitt, native of Co Leitrim Ireland died 1 January 1877, age 45 years
03	James Dewire, native of Parish Tunie Co Galway Ireland died 10 July 1872, age 40 years
02	Margaret Herward, wife of Thomas Dewire died 7 February 1877, age 43 years
11	Bridget, wife of John Dunn, died 29 June 1914, age 90 years
11	David Dunn 1862-1930
11	John Dunn, born in Queens Co Ireland 1831 died (?) 29 June 1880
11	William H., son of John and Bridget Dunn died 3 August 1878, age 3 years 17 days
02	John, son of Thomas and Margaret Dwyer 8 March 1867 - 22 September 1887
02	Patrick, son of Thomas and Margaret Dwyer 18 August 1862 - 5 September 1885
02	Thomas Dwyer, native of the Parish of Tuam (?) Co Galway Ireland died 1 May 1886, age 59 years
08	Carle Egle (?), died 12 February 1881, age 5 years 6 months
08	George Egle (?), died 8 June 1880, age 1 year 11 months 14 days
08	Lorenze Egle, died 8 October 1879, age 37 years
08	Lula, daughter of Lu and L. Egle, died 18 August 1877
08	Rosina Egle, died 28 October 1875, age 68 years 7 months 15 days
07	Kate Fahey 1868-1947
07	Mary Fahey 1865-1931

08	Patrick Fahey, native of Clougher Co Mayo Ireland
	died 30 May 1879, age 48 years
08	Patrick H. Fahey 25 August 1876 - 1 March 1899
	age 22 years 6 months 6 days
08	Sarah, wife of ? Featherly (?), died 23 December 1876, age 30 years
13	Winifred Finn, died 15 August 1883, age 33 years
03	John Finnegan, native of the parish of Ballaghaderreen Co Mayo Ireland
	24 June 1815 - 4 August 1885
13	Cecelia Gallagher (?), died 27 March 1879, age 22 years
13	Nora Gallagher (?), died 13 August 1887, age 20 years
13	Patrick Gallagher (?), died 25 December 1882, age 21 years
13	Terrance Gallagher, died 9 January 1886, age 64 years
13	? Atheri ? (Catherine ?), daughter of Philip and Catherine Garon
	15 April 1875 - 29 May 1881
10	Little Pat, son of John and Mary G/Carvey
	6 May 1876 - 7 February 1881
03	Thomas G/Carvey, native of the parish of Dunmore Co Ireland
	died 1 June 1877, age 63 years
09	Patrick H., child of J.C. and Bridget Geraghty
	15 September 1881 - 11 August 1882 (?)
09	Robert J., child of J.C. and Bridget Geraghty
	3 April 1878 - ? March 1879
03	Mary, child of John and Ann Gibbons
	7 April 1872 - 7 April 1872
02	Mary, wife of Patrick Gibbons, died 22 February 1873, age 35 years
02	Patrick Gibbons, died 19 June 1879, age 34 years
03	Willie, child of John and Ann Gibbons
	15 June 1871 (?) - 16 June 1871 (?)
10	George Gilbert, died 13 November 1871, age 11 years (?) 11 months
10	John Gilbert, died 3 November 1877, age 58 years
05	James Glynn, native of Co Mayo Ireland
	died 29 November 1880, age 25 years
05	Katie, daughter of J. and B. Glynn, a native of Coug(?) Co Mayo Ireland
	died 30 August 1875, age 24 years
04	Emma, daughter of Frank and Mar.(?) Gollon (?)
	died 27 May 1864 (?), age ?
04	James Hanaughan, native of Co Mayo Ireland
	died 2 May 1881, age 81 years
11	Hannah McCrath, wife of James Haverty, native of Co Mayo Ireland
	died 23 March 1880, age 35 years
12	Kate Sheridan, wife of James Higgins 1859-1882
05	Edward Highland, native of parish of Gilmore Co Mayo Ireland
	died 29 June 1877, age 90 years
07	Edward, child of Patrick and Mary Hyland

	3 July 1867 - 30 July 1870
05	Edward M., son of Thomas and Mary Hyland
	22 August 1855 - 25 October 1872
04	Frank Hyland, native of the parish Killman Co Mayo Ireland
	died 12 July 1880, age 30 years
04	James J. Hyland, died 18 September 1888, age 4 months
07	Mary Dwyer Hyland 1855-1932
07	Mary Ki?(rest is cemented over), wife of Patrick Hyland
	died 30 October (?) (year cemented over), age 32 years
07	Patrick H., child of Patrick and Mary Hyland
	7 March 1869 - 28 July 1870
05	Thomas, son of T. and M. Hyland 8 June 1862 - 15 October 1862
11	John Kane, native of Co Galway Ireland
	died 16 October 1880, age 75 years
06	John H. Keefe, died 25 January 1869, age 24 years 25 days
06	Bridget, wife of John Keeffe, died 10 March 1879, age 55 years
11	Margaret Burke, wife of Thomas Kelly, native of Co Mayo Ireland
	died 4 July 1879, age 66 years
11	Margaret Toolan, wife of Patrick Kelly, native of Co Mayo Ireland
	died 19 July 1879, age 55 years
05	Annie, wife of John Kennedy, native of Killabeg Co Donigaire
	died 2 September 1884, age 35 years
05	Edward, son of Annie and James Kennedy
	died 8 December 1876, age 5 months
05	James Kennedy, native of Parish of Inver Co Donigalire
	died 5 February 1885, age 42 years
04	Margaret Kennedy 1878-1928
04	Mary E. Kennedy 1873-1947
08	Martin Kilroy, native of Co Mayo Ireland
	died 5 November 1875, age 75 years
08	Mary Kilroy, native of Co Mayo Ireland
	died 7 August 1870, age 70 years
00	Emma, daughter of Frank and Mathilda Langer
	8 May 1883 - 5 November 1883
10	Annie E. Leach - born 30 July 1858
10	Mary Olive Leach 28 September 1882 - 9 September 1883
09	John Lenihan, native of Co Kerry Ireland
	17 March 1812 - 24 April 1881
09	Mary Lynch, wife of John Lenihan, native of Co Kerry Ireland
	died 16 May 1880, age 56 years
07	Patrick Loftus, native of Co Galway Ireland
	died 9 September 1874, age 25 years
06	Susan Loftus, daughter of Andrew and Ellen Loftus
	native of Co Galway Ireland, died 15 February 1871, age 21 years

10	John, son of Thomas and Maria Mangan
	died 6 June 1873, age 15 years 11 months 23 days
13	? child (?) ? (hard to read) born 1880 (?) died 1880 (?) McCarthy (?)
13	Catherine McCarthy, wife of Barthol.
	died 3 October 1883, age 64 years
02	Edward McCarthy 29 April 1831 - 19 July 1907
06	Edward McCarthy 1867-1928
03	James, son of Edward McCarthy (?) and Catherine Hyland
	native of Parish of ? Co Mayo Ireland, born in St Paul
	22 August 1859 - 22 August (?) 1881
02	Mary, born McCarthy, of the Parish of ? Co Kerrn(?) Ireland
	22 December 1827 (?) - ?? 1885 (?)
13	Timothy McCarthy, died 25 February 1886, age 35 years
06	Ellen McCugh, died 1 August 1886, age 11 years
06	Katie E. McCugh, died 3 February 1888 (?), age 8 years
11	Mary McDuillan, died 5 February 1876, age 87 years
04	Ann, daughter of Bartholemew and Bridget McGovran
	died 20 July 1873, age 5 years
04	Bridget, wife of Bartholemew McGovran
	died 12 December 1871, age 23 years
03	? McGrath (?), died 9 July 1874, age 16 years 10 months
03	Bernard McGrath 1859-1874
03	Hanora McGrath 1838-1903
03	Michael McGrath 1812-1892
12	Rose A. McNiskern 17 April 1859 - 24 May 1881
12	Bernard McSherry 1878-1927
12	John McSherry 1829-1913
12	Margaret Hyland, wife of John McSherry
	died 30 May 1888, age 54 years
11	Catherine Martin, died 4 March 1905, age 79 years
11	John Martin, native of Co Kilkenny Ireland
	died 7 June 1879, age 63 years
05	Philip J. Mathers - no dates
03	Arthur J. Walsh Moran 13 December 1903 - 20 April 1925
02	Mary, wife of John Murphy, died 9 August 1872, age 52 years
09	Michael Murnan, native of Co Limerick Ireland
	died 9 April 1872, age 48 years
09	Kattie Jane, daughter of Thos. and Bridget Murry
	died 20 August 1868, age 4 years 1 month 5 days
12	Joseph Edward Niskern 2 August 1880 - 18 September 1880
09	Ann, native of Co Mayo Parish of Ballycastle Ireland
	wife of Patrick Nolan, died 31 December 1877, age 44 years
09	Patrick Nolan, native of Co Mayo Ireland
	died 20 April 1878, age 53 years

09	John O'Connell, native of Taum Parish Co Galway Ireland
	died 11 February 1878, age 56 years
10	W.B. O'Donohoe, native of Sligo Ireland
	died 26 March 1878, age 35 years
13	Andrew O'Grady, died 1 January 1871, age 26 years
13	B. (?) H. O'Grady, died 20 February 1878, age 25 years
02	Michael O'Neil, native of Tipererarry of ? Ireland
	died 27 December 1872, age 25 years

| 04 | Thomas P., son of Sylvester and Maggey Parisa |
| | 29 August 1867 - 29 April 1871 |

| 09 | Joseph Quinn 22 April 1873 - 23 February 1875 |
| 09 | Nellie Quinn 10 November 1870 - 11 August 1873 |

01	Catherine M., daughter of Thomas and Mary Shaughnessy
	4 August 1858 - 2 July 1881
06	
Ellen, child of Thomas and Mary Shaughnessy
	died 31 May (?) 1862
06	Martin (?), child of Thomas and Mary Shaughnessy
	died 21 September 1863
01	Mary Shaughnessy 1834-1914
11	John Sheridan, died 30 May 1877, age 36 years
11	John M., son of John and Mary Sheridan (?)
	died 15 February 1881, age 14 years
05	Delia E. Smith, died 22 November 1872, age 21 years
08	Anna Sullivan, died 18 April 1872, age 53 years

06	Margaret A., wife of J.W. Tomson
	28 February 1867 - 1 March 1888
06	Rhoda Grace, daughter of J.W. and M.A. Tomson
	21 February 1888 - 5 September 1888

06	Mrs. Ann Walsh, born in Co Galway Ireland
	died 25 February 1892, age 78 years
07	Annie, daughter of P. and B. Walsh
	died 5 April 1888, age 1 year
07	Bernard, son of P. and B. Walsh
	died 31 March 1888, age 6 years 2 months
07	John, son of P. and B. Walsh
	died 17 July 1880, age 10 months 5 days
08	John M., son of J. and M. Walsh
	14 April 1878 - 23 April 1879
02	Joseph Thomas Walsh 20 April 1925

Minn. Seaman 2 CL US NRF

07   Thomas, son of P. and B. Walsh
          died 5 April 1888, age 5 years

02   Mary Welby, native of Co Galway Ireland
          died 2 January 1885, age 69 years
          erected by her sons J. and M. Hynes

I was not able to get a complete reading of the following stones.

12   ??? 1888 - all that remains of the stone

13   Katherine ?, died 6 August 1881 (?), age ?
          - worn and hard to read

Highland Cemetery
Lakeville Township T114N-R20W
Section 1

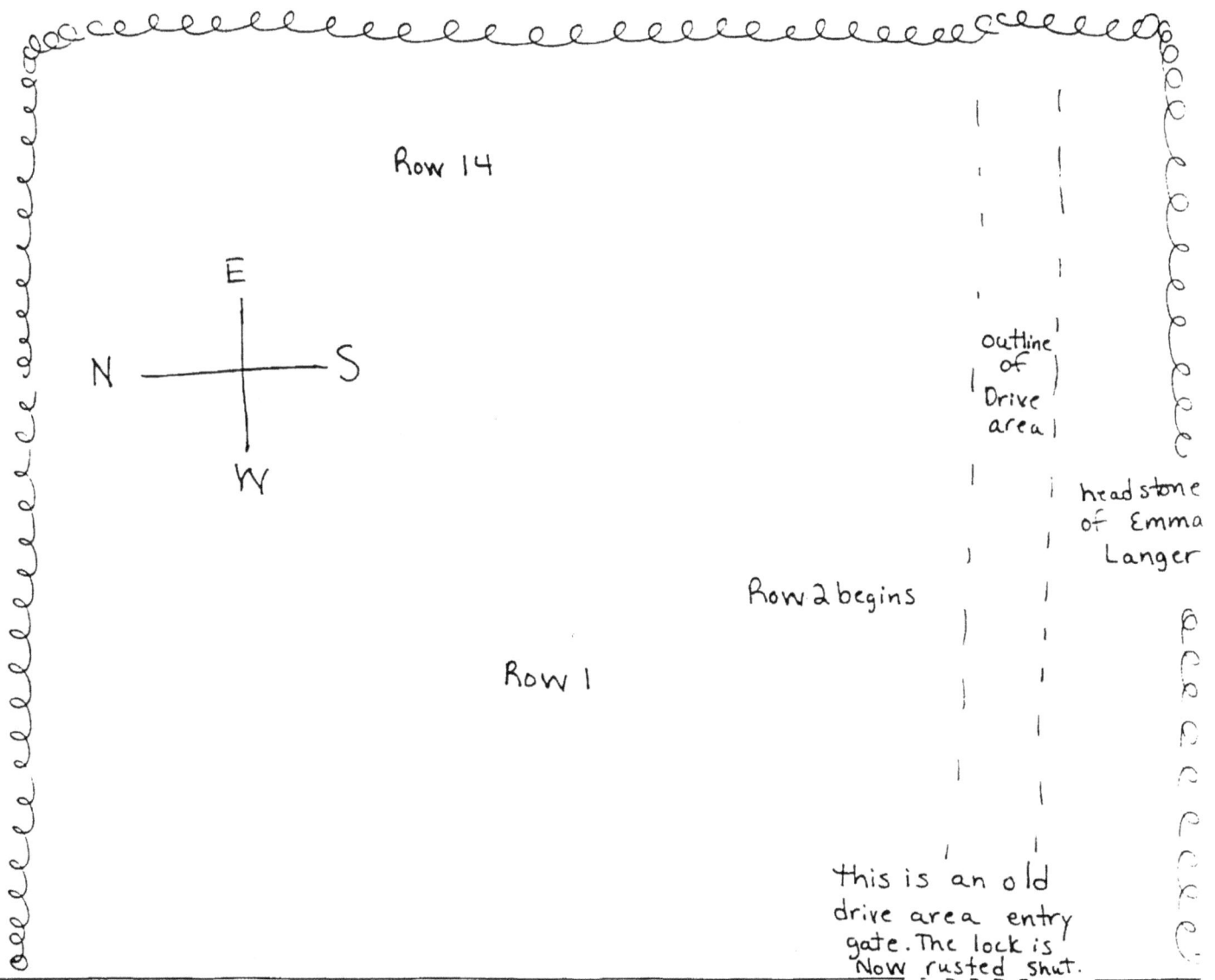

Row 14

E

N ———|——— S

W

Row 14

outline
of
Drive
area

headstone
of Emma
Langer

Row 2 begins

Row 1

this is an old
drive area entry
gate. The lock is
Now rusted shut.

County Road 31 or Pilot Knob Road

FARMINGTON PRESBYTERIAN CEMETERY

Farmington City, Dakota County, Minnesota: T114N-R20W, Section 25

This cemetery has not been upkept in a long time and is in poor shape. The cemetery was overtaken by the forest quite some time ago. There are many small to medium sized trees that cover the area. At the time I visited the cemetery during June 1997 the cemetery area was not marked by any type of sign, nor any obvious fence. There is no sign of any recent upkeep. There did appear to be an old cart path heading south from the burial area. This to has become overgrown.

There were about half a dozen various monument stone bases with no data on them. These monument stone bases appear to have been knocked around and are most likely not over the original graves anymore.

I did find one stone base with the surname SEWARD on it. There were also three names with data on another stone. The stone with data appeared to have possibly gone with the SEWARD stone base. I was not able to determine this to be correct or not. This cemetery was visited during 1996. The names and dates were:

Charles, died 28 February 1901, age 8 years 10 months 6 days

S. Anderson, died 10 October 1859, age 2 years 3 months

Caroline, died 10 April 1860, age 28 days

In 'History of Dakota County and the city of Hastings, ...' by Rev. Edward D. Neill, written in 1881, he wrote ... In July, 1868, one acre of land was given by Samuel Osborn to the trustees of the Presbyterian church for a cemetery. The grounds are pleasantly located on a hill-side in the south-east quarter of section 25, ... The body of Miss Ada Bacon was laid here first in 1859, before the land was formerly devoted to its present use. The officers of the Presbyterian church, act as officers of the cemetery. (page 417).

The Dakota county cemetery records compilation lists this cemetery as: Farmington Presbyterian Cemetery, established 1868. 1 acre. Section 25, SE1/4. Akin Road and Eve's Way. On hill behind houses on Eve's Way. (Abandoned)

N
W———E
S

Eaves Way

AKIN Road

(Northern Road Area is Pilot Knob Road)

Eaves Court

House

House

Old Cemetery Area

city utility?

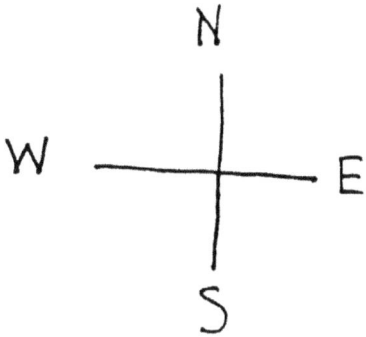

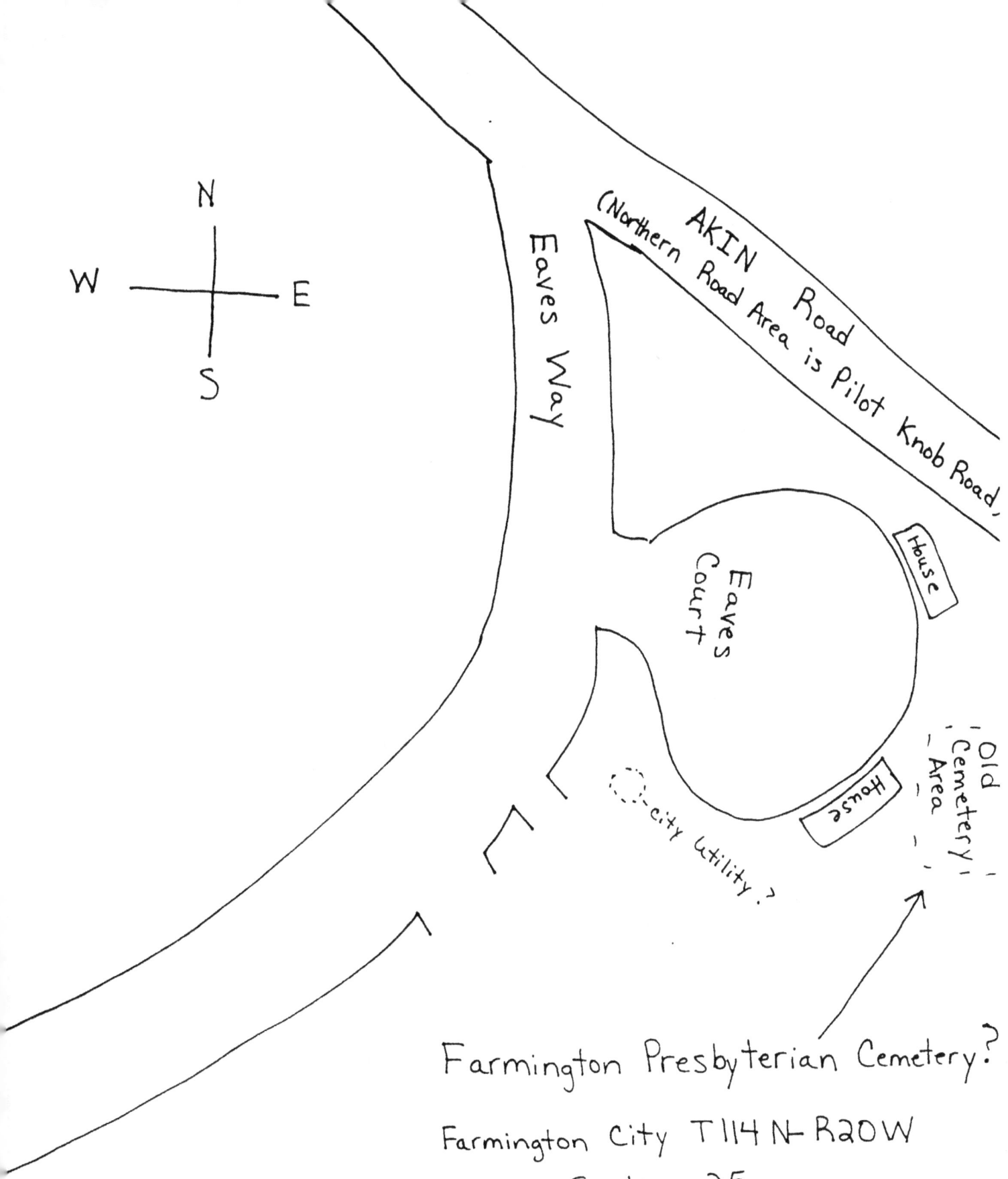

Farmington Presbyterian Cemetery?

Farmington City T114N-R20W
Section 25

349

Lakeville Grove Cemetery

City of Lakeville, Dakota County, Minnesota: T114N - R20W, section 28

This cemetery is upkept and in good shape. Row 1 begins along the east edge and just outside of the back loop. The main gates have separate memory dedications. They are for Mr. and Mrs. V.E. Lorentson and The Cross Family.

The Dakota county cemetery compilation lists this cemetery as: Lakeville Grove Cemetery. (Formerly Perkin's Cemetery). Owned by St. John's Lutheran Church of Lakeville. Established in ?. 3.67 acres. Located in the SW corner of NW 1/4 of Section 28.

Everyone is listed in alphabetical order. The number before each entry is the row number. There is a map at the back of this section.

These cemetery burial monuments were transcribed during 1996.

09	Ralph Ackerman 1929-1981
	married Anita 27 June 1953
15	Gustaous F. Ackley 1821-1898
15	Nellie A. Ackley or McGrail 1862-1964
15	Sara J. Ackley or McGrail 1836-1866
05	Victoria Alexson 1888-1922
13	Alan Allstopp 1954-1976
11	Mark L. Alstrom 15 December 1967 - 14 October 1971
03	Anderson twins - 1947 -
02	Alexander V. Anderson (?) 1877-1956
12	Alfred Anderson 1905-1950
11	Arthur Anderson 1889-1906
14	Augusta Anderson (?) 1850-1935
03	Catherine Anderson (?) 1847-1925
11	Ellen Anderson (?) 1855-1929
11	Ellen Anderson 17 August 1855 - 1 February 1929
12	Eric D. Anderson 27 March 1971 - 2 June 1971
10	Ethel M. Anderson 1907-1923
02	Francis W. Anderson (?) 1918-1978
15	Gladys C. Anderson - no dates
11	Harry Anderson (?) 1885-1955
14	Henry Anderson (?) 1863-1936
11	John Anderson (?) 1858-1941
02	Lova L. Anderson (?) 1922 - _____
02	Lucy A. Anderson (?) 1884-1972
11	Mamie Anderson (?) 1887-1975
12	Nellie Anderson 1915-1990
10	Peter Anderson 1830-1902

03   Peter Anderson (?) 1840-1924
05   Tena C. Anderson 1892-1922
10   Meghan Danielle Aug 30 January 1996 - 15 May 1996
16   Ardella I. Austad 1917-____
16   Kris E. Austad 1916-1989

09   Dan W. Balch 1844-1904
13   Della M. Balch 6 October 1889 - 28 January 1892
14   Etta M. Balch 18 August 1862 - 29 November 1919
14   Fred K. Balch 2 March 1847 - 22 October 1930
08   Louie Balch 1872-1873
09   Maria S. Balch 1849-1926
33   Dale L. Baldus 1915-____
33   Wilbert T. Baldus 1917-1992
26   Loren M. 'Red' Barsness
                26 January 1939 - 25 December 1990
02   Manton G. Barsness 1907-1984
02   Nina A. Barsness 1919-1978
03   Joe L. Battles 1853-1938
12   Anna M. Baudin 1895-1928
12   H.J. Baudin 1851-1920
12   Marie C. Baudin 1857-1932
01   David K. Bauer 1968-1986
10   Ean J. Beaumaster 24 January 1989 - 5 May 1989
14   Gladys E. Belford 1914-1979
14   William W. Belford 1902-1979
08   A. Leonard Bentson 23 December 1917-____
08   LaSalle H. Bentson 3 April 1919 - 20 October 1987
28   Kathleen A. Benz 17 June 1949 - 5 February 1996
36   Norma E. Berglund 15 April 1939 - 29 June 1994
                married Warren J. 20 September 1958
34   Debbie 'Suelter' Besmehn - no dates
09   'Father' Betz (?) 1826-1912
13   Helen Blackford 1915-1971
13   J.L. Blackford 1908-1960
01   Michael Dean Blackford - 1952 -
12   Robert Blackford 11 April 1935 - 9 March 1973
05   Edward William Blazek 1905-1980
05   Helen Haglund Blazex 1907-1995
15   Sharon Blenkush (?) 1937-1979
08   Albert Borgen 1914-1988
08   Reggie Borgen 1919-1975
10   Nancy L. Bowman 1960-1975
11   Ann M., wife of J.J. Brackett 6 March 1819 - 23 April 1893
11   Joseph J. Brackett 8 February 1814 - 26 December 1889
13   Bernette Brandon 1904-1995

13	Glen M. Brandon 1903-1982
01	F. ' Kicky' Breitmeier 1915-1985
17	Oliver W. Brown 1909-1955
06	Myrtle A. Bruder 1902-1987
06	Orestes M. Bruder 1902-1990
12	A.L.C. - no dates
04	Arvid O. Carlson 1888-1964
05	Billie A. Carlson 1926-1932
04	Mabel Carlson 1899-1980
11	Michael D. Carrier - 1962 - age 1 year 2 months
11	Hannah Castle 1835-1900
11	James Castle 1839-1902
15	baby Cederblade - 1953 -
15	Harold J. Cederblade 1913-1966
15	Hazel C. Cederblade 1925-1981
13	Cummings Cherry 1846-1936
13	Lydia Cherry 1860-1936
03	Edward Christensen 4 May 1932-____ MN Corp 7 Engrs 5 Div
14	Jens Christensen 1865-1934
14	Mabel C. Christensen 1894-1899
14	Marie C. Christensen 1868-1943
01	Christian P. Christiansen 1884-1964
01	Dorthea Christiansen 1883-1958
01	Russell A. Christiansen 1908-1990
07	Earl Lee Clay 1938-1986
	married Evonne A. 17 September 1960
09	Edward A. Coburn, son of Robert and Audrey 1955-1986
09	Isaac Coburn 1835-1910
01	Paul E. Colburn 1900-1976
25	Curtis A. Cole 1924-1996
	married Zelda F. 17 June 1946
13	? (first name buried to deep to read) Coles
	11 July 1898 - 30 January 1899
12	Anabell L. Conway 19 April 1834 - 19 March 1896
12	Lillie Cook 1 June 1894 - 1 June 1894
12	Samuel Cook 12 February 1897 - 10 March 1897
12	Wm Gladstone Cook 17 December 1895 - 10 January 1896
11	Wesley Alan Cotton 15 February - 10 May 1961
09	Elsie Cox 1915-____
09	Sam Cox 1914-1996
17	Christine E. Cross 1877-1954
17	Clinton F. Cross 1908-1982 T Sgt US Army WW2
18	Dale R. Cross 1963-1985
17	Florence B. Cross 1911-1994
17	Frank Edward Cross 1 May 1877 - 2 June 1961

MN Pvt Co I 15 Regt Minn Inf - Spanish American War
17   Richard E. Cross 1913-____

20   Robert W. Dahlke 22 February 1956 - 27 May 1993
16   Claude Rexford Damann 1 February 1914 - 31 December 1993
16   Elaine Rebecca Damann 10 September 1917 - 30 January 1993
10   Shawntay Marie Davis - 3 months old - 1984 -
10   Courtney Lynn Dawson - 13 December 1996 -
08   Jennett Deconing 1879-1906 - erected by brother Art
05   Lewis Kurtz Deibler 1859-1932
05   Marie Deibler 1861-1927
08   Huiebrecht (?) Dekoning 1875-1945
33   Mackenzie Katherine Ross Dickey, daughter of Dale and Val
             20 November 1992 - 12 August 1996
05   C. Elmar Diebler 1889-1919
02   Martha J. Dimond 1854-1937
02   Reuben B. Dimond 1848-1933
11   Adelbert D. Doland 1892-1982
11   Florence M. Doland 1891-1950
11   Viola E. Doland 1897-1973
09   Horace W. Donaldson 1878-1932
09   Louisa Donaldson 1872-1917 (?)
08   Edna Dufresne 1916-1981
30   Timothy Joseph Dugan 12 July 1977 - 12 April 1995
13   Blanche M. Dunham 1892-1969
13   Charles H. Dunham 1850-1942
13   Clayton D. Dunham 1917-1986 WW2
13   Clayton H. Dunham 4 December 1897 - 7 September 1917
13   Cora E. Dunham 1864-1945
13   Harry A. Dunham 1884-1973
13   Laverna M. Dunham 1913-1988
13   Richard S. Dunham 1903-1907

11   George Edwards 1873-1895
11   Joseph Edwards 1844-____
11   'Mother' Edwards (?) 1843-1906
03   Mary Jayne Elgersma 20 April 1922 - 4 January 1982
             Sgt US Army WW2
14   Elmer G. Emmons, died 12 March 189? - rest of stone cemented over
14   George H. Emmons 4 May 1884 - rest of stone cemented over
13   Harry L. Emmons 1875-1907
13   Lizzie M., wife of C.S. Emmons 1 April 1853 - 4 May 1882
16   Bert E. Enggren (?) 1858-1938
16   Evelyn Enggren 1907-1994
16   Ingeborg Enggren (?) 1871-1956
16   John G. Enggren 1901-1966

30	Melroy Engle 1903-1987
01	Richard R. Engle 1936-1951
30	Sereine Engle 1904-____
07	Edward N. Erickson 1876-1922
27	Sophia Victoria Erickson 26 March 1993 - 15 March 1995
04	Arthur L. Ersfeld 1906-1988
	married Helen 5 April 1929
05	Caroline Ersfeld (?) 1876-1951
04	Fred W. Ersfeld (?) 1902-1993
04	Helen Ersfeld 1909-____
	married Arthur L. 5 April 1929
02	Lawrence Ersfeld 1956-1979
05	Richard M. Ersfeld 1917-1921
05	Stephen M. Ersfeld (?) 1874-1953
05	Walter L. Ersfeld 1901-1969
36	John Curtis Everson 1959-1991
36	Julie Ann Everson 1961-1990
18	Chester J. Eugene 1905-1993
18	Violet A. Eugene 1908-1993
02	Emil Figura 1907-1929
04	Paul Figura 1877-1934
21	Jeremy 'Jay' Fischer 27 December 1973 - 27 October 1991
10	George L. Fisher 1892-1971
13	Dacy Dow Fladager 1888-1979
01	Thomas Edward Fleet 16 July 1956 - 7 August 1974
11	Kelly Rae Forbrook 18 June 1965 - 12 June 1979
03	John Forss 5 May 1890 - 7 January 1949
	MN Pvt 137 Inf 35 Div WW1
05	Margaret Forss - 1926 -
01	Robert B. Forstrom 1884-1959
14	Christopher S. Frank - 17 May 1983 -
06	Clara Frank 1908-1987
14	Cleone L. Frank 1905-1985
14	Denny Frank (?) 1928-1950
14	Patsy J. Frank 1930-1934
14	Richard N. Frank 1904-1984
06	Wilber Frank 1907-1989
10	Sarah Franzier 1 June 1819 - 22 December 1864
01	Arthur Fredrickson 1916-____
01	Jackie Fredrickson 1957-1957
01	Norma Fredrickson 1917-1992
21	Mildred V. Gaither 1907-1994
18	Elaine A. Gardner 1920-1985
15	Frank Gates 1884-1942

15	Lillian M. Gates 1897-1984
03	Ada Marie Geldman 12 August 1886 - 15 November 1973
15	Albert Leo Gembe 1888-1932
15	Charlotte R. Gembe 1898-1984
09	Bjarne E. German 1908-1974
11	Kenneth B. German 1940-1971
11	Patricia D. German - 5 August 1988 -
04	Ivester Gillespie 1932-1980
17	Samuel Neil Gladwin 4 October 1914 - 22 May 1988
	Sgt US Air Force WW2
16	Eva L. Glenn 1897-1971
16	John W. Glenn 1901-1974
08	Ella J. Gramsey 1896-1967
09	Kenneth Gramsey 1928-1928
09	Louis Gramsey 1924-1924
08	Louis C. Gramsey 1890-1952
09	Ralph Gramsey 1919-1919
23	Chantal L. Orcutt Gramstad - 8 February 1991 -
23	Diane L. Orcutt Gramstad 1950-1989
05	Herman F. Grapper 1877-1958
05	Raymond W. Grapper 1910-1924
10	David J. Graupmann 1856-1949
10	Deidrick Graupmann 1897-1952
10	Mary A. Graupmann 1862-1942
02	Ruth A. Grey 1890-1944
05	Willard H. Haase 29 April 1911 - 25 August 1921
03	John J. Hack 1873-1934
03	Lena P. Hack 1877-1967
03	Louis J. Hack 1900-1931
05	Carl A. Haglund 1904-1973
05	Erick Haglund 1879-1954
12	Laura C. Haglund 27 August 1902 - 1 March 1989
05	Mary E. Haglund 1878-1945
08	William W. Haglund 1903-1918
01	Edna M. Haiker 1911-____
	married Herman F. 5 June 1937
01	Herman F. Haiker 1902-1984
	married Edna M. 5 June 1937
01	Darwin F. Hamilton 1916-1935
	this grave is actually before row 1 - along the back or the east fence
10	Jesse J. Halbert 9 May 1986 - 12 July 1986
03	baby Hammer - 1945 -
03	Henry R. Hammer 1900-1969
03	Janet L. Hammer 1910-____

16	Anne C. Hansen 1862-1937
13	Charles R. Hansen 1896-1980
13	Clara M.J. Hansen 1899-1994
13	Connie Lin Hansen 1959-1961
16	Jacob Hansen 1860-1936
13	James Charles Hansen 1949-1950
13	Pamela Kay Hansen 1952-1954
13	Steven Oren Hansen Jr. - 15 January 1991 -
01	Olive K. Harfield 1913-1976
09	Robert D. Harris 1930-1981
17	Walter R. Hartman 1894-1983
17	Wilhelmina A. Hartman 1887-1980
05	August H. Haverland 1857-1918
05	baby Haverland - 1943 -
05	Caroline Haverland 1865-1952
05	Charles W. Haverland 1886-1949
05	Ernest W. Haverland 1882-1959
04	Florence B. Haverland 1898-1952
04	Fred W. Haverland 1893-1964
04	Hattie Haverland (?) 1872-1936
04	John Haverland 1866-1942
05	Lillian J. Haverland 1896-1989
05	Marie A. Haverland 1888-1982
04	Rosemarie Haverland 1926-1926
07	Sigurd Haug 28 November 1883 - 3 December 1918
01	Opal Kris (?) Hein 1932-1984
12	Elizabeth Heinold 1889-1984
11	baby girl Heintz - 4 October 1951 -
13	Arthur Heinz 1910-1996
13	Phyllis Heinz 1913-1978
08	Eleanor Henderson 1911-1987
06	Katie Ellen Henry, daughter of Michael - 1988 -
06	Laura Ann Henry, daughter of Michael - 1988 -
06	Valerie L. Henry, wife of Michael 1956-1988
07	Frank Henwood 1871-1935
07	Fred Henwood 1903-1944
07	Gertrude (?) Henwood 1897-1939
07	Harry Henwood 1917-1990
07	Jennie Henwood 1880-1917 (?)
07	Viola Henwood 1921-1965
04	Gordon W. Hetlinger 1911-1976
04	Myrtle H. Hetlinger 1905-1974
29	Olive M. Hillmer 18 October 1912 - _____
01	Earl Hobbs 1905-1964
01	Margaret J. Hobbs 1923-1992
14	Geo. Hoffman 1833-1900

10	Chris Charles Holen 3 August 1990 - 27 September 1990
02	Bertha B. Holmen 1893-1972
02	Ingval Holmen 1888-1931
14	Dean A. Holt 1923-1986
10	baby Hooker - 1949 -
10	Brownell Horn - 13 September 1988 -
12	Cora A. Hostetle 1870-1945
12	Maurice W. Hostetle 1863 (?) - 1934
14	Carrie A., wife of H.E. Howard 7 May 1859 - 12 September 1888
23	Michael W. Howe 22 May 1955 - 26 June 1995
12	Betty Hoyt 1910-1986
12	George Hoyt 1908-1974
12	Nettie O. Hoyt 1886-1955
12	Samuel Hullett 1833-1910
02	Anneliese Hummel 1921-____
02	Karl F. Hummel 1913-____
03	Thomas K. Hummel 1955-1980
04	Michele L. Isaacson 8 October 1970 - 5 August 1984
18	Austin W. Jacobson 27 - 29 July 1985
11	Patricia German Jacobson 1947-1982
09	Brenda J. Jasper 1944-1988
02	John P. Jensen 10 April 1889 - 12 March 1979
02	Nora L. Jensen 2 May 1895 - 27 September 1972
09	Alice J. Johnson 1882-1975
09	Austin L. Johnson 21 May 1917 - 1 December 1951
	MN MM1 US Navy WW2
12	Carralina O. Johnson 26 October 1886 - 20 January 1962
12	D.C. Johnson 16 October 1816 - 6 June 1894
12	H.E. Johnson 22 April 1830 - ____
09	John W. Johnson 1870-1949
09	William Lee Johnson 13 October 1960 - 7 November 1988
02	Emma Jones 1880-1937
02	John G. Jones 1881-____
11	Marie L. Kellington - October 1982 -
03	Emma B. Kerr 1858-1932
12	Mary Etta Kessel 1867-1961
10	?.B. Kilbourn 1803-1892
10	?.E. Kilbourn 1801-1894
12	Nelle D. Killmer 1884-1966
12	Roswell C. Killmer 1883-1969
10	Nancy Irene King - 1949 -
12	Ambrose O. Kinn 1904-1975
12	Andrew Kinn 1865-1928

12	Anna Kinn 1875-1959
12	Austin George Kinn 6 January 1914 - 21 February 1971
	MN Pvd 24 QM Co WW2
12	Howard Carl Kinn 9 August 1912 - 18 July 1969
	MN Cpl 312 Bomb GP AF WW2
12	Gladys P. Kinn 1906-1986
12	Joyce Kenneth Kinn 11 August 1909 - 22 December 1964
	MN Sgt 75 Signal Co Ph WW2
03	George Klemenhagen 1852-1924
03	Karl Klemenhagen (?) 1891-1981
02	Mabel M. Klemenhagen 1884-1968
02	Rudolph Klemenhagen 1889-1976
03	Sarah Klemenhagen 1857-1942
09	'Father' Luckert or Kleve (?) 1843 - 1926
09	Irene Kleve 1920-____
09	Maurice Kleve 1919-1983
09	'Mother' Luckert or Kleve (?) 1844-1907
37	Lawrence K. Kloster 1940-1991
17	Michael E. Knisely 4 August 1955 - 14 April 1991
03	Chuckie Knutson 1939-1941
02	Jarl R. Knutson 1878-1954
03	L.C. Lefty Knutson 1908-1988
02	Mabel C. Knutson 1886-1959
08	Herbert R. Koentopf 1907-1981
08	Ruth E. Koentopf 1908-1984
06	Eleanor C. Kohls 1904-1974
06	Henry J. Kohls 1892-1946
06	Margaret A. 'Peggy' Kohls 1938-1994
01	Raymond R. Kolbe 1936-1984
	'Lakeville Teacher 1958-1984'
03	John C. Kop 1881-1933
03	Minnie G. Hack Kopernick 1916-1952
03	Otto F. Kopernick 1907-1957
02	baby boy Kraft - 1 December 1931 -
02	Frances Kraft 1910-____
02	Leslie H. Kraft 1934-1945
02	Lucinda Frances Kraft - 17 August 1959
02	Paul Kraft 1889-1979
15	Alpha E. Kuehn 1913-1995
15	Roy W. Kuehn 1911-1987
12	Marie H. Kulstad 1881-1964
12	Oscar Kulstad 1876-1953
06	Betty Ann Lackey 1923-1940
06	Floyd B. Lackey 1897-1963
06	Ruth O. Lackey 1898-1953

01	Terrance Frank Langhorst 16 October 1938 - 3 May 1996
	US Army
03	Carl Marcus Larsen 1908-1991
02	Margarethe 'GOM' Petrea Larsen 1910-____
12	Oscar A. Larson 1890-1965
12	Margaret A. Larson 1891-1973
03	Samuel Larson 1878-1942
02	Chris Laursen 1884-1963
02	Ida Laursen 1897-1944
01	Emma Leese 1894-1978
01	Harry F. Leese 21 March 1923 - 29 September 1989
01	Jacob Leese 1885-1959
01	Mamie A. Leese (?) 1920-1961
14	Harry Lewis 1899-1960
14	Mayme Lewis 1900-1980
02	Bertha Lidgerding 1864-1931
02	Willia A. Lidgerding 1869-1932
01	Daniel J. Locker 1913-1986
01	Kathleen E. Locker 1915-1986
08	Pernelia J. Lorentson 1907-1978
08	Victor E. Lorentson 1895-1987
01	Chester C. Lovelace 1905-1954
01	Ruby M. Lovelace 16 August 1916 - 18 December 1984
08	?.H. Lucke 1846-1914
13	Aquina L. Lucken 5 July 1905 - 2 August 1965
09	'Father' Luckert or Kleve (?) 1843-1926
09	'Mother' Luckert or Kleve (?) 1844-1907
16	Robert H. Luckman 1913-1985 Sgt US Army WW2
15	Robert H. Luckman 1913-1985
16	Verna M. Luckman 1912-1988
15	Verna M. Luckman 1912-1988
10	baby girl Lynch - 10 January 1979 -
02	Alice Ann Madson 1910-1980
02	Ernest Madson 1908-1974
11	Alfred C. Markison 1897-1977
11	Bertha M. Markison 1898-1997
21	Milo Matthews 4 December 1938 - 24 April 1992
15	Cora A. Matzoll 1897-1982
15	John J. Matzoll 1898-1980
16	John J. Matzoll 14 June 1898 - 18 May 1980
	US Marine Corps WW1
01	Jane McCarthy 1 April 1914 - ___
10	Jody K. McCarthy 1949-1950
01	Joseph M. McCarthy 1 April 1895 - 24 December 1970
15	baby McClintock (?) 1928-1928

16	Clyde McClintock (?)	1872-1938
16	Elizabeth McClintock (?)	1837-1929
08	Ella A. McClintock	1874-1953
16	Erving McClintock (?)	1891-1891
15	Etta McClintock (?)	1877-1954
15	Gussie McClintock (?)	1869-1889
15	Helga McClintock (?)	1889-1948
15	John P. McClintock (?)	1862-1872
16	Richard McClintock (?)	1833-1913
15	Richard McClintock (?)	1880-1967
08	Ruth E. McClintock	1906-____
08	T.W. McClintock	1867-1927
01	Harry McCowen	1863-1951
03	Christian McDougall	1883-1925
16	Alice A. McGrail	1901-1988
15	Alice A. McGrail	1901-1988
16	Cortland S. McGrail	1904-1980
15	Cortland S. McGrail	1904-1980
15	Edward Charles McGrail	22 February 1858 - 2 May 1921
16	E.C. McGrail	
15	Lillian H. McGrail	9 August 1859 - 13 February 1914
16	Lillian H. McGrail - no dates	
15	Nellie A. Ackley or McGrail (?)	1862-1864
15	Phillip C. McGrail	1891-1894
15	Sara J. Ackley or McGrail (?)	1836-1866
06	J.C. McKennett	1874-1925
12	Edwin M. McLain	1877-1952
12	Ella C. McLain	1887-1969
12	Rosetta A. McLain	1907-1994
12	Samuel E. McLain	1906-1990
02	Astrid Melby	1888-1954
01	Edward T. Melby	1910-1986
01	Inez M. Melby	1913-____
02	Theodore Melby	1876-1940
01	Paul O. Melting	1898-1957
01	Ruth A. Melting	1899-1977
15	Virgil A. Merincourt	1906-1921
01	David Lee Messerll	1951-1953
08	Berniece Meyer	1914-____
07	Herman J. Meyer	1916-1988
08	Raymer Meyer	1907-1994
07	Ruth V. Smith Meyer	1915-1969
13	Esther R. Midvedt	1894-1982
13	Olaf H. Midvedt	1884-1961
02	Joseph P. Miles	1918-1937
10	baby boy Miller - 1972 -	

05	Charles T. Miller (?) 1854-1930
13	Edna B. Miller 24 December 1883 - 5 April 1975
05	Elsie L. Miller (?) 1903-1978
04	George A. Miller (?) 1876-1940
05	Herbert W. Miller (?) 1889-1948
02	Joseph Miller 1861-1940
05	Katherine Miller (?) 1853-1922
09	Katie, wife of George Miller 1879-1904
17	Lawrence M. Miller (?) 1897-1958
02	Minna L. Miller 1872-1958
04	Maud E. Miller (?) 1878-1966
16	R.R. Miller 1840-1929
16	Mrs. R. Miller (?) 1840-1929
13	Ralph Miller 21 June 1878 - 18 July 1966
02	Paul J. Mills 11 May 1904 - 23 October 1934
10	Heather Joanna Moe 8 November 1975 - 10 November 1975
14	Andrew Moen 1902-1975
14	Mildred Moen 1909-1984
10	Penny Sue Molter 1970-1970
22	Ella L. Monson 1901-1994
33	Kathryn Mi (Hickey) Murphy, wife of Lawrence W. 24 August 1958 - 26 May 1989
06	Sandy Murrell 1948-1985
18	William F. Nagel 1933-1989 married Marjorie M. 17 August 1952
10	Albert Nason 30 November 1847 - 19 March 1927
10	Ida Nason 1892-1987
10	Emily Nason 23 March 1859 - 4 May 1952
10	Rinaldo Nason 1884-1957
03	Frank L. Nau 1890-1970
07	Bergetha Nelsen (?) 1856-1928
07	Merel Nelsen (?) 1928-1943
07	Nels Nelsen (?) 1857-1940
07	Otto Nelsen (?) 1896-1918
07	Victor Nelsen (?) 1940-1941
06	Arne C. Nelson 11 March 1921 - 12 October 1990 Tec 3 US Army WW2
06	Arne N. Nelson 1889-1963
03	Clarence A. Nelson 17 April 1894 - 2 August 1984
06	Daisy G. Nelson 1898-1984
02	Dennis L. Nelson 18 April 1940 - 15 April 1993
01	Henry Nelson 3 December 1894 - 5 October 1971
06	Herman N. Nelson 1896-1966
06	Pearl F. Nelson 1914-1967
15	Bertha A. Newcomb 1865-1939

16	Charles G. Newcomb, died 16 August 1876, age 53 years
16	Jane C. Newcomb, died 24 August 1903, age 79 years
15	William A. Newcomb 1859-1935
12	Amarius Nielsen 1881-1958
10	Audrey Kay Nielsen 1954-1977
12	Jensine Nielsen 1882-1975
09	John C. Nielsen 1880-1968
12	Lester A. Nielsen 1908-1962
	married June K. 20 August 1935
10	baby Nordstrom - 1959 -
04	Hjalmar A. Offrell 1883-1942
04	Sadie A. Offrell 1887-1968
15	Kathryn A. Olmsted 1912-1977
15	Keith E. Olmsted 1910-1971
12	Bessie Marie Olson 1921-1922
07	Gust Olson 1870-1917
07	Karna Olson 1841-1920
07	Nels Olson 1840-____
37	Michael D. Osborne 28 October 1955 - 20 June 1995
08	Anton J. Osfeld 1883-1969
12	Owens, died 12 January 1901 (?)
01	Terrance R. Paulson 30 January 1944 - 7 May 1991
03	Renee E. Pearson 1914-1974
03	Roland W. Pearson 1901-1987
01	Michael J. Pepple 16 July 1962 - 8 April 1984
16	Alfred Perkins, died 18 July 1883 (?), age 86 years
16	Alfred N. Perkins, died 8 May 1893 (?), age 34 years
16	Anna Bell, daughter of Irenus and Sarah Perkins
	13 August 1862 - 3 September 1865
14	Eva M. Perkins 1880-1939
12	H.J. Perkins (?) 25 October 1850 - 17 January 1887
12	Henry T. Perkins 21 April 1845 - 3 September 1898
16	Irenus Perkins 2 May 1817 - 23 January 1904
16	Jane W., wife of A. Perkins, died 30 August 1880, age 83 years
14	Lucile Perkins 1891-1981
14	Lucina O. Perkins 1834-1907
14	Matilda Perkins 1859-1941
12	Orlo Perkins 22 May 1877 - 18 February 1900
14	Owen A. Perkins (?) 1852-1907
14	Samuel A. Perkins 1831-1901
16	Sarah, wife of Irenus (?) Perkins 18 June 1819 (?) - 5 August 1907
12	Harlan W. Persons 1936-1987
12	Inga (?) Peterson 1883-1909
07	John Peterson 1893-1976

10	Beatrice K. Pettet 1959-1967
10	Eugene Pettet 1915-1977
10	Wilma Pettet 1925-____
02	Arthur Leonard Pettis 1922-1985
	Pfc US Marine Corps WW2
03	Carrie Pettis 1881-1983
02	Donna Lee Pettis 1945-1947
03	Henry C. Pettis 1875-1956
03	Jack H. Pettis 1920-1942
05	Bruno Peuschel (?) 1855-1930
05	Margaret Peuschel (?) 1857-1941
14	Griffin Phelps 1826-1914
14	Harriet Phelps 1838-____
14	Sarah J. Phelps 1818-1888
14	Sarah J. Phelps, wife of G. Phelps
	7 March 1818 - 19 February 1888
11	Leone Phillips 2 years 5 months - no dates - hard to read
01	Anna G. Plaisted 1905-1970
14	Henry (?) B. (?) Pond (?), died 9 August 1880, age 63 years (?)
14	Maria H. Pond (?), died 17 January 1895, age 75 years
31	Carl M. Prevette 22 March 1937 - 2 November 1994
38	Marie Prochnow 1952-1989
38	Walter Prochnow 1920-1990
26	Joshua Myles Renken 21 May 1986 - 18 January 1997
15	Herschell L. Revell 1897-1917
12	Midred Rice 1894-1996
12	Mildred L. Rice 1884-1996
17	Lyle E. Ringeisen 1917-1961
34	Ronald L. Risdon 5 February 1944 - 5 March 1991
02	Mary Jane Roehl - 1936 -
10	baby boy Rose 1950-1950
05	Joanne G. Rowe 1936-1997
12	Esther C. Ruh 1898-1966
12	Juel O. Ruh 1900-1965
11	Herbert H. Rushlow 1895-1907
02	William Scheiman - no dates
15	Nancy J. Seebeck 1889-1971
15	Oscar W. Seebeck 1893-1957
01	baby Seikkula 1956-1956
07	Alice R. Seivers (?) 1900-1958
07	Anna C. Seivers (?) 1896-1978
06	Clarence T. Seivers (?) 1908-1963
07	Dorothy Seivers (?) 1905-1986
07	'Father' Seivers (?) 1875-1942

07	'Mother' Seivers (?) 1871-1914
07	Rodney L. Seivers (?) 1911-1939
13	Robert D. Sellner 1938-1995 US Army
13	Scott M. Sellner 4 August 1965 - 30 January 1966
05	baby daughter Serum, born and died 1925
05	Lillie Deibler Serum 1885-1925
10	Verna H. Gyrion Shaurette 11 August 1923 - 8 October 1987
10	Catherine Shen 19 October 1825 (?) - 2 June 1897 (?)
07	Ella Shen (?) 1853-1925
07	Harry Shen (?) 1878-1913
07	Henry Shen (?) 1853-1929
07	Robert Shen (?) 1881-1945
10	Walter C. Shen 20 April 1885 - 29 July 1885 (?)
07	William Shen (?) 1876-1941
01	Anna Sherburne 1876-1954
01	Georg Sherburne 1878-1962
01	Mary F. Jenkins Shirl 1948-1984
12	? (buried to deep to read) Silsbee (?)
	16 November 1881 - 2 October 1886
12	E.B. Silsbee 16 June 1886 - 2 October 1886
12	Herbert H. Silsbee 1889-1967
12	Rae Silsbee 1894-1973
04	T.B. Simmons 1886-1925
17	Brad A. Skoglund 13 October 1962 - 13 November 1987
10	Travis L. Skogman 30 January 1987 - 5 April 1987
09	Alfred Sletten 1921-____
09	Viola Sletten 1923-____
04	Amie Sorensen 1894-1977
07	Angus E. Sorensen 1900-1978
07	Anton P. Sorensen (?) 1861-1953
04	Harlan W. Sorensen 1924-1945
07	Mamie Sorensen (?) 1896-1914
07	Margaret Sorensen 1887-1970
07	Myrtle R. Sorensen 1893-1984
07	Pauline Sorensen (?) 1864-1953
04	Roscoe Sorensen 1888-1952
08	Alvin R. Smith 1913-1995
08	Bertrand L. Smith (?) 1912-1977
12	Charles W. Smith 6 July 1882 - 1 February 1964
08	Evelyn Smith (?) 1907-1936
07	Frank Smith 1875-1924
06	Fred Smith 1868-1936
08	George A. Smith (?) 1872-1941
08	Helen O. Smith 1906-1994
08	Helene P. Smith 1906-____
08	Margaret O. Smith (?) 1881-1970

07   Maude Smith 1895-1951
12   Minnie I. Smith 27 May 1890 - 26 February 1966
08   Orrin Smith 1909-1982
24   Ruth M. Smith 1912-1991
06   Stella Smith 1876-1963
05   Thomas C. Smith (?) 1842-1927
14   Carol Snow 1940-1971
11   baby girl, daughter of Wm. and Julia Somero - January 1960 -
05   Selma A. Sorg 1885-1970
04   Clarice M. Sperling 1899-1959
04   John J. Sperling 1904-1959
10   Anna Marie Stanton 1897-1976
10   John Earl Stanton 1898-1985
02   Floyd Steele 1904-1952
08   Grace Steele 1904-1971
08   John Steele 1899-1969
15   Katherine Steele 1883-1958
15   Thomas P. Steele 1883-1973
02   Thos. Steele 1875-1952
02   Winnie Steele 1880-1933
03   Julia Steen 1856-1932
32   Susan A. Steiner 16 January 1955 - 29 December 1991
05   Fannie Stewart 1842-1922
23   Robert L. Stoneberg 22 August 1892 - 9 January 1990
             Pvt US Army WW1
31   A. Martin Storlie 1901-1993
31   Dorothy A. (Svenning) Storlie 1928-1995
31   Marlin L. 'Sid' Storlie 1927-1997
31   Myra Storlie 1905-1994
09   Arie Streefland 1869-1953
09   Arie Streefland 1892-1969
09   Bernard Henry Streefland (?) 1910-1931
09   Christina Streefland (?) 9 days - no dates
09   Jansje Streefland 1871-1958
09   Jennie Streefland (?) 10 weeks - no dates
01   Herman Stricker 1870-1953
01   Ida J. Stricker 1877-1934
09   baby Swanson - no dates
08   Earl Swanson 1901-1960
09   John Swanson 1869-1956
08   Lena Swanson 1886-1966
09   Minnie Swanson 1870-1926

10   Clara C. Thies 1893-1976
11   Lillian C. Thies 1920-____
11   Wilbur F. Thies 1918-1993

05	Steven Ray Thomason 11 July 1960 - 8 June 1987
11	C.P. Thompson 15 October 1840 - 22 December 1899
11	Lynn M. Thompson 1959-1959
19	Marlene A. Thompson 4 April 1941 - 28 October 1991
11	R. Thompson 10 February 1827 - 7 March 1864
03	Mary Louise Todd 22 October 1932 - 23 October 1932
05	Catherine Elizabeth Hale Trygstad 27 January 1899 - 29 January 1980
05	Richard Melvin Trygstad 24 January 1904 - 12 June 1991
12	F.A.V. - no dates
12	J.H.V. - no dates
38	Thomas John Vereide 17 August 1967 - 6 October 1995
26	Janice Anne Rice Vigen 1969-1993
26	Katie Lyn Vigen - 1 November 1993 -
10	Jesse J. Vincent 18 January 1976 - 7 July 1976
10	baby boy Vogen 14 April 1972 - 15 April 1972
17	Ruth Jean Vopat 14 October 1983 - 15 May 1989
12	Earle Vrooman (?) - no dates
12	James H. Vrooman, born 5 March 1836, Co F 1st Wis. Calvalry, died at Farmington, MN 7 May 1895
12	Mabel V. Walker 1878-1953
03	Maxine M. Walker 1919-1928
12	Orin E. Walker 1878-1953
04	Edith J. Wallin 1892-1974
04	Edward H. Wallin 1890-1945
04	Marie Wallin 1862-1931
05	Mark A. Wallin 1955-1981
04	Nels Wallin 1865-1940
10	Matthew Walter 1961-1981
03	Anna Wastrom 1880-1947
03	Sven Wastrom 1883-____
03	Orville E. Watson 1919-1945 (?)
05	Alice G. Way 1910-1983
05	LeRoy D. Way 1909-1983
15	Clarice E. Weichselbaum 1912-1979
15	Edythe M. Weichselbaum 1905-1962
15	Frank Weichselbaum 1868-1939
16	John Weichselbaum 1831-1900
16	John Weichselbaum (?) 1865-1869
16	John F. Weichselbaum 1907-1968
15	Mamie C. Weichselbaum 1872-1941
16	Margaret Weichselbaum 1827-1900
16	Margaret L. Weichselbaum 1897-1964
16	Saubina Weichselbaum (?) 1853-1868
13	Anita Joyce Weirke 1968-1984

06   Vernon P. Westveer 22 July 1923 - 1 February 1983
01   Bernard Lowell Wetterlund 1941-1983 A DR3 US Navy
10   Connie White - 24 November 1981
13   Caroline Wilson 1815-1899
13   Ezkiel Wilson 1812-1895
25   Gene W. Wischmann 1935-1991
04   Harry Wisner 1925-1983
04   Harry Lukes Wisner 1925-1983 PHM2 US navy WW2
17   Dean F. Wolf September 1966 - September 1990
07   Louisa S. Wood 1843-1928
07   R.B. Wood 1840-1921 Co A 10th Wis. Inf.
14   Charles A. Wright 1928-1987
14   Richard C. Wright 1956-1987

10   Steven Young - 16 April 1983 -

01   Molly Ziebarth 1897-1970

Lakeville Grove Cemetery
City of Lakeville / Lakeville Township
T 114 N - R 20 W   Section 28

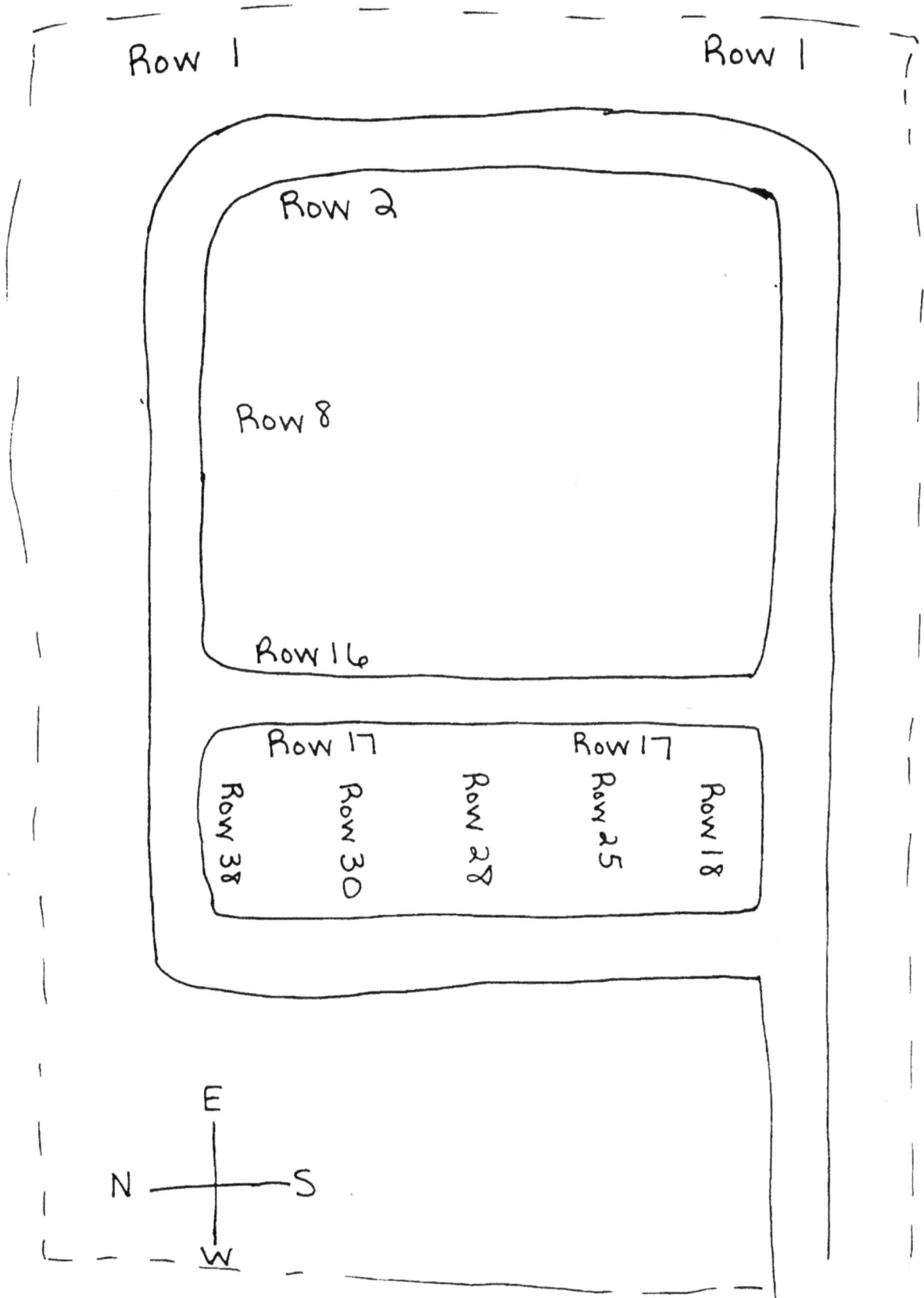

Row 1

Row 1

Row 2

Row 8

Row 16

Row 17

Row 17

Row 38

Row 30

Row 28

Row 25

Row 18

E

N ——+—— S

W

369

ALL SAINTS CEMETERY

Lakeville city, Dakota County, Minnesota: T114 - R20, section 32

     This cemetery is upkept and in good shape. Row 1 begins along the east edge of the cemetery. This cemetery contains a couple street signs to mark drive areas. Located between rows 10 and 11 is the St. Mark drive area. Located between rows 14 and 15 is the St. Thaddeus drive area. Row 29 is a burial area that runs east and west along the north end of the cemetery and comprises a couple of rows. The north entrance gate was dedicated to the memory of P.F. Donnelly.

     In "History of Dakota County and the city of Hastings", By Rev. Edward D. Neill, written in 1881, he lists two references to the All Saints [Catholic] Church congregation. 1) As an off-shoot of St. Joseph's church in 1877, the church of All Saints was formed, and two acres of land were purchased from the railroad company situated in the south-east quarter of section 29. (page 417). 2) All Saint's Cemetery is situated about half a mile south of the village of Lakeville, and comprises three acres of land, set aside for this purpose in 1880. (page 417).

     The Dakota county cemetery records compilation lists this cemetery as: All Saints Catholic Cemetery, established 1880. 3 acres. Located NE1/4 of Section 32. Highway 15 south of Highway 70.

     Everyone is listed in alphabetical order. The number before each entry is the row number. There is a map at the back of this section.

     These cemetery burial monuments were transcribed during 1996.

10	Cecelia Ackerman 1863-1956
10	'Father' Ackerman (?) 1824-1907
09	John Ackerman (?) 1910-1910
09	Lou J. Ackerman (?) 1877-1919
09	Mae A. Ackerman (?) 1887-1974
10	Magna M. Ackerman (?) 1907-1989
10	Margaret Ackerman 1876-1941
10	Mary Ackerman 1872-1961
09	Mildred Ackerman (?) 1911-1913
09	Mildred I. Ackerman 1910-1976
10	'Mother' Ackerman (?) 1837-1911
10	Rose Mary Ackerman (?) 1901-1994
09	Vern J. Ackerman (?) 1913-1928
09	Willard O. Ackerman 1909-1990
10	William C. Ackerman 1875-1941
01	Margaret Adelmann 1918-____
01	Nicholas Adelmann 1924-____
01	Nick P. Adelmann 1890-1961

01	Rose F. Adelmann 1893-1962
22	Carol A. Alexander 1937-1981
18	baby boy Alich - 21 January 1959 -
12	Florence A. Allis 20 October 1895 - 2 October 1990
12	Louis H. Allis, Minnesota PFC 357 Ambulance Co. WW1 PH
	19 August 1894 - 31 August 1962
22	Daniel Louis Allmann 1964-1979
07	John Alton (?) 1847-1942
07	Margaret Alton (?) 1848-1934
16	Rose Ammerman 1869-1930
08	Agnes Mary Anderson 8 January 1918 - 29 May 1990
12	Kathleen Anderson 16-29 March 1968
29	Robert S. 'Andy' Anderson 1942-1985
08	V. Edward Anderson 18 April 1923-____
03	Edward C. Antil 1894-1951
03	Ethel Antil 1899-1990
14	Michael F. Arndt 1869-1927
16	Margaret H. Awe 1891-1983
12	Margaret Friedges Ball 1885-1980
19	Raymond C. Barlage 1904-1953
19	Thelma L. Barlage 1909-____
29	Ashley Ann Barron 5 March 1987 - 9 March 1987
11	Dorothy A. Baudin 1901-1980
11	Mary Agnes Baudin 1876-1939
09	infant John Beckius - no dates
09	John Beckius 1847-1885
10	Joseph Beckius 1883-1939
09	infant Peter Beckius - no dates
21	Stephen Berdan 14 August 1966 - 27 June 1989
22	Robert C. 'Bob' Bernard 5 July 1957 - 1 November 1987
10	Anna Maria Bendel, wife of Thomas Berres
	27 August 1828 - 10 May 1883
09	baby Berres - no dates
16	Bert Berres 1892-1963
17	Casper Berres (?) 1844-1916
09	Catherine Berres 1862-1950
16	Christina Berres (?) 1894-1914
09	Elizabeth, wife of Mathius Berres
	16 October 1834 (?) at Gilleufeld (?) Germany, died 1 August 1901
09	Elizabeth Berres 1834-1901
14	Emma Berres 1846-1912
18	Frank J. Berres 1905-1989
09	George J. Berres (?) 1871-1935
18	Isabelle V. Berres 1901-1975
15	Jacob J. Berres 11 June 1860 - 9 March 1930

15	Jacob J. Berres (?) 1860-1930
09	Joseph Berres 8 August 1864 - 25 June 1895
10	Joseph J. Berres 1864-1895
09	Leo J. Berres (?) 1903-1946
17	Margaret Berres (?) 1855-1936
09	Margaret Berres (?) 1873-1949
09	Mary Berres 1873-1934
15	Mary E. Berres 26 May 1865 - 19 October 1947
15	Mary E. Berres (?) 1865-1947
09	Mathius Berres 21 October 1821 - 26 June 1896 (?)
09	Mathius Berres 1821-1896
17	Mat. (?) B. Berres (?) 1876-1947
09	Matt T. Berres 1904-1960
16	Mayme Berres 1901-1981
09	Michael Berres 1863-1937
14	Nick Berres 1876-1964
14	Peter Berres 1837-1912
17	Susan Berres (?) 1880-1958
10	Thomas Berres 8 May 1831 - 26 January 1898
17	Vera Berres 1912-1959
01	Gustave W. Betz, died 29 October 1909, aged 41 years
01	Josephine Betz, died 11 November 1930
20	Elizabeth M. Beuch 1917-____
20	Erich C. Beuch 1907-1995
11	Anna Bies 1883-1914
12	Edward J. Bies 8 March 1920 - 10 February 1991
	CM1 US Navy WW2
11	Hanora Bies 1850-1907
11	Henry Bies 1838-1906
14	Fred J. Blaschke 1894-1980
09	Francis Blazek 1876-1946
09	Michael Blazek 1876-1969
21	Robert A. Boenish (?) 1960-1973
22	Henry B. Bornhofen 1929-1975
19	Frances A. Bousquel 1886-1964
19	Frederick G. Bousquel 1880-1964
29	Chloe E. Boyum - 12 December 1992 -
10	John Brandl 26 November 1889 - 19 August 1965
	MN Cpl Co I 345 Infantry WW1
09	Mildred M. Brandl (?) 1922- ____
09	Robert A. Brandl (?) 1925-____
10	Christine B. Brandle 1897-1966
13	F.P. Breher 1855-1910
13	'Mother' Breher (?) 1858-1918
06	Bella C. Brennan 1897-1984
04	Bridgel Brennan 1828-1914

07	Catherine Connelly Brennan 1899-1942
05	children of J.E. and Mary Brennan - no names and dates
05	Ellen, daughter of Mr. and Mrs. Wm. Brennan 1921-1930
05	John E. Brennan 1858-1913
06	John F. Brennan 1891-1968
04	John L. Brennan 1825-1908
07	Joseph M. Brennan 1889-1962
07	Katheryne J. Brennan 1905-1986
05	Mary A. Brennan 1862-1948
06	Mary A. Brennan 1895-1970
05	Mary C. Brennan (?) 1872-1950
05	Michael P. Brennan (?) 1863-1947
04	William Brennan (?) - no dates
06	William E. Brennan 1895-1978
18	baby Bresnahan 1959-1959
18	baby Mary Bresnahan 1958-1958
23	Lawrence V. Brezinka 1936-1987
	married Rosalyn M. 6 July 1959
08	Baltasar Brost 1857-1930
07	Josephine Patient Brost (?) 27 June 1882 - 10 June 1914
08	Mary Brost 1867-1943
16	Mary R. Brown 1878-1941
16	Theodore Brown 1866-1945
24	Henry G. Buerke 1915-1983
02	Bridget Burns (?) 23 February 1872 - 28 April 1881
	child of - buried to deep to read
16	Bridget M. Burns - no dates
07	Daniel P. Burns (?) 1877-1901
16	James Burns - no dates
07	Margaret Burns (?) 1854-1916
07	Thomas Burns (?) 1853-1932
02	William Burns (?) 12 May 1877 - 22 April 1881
	child of - buried to deep to read
10	Isabelle Butler 1840-1920
10	John L. Butler 1845-1919
15	Agnes Byrne (?) 1895-1983
06	Dorothy Byrne 1917-____
	married Francis L. 11 September 1948
15	Francis Byrne (?) 1890-1945
06	Francis L. Byrne 1918-1971
	married Dorothy 11 September 1948
15	John Thomas Byrne 24 June 1929 - 5 April 1978
	SN US Navy
05	Margaret M. Byrne (?) 1866-1920
05	Michael F. Byrne (?) 1861-1935
15	Raymond F. Byrne 22 December 1921 - 5 June 1994

PHM2 US Navy WW2

02	Blanche C. Campion 1902-1995
16	Daniel Campion 1911-1949
01	'Father' Campion (?) 1856-1918
01	J. Francis Campion 1900-1961
01	James E. Campion 1899-1963
02	Jane Campion (?) 1862-1944
01	Joseph J. Campion (?) 1894-1927
15	Julia Campion 1875-1959
02	M. Edward Campion (?) 1862-1930
15	Michael Campion 1863-1946
01	'Mother' Campion (?) 1864-1924
02	Maurice V. Campion 1902-1969
01	Roy J. Campion (?) 1893-1957
01	William H. Campion (?) 1891-1963
29	Philip Carroll 1964-1991
05	Mary E., wife of Patrick Casey
	30 March 1850 - 20 November 1889
01	Mary Caspers 1840-1880
01	Mathias Caspers 1827-1909
01	Michael J. Caspers 1866-1916
17	Earl L. Cherry 1904-1967
05	Elizabeth V. Cherry 25 November 1900 - 27 March 1972
17	Lorraine Cherry 1907-1996
20	baby Faye D. Chisholm 1955-1955
20	Ida H. Chisholm 1918-____
20	Thomas A. Chisholm 1913-1986
17	Carl C. Christensen 1906-1976
18	Francis John, baby son of Carl and Lucille Christensen
	8 February - 5 December 1954
29	Heather Ann Christensen 18 July 1979 - 2 April 1984
17	Lucille E. Christensen 1910-____
05	Lawrence E. Christian 1898-1982
05	Mary M. Christian 1897-1988
21	Donald B. Coffing 1 December 1938 - 13 January 1985
19	Catherine Connelly 5 April 1891 - 17 May 1932
01	Elizabeth Connelly 1849-1925
01	John R. Connelly 1879-1933
01	Michael T. Connelly 1836-1913
02	'Our Brothers' Connelly - no names or dates
19	William F. Connelly 12 December 1885 - 22 April 1966
11	Isobel Conroy, died 18 August 1931, age 22 years
16	Mary Conroy 1879-1941
16	Michael Conroy 1869-1957
08	Patrick Conway 1855-1929

11	Ambrose C. Cool 1861-1934
11	Mary King Cool 1855-1934
19	Frank Corcoran 1889-1969
19	Nellie Corcoran 1891-1990
04	'Father' Coughlin (?) 1839-1892
03	Marie E. Coughlin 1916-1966
04	'Mother' Coughlin (?) 1845-1919
04	William Coughlin (?) 1872-1897
29	Timothy D. Cronin 18 August 1972 - 5 January 1973
11	Esther K. Courtney 1893-1968
11	Henry J. Courtney 1894-1968
22	Paul W. Cuta 21 April 1969 - 19 December 1990
14	Rose B. Daly 1886-1964
14	William E. Daly 1877-1948
16	Anna Dawson 1863-1931
16	baby Dawson born and died 11 February 1922
09	Elizabeth Dawson 1869-1901
16	Elizabeth Dawson 1890-1927
17	Elizabeth Dawson 1897-1986
09	Hannah MacMullen, wife of James Dawson 1827-1920
16	Hugh Dawson 1858-1933
17	Hugh Dawson 1896-1978
17	Gladys Simones Dawson 1924-1948
09	James Dawson 1817-1898
17	Lucille Dawson 1934-1936
09	Mary A. Dawson, died (?) 12 May 1885
	aged 21 years 3 months 12 days
24	John Francis Dean 25 May 1923 - 11 August 1976
	US Navy WW2
24	Magdalen M. Dean 27 December 1928 - 2 June 1974
19	Arthur L. Deconing 1906-1909
10	Alice Deegan (?) 1898-1951
08	Anna Deegan 1877-1950
09	Francis M. Deegan 1895-1924
07	James Melvin Deegan, died 1901, aged 1 year
09	Mary E. Deegan (?) 1862-1944
08	Michael J. Deegan 1867-1945
09	William Deegan (?) 1860-1943
10	William J. Deegan (?) Jr. 22 August 1897 - 14 April 1948
29	Chelsea Maria DeGroot 4 November 1986 - 27 March 1987
13	Donald W. DeJarlais 21 December 1928 - 4 February 1995
	US Marine Corps Korea
13	Mabel E. DeJarlais 1908-1958
13	William J. DeJarlais 1909-1990
05	Grace Milan Dekoning 1890-1929

13	Jake P. Derres 1874-1957
20	Stanley W. Dey 1916-1967
13	A. E. Dimond - no dates
20	Bernard J. Dircks 5 May 1935 - 30 November 1963
12	Arthur Doebel 1912-1980
12	Luella Doebel 1907-1985
21	Catherine Doetkott 1907-1980
21	Henry Doetkott 1895-1990
29	Maria Domjan - 16 August 1983 -
29	Peter Donkers 1956-1979
13	Catherine Donlon 1863-1942
15	Frances V. Donlon 10 June 1900 - 29 July 1992
14	George E. Donlon 1903-1979
12	Margaret Isabel Donlon 12 October 1878 - 3 October 1911
14	Mary Donlon 1897-1984
13	Michael J. Donlon 1897-1979
12	Peter J. Donlon 16 July 1863 - 19 April 1936
13	Peter R. Donlon 1894-1972
15	Robert F. Donlon 16 August 1935 - 2 February 1938
13	Thomas Donlon 1857-1934
15	Warren B. Donlon 26 May 1904 - 3 January 1990
05	Elizabeth Donnelly (?) 1903-1976
13	George E. Donnelly 1897-1967
13	Julia C. Donnelly 1893-1977
03	Marguerite Donnelly 1897-1988
03	Marguerite A. Donnelly 27 October 1897 - 1 January 1988
05	Martin J. Donnelly (?) 1895-1957
03	Patrick F. Donnelly 1890-1963
03	Patrick F. Donnelly 4 November 1890 - 14 March 1963
03	Robert J. Donnelly 21 August 1927 - 30 March 1988
03	Robert John Donnelly 21 August 1927 - 30 March 1988
	Cox US Navy WW2
05	James H. Donovan 1885-19__
05	John W. Donovan 1883-1959
05	P. Donovan 1827-1900
08	Patrick H. Duffy (?) 1869-1943
18	Alice M. Dunham - no dates
10	Anna Dunham 1892-1916
10	David W. Dunham 1886-1963
12	Eleanor M. Dunham 1893-1986
11	Frank Dunham 1884-1906
12	Gertrude M. Dunham 1892-1985 US Navy WW1
12	James J. Dunham 4 December 1897 - 25 December 1990
09	John L. Dunham 1888-1968
11	Mary A. Dunham 1857-1949
12	Mary A. Dunham 6 June 1904 - 24 November 1992

09	Mary T. Dunham 1888-1950
18	Philip L. Dunham 1895-1963
18	Philip L. Dunham 25 October 1895 - 12 March 1963
	Minnesota Pfc Co F 135 Infantry WW1 PH
11	Wright J. Dunham 1852-1944
10	James C. Dwyer, son of James M. and Mary Sullivan Dwyer
	7 June 1884 - 12 July 1901
23	Henry B. Ehnes 1913-1982
12	Peter M. Eischen 1888-1951
21	Louis L. Emond 1908-1978
22	Kenneth Eugen Enright 27 June 1944 - 14 February 1990
14	Louisa Hoheisel, wife of Nicholas Everote
	21 April 1852 - 10 March 1905
13	N. Everote 1850-1927
05	'Father' Feehan (?) 1862-1941
05	John J. Feehan 1893-1930
05	'Mother' Feehan (?) 1866-1926
05	Thomas L. Feehan (?) 1895-1935
07	Anna Irene Feely 1886-1915
07	'Mother' Feely (?) 1857-1926
07	Patrick H. Feely 1858-1935
19	Flora M. Felber 19 April 1888 - 8 February 1980
19	John A. Felber 6 June 1883 - 15 April 1966
19	Katherine M. Felber 1918-1946
19	M. Dorothy Felber 9 December 1912 - 8 October 1914
21	Bernard J. Feldman 1 August 1907 - 2 January 1989
	married Julia M. 1 July 1947
21	Julia M. Feldman 28 November 1918 - 16 March 1996
	married Bernard J. 1 July 1947
02	Edward Fitzgerald 1824-1897
02	Mrs. Edward Fitzgerald 1820-1887
01	Kate Fitzgerald 1860-1926
01	George Henry (?) 23 April 1880 - 4 September 1881
	- near White and Fitzgerald
01	Mary A. Fitzgerald 1885-1907
28	Ryan Edward Flaherty 23 March 1975 - 6 February 1993
02	Grace H. Flannery 1880-1970
16	Mary Forland - 1956 -
20	Gladys H. Fowler 1903-1985
20	E.J. Red Fowler 1906-1987
29	Erin Marie French 30 October 1978 - 17 September 1979
17	Mary J. Freundschuh 1933-1965
17	Alice M. Friedges 1909-1993
17	Nick F. Friedges 1898-1970

22	Peter B. Friedges 1927-1992
12	Peter J. Friedges 1890-1949
12	Sophia A. Friedges 1896-1971
11	Anna M. Friedges - Ring 1896-1972
11	Catherine Friedges - Ring 1859-1938
11	George P. Friedges - Ring 1892 -1990
11	Mathias Friedges - Ring 1855-1937
15	Madeline Gaffney 1879-1959
15	Dr. Thomas J. Gaffney 1869-1945
07	Margaret Gannon 1878-1956
03	'Father' Garot (?) 1852-1930
03	'Mother' Garot (?) 1849-1916
18	Margaret Gear (?) 1887-1959
12	Daniel Gephart (?) 1865-1915
06	Daniel M. Gephart 1902-1980
06	Evelyn M. Gephart 1900-1979
11	Fred Gephart 1900-1956
12	George Gephart 1893-1908
11	John C. Gephart 1891-1964
03	Josephine R. Gephart (?) 1895-1981
12	Kate A. Gephart (?) 1867-1956
04	Kris Ann Gephart 1955-1961
03	Leonard J. Gephart 9 September 1920 - 25 September 1991
	Cpl US Army WW2
03	Leonard N. Gephart (?) 1892-1963
05	Louis M. Rowan-Gephart 1879-1937
12	Mary E. Gephart 1861-1926
11	Mary T. Gephart 1892-1936
03	Raymond D. Gephart - 9 September 1959 -
11	Veronica Gephart 1898-1961
13	Alois Gerdesmeier 1916-1987
13	Alois George Gerdesmeier 19 March 1916 - 25 May 1987
	Tec 5 US Army WW2
13	Dolores Gerdesmeier 1922-____
13	John A. Gerdesmeier 16 December 1948 - 16 August 1968
	PFC US Marine Corps Vietnam PH
13	Joseph A. Gerdesmeier 29 August 1963 - 14 August 1993
	Sgt. US Marine Corp
03	Mary Gibbons 10 December 1853 - 22 December 1943
03	Walter Gibbons 2 July 1842 - 12 August 1923
03	Dan. Giles 1884-1931
03	Edward D. Giles 1876-1926
03	'Father' Giles (?) 1847-1923
04	Frank J. Giles 1898-1968
04	Helen M. Giles 1899-1967

04	Margaret A. Giles 1897-1983
03	'Mother' Giles (?) 1853-1918
25	Raphael J. Giles 1922-1970
03	Thomas Jerome Giles 1931-1969
04	William J. Giles 1894-1948
05	Agnes Gilmore 1861-1927
06	Edward Gilmore, native of Parish Bevenaugh Co. Galway Ireland died 14 November 1881, age 56 years
05	Gracie E., daughter of P.E. and Agnes Gilmore 18 September 1900 - 24 January 1901
06	John M. Gilmore 1880-1952
06	Margaret O'Connell, wife of Ed Gilmore, native of Parish Tuam Co Galway, Ireland, died 30 June 1897, age 80 years
05	Mary Gilmore 1862-1890
05	Mary O'Connell, wife of P.E. Gilmore, died 22 February 1890 28 years 10 months 22 days
05	Michael J. Gilmore 1881-1910
05	Patrick E. Gilmore 1857-1933
19	Therese A. Gitzen 1936-1968
11	Catherine Gleizner 1897-_____
11	Catherine Gleisner (?) 1893-1932
11	Sylvester Gleisner 1893-1976
21	Chris Gnerer 1914-1989
21	Edith Gnerer 1919-_____
10	Mayme M. Gomoll 1906-1963
10	Paul E. Gomoll 1904-1968
14	Georgie Gorman 1906-1926
22	E. Patrick Grandpre 1914-1975
22	Mary A. Grandpre 1918-_____
01	Anna Grady 1853-1931
02	Anna L. Grady 12 September 1883 - 21 January 1970 Minnesota Nurse Army Nurse Corps WW1
02	John F. Grady 28 December 1877 - 10 April 1965
02	Thomas E. Grady 7 September 1889 - 5 August 1954
01	William Grady, born in Co Mayo, Ireland 15 May 1845 - 23 August 1909
02	William J. Grady 1887-1953
09	Anna Leyden Graham 1891-1950
14	Emma Arendt Grapper 1880-1961
06	Francis D. Graves 1887-1961
06	Julie G. Graves 1896-1989
08	Catherine Green 1856-1946
08	Elizabeth Green 1874-1939
08	Henry Green 1847-1930
09	M. Agnes Green (?) 1887-1980
09	Marie Green 20 March 1920 - 19 June 1923

05	Martin Green, born in Co Gallway, Ireland
	died 1895, age 70 years
08	Thomas H. Green 1884-1952
09	William J. Green (?) 1880-1953
23	Nicholas G. Groff 1951-1993
29	Praxedis Grohoski 1893-1985
29	Walter Grohoski 1893-1981
28	Jana Gulbrandson - no dates - recent 1997 burial ?
28	Sharon Gulbrandson - no dates - recent 1997 burial ?
12	George J. Hack 1889-1935
12	Marie T. Hack 1884-1977
08	Stanley P. Hagan 1898-1974
01	Catherine V. Hagen 1905-____
01	Edwin O. Hagen 1897-1982
17	Dolores A. Haglund 1918-1975
17	Harold G. Haglund 1914-1979
29	Heather Marie Halbmaier - June 1985 -
29	Pat Haller 1917-1994
29	Stella A. 'Grandma Alice' Haller 1900-1983
19	Barbara Hammer (?) 1883-1970
19	Jamisen Michael Hammer - 27 December 1995 -
19	Joseph P. Hammer 1942-1947
07	Marie Hammer 1894-1991
19	Oscar Hammer (?) 1887-1959
07	Palmer Hammer 1891-1975
19	Patricia A. Hammer (?) 1910-1989
19	Paul N. Hammer (?) 1911-1970
10	Elizabeth Hammes 1801-1884
09	Elizabeth Hammes 21 August 1803 - 15 June (?) 1884
09	John Hammes 17 May (?) 1797 - 16 (?) 1883
10	John Hammes 1897-1883
19	Joseph P. Hannan 1890-1977
19	Joseph P. Hannan 20 October 1890 - 30 September 1977
	Pvt US Army WW1
19	Mary A. Hannan 1892-1977
19	Mary A. Hanzel 1891-1958
19	Peter P. Hanzel 1900-1976
21	Richard Hartmann 1914-____
21	Verna Hartmann 1912-____
08	Ambrose P. Hauer 1916-1967
08	Andrew M. Hauer 1891-1956
08	Anna K. Hauer 1889-1969
07	Jacob A. Hauer 1900-1988
08	James Rustan Hauer - 4 January 1970 -
	infant son of James and Christine

07	Mary E. Hauer 1899-1984
16	Floyd M. Hayes 1903-1941
01	Susan E. Hayes 1865-1944
29	Jennifer L. Haze 1967-1976
19	Dircks Hedlund (?) 1921-1982
19	Robert C. Hedlund 1940-1964
18	baby Tonya Heim - 1970 -
21	(Rocky) J.A. Heim 3 April 1922 - 7 August 1971
	S Sgt Co B 55 Armd Inf BN WW2
16	Barbara M. Heiman 1938-1938
16	Edward R. Heiman 1934-1935
16	Florence Heiman 1891-1963
16	Paul M. Heiman 1888-1974
22	Harold B. Hetletvedt 1920-1974
07	Mary Hickey 1863-1933
07	Wm. Hickey 1857-1935
17	Anna C. Higgins 1888-1950
18	baby boy Higgins - 8 December 1953 -
04	Bridget T. Higgins (?) 1864-1949
13	James L. Higgins 1889-1979
04	James P. Higgins (?) 1846-1934
13	Owen Higgins 1896-1938
08	Mrs. Geo. Hilstad 1898-1920
	daughter of Mr. and Mrs. P. J. Huberty
29	Tim Hirman 1965-1985
16	baby boy Hoffbeck - 8 August 1968 -
21	Blanche R. Hoffbeck 4 May 1918 - 10 September 1991
21	Elmer P. Hoffbeck 6 September 1916 - 18 June 1988
09	Anna C. Hogan 1887-1949
29	Steven Roger Horazuk 1 May 1970 - 9 October 1990
29	Ryan David Howe 7 November 1984 - 27 February 1985
07	baby girl Huberty, daughter of Clemens, - 25 January 1940 -
07	Clemens J. Huberty 1910-_____
08	Isabelle Huberty (?) 1907-1993
08	Peter J. Huberty (?) 1868-1956
08	Regina Huberty (?) 1876-1929
12	Albert C. Hullett (?) 1870-1940
16	Elizabeth E. Hullett 1914-1986
16	James Thomas Hullett 1912-1983 US Army WW2
16	James Hullett - 1946 -
11	Katherine A. Hullett (?) 1909 - _____
11	Lorena K. Hullett (?) 1907-1907
11	Lott Bernard Hullett 1878-1952
16	Margaret Hullett - 1947 -
07	Mary M. Hullett 1903-1978
11	Phylis K. Hullett (?) 1901-1902

11	Phylsie E. Hullett (?) 1901-1901
11	Raymond Frances Hullett 1908 - 1932
11	Rose Hullett 1881-1976
12	Susan A. Hullett (?) 1876-1949
07	Sylvester A. Hullett 1903-1973
16	Burdell Hystad 1903-1964
16	Katherine Hystad 1900-1964
25	Mary L. Ingersoll 1919-1987
25	Oscar M. Ingersoll 1899-1975
29	Frank N. Jackson 1928-1977
22	Leona F. Jackson 1926-1991
	married Arthur M. 11 October 1947
29	John P. Jay 2 November 1973 - 5 November 1973
04	Lauretta E. Jeffers 1891-1986
03	Tracy M. Jeffers 1899-1967
11	Asger M. Jensen 1907-1995
11	Elizabeth C. Jensen 1905-1987
09	James R. Jensen 1923-____
09	Ruth M. Jensen 1924-____
13	Catherine M. Johnson 1886-1971
18	Gilbert Johnson 1898-1981
01	Jason Patrick Johnson - 6 May 1969 -
18	Sadie Johnson 1900-1974
18	William Lawrence Johnson 1943-1981
29	Dale R. Kaisto 1969-1975
22	Ryan Jon Kalisch 6 July 1968 - 10 November 1994
06	Mary Ann Kean 1804-1880
06	William Kean 1807-1892
17	Albert J. Kehrer 1894-1986
11	Emma, daughter of Geo. (?) and Mary (?) Kehrer
	14 October 1874 (?) - 19 September 1901 (?)
11	George Kehrer 1846-1915
18	John M. Kehrer 26 May 1922 - 25 January 1923
17	Julian J. Kehrer 2 March 1924 - 28 February 1945
	Cpl US Army Air Corps WW2
17	Margaret Kehrer 1895-1979
11	Mary A. Kehrer 1849-1936
17	Michael J. Kehrer 23 July 1889 - 26 February 1966
23	Pamela A. Keith 18 October 1944 - 13 October 1989
	married Edwin E. 30 August 1961
04	Ann Kelly (?) 20 August 1855 - 20 January 1943
08	Anna L. Kelly 1885-1976
02	Bernard Kelly (?) 1889-1890

05	Catherine Kelly 1820-1883
02	Edward Kelly (?) 1898-1898
04	Edward Kelly (?) died (?) 14 April 1915 - age 47 years
05	Elizabeth M. Kelly (?) died (?) 1941
04	'Father' Kelly (?) 14 March 1823 - 5 June 1904
01	'Father' Kelly (?) 1857-1921
05	John Kelly 1827-1897
05	John Kelly 1868-1933
05	John F. Kelly - 1937 - died (?)
05	Joseph Kelly (?) 20 May 1900 - 29 May 1914
05	Margaret Kelly 1861-1946
05	Mary, wife of John Kelly 1833-1905
03	Mary Kelly (?) 20 May 1866 - 25 July 1939
01	'Mother' Kelly (?) 1859-1922
04	'Mother' Kelly (?) died (?) 18 April 1918 - age 82 years
05	Patrick Kelly 1857-1921
08	Patrick H. Kelly 1870-1953
02	Rose Kelly (?) 1885-1907
08	Sarah Kelly, wife of Timothy Kelly 1824-1896
08	Timothy Kelly 1910-1891
03	William D. Kelly (?) 15 December 1865 - 22 December 1943
29	J. Dayton Kempson 1910-1988
29	Rene R. Kempson 1957-1991
06	Clare C. Kennedy 9 November 1895 - 13 January 1975
06	John P. Kennedy 22 March 1886 - 23 May 1973
03	Emma Kill 1869-1941
04	John Kill 10 June 1875 - 19 February 1892
03	John Kill 1894-1979
04	Joseph Kill 12 February 1872 - 31 October 1890
04	Magdelena Kill 27 October 1836 - 25 May 1901
03	Nicholas Kill 1865-1957
03	Genevieve A. King 1905-1984
24	Harold E. King 1921-1995
11	Mary Ann King 1876-1935
11	Michael J. King 1868-1940
29	Nicole Ann King 7 January 1985 - 7 April 1985
03	Stephen M. King 1904-1970
19	Leo Kline 1903-1961
19	Mary Kline 1901-1976
22	Albert Kluzak - no dates
16	Mildred P. Knack 1921-1976
08	Eliz. Knapp 1870-1928
08	Lena Knapp 1851-1922
16	A. Cunnie Koehnen 1882-1956
16	Alouis M. Koehnen 1878-1959
15	Irene C. Koehnen 1933-1952

16	Debbie Koempel - 1951 -
17	Edward A. Korba 1916-1990
17	Genevieve C. Korba 1919-1986
22	Ann E. Kraft 1929-1983
14	Anton Kraft 1858-1929
16	Apollonia Kraft 1889-1967
14	Barbara Kraft 21 November 1887 - 25 July 1899 (?)
22	Corey C. Kraft 10 December 1973 - 3 February 1974
16	Henry J. Kraft 1883-1926
06	Lorraine A. Kraft 1919-1985
14	Mary Kraft 1861-1932
13	Mary Kraft 1896-1980
13	Robert F. Kraft 1897-1987
14	Veronika Kraft 15 February 1901 (?) - 11 March 1901
04	Carl W. Krause 1873-1967
04	Elizabeth Krause 1880-1948
03	Francis W. Krause 28 June 1906 - 16 January 1917
04	Jerome J. Krause 20 August 1915 - 25 September 1937
03	Raymond Krause 30 August 1912 - 18 October 1936
07	Albert Krejce 1897-1980
19	Anna Krejce 1889-1934
17	Charles Krejce 1893-1958
08	Daniel J. Krejce 1961-1982
23	Donald V. Krejce 1962-1991
07	Evelyn Krejce 1910-1975
08	Evelyn Marie Krejce 29 March 1933 - 23 January 1936
17	John P. Krejce 1903-1993
19	Joseph F. Krejce 1888-1952
21	Rosetta June Krejce 1932-1989
21	Vern Charles Krejce 1929-____
18	Veronica Krejce 1864-1951
11	Alois H. Kreuser 1901-1984
11	Bertha A. Kreuser 1904-1982
29	Thomas Edward Kroeninger 13 May 1989 - 23 June 1989
22	Virginia C. 'Ginger' Kroll 1938-1994
06	Judy Kubes - 1957 -
18	Ervin L. Kulzer 1918-1994
18	Lucille Kulzer 1922-1994
22	Keith E. Kurtz 2 March 1955 - 7 May 1991
18	Loretta E. Kurtz 1898-1953
12	Mary Ann Lahart 1849-1922
12	Matthew T. Lahart 1841-1917
05	William Lahart 27 January 1838 - 9 November 1892
11	Agatha V. Lander 1887-1895
12	Anna C. Lander 1893-1895

12	Anna J. Lander 1889-1889
11	Henry J. Lander 1903-1990
11	John Lander 1853-1935
11	Margaret Lander 1860-1948
17	Helen A. Lang 1876-1959
17	Patrick H. Lang 1871-1952
15	Catherine Larkin (?) 1867-1939
15	Michael Larkin (?) 1860-1928
17	Joseph W. Laverdiere 1896-1987
17	Mary Eva Laverdiere 1895-1990
21	Dianne L. Lebans 1950-1977
21	Robert A. Lebens 1923-1993
12	Ambrose J. Lenertz 1901-1969
12	Anna M. Lenertz (?) 1861-1941
12	Nicholas Lenertz (?) 1858-1919
07	Anton Lenhartz, born in Lux 15 June 1820, died 22 August 1893
07	Mary Lenhartz, born in Lux 6 January 1818, died 20 July 1902
09	Frank W. Lenihan 1885-1947
09	James M. Lenihan 1899-1973
09	John L. Lenihan 1893-1988
09	Josephine P. Lenihan 1895-1989
09	Josephine R. Lenihan 1926-1931
09	Josephine Rosemary Lenihan
	15 September 1926 - 14 August 1931
09	Kate J. Lenihan 1861-1947
09	Malichi James Lenihan 1857-1935
22	Judy C. LeTendre 1945-1986
	married Wayne L. 10 July 1965
13	baby V. Levern - 5 January 1918 -
22	Shirley V. LeVoir 4 October 1943 - 10 August 1976
10	A.T. Leyden 1891 - rest scrapped off the monument stone
09	Anna Leyden 1870-1943
09	Anthony Leyden 1870-1949
10	J.H. Leyden 1892-1893
29	Tanya Marie Littleton - 1978 -
14	Anna Lommel 15 June 1859 - 4 April 1908
13	John Lommel 1855-1932
13	Rose Lommell (?) 1887-1944
22	Barritt L. Lovelace 10 May 1939 - 6 November 1986
22	Barritt Lee Lovelace 1939-1986 Sp4 US Army
06	John F. Longtin 1931-1987
05	Mary C. Longtin 1902-1984
17	Gary Lucius (?) 1944-1983
17	Harold P. Lucius (?) 1917-1958
03	Anthony Ludden, died 22 April 1899, age 56 years
03	Ellen, wife of Anthony Ludden, died 25 July 1903, age 69 years

03	Mary Ellen, daughter of A. and E. Ludden
	died 15 May 1887, age 18 years 2 months
11	Ignaz Ludwig 1899-1963
11	Theresia Ludwig 1900-1990
18	Cecelia R. Lynch 1908-1995
15	Daniel E. Lynch 17 May 1940 - 27 May 1964
02	Edward C. Lynch 1899-1957
01	Ellen Lynch 1838-1912
16	Eugene E. Lynch 30 July 1888 - 8 January 1973
16	Helen M. Lynch 4 September 1910 - 17 December 1988
01	Irene Lynch 1898-1925
01	James J. Lynch 1858-1927
02	Joseph C. Lynch 1887-1943
18	Joseph W. Lynch 1902-1973
01	Mary E. Lynch 1860-1945
01	Mayme D. Lynch 1882-1934
01	Nelie A. Lynch 1884-1959
15	Prudence Kay Lynch 22 - 23 March 1961
02	Raymond W. Lynch 31 December 1893 - 31 August 1947 (?)
	MN Sgt 13 SN.TN. 13 Division
01	T. Lynch - no dates
01	Timothy Lynch - who departed this life 1 February 1890
	aged 61 years
02	Timothy Lynch 1891-1969
02	Thomas F. Lynch 1885-1937
02	Bridgel Lyons 27 June 1812 - 24 February 1897
22	Laura Lyons 1939-1985
29	Stephen J. Madden - 29 April 1981 -
18	Bernard J. Mahoney (?) 1911-1959
14	Charles F. Mahoney (?) 1884-1959
13	Elizabeth Mahoney 1887-1978
10	Ellen D. Mahoney 1860-1942
13	Florence Mahoney (?) 1906-1909
19	Francis Mahoney (?) 1908-1992
13	James Mahoney (?) 1888-1920
09	James Mahoney - died 21 September 1925
18	John H. Mahoney (?) 1879-1949
14	Joseph Mahoney (?) 1883-1917
19	Joseph Thomas Mahoney 1919-1985
	Cpl US Army WW2
13	Julia D. Mahoney 1891-1969
14	Loretta Mahoney (?) 1896-1920
13	Margaret Mahoney 1851-1913
18	Margaret A. Mahoney (?) 1886-1974
10	Margaret H. Mahoney 1896-1976

13	Michael Mahoney 1850-1931
19	Michael B. Mahoney 15 July 1910 - 29 October 1981
	Tec 5 US Army WW2
13	Michael J. Mahoney 18 April 1891 - 17 October 1959
	MN Horseshoer US Army WW1
14	Nora Mahoney (?) 1854-1908
09	Patrick H. Mahoney 1884-1964
19	Phillip L. Mahoney 1923-1996
18	Robert Leo Mahoney (?) 1922-1981
19	Sylvester Mahoney (?) 1913-1992
14	Thomas Mahoney (?) 1856-1906
13	Thomas Mahoney (?) 1892-1944
10	William Mahoney 1855-1898
10	William Mahoney, born 1855, died 28 February 1898
	aged 42 years 3 months 8 days
09	Amy Diane Mahowald 27 January 1966 - 17 April 1966
21	Ann Mahowald 1899-1991
16	Annie M. Berres, wife of John P. Mahowald
	20 December 1866 - 17 February 1891
09	Christina H. Mahowald 1897-1953
11	Clara Mahowald (?) 1872-1944
10	Francis G. Mahowald (?) 1918-_____
09	Frank M. Mahowald 1892-1967
16	Fransiska Mahowald 29 October 1889 - 18 January 1890
16	Fransiskus Mahowald, born and died 13 February 1891
11	Jacob Mahowald (?) 1867-1932
07	James J. Mahowald 1920-_____
11	Jerome H. Mahowald 1939-1994
10	Marcella A. Mahowald (?) 1921-1981
10	Marie E. Mahowald 1908-1987
10	Nich P. Mahowald 1905-1988
12	Patrick J. Mahowald 1966-1986
07	Phyllis D. Mahowald 1925-1967
21	Raymond J. Mahowald 1898-1970
21	Mary Nell Maloney, nee Conner
	24 January 1926 - 19 May 1988
08	James Mamer 12 January 1891 - 15 September 1983
	1st Lt US Army
08	Rose M. Mamer 1 May 1898 - 11 March 1985
17	Agnes Marek 1897-1990
17	Frank Marek 1895-1973
22	Steven J. Marek 1960-1986
18	Valene J. Marek 1932-1954
07	Catherine Marrinan 1872-1954
07	John J. Marrinan 1866-1950
18	Peggy Marrinan 1911-_____

07	J. E. Martin 4 March 1851 - 22 February 1923
12	Eric John Martinson 1974-1992
06	Anna McAndrew 1864-1964
05	James P. McAndrew 20 June 1839 - 1 July 1906
06	John J. McAndrew 1863-1946
05	Mary McAndrew 15 May 1843 - 26 June 1921
05	Richard McAndrew 22 January 1874 - rest buried to deep to read
10	Mary E. McAninch 1921-1974
03	Charles B. McBride (?) 1857-1927
03	Margaret T. McBride (?) 1857-1943
29	Daniel W. McCarthy 6 May 1911 - 25 October 1993
08	Catherine, wife of James McDonald, born in Co Galway Ireland 1823
	died 4 August 1879
08	James McDonald, born Co Galway Ireland 1816
	died 1 January 1881
17	John H. McFadden 1886-1950
17	Rose McFadden 1883-1951
21	Frank H. McGlone 1932-1982 Cpl US Army Korea
21	Frank H. McGlone 24 October 1932 - 10 June 1982
12	Marcella M. McGonagle 1900-1965
12	Stephen J. McGonagle 1880-1945
01	Catherine McInerney 1875-1942
05	Laura M. McNearney 1 July 1895 - 11 January 1989
05	Robert Leo McNearney 7 March 1896 - 19 December 1968
	MN Mech US Army WW1
22	Jennifer A. Meacham 1965-1982
29	Maria W. Meister 28 May 1909 - 2 October 1987
29	Ann J. Merten 1895-1982
29	Angela Mesmer - 25 April 1985 -
10	John M. Messenger 1921-1931
04	Harold N. Midtvedt 26 April 1916 - 10 January 1990
	Pvt US Army WW2
05	Elmer V. Mielke 1917-1985
05	Bertha C. Mielke 1879-1953
06	'Father' Mielke (?) 1840-1928
06	Francis G. Mielke 1905-1922
05	Joseph F. Mielke 1869-1924
09	May S. Mielke 1914-1916
06	'Mother' Mielke (?) 1850-1919
10	Alice Milan, born in Co Limerick Ireland - no dates
05	Anna Milan (?) 3 February 1863 - 25 July 1944
10	Annie Milan (?) 1873-1910
06	Balbina C. Milan 1891-1974
10	Bridget Milan (?) 1862-1949
10	Catherine Nye Milan 1880-1972
09	David J. Milan 26 January 1955 - 25 March 1980

10	Denis Milan, born in Co Limerick Ireland
	died 20 September 1907, aged 80 years
09	Dennis John Milan 25 August 1931 - 15 June 1978
03	Esther M. Milan 1896-1978
05	'Father' Milan (?), born is Springfield, Massachusetts
	31 October 1855 - 15 April 1916
10	Florence M. Milan 1889-1921
10	Gertrude A. Milan 1900-1903
21	James W. Milan 2 November 1924 - 1997 (?)
03	James L. Milan 1892-1944
10	John Milan (?) 1868-1922
10	Margaret M. Milan 1879-1958
12	Mary Milan - 10 October 1920 -
09	Mary K. Milan 1898-1952
10	Patrick H. Milan 1870-1954
09	Romuald P. Milan 1923-____
10	Thomas Milan 1861-1933
09	Walter F. Milan 1894-1981
06	William L. Milan 1886-1964
21	Margaret F. Miller 1912-1996
19	Patricia M. Miller 1918-____
	married Sidney O. 8 June 1943
19	Sidney O. Miller 1918-1987
	married Patricia M. 8 June 1943
21	Walter A. Miller 1912-___
24	William G. Moebius 1944-1986
12	Alfred N. Moes 1896-1960
15	Anna Moes 1871-1957
16	Dorothy Moes 1918-1989
16	Harold Moes 1911-1995
15	Nicholas Moes 1859-1953
12	Vivian M. Moes 1901-1981
02	Billy, son of J.M. and M.R. Mollers 1927-1928
02	Christine Mollers 1910-1929
18	Eugene P. Mollers 1908-1971
18	Hubert M. Mollers 1900-1977
18	John L. Mollers 1905-1947
02	Joseph M. Mollers 1902-1929
01	Mary Caspers Mollers 1868-1944
19	Mary Dores Mollers 1899-1961
19	Theodore P. Mollers 1904-1970
04	Emma Moore 1871-1953
04	John Moore 1869-1953
08	Alice, daughter of S.L. and M. Moran
	28 August 1888 - 12 March 1891
08	Elizabeth, child of L. and M. Moran - age 38 years - no dates

08	Francis M., daughter of J.D. and E. Moran
	31 January 1879 - 17 February 1879
08	Lawrence Moran 24 June 1801 - 16 January 1879
08	Margaret, wife of Lawrence Moran
	27 April 1810 - 29 September 1894
07	Mary A. Moran 1852-1934
08	Michael, child of L. and M. Moran - age 59 years - no dates
22	James E. Morrisey 1935-1990
	married Marjorie J. 14 June 1958
22	James E. Morrisey 22 March 1935 - 27 July 1990
	Pft US Army Korea
22	John A. Morrison 1924-1987 S Sgt US Army WW2
21	Frank I. Moudry 1913-1983
21?	Frank James Moudry 28 August 1940 - 6 December 1992
	US Air Force
21	Helen M. Moudry 1915-_____
19	Dorothy E. Mueller 1919-_____
19	William Mueller 1911-1962
03	Christopher Mulkern (?) 1860-1937
03	Elizabeth Mulkern (?) 1861-1951
04	Joseph B. Mulkern 7 June 1898 - 13 September 1963
	MN QM3 US Navy WW1
04	Rose Mulkern (?) 1884-1978
20	Bernice E. Murphy 1906-1997 (?)
19	Bertha E. Murphy 1891-1967
13	Bland Murphy 1879-1930
13	Evelyn B. Murphy 1916-_____
21	Gertrude M. Murphy 1894-1977
17	Hannah F. Murphy 1885-1952
21	James E. Murphy 1889-1990
19	John H. Murphy 1886-1954
09	Lillian Murphy 1910-1918
04	Mary J. Murphy (?) 1861-1953
04	Michael J. Murphy (?) 1856-1928
03	Michael J. Murphy 22 November 1900 - 9 July 1973
23	Michael J. Murphy 1925-1991
06	Patrick Leo Murphy 1912-1985 Tec 4 US Army WW2
17	Robert Murphy 1881-1978
13	Robert J. Murphy 1917-_____
20	Willard J. Murphy 1912-1975
20	Willard Jack Murphy 1912-1975
07	Bridget, wife of Thomas Murray, born in ? Co Galway
	died 21 June 1898, age 84 years
07	Margaret Murray, daughter of Thomas and Bridget Murray
	born in Neu Market, died 1 February 1885, age 25 years
07	Thomas Murray, Native of Dunmore Co. Galway Ireland

died 7 June 1892, age 88 years
01	Edward J. Myers (?) 1869-1923
02	'Father' Myers (?) 1831-1904
13	James Myers 1911-1988
13	John N. Myers 1871-1942
02	Lucy Myers (?) 1875-1927
13	Marcella Myers 1908-1993
01	Margaret Myers 1861-1934
13	Margaret I. Myers 1885-1948
02	'Mother' Myers (?) 1884-1917
01	Nora Myers (?) 1880-1935
01	Catherine Neary 1870-1941
01	Charles Neary 1854-1945
02	John Neary 1858-1919
02	Wm. F. Neary 1860-1931
02	Wm. F. Neary 1887-1975
14	Marie Redmond Nelson 1901-1982
14	Robert T. Nelson 12 March 1938 - 12 October 1992
	Tec 4 US Army
14	Charles O. Newcomb 1885-1968
14	Ella N. Newcomb 1886-1970
14	Ethyl M. Newcomb 1895-1944
14	Frank W. Newcomb 1886-1960
06	Leister E. Newcomb 1896-1984
06	Rita C. Newcomb 1897-1938
21	James A. Newhouse 1939-1981
21	Rita Mae Novak 1936-1978
05	Bridget O'Connell 1826-1911
18	Leo O'Connell 1894-1966
09	Louise M. O'Connell 1898-1974
05	Margaret O'Connell 1860-1944
06	Patrick O'Connell, native of Parish Tuan Co Galway Ireland
	died 8 October 1897, age 75 years
06	Thomas O'Connell, born in Parish Tuan Co Galway Ireland
	died 11 June 1899, age 74 years
05	Thomas O'Connell 1854-1945
05	Tom O'Connell Sr., died 11 June 1899, age 74 years
04	Michael O'Conners, died 10 February 1897, age 75 years
12	Bessie O'Donnell 1895-1964
12	Elizabeth O'Donnell 1863-1923
12	John O'Donnell 1862-1945
12	John Thomas O'Donnell 1889-1954
01	James D. O'Leary (?), died 10 August 1903, age 35 years
01	Julia O'Leary (?), died 16 December 1892, age 86 years

01	Julia F. O'Leary (?), died 13 March 1888, age 18 years
01	Mabel Grace O'Leary (?), died 4 January 1881, age 2 years
01	Mary F. O'Leary (?), died 25 December 1904, age 67 years
01	Timothy O'Leary (?), died 6 June 1922, age 84 years
01	William O'Leary (?), died 24 June 1873, age 24 years
21	Alexander Olsen 15 January 1928 - 26 October 1979
25	Adeline Olson 1911-1994
20	Lucille M. Olson 1918-1994
20	Orville W. Olson 1911-1968
29	Rosemary Olson 1930-1982
20	Louis Oster 1860-1905
22	Martin H. Otting 8 November 1932 - 12 July 1993
16	Michael J. Otting 1967-1968
24	Donald F. Oxborough 1914-1986
24	Dorothy A. Oxborough 1916-1982
29	Julia Mollers Paton 14 May 1894 - 18 September 1994
18	Francis M. Paulson - no dates
18	Josephine M. Paulson 1925-1931
19	Mary / Marie H. Paulson 16 June 1895 - 17 December 1977
19	Clara E. Pawlak 1908-1987
19	Edward F. Pawlak 1905-1969
09	Mary Penners 1852-1939
12	David Pepera 1959-1979
12	David Pepera Jr. - 1980 -
11	Evelyn J. Pepera 17 December 1902 - ____
11	George S. Pepera 6 April 1901 - 22 December 1993
12	James G. Pepera 9 January 1925 - 16 July 1992
	Tec 5 US Army WW2
11	LeRoy Joseph Pepera 23 September 1936 - 24 December 1989
12	Vicki Pepera 1953-1953
11	Joan Perepa 1930-1939
21	Florence Larson Peterson 1911-1995
21	Leslie Larson Peterson 1945-1990
12	Anna Peuschel 1882-1927
18	Emil B. Peuschel 1883-1942
18	Floy E. Peuschel 1880-1948
22	Geraldine Pfarr 1920-____
10	Mary Piperak - no dates
21	Timothy Pivek 1960-1980
29	Adelaide L. Plante 1915-1986
29	Gary E. Plante 1945-1982
12	Cally Pool 1892-1950
12	Eulalia Pool 1898-1983
11	Frank H. Pool 1920-1994
13	Elizabeth Prehall 1882-1953

13	William E. Prehall 1884-1959
13	'Father' Pudil (?) 1850-1932
14	Henrietta M. Pudil 1915-1933
13	'Mother' Pudil (?) 1852-1922

14	Elizabeth Quinn 1884-1909
14	James Quinn 1860-1932
14	James Quinn 1879-1943 (?)
14	John Quinn 1866-1903
10	John Quinn 11 May 1872 - 12 March 1908
14	Margaret Quinn - 1881 - 10 months
10	Mary Quinn 1841-1915
10	Michael Quinn 1841-1912
09	Michael F. Quinn 1883-1938
14	Rose Quinn 1843-1912
14	Thomas Quinn 1831-1888
09	William Quinn 1861-1926

29	Jacob Todd Rawson, son of Wanda and Terry - 29 March 1988 -
13	'Father' Redmond (?) 1860-1944
13	Frank Redmond (?) 1895-1975
13	James Redmond (?) 1899-1968
13	'Mother' Redmond (?) 1873-1952
16	Catherine V. Regan 1882-1970
12	John J. Regan 14 April 1909 - 11 April 1981
	Pvt US Army WW2
16	Joseph J. Regan 1885-1940
12	William J. Regan 5 August 1909 - 6 January 1983
08	Mary B. Reiley 1885-1951
08	Michael J. Reiley 1872-1954
15	Gertrude L. Reis 1918-1970
24	James G. 'Big Jim' Reisinger 13 November 1929 - 28 September 1994
	married Therese A. 'Tessie' 1 June 1949
23	Lauralee T. Restrepo 1945-1995
26	Jeffrey C. Rice 5 November 1965 - 16 September 1992
09	Lucille A. Rice, daughter of Catherine and Tom, 1904-1988
13	Anna C. Ring 1913-____
13	Clarence P. Ring 1909-1983
13	Elaine M. Ring 1937-1943
06	Elizabeth Margaret Ring 1907-1927
05	Hubert J. Ring 1905-1960
05	Joseph H. Ring 1883-1955
05	Katherine Ring 1875-1927
06	Lawrence George Ring 1921-1922
05	Marie V. Ring 1909-1958
06	Rosa Clara Ring 1911-1913

29	Yorkco L. Rivera 17 September 1977 - 1 January 1979
18	John G. Roehl 1897-1959
11	Mary M. Roehl 1895-1985
18	Mary E. Roehl 1916-____
22	Peter H. Roehl 1910-1974
05	John W. Rowan 1868-1937
01	Michael Rowan 1839-1915
01	Sarah Rowan 1841-1925
01	Sarah Rowan (?) 1881-1881
05	Sarah J. Rowan 1871-1935
05	Dominick Rowan-Akin 1870-1943
05	Ellen Rowan-Akin 1868-1958
06	'Mother' Rowan-Akin (?) 1894-1929
05	Michael J. Rowan-Gephart 1878-1947
13	Eugene Ruddle 23 February 1927 - 28 March 1973
13	George Ruddle (?) 1890-1974
13	Ida Ruddle (?) 1893-1955
13	Irene M. Ruddle 12 June 1928-____
14	Thomas Ruddle, son of Eugene and Irene 1955-1960
10	Aurelia Rushlow 18 June 1832 - 3 January 1911
10	Fred Rushlow (?) - no dates
10	Louis Rushlow 12 June 1827 - 6 August 1901
21	Agnes F. Ryan (?) 9 April 1930 - 20 August 1973
04	Anna Ryan, native of Co Clare Ireland, died 8 January 1884 age 87 years. Erected by Stephen Ryan, in memory of his mother
16	baby Ryan - 1953 -
16	Dorance Cyril Ryan 18 March 1924 - 18 March 1971 MN S Sgt Co C 796 MP BN WW2
08	John C. Ryan 1874-1951
15	Leo J. Ryan 1885-1956
08	Mary Ryan 1841-1929
15	Mary E. Ryan 1889-1978
08	William C. Ryan 1862-1948
04	Barbara Samels 1857-1920
03	Frank J. Samels (?) 1889-1973
04	John Samels 1851-1928
04	John P. Samels (?) 1882-1948
04	Katherine Samels (?) 1876-1945
03	Lucy C. Samels (?) 1895-1983
03	William F. Samels (?) 1890-1974
11	only Sauber - no dates
01	Aloysuis Sauber 1911-1934
01	Anna Sauber 1881-1957
11	Catherine Sauber 1845-1909

19	Eddie M. Sauber 1904-1995
19	Gertrude Sauber 1909-____
02	Grace Ruddle Sauber 13 February 1925-____
12	Henry Sauber 1869-1954
03	John Sauber (?) 1839-1912
12	John W. Sauber 1860-1913
02	Joseph P. Sauber 20 July 1951 - 24 August 1976
02	Louis P. Sauber 16 June 1921 - 19 January 1983
03	Margaret Sauber (?) 1887-1937
12	Mary Sauber 1862-1931
01	Mathias W. Sauber 1905-1987 Tec 5 US Army WW2
03	'Mother' Sauber (?) 1846-1922
03	Nicholas Sauber (?) 1882-1943
12	Nicolaus, son of N. and K. Sauber 26 November 1881 - 8 January 1884
01	Peter Sauber 1873-1953
11	William Sauber 1833-1913
04	William H. Sauber 1878-1968
18	Amelia S. Sauser 1908-____
10	Anna Sauser (?) - no dates
07	Charles M. Sauser 1884-1955
17	Edward F. Sauser 1892-1975
11	Edward M. Sauser 1895-1975
10	Francis Sauser (?) - no dates
11	Frank Sauser or VonBank 1856-1920
10	Florence Sauser (?) - no dates
03	Henry Sauser 1898-1962
09	John Sauser (?) 1853-1918
17	Joseph Sauser 1858-1946
07	Joseph E. Sauser (?) 1880-1948
03	Julia Sauser 1886-1962
18	Julius M. Sauser 1891-1958
03	Katherine Sauser (?) 1861-1943
12	Margaret Sauser 1849-1924
11	Margaret Sauser or VonBank 1888-1916
07	Mary Sauser (?) 1889-1914
07	Mary A. Sauser 1887-1973
11	Mary E. Sauser 1891-1978
17	Mary L. Sauser 1862-1952
07	Mary L. Hauer Sauser 1882-1974
11	Mat Sauser 1861-1911
03	Peter Sauser (?) 1860-1925
07	Peter J. Sauser 1910-1955
09	Regina Sauser (?) 1859-1957
18	Vicki Dee Sauser, daughter of Muggs and Dolly 5 December 1972 - 20 September 1975

29	James H. Schadeg 29 August 1947 - 22 March 1997
	Sp4 US Army
12	Frank C. Schlosser 1889-1947
24	Florence M. Schmitt 1917-1992
	married Wilfrid A. 28 September 1940
24	Wilfrid A. Schmitt 1915-____
	married Florence M. 28 September 1940
25	Marshall Schmit 20 February 1922 - 15 March 1973
26	Dolores Schmitz 2 August 1939 - 7 March 1996
08	John B. Schneider 12 November 1890 - 10 January 1950
18	Helen Schuhwerck (?) 1904-1968
18	Martin T. Schuhwerck (?) 1898-1962
15	David Schweich (?) - 1948 -
15	Jacob P. Schweich (?) 1889-1947
15	Jerome Jacob Schweich 8 June 1921 - 14 December 1944
	HA1 US Navy WW2
22	Joseph J. Schweich 1932-1988
	married Mary C. 5 January 1952
15	Margaret V. Schweich (?) 1896-1977
16	Marlys M. Schweich 1945-1985
15	Mary Schweich (?) - 1950 -
22	Lori A. Seuer 1961-1990
22	Raymond J. Seuer 10 June 1927 - 16 February 1989
	Pfc US Army Korea
22	Raymond J. Seuer 1927-1989
04	John Sheerien, born in Ballingary Parish Co. Limerick Ireland
	10 March 1810 - no death date listed
04	Mary C. Sheerien, native of Lestry Parish Co. Kerry Ireland
	died 9 September 1892, age 74 years
15	Scott D. Shepard 1952-1981
05	Barbara Sheridan, died 25 February 1881, age 60 years
01	'Father' Sheridan (?) 1862-1925
01	'Father' Sheridan (?) 1899-1941
02	Joseph J. Sheridan 1899-1983
02	Margaret L. Sheridan 1903-1993
01	'Mother' Sheridan (?) 1866-1944
18	Grace Sibell 1895-1944
15	Cecelia I. Sieber 1905-1967
15	Walter C. Sieber 1903-1984
25	Edward P. Simon 1906-1991
25	Josephine A. Simon 1913-____
15	Carolie Simones 1888-1981
15	Jacob Simones 1814-1894
15	Jacob J. Simones 1883-1946
16	Rita C. Simones 1921-____
16	Roland J. Simones 1914-____

19	Susanne Mary Slette - 1959 - 2 years 3 months
11	Joseph W. Smallwood 1899-1969
17	Anna Smith - rest of stone buried to deep to read
15	Verle Smith 1933-1990
	married David 18 September 1954
15	Gertrude R. Soucek 1915-1969
15	Gertrude S. Soucek 1891-1981
15	Louis J. Soucek 1889-1974
22	Albert Speiker 1899-1983
13	Alice O. Speiker 1907-____
19	Bernard A. Speiker 1901-1978
22	Danny Speiker 1967-1996
19	Edna T. Speiker 1910-1994
16	Francis Speiker 1909-1971
22	George A. Speiker 1915-1985
	married Myrtle R. 21 May 1941
29	Grace Speiker 1907-1973
13	Henry G. Speiker 1886-1946
17	John J. Speiker (?) 1891-1948
18	John L. Speiker 1922-1964
22	Louise Speiker 1902-1983
16	Margaret Speiker 1910-____
17	Marie A. Speiker (?) 1897-1990
15	Mary Speiker (?) 1870-1945
21	Myrtle R. Speiker 1921-____
	married George A. 21 May 1941
15	Paul Speiker (?) 1867-1948
13	Peter H. Speiker 1899-1982
13	William Speiker 1887-1960
14	Catherine N. Speikers (?) 1867-1922
14	Gerhard Speikers (?) 1862-1938
13	Henry G. Speikers 1886-1946
13	John H. Speikers, died 16 February 1901, age 77 years
13	Margaret Speikers 27 April 1872 - 9 June 1935
13	Robert Speikers 12 November 1865 - 17 March 1943
13	Susan, daughter of K. and J. Speikers
	26 February 1895 - 27 (?) February 1895
13	William Speikers 1887-1960
11	baby Spellacy - 1899 -
11	Ellen Spellacy (?) 1873-1953
11	Michael Spellacy (?) 1863-1932
13	Rose Spencer 1880-1914
25	George Stanek 1896-1972
19	Dale A. Staupe - 12 July 1965 -
21	Oberlin S. Staupe 22 April 1916 - 29 September 1971
	MN Pfc Btry A 775 FA BN WW2

21	Oberlin S. Staupe 1916-1971
21	Vivian V. Staupe 1921-____
17	Edward N. Zimmer or Stelter 27 October 1886 - 25 November 1916
17	George Stelter (?) - rest of stone buried to deep to read
16	Leo Gilbert Stelter 1903-1982 Pvt US Army WW2
16	Mae Stelter 1876-1950
16	Peter J. Stelter 1872-1946
17	Rose Stelter 1901-1923
08	Anna Stieger 24 December 1859 - 25 October 1951
08	Charles F. Stieger 17 April 1855 - 17 September 1907
24	Daniel M. Stommes 1960-1986
24	Patrick John Stommes 1957-1974
24	Wilfred F. Stommes 1924-1996
01	Clara F. Storlie 1907-____
01	Sidney O. Storlie 1906-1976
18	Alice Streefland 1909-1981
18	Art Streefland 1872-1946
18	Mary Streefland 1883-1972
21	Mary M. Streefland 1899-1984
21	Russell L. Streefland 1897-1978
17	'Father' Strong (?) - rest of stone buried to deep to read
16	George E. Strong 1870-1965
16	Jessica Eve Strong - 22 May 1986 -
16	Margaret Strong 1875-1967
17	'Mother' Strong (?) 12 May 1845 - 27 February (?) 1913
17	Susie Strong (?) 20 September 1863 - 16 November 1903
18	Amandus Studer 1886-1979
	married Hazel 25 April 1911
18	baby Studer - 8 January 1937 -
18	Hazel Studer 1892-1983
	married Amandus 25 April 1911
18	Joan Studer 1927-1929
18	Phyllis Studer 1922-1928
13	Catherine Sullivan (?) 5 February 1870 - 22 April 1944
01	Daniel Sullivan, born in Ireland 1830-1898
02	Daniel Sullivan, born in Ireland 1830, died 31 January 1898
14	Eleanor Sullivan 1916-____
	married William F. 15 September 1936
01	Ellen Sullivan (?) 8 June 1866 - 16 April 1947
07	'Father' Sullivan 22 March 1871 - 3 July 1916
13	George D. Sullivan (?) 1904-1992
01	John H. Sullivan (?) 28 February 1865 - 9 January 1929
01	Mary Sullivan, born in Ireland 1834-1888
02	Mary McCarthy, beloved wife of Daniel Sullivan
	born in Ireland 1834, died 29 March 1888
07	'Mother' Sullivan (?) 26 April 1877 - 7 September 1928

13	Patrick Sullivan (?) 20 March 1868 - 12 November 1948
02	Pearl Sullivan (?) 4 January 1898 - 27 September 1898
02	Raymond Sullivan (?) 4 November 1899 - 21 December 1899
13	Susan M. Sullivan (?) 1903-____
14	William F. Sullivan 1908-1963
	married Eleanor 15 September 1936
03	William H. Sullivan (?) 1891-1938
22	Lillian Sweno 1918-____
11	Edward L. Swift 1883-1909
11	Thomas Swift 1843-1913
29	John S. Sykora 1952-1986
08	Anna Tabaka 1885-1951
17	Anthony J. Tabaka 1872-1953
10	Frank Tabaka 1867-1934
21	Joseph A. Tabaka 1912-1994
10	Lucy Tabaka 1878-1962
10	Margaret Tabaka 1906-1984
21	Margaret Tabaka 1921-1997 (?)
17	Mary L. Tabaka 1873-1965
08	Nicholas Tabaka 1870-1950
21	Raymond Tabaka 1911-1989
21	Teresa M. Tabaka 1918-1989
18	William J. Tabaka 1906-1921
18	William J. Tabaka 14 January 1906 - 10 September 1921
24	Jean Louise Talley 14 June 1969 - 20 May 1996
24	Myrna M. Talley 1944-1975
05	Loretta A. Taylor 1898-1949
25	Anthony C. Thole 22 January 1913 - 1 August 1989
29	Galen M. Thomas 1967-1986
17	Margaret Thomas 1866-1943
18	Felix P. Tillges 1912-____
18	M. Gladys Tillges 1915-1967
16	Vella M. Tillges 1910-1996
16	Sylvester Tillges 1902-1958
09	Nicholas Chiam Tilsen 7 August 1951 - 13 August 1990
08	Elizabeth Timmons 23 February 1868 - 9 April 1962
07	'Father' Timmons (?) 1857-1914
07	Simon Timmons 1863-1945
08	William E. Timmons 22 May 1854 - 11 August 1938
20	Helen A. Tobey 1888-1969
20	Roy E. Tobey 1888-1960
	Robert Tourdot - 1985 -
21	Catherine A. Travis 1949-1985
22	Barbara Tritz 1896-1984
22	John Tritz 1897-1979

05	Ann Twohy 1858-1910
06	Catherine M. Twohy 1891-1970
05	Hubert Twohy 24 December 1857 - 24 November 1906
06	Michael J. Twohy 1886-1954
29	Margaret G. Valo 14 August 1890 - 24 April 1987
11	Mary Ellen Vizena 1931-1986
21	Mathew Voelker - 18 February 1986 -
11	Elizabeth VonBank 1859-1932
18	Frank VonBank 1889-1967
	married Fredericka 11 October 1932
11	Frank Sauser or VonBank 1856-1920
18	Fredericka VonBank 1909-1962
	married Frank 11 October 1932
11	Joseph VonBank 1892-1916
11	Margaret Sauser or VonBank 1888-1916
12	Mathias, son of Frank and Lizzie VonBank
	23 December 1886 - 1 August 1887
19	Eleanore Wagner 1914-1974
07	Grace Sauser Wagner 1912-____
07	John P. Wagner 1906-1968
13	Louis J. Wagner 1901-1993
13	Madelyn B. Wagner 1905-____
19	Mary A. Wagner 1883-1959
19	William P. Wagner 1882-1946
22	Beverly Kay Waller 3 August 1959 - 15 June 1987
22	John H. Wallin 1919-1990
11	Delia Catherine Walsh 25 January 1903 - 28 January 1928
29	Gerold M. Walsh 1944-1983
25	Helen Mae Walsh 1915-1996
	married Wilfrid W. 16 August 1938
18	M. George Walsh 1943-1944
12	Margaret Walsh 1869-1944
12	Martin Walsh 1870-1945
11	Roy M. Walsh 12 September 1904 - 12 August 1926
25	Wilfrid W. Walsh 1914-1977
	married Helen Mae 16 August 1938
21	Chad R. Walther 1975-1984
04	Catherine M. Weber (?) 1878-1962
04	Charles W. Weber (?) 1880-1961
04	Florence Weber 1910-1913
03	Francis C. Weber (?) 1906-1964
03	Letty D. Weber (?) 1912-1991
04	Louis N. Weber 1882-1967
22	Alice C. Wells 1901-1976

22	George H. Wells 1902-1977
24	Tom J. Werdan 1958-1991
25	Frank Wetch 6 January 1934 - 10 June 1992
03	James Edgar Wheaton 23 June 1925 - 13 April 1990 Ens US Navy WW2
02	Anna E., wife of Patrick White, died 7 May 1885, age 74 years
13	Earl White (?) - no dates
03	Flavian J. White (?) 1904-1990
01	George Henry White or Fitzgerald 23 April 1880 - 4 September 1881
13	Kate White 1874-1960
03	Louise V. White (?) 1907-____
01	Marguerite T. O'Leary (?), beloved wife of P.H. White died 2 August 1888, age 22 years
13	May White (?) - no dates
02	Patrick White, died 12 April 1884, age 68 years erected by his beloved wife Anna White
04	Robert Francis, son of Robert and Joan White (?) 19 November 1959 - 8 February 1960
18	Anna M. Wild 1902-1983
18	George D. Wild 1896-1960
12	Anna Wilde (?) 1861-1936
19	Bernard F. Wilde 1897-1975
19	Catherine M. Wilde 1901-1991
12	Jacob Wilde (?) 1866-1947
19	Raymond G. Wilde 1 January 1922 - 16 June 1990
22	Leander J. Lee Willner 1932-1989
12	John Wolf 1861-1938
18	Charles Wren 1921-1988
18	Frances Wren 1921-____
17	Vincent Wren 1902-1961
17	Wilhilmina Wren 1915-1958
07	John C. Yung (?) 1861-1939
19	Katherine Yung 1900-1952
08	Ludwig M. Yung 1890-1958
08	Margaret A. Yung 1897-1986
07	Mary Yung - 19 July 1923 -
07	Mary Magdalen Yung (?) 1861-1940
19	Michael J. Yung 1893-1959
07	Odelle Magdalen Yung (?) 1898-1954
16	Josephine Zelt 16 December 1879 - 28 October 1928
11	only Zimmer - no dates listed
18	Adon A. Zimmer (?) 1910-1966
12	Andrew J. Zimmer 1874-1948

12	Barbara Zimmer (?) 1854-1882
12	Brad Louis Zimmer - 1975 -
17	Edward N. Zimmer or Stelter 27 October 1886 - 25 November 1916
12	'Father' Zimmer (?) 1822-1882
18	Florence L. Zimmer (?) 1910-1973
11	Francis Zimmer (?) - 1902 - age 3 days
16	Frank A. Zimmer 1901-1992
16	Frank V. Zimmer 1858-1952
12	Helena Samels Zimmer 1879-1949
11	Irene M. Zimmer 1907-____
11	James Michael Zimmer 1945-1985
17	John H. Zimmer (?) 1876-1960
17	Josephine M. Zimmer (?) 1884-1953
11	Louis J. Zimmer 1907-1970
12	Margaret Wood Zimmer 1874-1914
17	Martha Zimmer 1907-1993
12	'Mother' Zimmer (?) 1833-1901
16	Suzanna Zimmer 1864-1928
17	Wilbert Zimmer 1906-1981
21	Phyllis J. Zurek 1930-1986
21	Alice K. Zweber 1928-1981
21	Francis J. Zweber 1926-1986
21	Helen M. Wermerskirchen Zweber (?) 1921-____
02	Joan Claire Zweber 1937-1961
21	Leroy Zweber 1918-1996
21	Leroy H. Zweber 16 May 1918 - 21 March 1996
	US Army WW2
21	Loretta Deutsch Zweber (?) 1909-1982
21	Wilfred Zweber 1911-____

I was not able to determine surnames for the following:

22	Cindy Ann 1958-1976
20	Margaret Ellen 24 December 1884 - 16 August 1885

All Saints Cemetery
Lakeville City T114-R20
Section 32

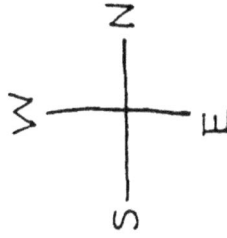

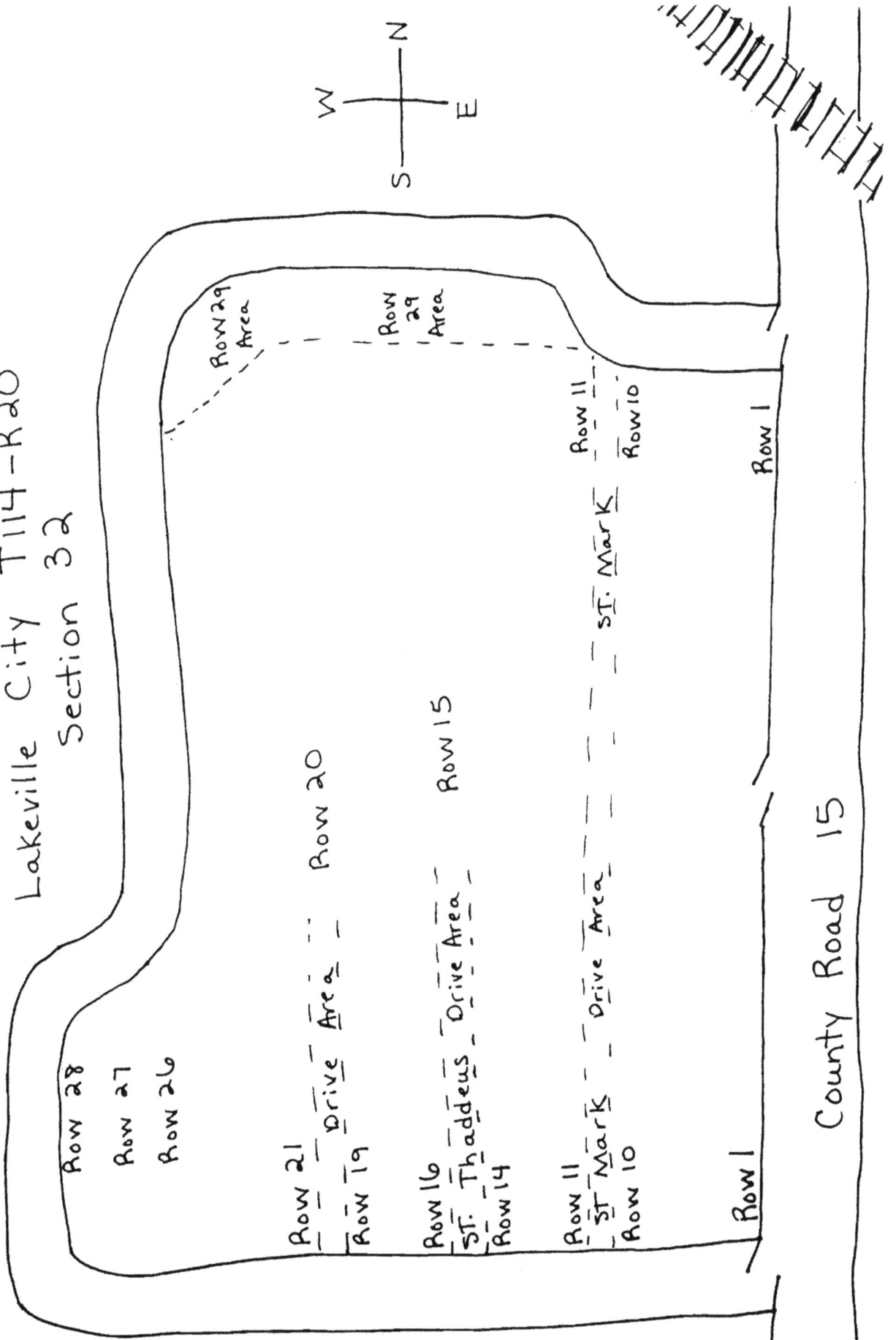

Row 28

Row 27

Row 26

Row 21
— Drive Area —
Row 19

Row 16
ST. Thaddeus Drive Area
Row 14

Row 11
ST. Mark — Drive Area
Row 10

Row 1

Row 20

Row 15

Row 29 Area

Row 29 Area

Row 11
Row 10
ST. Mark

Row 1

County Road 15

N
W — E
S